ELEMENTS OF CRITICISM

VOLUME I

NATURAL LAW AND
ENLIGHTENMENT CLASSICS

Knud Haakonssen
General Editor

Henry Home, Lord Kames

NATURAL LAW AND
ENLIGHTENMENT CLASSICS

Elements
of
Criticism

VOLUME I

Henry Home, Lord Kames

The Sixth Edition

Edited and with an Introduction by Peter Jones

Major Works of Henry Home, Lord Kames

LIBERTY FUND
Indianapolis

This book is published by Liberty Fund, Inc., a foundation established
to encourage study of the ideal of a society of free and responsible individuals.

The cuneiform inscription that serves as our logo and as the design motif for
our endpapers is the earliest-known written appearance of the word
"freedom" (*amagi*), or "liberty." It is taken from a clay document written
about 2300 B.C. in the Sumerian city-state of Lagash.

Introduction, annotations © 2005 Liberty Fund, Inc.

Printed in the United States of America

09 08 07 06 05 C 5 4 3 2 1
09 08 07 06 05 P 5 4 3 2 1

Frontispiece and cover (detail): Portrait of Henry Home, Lord Kames, by David Martin.
Reproduced with permission of the National Galleries of Scotland.

Library of Congress Cataloging-in-Publication Data
Kames, Henry Home, Lord, 1696–1782.
Elements of criticism / Henry Home, Lord Kames;
edited and with an introduction by Peter Jones.
p.   cm.—(Major works of Henry Home, Lord Kames)
(Natural law and enlightenment classics)
Originally published: 6th ed. Edinburgh: J. Bell and W. Creech;
London: T. Cadell and G. Robinson, 1785.
Includes bibliographical references.
ISBN 0-86597-466-7 (set: alk. paper)   ISBN 0-86597-469-1 (set: soft: alk. paper)
ISBN 0-86597-467-5 (v. 1: alk. paper)   ISBN 0-86597-470-5 (v. 1: sc: alk. paper)
1. Criticism.   2. Style, Literary.
I. Jones, Peter (Peter H.), 1935–   . II. Title. III. Series.
PN81.K3 2005
801'.95—DC22   2004063389

LIBERTY FUND, INC.
8335 Allison Pointe Trail, Suite 300
Indianapolis, Indiana 46250-1684

CONTENTS

INTRODUCTION

Henry Home was born in 1696 in the southeastern Scottish parish of Eccles, three miles from the English border; he died in 1782, in Edinburgh. Both of his parents came from prominent families divided by Whig, Presbyterian, and Episcopalian loyalties; Jacobite sympathies were also apparent. Because of his father's accumulating debts and large family burdens, Home was educated entirely at home; and he acquired the tenacity, energy, and encyclopedic range of many self-educated people. In 1741 Home proudly inherited his seventeenth-century family house, together with mill, brewhouse, and mixed arable farm, and until 1766, when he also took over his wife's property in Perthshire, delighted in taking friends there.

Home moved to Edinburgh in 1712, and over the next ten years studied, first, to be a solicitor, and later, an advocate: during that period he joined several clubs, especially those devoted to philosophy and to music. In 1732 he failed to secure the Edinburgh Chair of Civil Law, but by the later 1730s had become an established advocate, and had also attached himself to the political faction and patronage of the second duke of Argyll. Under the patronage of the third duke, he became a Scottish lawlord in 1752, when he was appointed to the supreme civil court, the Court of Session. In 1763 he was appointed to the highest criminal court, the High Court of Justiciary. Earlier, in 1755, he had also been appointed to the main government agencies controlling the Scottish economy after the 1745 Jacobite Rebellion: the Board of Trustees for Fisheries, Manufactures and Improvements in Scotland and the Commission for the Forfeited Estates. By that date, Kames was involved both in extensive farming improvements to his wife's estate and in patronage of other improvement schemes and artistic activities. For five years after 1737 he was a curator of the Advocates' Library in Edinburgh, whose keeper, Thomas Ruddiman, helped to establish it as one of the great collections: there, he was able to consult almost any significant ancient or modern work on law or philosophy, history or economics, architecture or rhetoric, the sciences or education.

From at least 1720 Home had taken an active interest in philosophical discussions, and in the late 1730s he planned a literary and political periodical with his distant cousin, David Hume (who was the first to change the spelling of the family name). In 1741 he became a member of the Philosophical Society of Edinburgh, becoming vice president in 1748 and president from 1769 until his death: through this society he made the valued friendship of Benjamin Franklin, who stayed with him and maintained a fruitful correspondence. Kames was an active founder member of the Select Society from 1755 onward and of two of its practical offshoots, the Edinburgh Society for the Encouragement of Arts, Sciences, Manufactures, and Agriculture, and the Society for Promoting the Reading and Speaking of the English Language in Scotland. Several of the discussions in the present book have their sources, or allude to recorded discussions, in these societies, the full titles of which, including their offshoots and subcommittees, varied, whether by accident or design.

Unlike Hume and Smith, Kames never lived in France, nor like a few of his richer colleagues did he undertake the Grand Tour. His information about the continent came from conversation, correspondence, and reading. Although he had a vast range of acquaintances, he was probably not a family man, as such: his self-imposed workload would have precluded it. By contemporaries he was held to have done more than anyone else in Scotland for a century to promote philosophy, *belles lettres,* and the arts.

The majority of Kames's works are concerned with the law of Scotland. During his attempts, in the early volumes, to assemble and classify court decisions by reference to the rules being applied, he became acutely aware of the historical evolution of Scots law. He was a pioneer in comparative legal history, and as his inquiries broadened to include property and rights, he was able to develop his long-standing philosophical interests. For Kames, the law is grounded in morality and human nature: on these topics he is an empiricist in the tradition of Shaftesbury and, to some extent, Hutcheson. He shared the hostility toward skepticism of Scottish common-sense philosophers such as Reid, but he drifts toward a form of determinism in which "the benevolent hand of the Creator" [1.351] has left the universe to run on its own. As he makes clear in *Elements of Criticism,* introspection is the key to understanding the mind, and the first edition of that work (1762) stands at the midpoint of his explicitly philosophical works. Kames believed that in this sphere of inquiry, his own major work was *Sketches of the History of Man* (1774), which analyzes the individual and social character of men and society, canvasing many insights adopted by later students of sociology, anthropology, social theory, and comparative history.

Cultural, Physical, and Social Context of Scotland

The cultural context of Scotland changed dramatically during Kames's lifetime, although two major factors ensured that it lagged behind developments in England generally and those in London and Paris most prominently: economic poverty and the dominating, though declining, influence of the Calvinist church. The latter discouraged all forms of costly display, personal or public, along with any self-indulgence associated with music and theater in general and dancing in particular. The former ensured that only a very few individuals were rich enough to act as patrons in any of the arts, and influential enough to ignore ecclesiastical pressures.

Nevertheless, at varying rates and with regional differences, by the 1760s much of Britain, including Scotland, was experiencing the benefits of an increasingly rich and stable political nation. The spread of wealth and increasing leisure among the middle classes, together with a greater ease of travel; the beginning of public concerts and museums in which works would be removed from their original contexts for special attention; a decline in individual patronage and the concomitant freedom of artists to satisfy a growing luxury market; the beginning of the formal study of the arts by nonpractitioners and nonowners; the greater availability of books and illustrations as secondary sources of information; the increasing influence of critics, through journals; the institutionalization of the arts and sciences and thus of professional distinctions between them—all these factors characterized, in various degrees, the contexts in which Kames's intended readership might attend to his views.

And in Scotland, especially, the self-conscious emphasis on education as the key to "improvement" justified the occasional pedagogic, if not didactic, tone of the argument. That alone, together with the relative inaccessibility to most Scots of notable paintings, architecture, or music, explained both the unusual interest readers took in Kames's discussions of those arts and also his central emphasis on topics concerning literature and language, about which they would be more familiar.

The physical, social, and intellectual context of Scotland also differed dramatically from that farther south. In 1762 fewer than one million people lived in Scotland, many at the level of bare subsistence, particularly in the Highlands where the population survived on a diet almost exclusively of oatmeal. The only large city, Edinburgh, was a derelict, medieval walled enclave of 140 acres, overcrowded with a population of around fifty-five thousand renting often unheated rooms in buildings up to fifteen stories high. Looking back to his youth, a younger colleague of Kames, Lord Cockburn, states that even in the 1770s there must have been "thousands of slaves" throughout Scotland, bought and sold like serfs of old. In spite of the Turnpike Act of 1751 there were, as yet, few roads outside Edinburgh: the coach journey to Glasgow took twelve hours, and the boat to London up to one month.

Most social life occurred, not in private apartments, but in rooms rented in the numerous local taverns; here took place not only all official commercial or legal business but also the countless discussion and drinking clubs, modeled on those that had been thriving in France and England since the later seventeenth century. In Edinburgh, Aberdeen, and Glasgow particularly, but even in smaller towns such as Perth, a major emphasis in discussion societies from the mid-eighteenth century was on "improvement"—that is, on any matters which directly or indirectly might lead to the increased health and wealth of the nation. The three central topics in Edinburgh societies around the 1750s were agriculture, mining, and banking; and the intensely practical debates in the Edinburgh Philosophical Society at that date, when Kames was vice president, ranged over such issues as mining and the ventilation of mines, the chemistry of various solutions, drainage systems, the uses of oxen (Kames favored them over horses), and later, as a communication with Benjamin Franklin testifies, the problems of smoky chimneys and lightning. Such practical debates accelerated awareness of changes in thinking about the world, for the scientific understanding of the day was extremely limited by our standards.

The first circulating library in Edinburgh opened in 1725, at the initiative of the bookseller and poet Allan Ramsay, but the few seasonal public balls and occasional plays were all condemned by a vocal minority of the clergy. The Musical Society, founded in 1728, and of which Kames was a member, became especially active after the opening of St. Cecilia's Hall in the 1760s. Music was made for and by amateurs (unaccompanied songs were widely enjoyed at family gatherings) and, like the discussion clubs, fostered participation: there were few public audiences as such, paying to enjoy passively the efforts of others. And apart from nature, about which Kames was one of the first Scottish philosophers to write appreciatively [1.127, 240], there was little visual stimulation or interest, which underlines the importance of his discussions of gardening, architecture, and painting. In 1756, for example, there were only two carpets in the whole town of Jedburgh, a Border market center a few miles from Kames's farm. At the same date, in the whole of Scotland, there were barely a dozen private collections of what today we regard as art.

The Argument of *Elements of Criticism*

Like many of his contemporaries, Kames states that he is investigating "the science of human nature" and, since "action is the aim of all our improvements," pleasure should be considered for "relaxation only" [1.305, 318, 361, 418]. The present book, therefore, addresses only one segment of our experience. Kames sets out to show that "the science of criticism"—essentially, discussion of the arts—is "a rational science," like morals: it is "a subject of reasoning as well as of taste" [1.7, 195]. Criticism is an "intermediate link" between mere corporeal pleasures and those of morality and religion, and requires more "circumspection" than the latter, where the common sense of mankind is more evident [2.499]. It is a secular practice, grounded in human nature, but one that contributes to the fulfillment of man's social nature, and thereby to the harmony and stability of society itself. The sources and nature of criticism can be explained only by reference to how the mind works, and to how and why people respond and behave as they do; such facts about context are important, because relations between things are often as important as their inherent properties. The fine arts are intended to entertain us, and they raise emotions of pleasure in us by means of their properties: the principles they employ or implement are "founded upon the sensitive part of our nature"; that helps to explain why music, gardening, and architecture humanize and polish the mind [1.13, 53].

Kames concentrates on our responses to the arts, not on the creative act itself. Like most philosophers, Kames usually differs only in detail and emphasis from those who most influenced him. Following Locke, Kames holds that we all experience a train of ideas in the mind, related to each other by a sense of order, resemblance, contiguity, and cause and effect. Such notions, of course, characterize Hume's analyses of causation and of the mind's workings, and Hume is the first silent interlocutor with whom Kames is constantly debating his ideas. The second silent partner is Adam Smith, to whom Kames was patron at the outset of his career. For example, Kames follows both Hume and Smith in assigning a central role to sympathy, without which no person could fully understand another, nor the bonds of society be secured [1.446]. He argues that whenever we turn our attention away from the immediate present, we create an "ideal presence" in our minds that enables us to be affected by any of our thoughts, "a waking dream" in which nothing at the time strikes us as inferior to daily life [1.91]. Like Shaftesbury, Francis Hutcheson, and especially Thomas Reid, Kames resorted to several allegedly common-sense assumptions, notably inherent internal senses—such as a moral sense, a sense of beauty, and so on [e.g., 1.378]. Here, Hume and Smith differ from Kames and Reid not on the facts, but on their explanation: none denies that most people, under common conditions, behave or respond in similar ways. Whereas Hume seeks to explain the responses in terms of a context of learning, habit, tradition, and social practice, Kames appeals to natural, God-given intuitions, while also denying innate ideas [2.516]. He accepts that there are obvious changes in practice and taste [1.206] and argues that the kind of rivalry often engendered by such changes can contribute to genuine improvement. Nevertheless, it remains necessary to establish standards of criticism [2.499]. This was a recurrent topic from the end of the seventeenth century, and was vigorously debated in Edinburgh in the 1750s. Two issues were usually debated in tandem: what are the relative roles of feeling and reasoning in matters of taste, and can there be a standard of taste?

The committee of the Edinburgh Society concerned with belles lettres and criticism announced in 1755 a prize for the "best essay on taste": the prize was won by Alexander Gerard, of Aberdeen, and his revised essay was published in 1759. In the meantime Allan Ramsay, the painter, had published his "Dialogue on Taste" in 1755 [*The Investigator,* CCCXXII], Hume brought out his essay "Of the Standard of Taste" in 1757, and passages in *The Theory of Moral Sentiments* of 1759 represent part of Smith's response to the topic. Kames was an active speaker in the Select Society committee, and chapters 24 and 25 of *Elements of Criticism* represent his deliberations on the topic itself and on these recent publications. Many of his references to architecture and the views of thinkers such as the French architect and translator of Vitruvius, Claude Perrault (1613–88), mirror those debates [1.179, 202; 2.465]. Kames had sponsored and discussed with Smith his lectures on rhetoric and belles lettres, given for the first time in Edinburgh in 1748 and, after 1752, in Glasgow, and there are numerous parallels between the two writers in their chosen topics and references. Discussions of other topics in Kames's text also allude to those in the Select Society and its northern equivalent, the Aberdeen Philosophical Society, known as The Wise Club [e.g., on ridicule, 1.114; on the sublime, 1.211].

Although he sharply separated himself in one respect from Hume's account of causation [2.86], Kames accepts all of Hume's main points about judgments of taste. Works of fine art are intentionally made by human beings but, because intentions are not visible, "it requires reflection to discover their true character" [1.37]. Accordingly, experience, learning, and comparative judgment are as essential in forming a taste as in any other social endeavor. Truly refined pleasures may be enjoyed by only a small number of people [1.111], largely because of the time, effort, and abilities needed, but almost everyone not struggling at the level of bare survival can derive some pleasure from the arts [2.499]. He agrees that the tendency of pleasant emotions is to prolong the pleasure and that the mind essentially seeks to create order out of its impressions and experiences [1.22]: at bottom, as classical writers had insisted, *propriety* is the ultimate criterion of merit and our pleasurable response to it [1.338], but it can be discerned only by means of judgment or reflection [2.478].

Kames adopts a standard distinction of the day between intrinsic beauty and relative beauty, deriving from discussions in Shaftesbury [*Characteristics*, "The Moralists," pt. III. sect. 2], Addison [*The Spectator*, no. 415], Francis Hutcheson [*An Inquiry into the Original of Our Ideas of Beauty and Virtue*], David Hume's *Treatise* [bk. II. pt. 2. sect. 5; bk. III. pt. 3. sect. 1], and Smith's *Theory of Moral Sentiments* [pt. IV. ch. 1, 2]. The central point is that all judgments about relative beauty require "an act of understanding and reflection," as is most obvious in "the beauty of utility" [1.197, 458]. In his own discussions of the sublime [1.211], Kames barely alludes to Edmund Burke's *A Philosophical Enquiry into the Origin of Our Ideas of the Sublime and Beautiful*, 1757, possibly to imply a distance from him; but he certainly knew John Baillie's *An Essay on the Sublime*, 1747, through Alexander Gerard's enthusiastic discussion of it in the prize essay that Kames had helped to judge. Gerard and Smith had also published their views on ridicule, to which Kames is adverting in his own discussion [1.114], although prominent French discussion in the seventeenth century had prompted the reflections of Shaftesbury, and those in *The Spectator* (by Addison in no. 249, and Steele in no. 422), which were particularly influential on current debate.

Gardening exercised the minds and purses of many prominent Scots from the 1720s onward, Kames even suggesting that, exceptionally, it may excel architecture in its impact on observers [2.430]. Sir John Clerk attracted attention by means of extensive circulation in manuscript of his poem "The Country Seat" in the late 1720s, and Sir John Dalrymple's *Essay on Landscape Gardening* was circulating widely in Edinburgh in the 1750s among his fellow lawyers and landowners. Dalrymple took part in the Select Society's discussions on taste, and he was a friend of Kames, Hume, Smith, Adam Ferguson, William Robertson, and Robert Adam. In an emerging context of seemingly abstract or theoretical debate, where buildings and gardens might be illustrated only by geometrical plans or elevations, Kames's practicality was widely appreciated: for example, Samuel

Bard recommended to his father in New York that he study Kames before embarking on any improvements. (Kames castigates architects who resort to "blind windows" when they cannot harmonize internal plan and external appearance: 2.458, 476.) By 1764 Dalrymple and Kames had established a dominant taste for the natural style in gardening, both admiring Kent and work at Stowe, and Daniel Paterson's gardens of 1756 for Inveraray. Among several publications on Stowe, Kames probably knew at least William Gilpin's *A Dialogue upon the Gardens . . . at Stow,* 1748 (published anonymously).

Scattered throughout the book are Kames's reflections on music and the most topical debate of the day throughout Europe, concerning the relation of music to emotions and to words [1.53, 138]. Reflections on music, and probably on such books as Charles Avison's *An Essay on Musical Expression* (1752), incline him to think of a natural language for the expression of emotions, and to view music as a unique language. He alludes to the vigorous debate about the respective merits of French and Italian opera [1.141], which much occupied Rousseau, whose essays we know Kames read. It is almost certain, in view of the proximity of their views, that he had discussed all these matters with Smith, who left unfinished a work on the imitative arts and the particular character of music. The discussions of beauty in language and of versification are partly concerned with how to speak poetry properly, that is, to harmonize "sound and sense" [2.94]: comparisons with music are inevitable. To distinguish pronunciation from singing, he notes that feet regulate pronunciation and hence melody, and feet are determined by pauses [2.108].

What kinds of reception did *Elements of Criticism* receive? Owen Ruffhead reviewed the book in volumes 26 and 27, for 1762 and 1763, of the *Monthly Review.* Eight editions within a twenty-year period testify to considerable interest for a book of this kind. Along with works on rhetoric by Hugh Blair, and later George Campbell, Kames's work, often in one of several abridged editions, entered the syllabus of American colleges founded on a Scottish model, in which almost all students took a general course in rhetoric. It was used throughout the nineteenth century in such courses. His book also entered the libraries of self-respecting intellectuals abroad, ranging from Franklin and Jefferson in America to Kant and Josef Haydn; it was helped, unusually, not by a French version but by a German translation issued only a year after the first edition had appeared, and itself reprinted four times before the end of the century.

Peter Jones

Selected Reading

Fleming, John. *Robert Adam and His Circle in Edinburgh and Rome.* London: John Murray, 1962.

Jones, Peter. "The Aesthetics of Adam Smith," in *Adam Smith Reviewed,* edited by Peter Jones and Andrew S. Skinner. Edinburgh: Edinburgh University Press, 1992.

———. "Hume on the Arts and 'The Standard of Taste': Texts and Contexts," in *The Cambridge Companion to Hume,* edited by David Fate Norton. 2nd ed. Cambridge: Cambridge University Press, 2005.

Lindsay, Ian, and Mary Cosh. *Inveraray and the Dukes of Argyll.* Edinburgh: Edinburgh University Press, 1973.

Ross, I. S. *Lord Kames and the Scotland of His Day.* Oxford: Clarendon Press, 1972.

Tait, A. A. *The Landscape Garden in Scotland, 1735–1835.* Edinburgh: Edinburgh University Press, 1980.

EDITOR'S NOTE

Henry Home, Lord Kames, published the first edition of *Elements of Criticism* in 1762, although he began writing it at least a decade earlier. There are no substantive differences between the first and last editions, although there are many stylistic changes. Kames frequently multiplied examples and he expanded some discussions, but the central doctrines remain unchanged. The present edition reproduces the text of the sixth edition, of 1785, which was the last authorized by Kames himself and appeared shortly after his death. A few variations between the first and sixth editions have been indicated, and printer's errors have been corrected. Page breaks in the sixth edition are indicated by the use of angle brackets. For example, page 112 begins after <112>.

All of Kames's original notes are indicated by asterisks, daggers, and other symbols; where editorial notes have been added, these are contained within brackets. All other new editorial notes and references are indicated by arabic numerals.

Editorial notes have been restricted to providing the dates of people mentioned by Kames in his text, together with the titles and authors of works not fully identified by him. These details are normally given at the first occurrence of a name or work, which is itself recorded in the original index.

References

Kames rarely indicated the editions he was using. For both Shakespeare and classical Latin authors, modern references have been provided. Kames used eighteenth-century editions of Shakespeare, which embodied editorial decisions by Rowe and Warburton, many of which have been rejected by later scholars. Modern act and scene divisions have been provided.

In his extensive discussion of poetry in volume 2, Kames frequently cites single lines of Latin, Italian, French, or English, without indicating their author or the work in which the quotation occurs. Although he explicitly states that "thought and expression have a great influence on expression" [2.143], many of the single lines, extracted from their contexts, are almost meaningless, and translations have not been provided. Kames is interested essentially in how lines should, or could, be properly spoken, and his discussion is about accent, rhythm, and meter.

Translations

Kames read Latin, French, and Italian fluently, and quoted texts in the original language: his comments are on works in their original language, not on any translation that may be provided. He himself particularly admired the translations of Alexander Pope and John Dryden, and these have been used where possible, together with some other translations of the time. Details are:

Ariosto, Lodovico. *Orlando Furioso* (1532). Translated by William Stewart Rose. London: J. Murray, 1823–31.

Boileau Despréaux, Nicolas. *The Works of Monsieur Boileau*. Translated by Nicholas Rowe. London: E. Sanger and E. Curll, 1712.

Catullus, Gaius Valerius. *The Poems of Catullus*. Translated by Peter Whigham. Baltimore: Penguin Books, 1966.

Corneille, Pierre. *The Cid, Cinna, The Theatrical Illusion*. Translation and introduction by John Cairncross. Harmondsworth, Middlesex, England: Penguin Books, 1975.

———. *Pompey the Great, a Tragedy*. Translated out of French by certain persons of honor. London: Herringman, 1664.

Dryden, John, trans. *Works of Virgil: Containing His Pastorals, Georgics, and Aeneid*. London: J. Tonson, 1697.

Fénelon, François de Salignac de la Mothe-, *The Adventures of Telemachus, the Son of Ulysses*. Translated by Tobias Smollett. London, 1776.

Guarini, Battista. *Il Pastor Fido*. Translated by Richard Fanshawe. London: Bently et al., 1692.

Pope, Alexander, trans. *The Iliad of Homer*. London: for Bernard Lintott, 1715–20.

———. *Imitations of Horace.* Edited by John Butt. London: Methuen, 1939.

———. *The Odyssey of Homer.* London: for Bernard Lintott, 1725–26.

———. *The Poetical Works.* Edited by A. W. Ward. London: Macmillan, 1873.

Quintus Curtius Rufus. *The History of Alexander.* Translated by John Yardley. Hammondsworth, Middlesex, England: Penguin Books, 1984.

Racine, Jean. *Bajazet.* Translated by Y. M. Martin. London: George Gill, 1964.

———. *Iphigenia, Phaedra, Athaliah.* Translation and introduction by John Cairncross. Harmondsworth, Middlesex, England: Penguin Books, 1970.

Tasso, Torquato. *Gerusalemme Liberata.* Translated by Edward Fairfax. Published in 1600 as *Godfrey of Bulloigne, or the Recovery of Jerusalem.* Oxford: Clarendon Press, 1981.

———. *Aminta.* Translated by E. Grillo. London: Dent, 1924.

Vida, Marco Girolamo. *Vida's Art of Poetry.* Translated by Christopher Pitt. London: Sam. Palmer for A. Bettersworth, 1725.

The classical texts quoted by Kames differ in countless minor details from modern editions: the variations have not been noted. The following classical works are cited in translations from the Loeb Classical Library published by Heinemann, London, and Harvard University Press, various dates:

Cicero: *De Finibus,* H. Rackham

Cicero: *De Officiis,* Walter Miller

Cicero: *De Oratore,* E. W. Sutton and H. Rackham

Cicero: *Tusculan Disputations,* J. E. King

Cicero: *Verrine Orations* (Against Caecilius), L. H. G. Greenwood

Horace: *Odes and Epodes,* C. E. Bennett

Horace: *Satires, Epistles, Ars Poetica,* H. R. Fairclough

Livy: B. O. Foster, F. G. Moore, Evan T. Sage, A. C. Schlesinger, R. M. Geer

Lucan: *The Civil War* [Pharsalia], J. D. Duff

Martial: *Epigrams,* D. R. Shackleton Bailey

Ovid: *The Art of Love and Other Poems,* J. H. Mozley

Ovid: *Heroides and Amores,* Grant Showerman

Quintilian: *The Institutio Oratoria,* H. E. Butler

Terence: *The Self-Tormentor, The Eunuch,* John Barsby

Virgil: *Eclogues, Georgics, Aeneid, The Minor Poems,* H. R. Fairclough

In a few cases I have provided my own version.

ACKNOWLEDGMENTS

Most editors exhaust their own resources in chasing down unidentified books and quotations and appropriate translations. Without the unstinting help of friends there would remain many more gaps in notes to the text than still exist, and I wish to thank most warmly William Desmond, Jean Jones, Emilio Mazza, Åsa Söderman, and Robert Wokler.

ELEMENTS OF CRITICISM

VOLUME I

ELEMENTS

<iii>

OF

CRITICISM.

The SIXTH EDITION.

WITH THE

AUTHOR'S LAST CORRECTIONS
AND ADDITIONS.

VOLUME I

EDINBURGH:

Printed for JOHN BELL and WILLIAM CREECH,
And for T. CADELL and G. ROBINSON, *London.*

M,DCC,LXXXV.   <iv><v>

TO THE
KING

Sir,

The Fine Arts have ever been encouraged by wise Princes, not singly for private amusement, but for their beneficial influence in society. By uniting different ranks in the same elegant pleasures, they promote benevolence: by cherishing love of order, they enforce submission to government: and by inspiring delicacy of feeling, they make regular government a double blessing. <vi>

These considerations embolden me to hope for your Majesty's patronage in behalf of the following work, which treats of the Fine Arts, and attempts to form a standard of taste, by unfolding those principles that ought to govern the taste of every individual.

It is rare to find one born with such delicacy of feeling, as not to need instruction: it is equally rare to find one so low in feeling, as not to be capable of instruction. And yet, to refine our taste with respect to beauties of art or of nature, is scarce endeavoured in any seminary of learning; a lamentable defect, considering how early in life taste is susceptible of culture, and how difficult to reform it if unhappily perverted. To furnish materials for supplying that defect, was an additional motive for the present undertaking. <vii>

To promote the Fine Arts in Britain, has become of greater importance than is generally imagined. A flourishing commerce begets opulence; and opulence, inflaming our appetite for pleasure, is commonly vented on luxury, and on every sensual gratification: Selfishness rears its head; becomes fashionable; and, infecting all ranks, extinguishes the *amor patriae,*[1] and

1. Love of one's country.

3

every spark of public spirit. To prevent or to retard such fatal corruption, the genius of an Alfred cannot devise any means more efficacious, than the venting opulence upon the Fine Arts: riches so employ'd, instead of encouraging vice, will excite both public and private virtue. Of this happy effect, ancient Greece furnishes one shining instance; and why should we despair of another in Britain?

In the commencement of an auspicious reign, and even in that early period of life when pleasure commonly is the <viii> sole pursuit, your Majesty has uniformly display'd to a delighted people, the noblest principles, ripen'd by early culture; and for that reason, you will be the more disposed to favour every rational plan for advancing the art of training up youth. Among the many branches of education, that which tends to make deep impressions of virtue, ought to be a fundamental object in a well-regulated government: for depravity of manners will render ineffectual the most salutary laws; and in the midst of opulence, what other means to prevent such depravity but early and virtuous discipline? The British discipline is susceptible of great improvements; and if we can hope for them, it must be from a young and accomplished Prince, eminently sensible of their importance. To establish a complete system of education, seems reserved by Providence for a Sovereign who commands the hearts of his subjects. Success will crown the undertaking, and endear <ix> GEORGE THE THIRD to our latest posterity.

The most elevated and most refined pleasure of human nature, is enjoy'd by a virtuous prince governing a virtuous people; and that, by perfecting the great system of education, your Majesty may very long enjoy this pleasure, is the ardent wish of

> Your Majesty's
>
> Devoted Subject,
>
> HENRY HOME,

December 1761. <x><xi>

PREFACE TO
THE SECOND EDITION

Printing, by multiplying copies at will, affords to writers great opportunity of receiving instruction from every quarter. The author of this treatise, having always been of opinion that the general taste is seldom wrong, was resolved from the beginning to submit to it with entire resignation: its severest disapprobation might have incited him to do better, but never to complain. Finding now the judgement of the public to be favourable, ought he not to draw satisfaction from it? He would be devoid of sensibility were he not greatly satisfied. Many criticisms have indeed reached his ear; but they are candid and benevolent, if not always just. Gratitude therefore, had there been no other motive, must have rous'd his utmost industry to clear this edition from all the defects of the former, so far as suggested by others, or discovered by himself. In a work, containing many particulars both new and abstruse, it was difficult to express every article with sufficient perspicuity; and <xii> after all the pains bestow'd, there remained certain passages which are generally thought obscure. The author giving an attentive ear to every censure of that kind, has, in the present edition, renewed his efforts to correct every defect; and he would gladly hope that he has not been altogether unsuccessful. The truth is, that a writer, who must be possessed of the thought before he can put it into words, is but ill qualified to judge whether the expression be sufficiently clear to others: in that particular, he cannot avoid the taking on him to judge for the reader, who can much better judge for himself.

June 1763. <xiii>

CONTENTS[1]

1. The original page numbers from the sixth edition are retained here.

That nothing external is perceived till first it make an impression upon the organ of sense, is an observation that holds equally in every one of the external senses. But there is a difference as to our knowledge of that impression: in touching, tasting, and smelling, we are sensible of the impression;[1] that, for example, which is made upon the hand by a stone, upon the palate by an apricot, and upon the nostrils by a rose: it is otherwise in seeing and hearing; for I am not sensible of the impression made upon my eye, when I behold a tree; nor of the impression made upon my ear, when I listen to a song.* That difference in the manner of perceiving external objects, distinguisheth remarkably hearing and seeing from the other senses; and I am ready to show, that it distinguisheth still more remarkably the feelings of the former from those of the latter: every feeling, pleasant or painful, must be in the mind; and yet because in tasting, touching, and smelling, we are sensible of the impression made upon the organ, we are led to place there also the pleasant or painful feeling caused by that impres-<2>sion;† but with respect to seeing and hearing, being insensible of the organic impression, we are not misled to assign a wrong place to the pleasant

---

* See the Appendix, § 13.

† After the utmost efforts, we find it beyond our power to conceive the flavour of a rose to exist in the mind: we are necessarily led to conceive that pleasure as existing in the nostrils along with the impression made by the rose upon that organ. And the same will be the result of experiments with respect to every feeling of taste, touch, and smell. Touch affords the most satisfactory experiments. Were it not that the delusion is detected by philosophy, no person would hesitate to pronounce, that the pleasure arising from touching a smooth, soft, and velvet surface, has its existence at the ends of the fingers, without once dreaming of its existing any where else.

1. First edition reads: "But there is a difference as to our consciousness of that impression. In touching, tasting, and smelling, we are conscious of the impression."

or painful feelings caused by that impression; and therefore we naturally place them in the mind, where they really are: upon that account, they are conceived to be more refined and spiritual, than what are derived from tasting, touching, and smelling; for the latter feelings, seeming to exist externally at the organ of sense, are conceived to be merely corporeal.

The pleasures of the eye and the ear, being thus elevated above those of the other external senses, acquire so much dignity as to become a laudable entertainment. They are not, however, set on a level with the purely intellectual; being no less inferior in dignity to intellectual pleasures, than superior to the organic or corporeal: they indeed <3> resemble the latter, being, like them, produced by external objects; but they also resemble the former, being, like them, produced without any sensible organic impression. Their mixt nature and middle place between organic and intellectual pleasures, qualify them to associate with both: beauty heightens all the organic feelings, as well as the intellectual: harmony, though it aspires to inflame devotion, disdains not to improve the relish of a banquet.

The pleasures of the eye and the ear, have other valuable properties beside those of dignity and elevation; being sweet and moderately exhilarating, they are in their tone equally distant from the turbulence of passion, and the languor of indolence; and by that tone are perfectly well qualified, not only to revive the spirits when sunk by sensual gratification, but also to relax them when overstrained in any violent pursuit. Here is a remedy provided for many distresses; and to be convinced of its salutary effects, it will be sufficient to run over the following particulars. Organic pleasures have naturally a short duration; when prolonged, they lose their relish; when indulged to excess, they beget satiety and disgust: and to restore a proper tone of mind, nothing can be more happily contrived than the exhilarating pleasures of the eye and ear. On the other hand, any intense exercise of intellectual powers, becomes painful by overstraining the mind: cessation from such exercise gives <4> not instant relief; it is necessary that the void be filled with some amusement, gently relaxing the spirits:* organic

* Du Bos judiciously observes, that silence doth not tend to calm an agitated mind: but that soft and slow music hath a fine effect. [Jean-Baptiste Du Bos (1670–1742): historian, critic, secretary of the French Academy 1723–42, friend of Pierre Bayle (1647–

pleasure, which hath no relish but while we are in vigour, is ill qualified for that office; but the finer pleasures of sense, which occupy without exhausting the mind, are finely qualified to restore its usual tone after severe application to study or business, as well as after satiety from sensual gratification.

Our first perceptions are of external objects, and our first attachments are to them. Organic pleasures take the lead: but the mind, gradually ripening, relisheth more and more the pleasures of the eye and ear; which approach the purely mental, without exhausting the spirits; and exceed the purely sensual, without danger of satiety. The pleasures of the eye and ear have accordingly a natural aptitude to draw us from the immoderate gratification of sensual appetite; and the mind, once accustomed to enjoy a variety of external objects without being sensible of the organic impression, is prepared for enjoying internal objects where there cannot be an organic impression. Thus the author of nature, by qualifying the human mind for a succession of enjoyments from low to high, leads it by gentle steps from the most grov-<5>eling corporeal pleasures, for which only it is fitted in the beginning of life, to those refined and sublime pleasures that are suited to its maturity.

But we are not bound down to this succession by any law of necessity: the God of nature offers it to us, in order to advance our happiness; and it is sufficient, that he hath enabled us to carry it on in a natural course. Nor has he made our task either disagreeable or difficult: on the contrary, the transition is sweet and easy, from corporeal pleasures to the more refined pleasures of sense; and no less so, from these to the exalted pleasures of morality and religion. We stand therefore engaged in honour as well as interest, to second the purposes of nature, by cultivating the pleasures of the eye and ear, those especially that require extraordinary culture,* such as arise

---

1706) and John Locke (1632–1704). His *Réflexions critiques sur la poésie et sur la peinture*, 1719 (Eng. trans. 1748), was cited throughout the century.]

* A taste for natural objects is born with us in perfection; for relishing a fine countenance, a rich landscape, or a vivid colour, culture is unnecessary. The observation holds equally in natural sounds, such as the singing of birds, or the murmuring of a brook. Nature here, the artificer of the object as well as of the percipient, hath accurately suited

from poetry, painting, sculpture, music, gardening, and architecture. This especially is the duty of the opulent, who have leisure to improve their minds and <6> their feelings. The fine arts are contrived to give pleasure to the eye and the ear, disregarding the inferior senses. A taste for these arts is a plant that grows naturally in many soils; but, without culture, scarce to perfection in any soil: it is susceptible of much refinement; and is, by proper care, greatly improved. In this respect, a taste in the fine arts goes hand in hand with the moral sense, to which indeed it is nearly allied: both of them discover what is right and what is wrong: fashion, temper, and education, have an influence to vitiate both, or to preserve them pure and untainted: neither of them are arbitrary nor local; being rooted in human nature, and governed by principles common to all men. The design of the present undertaking, which aspires not to morality, is, to examine the sensitive branch of human nature, to trace the objects that are naturally agreeable, as well as those that are naturally disagreeable; and by these means to discover, if we can, what are the genuine principles of the fine arts. The man who aspires to be a critic in these arts, must pierce still deeper: he must acquire a clear perception of what objects are lofty, what low, what proper or improper, what manly, and what mean or trivial. Hence a foundation for reasoning upon the taste of any individual, and for passing sentence upon it: where it is conformable to principles, we can pronounce with certainty that it is correct; otherwise, that it is incorrect, <7> and perhaps whimsical. Thus the fine arts, like morals, become a rational science; and, like morals, may be cultivated to a high degree of refinement.

Manifold are the advantages of criticism, when thus studied as a rational science. In the first place, a thorough acquaintance with the principles of the fine arts, redoubles the pleasure we derive from them. To the man who resigns himself to feeling without interposing any judgement, poetry, music, painting, are mere pastime. In the prime of life indeed they are delightful, being supported by the force of novelty, and the heat of imagination: but in time they lose their relish; and are generally neglected in the maturity of life, which disposes to more serious and more important occupations.

---

them to each other. But of a poem, a cantata, a picture, or other artificial production, a true relish is not commonly attained without some study and much practice.

To those who deal in criticism as a regular science, governed by just principles and giving scope to judgement as well as to fancy, the fine arts are a
favourite entertainment; and in old age maintain that relish which they
produce in the morning of life.*

In the next place, a philosophic inquiry into the principles of the fine
arts, inures the reflecting <8> mind to the most enticing sort of logic: the
practice of reasoning upon subjects so agreeable, tends to a habit; and a
habit, strengthening the reasoning faculties, prepares the mind for entering
into subjects more intricate and abstract. To have, in that respect, a just
conception of the importance of criticism, we need but reflect upon the
ordinary method of education; which, after some years spent in acquiring
languages, hurries us, without the least preparatory discipline, into the most
profound philosophy. A more effectual method to alienate the tender mind
from abstract science, is beyond the reach of invention: and accordingly,
with respect to such speculations, our youth generally contract a sort of
hobgoblin terror, seldom if ever subdued. Those who apply to the arts, are
trained in a very different manner: they are led, step by step, from the easier
parts of the operation, to what are more difficult; and are not permitted to
make a new motion, till they are perfected in those which go before. Thus
the science of criticism may be considered as a middle link, connecting the
different parts of education into a regular chain. This science furnisheth
an inviting opportunity to exercise the judgement: we delight to reason
upon subjects that are equally pleasant and familiar: we proceed gradually
from the simpler to the more involved cases: and in a due course of discipline, custom, which improves all our faculties, bestows acuteness on that
of rea-<9>son, sufficient to unravel all the intricacies of philosophy.

Nor ought it to be overlooked, that the reasonings employed on the fine
arts are of the same kind with those which regulate our conduct. Mathematical and metaphysical reasonings have no tendency to improve our

* "Though logic may subsist without rhetoric or poetry, yet so necessary to these last
is a sound and correct logic, that without it they are no better than warbling trifles."
Hermes, p. 6. [James Harris (1709–80): member of parliament, author, prominent am-
ateur musician. *Hermes; Or, a Philosophical Inquiry Concerning Universal Grammar, Logic
and Poetry* (1751) was the second of his three works on language, poetics, and aesthetics.
The reference is to part 1, chap. 1.]

knowledge of man; nor are they applicable to the common affairs of life: but a just taste of the fine arts, derived from rational principles, furnishes elegant subjects for conversation, and prepares us for acting in the social state with dignity and propriety.

The science of rational criticism tends to improve the heart no less than the understanding. It tends, in the first place, to moderate the selfish affections: by sweetening and harmonizing the temper, it is a strong antidote to the turbulence of passion and violence of pursuit: it procures to a man so much mental enjoyment, that in order to be occupied, he is not tempted to deliver up his youth to hunting, gaming, drinking;* nor his middle age to ambition; nor his old age to avarice. Pride and envy, two disgustful passions, find in the constitution no enemy more formidable than a delicate and <10> discerning taste: the man upon whom nature and culture have bestowed this blessing, delights in the virtuous dispositions and actions of others: he loves to cherish them, and to publish them to the world: faults and failings, it is true, are to him no less obvious; but these he avoids, or removes out of sight, because they give him pain. On the other hand, a man void of taste, upon whom even striking beauties make but a faint impression, indulges pride or envy without controul, and loves to brood over errors and blemishes. In a word, there are other passions, that, upon occasion, may disturb the peace of society more than those mentioned; but not another passion is so unwearied an antagonist to the sweets of social intercourse: pride and envy put a man perpetually in opposition to others; and dispose him to relish bad more than good qualities, even in a companion. How different that disposition of mind, where every virtue in a companion or neighbour, is, by refinement of taste, set in its strongest light; and defects or blemishes, natural to all, are suppressed, or kept out of view!

In the next place, delicacy of taste tends no less to invigorate the social affections, than to moderate those that are selfish. To be convinced of that tendency, we need only reflect, that delicacy of taste necessarily heightens

---

* If any youth of a splendid fortune and English education stumble perchance upon this book and this passage, he will pronounce the latter to be empty declamation. But if he can be prevailed upon to make the experiment, he will find, much to his satisfaction, every article well founded.

our feeling of pain and pleasure; and of course our sympathy, which is the capital branch of every social passion. Sym-<11>pathy invites a communication of joys and sorrows, hopes and fears: such exercise, soothing and satisfactory in itself, is necessarily productive of mutual good-will and affection.

One other advantage of rational criticism is reserved to the last place, being of all the most important; which is, that it is a great support to morality. I insist on it with entire satisfaction, that no occupation attaches a man more to his duty, than that of cultivating a taste in the fine arts: a just relish of what is beautiful, proper, elegant, and ornamental, in writing or painting, in architecture or gardening, is a fine preparation for the same just relish of these qualities in character and behaviour. To the man who has acquired a taste so acute and accomplished, every action wrong or improper must be highly disgustful: if, in any instance, the overbearing power of passion sway him from his duty, he returns to it with redoubled resolution never to be swayed a second time: he has now an additional motive to virtue, a conviction derived from experience, that happiness depends on regularity and order, and that disregard to justice or propriety never fails to be punished with shame and remorse.* <12>

Rude ages exhibit the triumph of authority over reason: Philosophers anciently were divided into sects, being Epicureans, Platonists, Stoics, Pythagoreans, or Sceptics: the speculative relied no farther on their own judgement but to chuse a leader, whom they implicitly followed. In later times, happily, reason hath obtained the ascendant: men now assert their native privilege of thinking for themselves; and disdain to be ranked in any sect, whatever be the science. I am forc'd to except criticism, which, by what fatality I know not, continues to be no less slavish in its principles nor less submissive to authority, than it was originally. Bossu,[2] a celebrated French

---

* Genius is allied to a warm and inflammable constitution, delicacy of taste to calmness and sedateness. Hence it is common to find genius in one who is a prey to every passion; but seldom delicacy of taste. Upon a man possessed of that blessing, the moral duties, no less than the fine arts, make a deep impression, and counterbalance every irregular desire: at the same time, a temper calm and sedate is not easily moved, even by a strong temptation.

2. René Le Bossu (1635–80): French critic, author of *Traité du poëme épique,* 1675 (Eng. trans. 1695).

critic, gives many rules; but can discover no better foundation for any of them, than the practice merely of Homer and Virgil, supported by the authority of Aristotle: Strange! that in so long a work, he should never once have stumbled upon the question, Whether, and how far, do these rules agree with human nature. It could not surely be his opinion, that these poets, however eminent for genius, were intitled to give law to mankind; and that nothing now remains, but blind obedience to their arbitrary will: if in writing they followed no <13> rule, why should they be imitated? if they studied nature and were obsequious to rational principles, why should these be concealed from us?

With respect to the present undertaking, it is not the author's intention to compose a regular treatise upon each of the fine arts; but only, in general, to exhibit their fundamental principles, drawn from human nature, the true source of criticism. The fine arts are intended to entertain us, by making pleasant impressions; and, by that circumstance, are distinguished from the useful arts: but in order to make pleasant impressions, we ought, as above hinted, to know what objects are naturally agreeable, and what naturally disagreeable. That subject is here attempted, as far as necessary for unfolding the genuine principles of the fine arts; and the author assumes no merit from his performance, but that of evincing, perhaps more distinctly than hitherto has been done, that these principles, as well as every just rule of criticism, are founded upon the sensitive part of our nature. What the author hath discovered or collected upon that subject, he chuses to impart in the gay and agreeable form of criticism; imagining that this form will be more relished, and perhaps be no less instructive, than a regular and laboured disquisition. His plan is, to ascend gradually to principles, from facts and experiments; instead of beginning with the former, handled abstractedly, and descending to the latter. But <14> though criticism is thus his only declared aim, he will not disown, that all along it has been his view, to explain the nature of man, considered as a sensitive being capable of pleasure and pain: and though he flatters himself with having made some progress in that important science, he is however too sensible of its extent and difficulty, to undertake it professedly, or to avow it as the chief purpose of the present work.

To censure works, not men, is the just prerogative of criticism; and accordingly all personal censure is here avoided, unless where necessary to illustrate some general proposition. No praise is claimed on that account; because censuring with a view merely to find fault, cannot be entertaining to any person of humanity. Writers, one should imagine, ought, above all others, to be reserved on that article, when they lie so open to retaliation. The author of this treatise, far from being confident of meriting no censure, entertains not even the slightest hope of such perfection. Amusement was at first the sole aim of his inquiries: proceeding from one particular to another, the subject grew under his hand; and he was far advanced before the thought struck him, that his private meditations might be publicly useful. In public, however, he would not appear in a slovenly dress; and therefore he pretends not otherwise to apologise for his errors, than by observing, that in a new subject, no less nice than extensive, errors <15> are in some measure unavoidable. Neither pretends he to justify his taste in every particular: that point must be extremely clear, which admits not variety of opinion; and in some matters susceptible of great refinement, time is perhaps the only infallible touchstone of taste: to that he appeals, and to that he chearfully submits.

N.B. THE ELEMENTS OF CRITICISM, meaning the whole, is a title too assuming for this work. A number of these elements or principles are here unfolded: but as the author is far from imagining that he has completed the list, a more humble title is proper, such as may express any number of parts less than the whole. This he thinks is signified by the title he has chosen, *viz.* ELEMENTS OF CRITICISM. <16><17>

ELEMENTS
OF
CRITICISM.

∞ CHAPTER I ∞

Perceptions and Ideas in a Train

A man while awake is conscious of a continued train of perceptions and ideas passing in his mind. It requires no activity on his part to carry on the train: nor can he at will add any idea to the train.* At the same time we learn from daily <18> experience, that the train of our thoughts is not regulated by chance: and if it depend not upon will, nor upon chance, by what law is it governed? The question is of importance in the science of human nature; and I promise beforehand, that it will be found of great importance in the fine arts.

It appears, that the relations by which things are linked together, have a great influence in directing the train of thought. Taking a view of external objects, their inherent properties are not more remarkable, than the various

---

* For how should this be done? what idea is it that we are to add? If we can specify the idea, that idea is already in the mind, and there is no occasion for any act of the will. If we cannot specify any idea, I next demand, how can a person will, or to what purpose, if there be nothing in view? We cannot form a conception of such a thing. If this argument need confirmation, I urge experience: whoever makes a trial will find, that ideas are linked together in the mind, forming a connected chain: and that we have not the command of any idea independent of the chain.

21

relations that connect them together: Cause and effect, contiguity in time or in place, high and low, prior and posterior, resemblance, contrast, and a thousand other relations, connect things together without end. Not a single thing appears solitary and altogether devoid of connection; the only difference is, that some are intimately connected, some more slightly; some near, some at a distance.

Experience will satisfy us of what reason makes probable, that the train of our thoughts is in a great measure regulated by the foregoing relations: an external object is no sooner presented to us in idea, than it suggests to the mind other objects to which it is related; and in that manner is a train of thoughts composed. Such is the law of succession; which must be natural, because it governs all human beings. The law however seems not to be inviolable: it sometimes happens that an idea <19> arises in the mind without any perceived connection; as for example, after a profound sleep.

But though we cannot add to the train an unconnected idea, yet in a measure we can attend to some ideas, and dismiss others. There are few things but what are connected with many others; and when a thing thus connected becomes a subject of thought, it commonly suggests many of its connections: among these a choice is afforded; we can insist upon one, rejecting others; and sometimes we insist on what is commonly held the slighter connection. Where ideas are left to their natural course, they are continued through the strictest connections: the mind extends its view to a son more readily than to a servant; and more readily to a neighbour than to one living at a distance. This order, as observed, may be varied by will, but still within the limits of related objects; for tho' we can vary the order of a natural train, we cannot dissolve the train altogether, by carrying on our thoughts in a loose manner without any connection. So far doth our power extend; and that power is sufficient for all useful purposes: to have more power, would probably be hurtful instead of being salutary.

Will is not the only cause that prevents a train of thought from being continued through the strictest connections: much depends on the present tone of mind; for a subject that accords with that tone is always welcome. Thus, in good spi-<20>rits, a chearful subject will be introduced by the slightest connection; and one that is melancholy, no less readily in low spirits: an interesting subject is recalled, from time to time, by any connection indifferently, strong or weak; which is finely touched by Shakespear, with relation to a rich cargo at sea:

> My wind, cooling my broth,
> Would blow me to an ague, when I thought
> What harm a wind too great might do at sea.
> I should not see the sandy hour-glass run,
> But I should think of shallows and of flats;
> And see my wealthy Andrew dock'd in sand,
> Vailing her high top lower than her ribs,
> To kiss her burial. Should I go to church,
> And see the holy edifice of stone,
> And not bethink me strait of dangerous rocks?
> Which touching but my gentle vessel's side,
> Would scatter all the spices on the stream,
> Enrobe the roaring waters with my silks;
> And, in a word, but now worth this,
> And now worth nothing.
>
> *Merchant of Venice, act* I. *sc.* I.

Another cause clearly distinguishable from that now mentioned, hath also a considerable influence to vary the natural train of ideas; which is, that in the minds of some persons, thoughts and circumstances crowd upon each other by the slightest connections. I ascribe this to a bluntness in the discerning faculty; for a person who cannot accu-<21>rately distinguish between a slight connection and one that is more intimate, is equally affected by each: such a person must necessarily have a great flow of ideas, because they are introduced by any relation indifferently; and the slighter relations, being without number, furnish ideas without end. This doctrine is, in a lively manner, illustrated by Shakespear:

> *Falstaff.* What is the gross sum that I owe thee?
> *Hostess.* Marry, if thou wert an honest man, thyself and thy money too. Thou didst swear to me on a parcel-gilt goblet, sitting in my Dolphin-chamber, at the round table, by a sea-coal fire, on Wednesday in Whitsun-week, when the Prince broke thy head for likening him to a singing man of Windsor, thou didst swear to me then, as I was washing thy wound, to marry me, and make me my Lady thy wife. Canst thou deny it? Did

not Goodwife Keech, the butcher's wife, come in then, and call me Gossip Quickly? coming in to borrow a mess of vinegar; telling us she had a good dish of prawns; whereby thou didst desire to eat some; whereby I told thee they were ill for a green wound. And didst not thou, when she was gone down stairs, desire me to be no more so familiarity with such poor people, saying, that ere long they should call me Madam? And didst thou not kiss me, and bid me fetch thee thirty shillings? I put thee now to thy book-oath, deny it if thou canst?

Second part, Henry IV. *act* 2. *sc.* 2.[1]

On the other hand, a man of accurate judgement cannot have a great flow of ideas; because <22> the slighter relations, making no figure in his mind, have no power to introduce ideas. And hence it is, that accurate judgement is not friendly to declamation or copious eloquence. This reasoning is confirmed by experience; for it is a noted observation, That a great or comprehensive memory is seldom connected with a good judgement.

As an additional confirmation, I appeal to another noted observation, That wit and judgement are seldom united. Wit consists chiefly in joining things by distant and fanciful relations, which surprise because they are unexpected: such relations, being of the slightest kind, readily occur to those only who make every relation equally welcome. Wit, upon that account, is in a good measure incompatible with solid judgement; which, neglecting trivial relations, adheres to what are substantial and permanent. Thus memory and wit are often conjoined: solid judgement seldom with either.

Every man who attends to his own ideas, will discover order as well as connection in their succession. There is implanted in the breast of every man a principle of order, which governs the arrangement of his perceptions, of his ideas, and of his actions. With regard to perceptions I observe, that in things of equal rank, such as sheep in a fold, or trees in a wood, it must be indifferent in what order they be surveyed. But in things of <23> unequal rank, our tendency is, to view the principal subject before we descend to its accessories or ornaments, and the superior before the inferior or dependent: we are equally averse to enter into a minute consideration

1. Act 2, sc. 1.

of constituent parts, till the thing be first surveyed as a whole. It need scarce be added, that our ideas are governed by the same principle; and that in thinking or reflecting upon a number of objects, we naturally follow the same order as when we actually survey them.

The principle of order is conspicuous with respect to natural operations; for it always directs our ideas in the order of nature: thinking upon a body in motion, we follow its natural course; the mind falls with a heavy body, descends with a river, and ascends with flame and smoke: in tracing out a family, we incline to begin at the founder, and to descend gradually to his latest posterity: on the contrary, musing on a lofty oak, we begin at the trunk, and mount from it to the branches: as to historical facts, we love to proceed in the order of time; or, which comes to the same, to proceed along the chain of causes and effects.

But tho', in following out an historical chain, our bent is to proceed orderly from causes to their effects, we find not the same bent in matters of science: there we seem rather disposed to proceed from effects to their causes, and from particular propositions to those which are more general. Why this difference in matters that appear so nearly re-<24>lated? I answer, The cases are similar in appearance only, not in reality. In an historical chain, every event is particular, the effect of some former event, and the cause of others that follow: in such a chain, there is nothing to bias the mind from the order of nature. Widely different is science, when we endeavour to trace out causes and their effects: many experiments are commonly reduced under one cause; and again, many of these causes under one still more general and comprehensive: in our progress from particular effects to general causes, and from particular propositions to the more comprehensive, we feel a gradual dilatation or expansion of mind, like what is felt in an ascending series, which is extremely pleasing: the pleasure here exceeds what arises from following the course of nature; and it is that pleasure which regulates our train of thought in the case now mentioned, and in others that are similar. These observations, by the way, furnish materials for instituting a comparison between the synthetic and analytic methods of reasoning: the synthetic method, descending regularly from principles to their consequences, is more agreeable to the strictness of order; but in following the opposite course in the analytic method, we have a sensible pleasure, like mounting upward, which is not felt in the other: the analytic method is more agreeable to the imagination; the other method will be preferred by those only who with rigidity ad-<25>here to order, and give no indulgence to natural emotions.*

It now appears that we are framed by nature to relish order and connection. When an object is introduced by a proper connection, we are conscious of a certain pleasure arising from that circumstance. Among objects of equal rank, the pleasure is proportioned to the degree of connection: but among unequal objects, where we require a certain order, the pleasure arises chiefly from an orderly arrangement; of which one is sensible, in tracing objects contrary to the course of nature, or contrary to our sense of order: the mind proceeds with alacrity down a flowing river, and with the same alacrity from a whole to its parts, or from a principal to its accessories; but in the contrary direction, it is sensible of a sort of retrograde motion, which is unpleasant. And here may be remarked the great influence of order upon the mind of man: grandeur, which makes a deep impression, inclines us, in running over any series, to proceed from small to great, rather than from great to small; but order prevails over that tendency, and affords pleasure as well as facility in passing from a whole to its parts and from a subject to its ornaments, which are not felt in the opposite course. Elevation touches the mind no less <26> than grandeur doth; and in raising the mind to elevated objects, there is a sensible pleasure: the course of nature, however, hath still a greater influence than elevation; and therefore, the pleasure of falling with rain, and descending gradually with a river, prevails over that of mounting upward. But where the course of nature is joined with elevation, the effect must be delightful: and hence the singular beauty of smoke ascending in a calm morning.

I am extremely sensible of the disgust men generally have to abstract speculation; and I would avoid it altogether, if it could be done in a work that professes to draw the rules of criticism from human nature, their true source. We have but a single choice, which is, to continue a little longer in the same train, or to abandon the undertaking altogether. Candor obliges

---

* A train of perceptions or ideas, with respect to its uniformity and variety, is handled afterward, chap. 9.

me to notify this to my readers, that such of them as have an invincible aversion to abstract speculation, may stop short here; for till principles be unfolded, I can promise no entertainment to those who shun thinking. But I flatter myself with a different bent in the generality of readers: some few, I imagine, will relish the abstract part for its own sake; and many for the useful purposes to which it may be applied. For encouraging the latter to proceed with alacrity, I assure them beforehand, that the foregoing specu-lation leads to many important rules of criticism, which shall be unfolded in the <27> course of this work. In the mean time, for instant satisfaction in part, they will be pleased to accept the following specimen.

Every work of art that is conformable to the natural course of our ideas, is so far agreeable; and every work of art that reverses that course, is so far disagreeable. Hence it is required in every such work, that, like an organic system, its parts be orderly arranged and mutually connected, bearing each of them a relation to the whole, some more intimate, some less, according to their destination: when due regard is had to these particulars, we have a sense of just composition, and so far are pleased with the performance. Homer[2] is defective in order and connection; and Pindar[3] more remark-ably. Regularity, order, and connection, are painful restraints on a bold and fertile imagination; and are not patiently submitted to, but after much cul-ture and discipline. In Horace[4] there is no fault more eminent than want of connection: instances are without number. In the first fourteen lines of ode 7. lib. 1. he mentions several towns and districts, more to the taste of some than of others: in the remainder of the ode, Plancus is exhorted to drown his cares in wine. Having narrowly escaped death by the fall of a

2. Homer: one or more Greek authors of the epic poem the *Iliad,* of unknown iden-tity and date, although probably about 800 B.C. The poem describes the war waged against Troy, the anger of Achilles toward Agamemnon, and the slaying of Hector.

3. Pindar (ca. 522–442 B.C.): Greek lyric poet, author of odes celebrating winners at the Olympic Games. He influenced Horace and, later, John Dryden (1631–1700).

4. Quintus Horatius Flaccus (65–8 B.C.): Roman poet, who studied philosophy in Athens; author of the *Satires* (35 and 30 B.C.) and *Odes* (23 B.C.). "Let others praise famed Rhodes, or Mitylene, or Ephesus, or the walls of Corinth, that overlooks two seas, or Thebes renowned for Bacchus, Delphi for Apollo, or Thessalian Tempe" (*The Odes and Epodes,* bk. 1.7).

tree, this poet* takes occasion to observe justly, that while we guard against some dangers, <28> we are exposed to others we cannot foresee: he ends with displaying the power of music. The parts of ode 16. lib. 2. are so loosely connected as to disfigure a poem otherwise extremely beautiful. The 1st, 2d, 3d, 4th, 11th, 24th, 27th odes of the 3d book, lie open all of them to the same censure. The first satire, book 1. is so deformed by want of connection, as upon the whole to be scarce agreeable: it commences with an important question, How it happens that people, though much satisfied with themselves, are seldom so with their rank or condition. After illustrating the observation in a sprightly manner by several examples; the author, forgetting his subject, enters upon a declamation against avarice, which he pursues till the line 108.: there he makes an apology for wandering, and promises to return to his subject; but avarice having got possession of his mind, he follows out that theme to the end, and never returns to the question proposed in the beginning.

Of Virgil's *Georgics,*[5] tho' esteemed the most complete work of that author, the parts are ill connected, and the transitions far from being sweet and easy. In the first book† he deviates from his subject to give a description of the five zones: the want of connection here, as well as in the description of the prodigies that accompanied the death of Caesar, are scarce pardonable. A digression on <29> the praises of Italy in the second book,‡ is not more happily introduced: and in the midst of a declamation upon the pleasures of husbandry, which makes part of the same book,§ the author introduces himself into the poem without the slightest connection. In the *Lutrin,*[6] the Goddess of Discord is introduced without any connection: she is of no consequence in the poem; and acts no part except that of lavishing

* Lib. 2. ode 13.
† Lin. 231.
‡ Lin. 136.
§ Lin. 475.

5. Publius Vergilius Maro (70–19 B.C.): Roman poet, whose epic poem the *Aeneid* recounts the adventures of Aeneas and the Trojans; his *Georgics* is a didactic poem on agriculture. In Dryden's verse translation the references are 1.322; 2.207, 673.

6. *The Lutrin* (1674): a satirical poem by Nicolas Boileau (1636–1711), French poet and critic, and a friend of Molière (1622–73), La Fontaine (1621–95), and Racine (1639–99), to all of whom Kames refers.

praise upon Lewis the Fourteenth. The two prefaces of Sallust[7] look as if by some blunder they had been prefixed to his two histories: they will suit any other history as well, or any subject as well as history. Even the members of these prefaces are but loosely connected: they look more like a number of maxims or observations than a connected discourse.

An episode in a narrative poem, being in effect an accessory, demands not that strict union with the principal subject, which is requisite between a whole and its constituent parts: it demands, however, a degree of union, such as ought to subsist between a principal and accessory; and therefore will not be graceful if it be loosely connected with the principal subject. I give for an example the descent of Aeneas into hell, which employs the sixth book of the Aeneid: the reader is not prepared for that important event: no cause is assigned that can make it appear necessary, or even natural, <30> to suspend for so long a time the principal action in its most interesting period: the poet can find no pretext for an adventure so extraordinary, but the hero's longing to visit the ghost of his father recently dead: in the mean time the story is interrupted, and the reader loses his ardor. Pity it is that an episode so extremely beautiful, were not more happily introduced. I must observe at the same time, that full justice is done to this incident, by considering it to be an episode; for if it be a constituent part of the principal action, the connection ought to be still more intimate. The same objection lies against that elaborate description of Fame in the Aeneid:* any other book of that heroic poem, or of any heroic poem, has as good a title to that description as the book where it is placed.

* Lib. 4. lin. 173.

[Fame, the great Ill, from small beginnings grows.
Swift from the first; and ev'ry Moment brings
New Vigour to her flights, new Pinnions to her Wings.
Soon grows the Pygmee to Gigantic size;
Her Feet on Earth, her Forehead in the Skies.
(Dryden, IV.251)]

7. Gaius Sallustius Crispus (86–35 B.C.): Roman historian and associate of Caesar in the civil war. Frequently translated into English; it was commonplace to regret the prefaces (for example, the 1709 translation by John Rowe, p. xix).

In a natural landscape we every day perceive a multitude of objects connected by contiguity solely; which is not unpleasant, because objects of sight make an impression so lively, as that a relation even of the slightest kind is relished. This however ought not to be imitated in description: words are so far short of the eye in liveliness of impression, that in a description connection ought to be carefully studied; for new objects introduced in description are made more or less welcome in proportion to the degree of their connec-<31>tion with the principal subject. In the following passage, different things are brought together without the slightest connection, if it be not what may be called verbal, *i.e.* taking the same word in different meanings.

> Surgamus: solet esse gravis cantantibus umbra.
> Juniperi gravis umbra: nocent et frugibus umbrae.
> Ite domum saturae, venit Hesperus, ite capellae.
>
> *Virg. Buc.* x. 75.[8]

The introduction of an object metaphorically or figuratively, will not justify the introduction of it in its natural appearance: a relation so slight can never be relished:

> Distrust in lovers is too warm a sun;
> But yet 'tis night in love when that is gone.
> And in those climes which most his scorching know,
> He makes the noblest fruits and metals grow.
>
> *Part 2. Conquest of Granada, act* 3.[9]

---

8. Now let us rise, for Hoarseness oft invades
   The Singer's Voice, who sings beneath the Shades.
   From Jupiter, unwholsom Dews distill,
   That blast the sooty Corn; the with'ring Herbage kil;
   Away, my Goats, away: for you have browz'd your fill.
                    (Dryden, *The Pastorals,* X.110)

9. *The Conquest of Granada, or Almanzor and Almahide,* 1670, by John Dryden, satirized in *The Rehearsal,* 1672, written in part by George Villiers, second Duke of Buckingham (1628–87), and from which Kames also quotes.

The relations among objects have a considerable influence in the gratification of our passions, and even in their production. But that subject is reserved to be treated in the chapter of emotions and passions.*

There is not perhaps another instance of a building so great erected upon a foundation so slight in <32> appearance, as the relations of objects and their arrangement. Relations make no capital figure in the mind, the bulk of them being transitory, and some extremely trivial: they are however the links that, by uniting our perceptions into one connected chain, produce connection of action, because perception and action have an intimate correspondence. But it is not sufficient for the conduct of life, that our actions be linked together, however intimately: it is beside necessary that they proceed in a certain order; and this also is provided for by an original propensity. Thus order and connection, while they admit sufficient variety, introduce a method in the management of affairs: without them our conduct would be fluctuating and desultory; and we should be hurried from thought to thought, and from action to action, entirely at the mercy of chance. <33>

* Chap. 2. part I. sect. 4.

CHAPTER II

Emotions and Passions

Of all the feelings raised in us by external objects, those only of the eye and the ear are honoured with the name of *passion* or *emotion:* the most pleasing feelings of taste, or touch, or smell, aspire not to that honour. From this observation appears the connection of emotions and passions with the fine arts, which, as observed in the Introduction, are all of them calculated to give pleasure to the eye or the ear; never once condescending to gratify any of the inferior senses. The design accordingly of this chapter is to delineate that connection, with the view chiefly to ascertain what power the fine arts have to raise emotions and passions. To those who would excel in the fine arts, that branch of knowledge is indispensable; for without it the critic, as well as the undertaker, ignorant of any rule, have nothing left but to abandon themselves to chance. Destitute of that branch of knowledge, in vain will either pretend to foretell what effect his work will have upon the heart.

The principles of the fine arts, appear in this view to open a direct avenue to the heart of man. <34> The inquisitive mind beginning with criticism, the most agreeable of all amusements, and finding no obstruction in its progress, advances far into the sensitive part of our nature; and gains imperceptibly a thorough knowledge of the human heart, of its desires, and of every motive to action; a science, which of all that can be reached by man, is to him of the greatest importance.

Upon a subject so comprehensive, all that can be expected in this chapter, is a general or slight survey: and to shorten that survey, I propose to handle separately some emotions more peculiarly connected with the fine arts. Even after that circumscription, so much matter comes under the present chapter, that, to avoid confusion, I find it necessary to divide it into many parts: and though the first of these is confined to such causes of emotion or passion as are the most common and the most general; yet upon examination I find this single part so extensive, as to require a subdivision into several sections. Human nature is a complicate machine, and is unavoidably so in order to answer its various purposes. The public indeed have been entertained with many systems of human nature that flatter the mind by their simplicity: according to some writers, man is entirely a selfish being; according to others, universal benevolence is his duty: one founds morality upon sympathy solely, and one upon utility. If any of these systems were copied from nature, the pre-<35>sent subject might be soon discussed. But the variety of nature is not so easily reached: and for confuting such Utopian systems without the fatigue of reasoning, it appears the best method to take a survey of human nature, and to set before the eye, plainly and candidly, facts as they really exist.

PART I

Causes unfolded of the Emotions and Passions.

SECTION I

Difference between Emotion and Passion.————*Causes that are the most common and the most general.*————*Passion considered as productive of Action.*

These branches are so interwoven, that they cannot be handled separately. It is a fact universally admitted, that no emotion or passion ever starts up in the mind, without a cause: if I love a person, it is for good qualities or good offices: if I have resentment against a man, it must be for some injury he has done me: and I cannot pity any one who is under no distress of body nor of mind.

The circumstances now mentioned, if they raise an emotion or passion, cannot be entirely indiffer-<36>ent; for if so, they could not make any impression. And we find upon examination, that they are not indifferent:

looking back upon the foregoing examples, the good qualities or good offices that attract my love, are antecedently agreeable: if an injury did not
give uneasiness, it would not occasion resentment against the author: nor
would the passion of pity be raised by an object in distress, if that object
did not give pain.

What is now said about the production of emotion or passion, resolves
into a very simple proposition, That we love what is agreeable, and hate
what is disagreeable. And indeed it is evident, that a thing must be agreeable
or disagreeable, before it can be the object either of love or of hatred.

This short hint about the causes of passion and emotion, leads to a more
extensive view of the subject. Such is our nature, that upon perceiving certain external objects, we are instantaneously conscious of pleasure or pain:
a gently-flowing river, a smooth extended plain, a spreading oak, a towering
hill, are objects of sight that raise pleasant emotions: a barren heath, a dirty
marsh, a rotten carcass, raise painful emotions. Of the emotions thus produced, we enquire for no other cause but merely the presence of the object.

The things now mentioned, raise emotions by means of their properties
and qualities: to the emotion raised by a large river, its size, its force, <37>
and its fluency, contribute each a share: the regularity, propriety, and convenience of a fine building, contribute each to the emotion raised by the
building.

If external properties be agreeable, we have reason to expect the same
from those which are internal; and accordingly power, discernment, wit,
mildness, sympathy, courage, benevolence, are agreeable in a high degree:
upon perceiving these qualities in others, we instantaneously feel pleasant
emotions, without the slightest act of reflection, or of attention to consequences. It is almost unnecessary to add, that certain qualities opposite to
the former, such as dullness, peevishness, inhumanity, cowardice, occasion
in the same manner painful emotions.

Sensible beings affect us remarkably by their actions. Some actions raise
pleasant emotions in the spectator, without the least reflection; such as
graceful motion and genteel behaviour. But as *intention,* a capital circumstance in human actions, is not visible, it requires reflection to discover their
true character: I see one delivering a purse of money to another, but I can
make nothing of that action, till I learn with what intention the money is

given: if it be given to discharge a debt, the action pleases me in a slight degree; if it be a grateful return, I feel a stronger emotion; and the pleasant emotion rises to a great height, when it is the intention of the giver to relieve a virtuous fa-<38>mily from want. Thus actions are qualified by intention: but they are not qualified by the event; for an action well intended gives pleasure, whatever the event be. Further, human actions are perceived to be *right* or *wrong;* and that perception qualifies the pleasure or pain that results from them.* <39>

Emotions are raised in us, not only by the qualities and actions of others, but also by their feelings: I cannot behold a man in distress, without partaking of his pain; nor in joy, without partaking of his pleasure.

The beings or things above described, occasion emotions in us, not only in the original survey, but also when recalled to the memory in idea: a field laid out with taste, is pleasant in the recollection, as well as when under our eye: a generous action described in words or colours, occasions a sensible emotion, as well as when we see it performed: and when we reflect upon the distress of any person, our pain is of the same kind with what we felt when eye-witnesses. In a word, an agreeable or disagreeable object recalled

---

* In tracing our emotions and passions to their origin, my first thought was, that qualities and actions are the primary causes of emotions; and that these emotions are afterward expanded upon the being to which these qualities and actions belong. But I am now convinced that this opinion is erroneous. An attribute is not, even in imagination, separable from the being to which it belongs; and for that reason, cannot of itself be the cause of any emotion. We have, it is true, no knowledge of any being or substance but by means of its attributes; and therefore no being can be agreeable to us otherwise than by their means. But still, when an emotion is raised, it is the being itself, as we apprehend the matter, that raises the emotion; and it raises it by means of one or other of its attributes. If it be urged, That we can in idea abstract a quality from the thing to which it belongs; it might be answered, That such abstraction may serve the purposes of reasoning, but is too faint to produce any sort of emotion. But it is sufficient for the present purpose to answer, That the eye never abstracts: by that organ we perceive things as they really exist, and never perceive a quality as separated from the subject. Hence it must be evident, that emotions are raised, not by qualities abstractly considered, but by the substance or body so and so qualified. Thus a spreading oak raises a pleasant emotion, by means of its colour, figure, umbrage, *&c.:* it is not the colour, strictly speaking, that produces the emotion, but the tree coloured: it is not the figure abstractly considered that produces the emotion, but the tree of a certain figure. And hence by the way it appears, that the beauty of such an object is complex, resolvable into several beauties more simple.

to the mind in idea, is the occasion of a pleasant or painful emotion, of
the same kind with that produced when the object was present: the only
difference is, that an idea being fainter than an original perception, the
pleasure or pain produced by the former, is <40> proportionably fainter
than that produced by the latter.

Having explained the nature of an emotion, and mentioned several
causes by which it is produced, we proceed to an observation of considerable importance in the science of human nature, which is, That desire
follows some emotions, and not others. The emotion raised by a beautiful
garden, a magnificent building, or a number of fine faces in a crowded
assembly, is seldom accompanied with desire. Other emotions are accompanied with desire; emotions, for example, raised by human actions and
qualities: a virtuous action raiseth in every spectator a pleasant emotion,
which is commonly attended with desire to reward the author of the action:
a vicious action, on the contrary, produceth a painful emotion, attended
with desire to punish the delinquent. Even things inanimate often raise
emotions accompanied with desire: witness the goods of fortune, which
are objects of desire almost universally; and the desire, when immoderate,
obtains the name of *avarice*. The pleasant emotion produced in a spectator
by a capital picture in the possession of a prince, is seldom accompanied
with desire; but if such a picture be exposed to sale, desire of having or
possessing is the natural consequence of a strong emotion.

It is a truth verified by induction, that every passion is accompanied with
desire; and if an <41> emotion be sometimes accompanied with desire,
sometimes not, it comes to be a material enquiry, in what respect a passion
differs from an emotion. Is passion in its nature or feeling distinguishable
from emotion? I have been apt to think that there must be such a distinction; but after the strictest examination, I cannot perceive any: what is love,
for example, but a pleasant emotion raised by a sight or idea of the beloved
female, joined with desire of enjoyment? in what else consists the passion
of resentment, but in a painful emotion occasioned by the injury, accompanied with desire to chastise the guilty person? In general, as to passion
of every kind, we find no more in its composition, but the particulars now
mentioned, an emotion pleasant or painful, accompanied with desire.
What then shall we say? Are *passion* and *emotion* synonymous terms? That

cannot be averred; because no feeling nor agitation of the mind void of desire, is termed a passion; and we have discovered, that there are many emotions which pass away without raising desire of any kind. How is the difficulty to be solved? There appears to me but one solution, which I relish the more, as it renders the doctrine of the passions and emotions simple and perspicuous. The solution follows. An internal motion or agitation of the mind, when it passeth away without desire, is denominated *an emotion:* when desire follows, the motion or agitation is denominated *a passion.* <42> A fine face, for example, raiseth in me a pleasant feeling: if that feeling vanish without producing any effect, it is in proper language an emotion; but if the feeling, by reiterated views of the object, become sufficiently strong to occasion desire, it loses its name of emotion, and acquires that of passion. The same holds in all the other passions: the painful feeling raised in a spectator by a slight injury done to a stranger, being accompanied with no desire of revenge, is termed an emotion; but that injury raiseth in the stranger a stronger emotion, which being accompanied with desire of revenge, is a passion: external expressions of distress produce in the spectator a painful feeling, which being sometimes so slight as to pass away without any effect, is an emotion; but if the feeling be so strong as to prompt desire of affording relief, it is a passion, and is termed *pity:* envy is emulation in excess; if the exaltation of a competitor be barely disagreeable, the painful feeling is an emotion; if it produce desire to depress him, it is a passion.

To prevent mistakes, it must be observed, that desire here is taken in its proper sense, namely, that internal act, which, by influencing the will, makes us proceed to action. Desire in a lax sense respects also actions and events that depend not on us, as when I desire that my friend may have a son to represent him, or that my country may flourish in <43> arts and sciences: but such internal act is more properly termed a *wish* than a *desire.*

Having distinguished passion from emotion, we proceed to consider passion more at large, with respect especially to its power of producing action.

We have daily and constant experience for our authority, that no man ever proceeds to action but by means of an antecedent desire or impulse. So well established is this observation, and so deeply rooted in the mind, that we can scarce imagine a different system of action: even a child will say familiarly, What should make me do this or that, when I have no desire to do it? Taking it then for granted, that the existence of action depends on antecedent desire; it follows, that where there is no desire there can be no action. This opens another shining distinction between emotions and passions. The former, being without desire, are in their nature quiescent: the desire included in the latter prompts one to act in order to fulfil that desire, or, in other words, to gratify the passion.

The cause of a passion is sufficiently explained above: it is that being or thing, which, by raising desire, converts an emotion into a passion. When we consider a passion with respect to its power of prompting action, that same being or thing is termed its *object:* a fine woman, for example, raises the passion of love, which is directed to her as its object: a man, by injuring me, raises my resentment, and becomes thereby the <44> object of my resentment. Thus the cause of a passion, and its object, are the same in different respects. An emotion, on the other hand, being in its nature quiescent, and merely a passive feeling, must have a cause; but cannot be said, properly speaking, to have an object.[1]

The objects of our passions may be distinguished into two kinds, general and particular. A man, a house, a garden, is a particular object: fame, esteem, opulence, honour, are general objects, because each of them comprehends many particulars. The passions directed to general objects are commonly termed *appetites,* in contradistinction to passions directed to particular objects, which retain their proper name: thus we say an appetite for fame, for glory, for conquest, for riches; but we say the passion of friendship, of love, of gratitude, of envy, of resentment. And there is a material difference between appetites and passions, which makes it proper to distinguish them by different names: the latter have no existence till a proper object be presented; whereas the former exist first, and then are directed to an object: a passion comes after its object; an appetite goes before it, which is obvious in the appetites of hunger, thirst, and animal love, and is the same, in the other appetites above mentioned.

By an object so powerful as to make a deep impression, the mind is inflamed, and hurried to action with a strong impulse. Where the object is less powerful, so as not to inflame the mind, no-<45>thing is felt but desire

1. The next five paragraphs did not appear in the first edition.

without any sensible perturbation. The principle of duty affords one instance: the desire generated by an object of duty, being commonly moderate, moves us to act calmly, without any violent impulse; but if the mind happen to be inflamed with the importance of the object, in that case desire of doing our duty becomes a warm passion.

The actions of brute creatures are generally directed by instinct, meaning blind impulse or desire, without any view to consequences. Man is framed to be governed by reason: he commonly acts with deliberation, in order to bring about some desireable end; and in that case his actions are means employed to bring about the end desired: thus I give charity in order to relieve a person from want: I perform a grateful action as a duty incumbent on me: and I fight for my country in order to repel its enemies. At the same time, there are human actions that are not governed by reason, nor are done with any view to consequences. Infants, like brutes, are mostly governed by instinct, without the least view to any end, good or ill. And even adult persons act sometimes instinctively: thus one in extreme hunger snatches at food, without the slightest consideration whether it be salutary: avarice prompts to accumulate wealth, without the least view of use; and thereby absurdly converts means into an end: and animal love often hurries to fruition, without a thought even of gratification. <46>

A passion when it flames so high as to impel us to act blindly without any view to consequences, good or ill, may in that state be termed *instinctive;* and when it is so moderate as to admit reason, and to prompt actions with a view to an end, it may in that state be termed *deliberative.*

With respect to actions exerted as means to an end, desire to bring about the end is what determines one to exert the action; and desire considered in that view is termed a *motive:* thus the same mental act that is termed *desire* with respect to an end in view, is termed a *motive* with respect to its power of determining one to act. Instinctive actions have a cause, namely, the impulse of the passion; but they cannot be said to have a motive, because they are not done with any view to consequences.

We learn from experience, that the gratification of desire is pleasant; and the foresight of that pleasure becomes often an additional motive for acting. Thus a child eats by the mere impulse of hunger: a young man thinks of the pleasure of gratification, which being a motive for him to eat, fortifies the original impulse: and a man farther advanced in life, hath the additional motive, that it will contribute to his health.* <47>

From these premisses, it is easy to determine with accuracy, what passions and actions are selfish, what social. It is the end in view that ascertains the class to which they belong: where the end in view is my own good, they are selfish; where the end in view is the good of another, they are social. Hence it follows, that instinctive actions, where we act blindly and merely by impulse, cannot be reckoned either social or selfish: thus eating, when prompted by an impulse merely of nature, is neither social nor selfish; but add a motive, That it will contribute to my pleasure or my health, and it becomes in a measure selfish. On the other hand, when affection moves me to exert an action to the end solely of advancing my friend's happiness, without regard to my own gratification, the action is justly denominated *social;* and so is also the affection that is its cause: if another motive be added, That gratifying the affection will also contribute to my own happiness, the action becomes partly selfish. If charity be given with the single view of relieving a person from distress, the action is purely social; but if it be partly in view to enjoy the pleasure of a virtuous act, the action is so far selfish.† Animal <48> love when carried into action by natural impulse singly, is neither social nor selfish: when exerted with a view to gratification, it is selfish: when the motive of giving pleasure to its object is superadded, it is partly social, partly selfish. A just action, when prompted by the principle of duty solely, is neither social nor selfish. When I perform an act of justice with a view to the pleasure of gratification, the action is selfish: I pay debt for my own sake, not with a view to benefit my creditor. But suppose the money has been advanced by a friend without interest, purely

---

* One exception there is, and that is remorse, when it is so violent as to make a man desire to punish himself. The gratification here is far from being pleasant. See p. 188. of this volume. But a single exception, instead of overturning a general rule, is rather a confirmation of it.

† A selfish motive proceeding from a social principle, such as that mentioned, is the most respectable of all selfish motives. To enjoy the pleasure of a virtuous action, one must be virtuous; and to enjoy the pleasure of a charitable action, one must think charity laudable at least, if not a duty. It is otherwise where a man gives charity merely for the sake of ostentation; for this he may do without having any pity or benevolence in his temper.

to oblige me: in that case, together with the motive of gratification, there arises a motive of gratitude, which respects the creditor solely, and prompts me to act in order to do him good; and the action is partly social, partly selfish. Suppose again I meet with a surprising and unexpected act of generosity, that inspires me with love to my benefactor, and the utmost gratitude: I burn to do him good: he is the sole object of my desire; and my own pleasure in gratifying the desire, vanisheth out of sight: in this case, the action I perform is purely <49> social. Thus it happens, that when a social motive becomes strong, the action is exerted with a view singly to the object of the passion, and self never comes in view. The same effect of stifling selfish motives, is equally remarkable in other passions that are in no view social. An action, for example, done to gratify my ambitious views, is selfish; but if my ambition become headstrong, and blindly impell me to action, the action is neither selfish nor social. A slight degree of resentment, where my chief view in acting is the pleasure arising to myself from gratifying the passion, is justly denominated *selfish:* where revenge flames so high as to have no other aim but the destruction of its object, it is no longer selfish; but, in opposition to a social passion, may be termed *dissocial.**

When this analysis of human nature is considered, not one article of which can with truth be controverted, there is reason to be surprised at the blindness of some philosophers, who, by dark and confused notions, are led to deny all motives <50> to action but what arise from self-love. Man, for aught appears, might possibly have been so framed as to be susceptible of no passions but what have self for their object: but man thus framed, would be ill fitted for society: his constitution, partly selfish partly social, fits him much better for his present situation.†

* This word, hitherto not in use, seems to fulfil all that is required by Demetrius Phalereus [*Of Elocution, sect. 96.*] in coining a new word: first, that it be perspicuous; and next, that it be in the tone of the language; that we may not, says our author, introduce among the Grecian vocables, words that sound like those of Phrygia or Scythia. [Demetrius Phalereus: Greek author of unknown identity and date. The Latin title of the work is *De Elocutione;* the English title is *On Style.*]

† As the benevolence of many human actions is beyond the possibility of doubt, the argument commonly insisted on for reconciling such actions to the selfish system, is,

Of self, every one hath a direct perception; of other things we have no knowledge but by means of their attributes: and hence it is, that of self the perception is more lively than of any other thing. Self is an agreeable object; and, for the reason now given, must be more agreeable than any other object. Is this sufficient to account for the prevalence of self-love?

In the foregoing part of this chapter it is suggested, that some circumstances make beings or things fit objects for desire, others not. This hint ought to be pursued. It is a truth ascertained by univer-<51>sal experience, that a thing which in our apprehension is beyond reach, never is the object of desire; no man, in his right senses, desires to walk on the clouds, or to descend to the centre of the earth: we may amuse ourselves in a reverie, with building castles in the air, and wishing for what can never happen; but such things never move desire. And indeed a desire to do what we are sensible is beyond our power, would be altogether absurd. In the next place, though the difficulty of attainment with respect to things within reach, often inflames desire; yet where the prospect of attainment is faint, and the event extremely uncertain, the object, however agreeable, seldom raiseth any strong desire: thus beauty or any other good quality in a woman of rank, seldom raises love in a man greatly her inferior. In the third place, different objects, equally within reach, raise emotions in different degrees; and when desire accompanies any of these emotions, its strength, as is natural, is proportioned to that of its cause. Hence the remarkable difference among desires directed to beings inanimate, animate, and rational: the emotion caused by a rational being, is out of measure stronger than any caused by an animal without reason; and an emotion raised by such an animal, is stronger than what is caused by any thing inanimate. There is a separate reason why desire of which a rational being is the object, should be the strongest: our desires swell by par-<52>tial gratification; and the means we have of gratifying desire by benefiting or harming a rational be-

---

that the only motive I can have to perform a benevolent action, or an action of any kind, is the pleasure that it affords me. So much then is yielded, that we are pleased when we do good to others: which is a fair admission of the principle of benevolence; for without that principle, what pleasure could one have in doing good to others? And admitting a principle of benevolence, why may it not be a motive to action, as well as selfishness is, or any other principle?

ing, are without end: desire directed to an inanimate being, susceptible neither of pleasure nor pain, is not capable of a higher gratification than that
of acquiring the property. Hence it is, that though every emotion accompanied with desire, is strictly speaking a passion; yet commonly none of
these are denominated passions, but where a sensible being capable of pleasure and pain, is the object.

SECTION II[2]

Power of Sounds to raise Emotions and Passions.

Upon a review, I find the foregoing section almost wholly employed upon
emotions and passions raised by objects of sight, though they are also raised
by objects of hearing. As this happened without intention, merely because
such objects are familiar above others, I find it proper to add a short section
upon the power of sounds to raise emotions and passions.

I begin with comparing sounds and visible objects with respect to their
influence upon the mind. It has already been observed, that of all external
objects, rational beings, especially of our own species, have the most powerful influence in raising emotions and passions; and as speech is the most
<53> powerful of all the means by which one human being can display
itself to another, the objects of the eye must so far yield preference to those
of the ear. With respect to inanimate objects of sight, sounds may be so
contrived as to raise both terror and mirth beyond what can be done by
any such object. Music has a commanding influence over the mind, especially in conjunction with words. Objects of sight may indeed contribute
to the same end, but more faintly; as where a love-poem is rehearsed in a
shady grove, or on the bank of a purling stream. But sounds, which are
vastly more ductile and various, readily accompany all the social affections
expressed in a poem, especially emotions of love and pity.

Music having at command a great variety of emotions, may, like many
objects of sight, be made to promote luxury and effeminacy; of which we
have instances without number, especially in vocal music. But with respect

2. This section is not in the first edition.

to its pure and refined pleasures, music goes hand in hand with gardening and architecture, her sister-arts, in humanizing and polishing the mind;* of which none can doubt who have felt the charms of music. But if authority be required, the following passage from a grave historian, eminent for solidity of judgement, must have the greatest weight. Polybius,[3] speaking of the people of Cynaetha, an Arcadian <54> tribe, has the following train of reflections. "As the Arcadians have always been celebrated for their piety, humanity, and hospitality, we are naturally led to enquire, how it has happened that the Cynaetheans are distinguished from the other Arcadians, by savage manners, wickedness, and cruelty. I can attribute this difference to no other cause, but a total neglect among the people of Cynaetha, of an institution established among the ancient Arcadians with a nice regard to their manners and their climate: I mean the discipline and exercise of that genuine and perfect music, which is useful in every state, but necessary to the Arcadians; whose manners, originally rigid and austere, made it of the greatest importance to incorporate this art into the very essence of their government. All men know, that in Arcadia, the children are early taught to perform hymns and songs composed in honour of their gods and heroes; and that when they have learned the music of Timotheus and Philoxenus, they assemble yearly in the public theatres, dancing with emulation to the sound of flutes, and acting in games adapted to their tender years. The Arcadians, even in their private feasts, never employ hirelings, but each man sings in his turn. They are also taught all the military steps and motions to the sound of instruments, which they perform yearly in the theatres, at the pu-<55>blic charge. To me it is evident, that these solemnities were introduced, not for idle pleasure, but to soften the rough and stubborn temper of the Arcadians, occasioned by the coldness of a high country. But the Cynaetheans, neglecting these arts, have become so fierce and savage, that there is not another city in Greece so remarkable for frequent and great enormities. This consideration ought to engage the Arcadians never to relax in any degree their musical discipline; and it ought to open the eyes of the

---

* See chapter 24.

3. Polybius (ca. 200–118 B.C.): Greek historian of Rome's rise to power, covering the period 264–146 B.C.

Cynaetheans, and make them sensible of what importance it would be to restore music to their city, and every discipline that may soften their manners; for otherwise they can never hope to subdue their brutal ferocity."*

No one will be surprised to hear such influence attributed to music, when, with respect to another of the fine arts, he finds a living instance of an influence no less powerful. It is unhappily indeed the reverse of the former; for it has done more mischief by corrupting British manners, than music ever did good by purifying those of Arcadia.

The licentious court of Charles II. among its many disorders, engendered a pest, the virulence of which subsists to this day. The English comedy, copying the manners of the court, became abominably licentious; and continues so with very <56> little softening. It is there an established rule, to deck out the chief characters with every vice in fashion, however gross. But as such characters viewed in a true light would be disgustful, care is taken to disguise their deformity under the embellishments of wit, sprightliness, and good-humour, which in mixt company make a capital figure. It requires not much thought to discover the poisonous influence of such plays. A young man of figure, emancipated at last from the severity and restraint of a college-education, repairs to the capital disposed to every sort of excess. The playhouse becomes his favourite amusement; and he is enchanted with the gaiety and splendor of the chief personages. The disgust which vice gives him at first, soon wears off, to make way for new notions, more liberal in his opinion; by which a sovereign contempt of religion, and a declared war upon the chastity of wives, maids, and widows, are converted from being infamous vices to be fashionable virtues. The infection spreads gradually through all ranks, and becomes universal. How gladly would I listen to any one who should undertake to prove, that what I have been describing is chimerical! but the dissoluteness of our young men of birth will not suffer me to doubt of its reality. Sir Harry Wildair[4] has completed many a rake; and in the *Suspicious Husband,* Ranger,[5] the humble imitator

---

* Polybius, lib. 4. cap. 3.

4. Sir Harry Wildair was the chief character in both *The Constant Couple, or a Trip to the Jubilee,* 1700, and *Sir Harry Wildair,* 1701, by George Farquhar (1678–1707).

5. Ranger was a part made famous by the leading English actor, David Garrick (1717–79), in *The Suspicious Husband,* 1747, by Dr. Benjamin Hoadly (1706–57).

of Sir Harry, has had no slight influence in spreading that character. <57>
What woman tinctured with the playhouse-morals, would not be the
sprightly, the witty, though dissolute Lady Townly, rather than the cold,
the sober, though virtuous Lady Grace?[6] How odious ought writers to be
who thus employ the talents they have from their Maker most traitorously
against himself, by endeavouring to corrupt and disfigure his creatures! If
the comedies of Congreve[7] did not rack him with remorse in his last moments, he must have been lost to all sense of virtue. Nor will it afford any
excuse to such writers, that their comedies are entertaining; unless it could
be maintained, that wit and sprightliness are better suited to a vicious than
a virtuous character. It would grieve me to think so; and the direct contrary
is exemplified in the *Merry Wives of Windsor,*[8] where we are highly entertained with the conduct of two ladies, not more remarkable for mirth and
spirit than for the strictest purity of manners.

SECTION III

Causes of the Emotions of Joy and Sorrow.

This subject was purposely reserved for a separate section, because it could
not, with perspicuity, be handled under the general head. An emotion accompanied with desire is termed *a* <58> *passion;* and when the desire is
fulfilled, the passion is said to be gratified. Now, the gratification of every
passion must be pleasant; for nothing can be more natural, than that the
accomplishment of any wish or desire should affect us with joy: I know of
no exception but when a man stung with remorse desires to chastise and
punish himself. The joy of gratification is properly called *an emotion;* because it makes us happy in our present situation, and is ultimate in its na-

6. Lady Townly and Lady Grace are characters in *The Provok'd Husband,* 1728, by Sir
John Vanbrugh (1664–1726), who was both a successful dramatist and a leading architect,
responsible for Castle Howard, Blenheim Palace, and the Haymarket Theatre, London.
    7. William Congreve (1670–1729): author of *The Old Bachelor,* 1693; *The Double
Dealer,* 1694; *Love for Love,* 1695; and *The Mourning Bride,* 1697; to all of which Kames
refers. Henry Purcell (1659–95) wrote incidental music and songs for the first two plays;
the Moravian-born Gottfried Finger (1660–1730), for the fourth.
    8. *Merry Wives of Windsor,* ca. 1600, by William Shakespeare (1564–1616).

ture, not having a tendency to any thing beyond. On the other hand, sorrow must be the result of an event contrary to what we desire; for if the accomplishment of desire produce joy, it is equally natural that disappointment should produce sorrow.

An event, fortunate or unfortunate, that falls out by accident, without being foreseen or thought of, and which therefore could not be the object of desire, raiseth an emotion of the same kind with that now mentioned: but the cause must be different; for there can be no gratification where there is no desire. We have not however far to seek for a cause: it is involved in the nature of man, that he cannot be indifferent to an event that concerns him or any of his connections; if it be fortunate, it gives him joy; if unfortunate, it gives him sorrow.

In no situation doth joy rise to a greater height, than upon the removal of any violent distress of mind or body; and in no situation doth sorrow <59> rise to a greater height, than upon the removal of what makes us happy. The sensibility of our nature serves in part to account for these effects. Other causes concur. One is, that violent distress always raises an anxious desire to be free from it; and therefore its removal is a high gratification: nor can we be possessed of any thing that makes us happy, without wishing its continuance; and therefore its removal, by crossing our wishes, must create sorrow. The principle of contrast is another cause: an emotion of joy arising upon the removal of pain, is increased by contrast when we reflect upon our former distress: an emotion of sorrow, upon being deprived of any good, is increased by contrast when we reflect upon our former happiness:

> *Jaffier.* There's not a wretch that lives on common charity,
> But's happier than me. For I have known
> The luscious sweets of plenty: every night
> Have slept with soft content about my head,
> And never wak'd but to a joyful morning.
> Yet now must fall like a full ear of corn,
> Whose blossom 'scap'd, yet's withered in the ripening.
>
> *Venice preserv'd, act* I. *sc.* I.[9]

9. Thomas Otway (1652–85): actor, soldier, and dramatist. *The Orphan,* 1680, and

It hath always been reckoned difficult to account for the extreme pleasure that follows a cessation of bodily pain; as when one is relieved from the rack, or from a violent fit of the stone. What <60> is said explains this difficulty, in the easiest and simplest manner: cessation of bodily pain is not of itself a pleasure, for a *non-ens* or a negative can neither give pleasure nor pain; but man is so framed by nature as to rejoice when he is eased of pain, as well as to be sorrowful when deprived of any enjoyment. This branch of our constitution is chiefly the cause of the pleasure. The gratification of desire comes in as an accessory cause: and contrast joins its force, by increasing the sense of our present happiness. In the case of an acute pain, a peculiar circumstance contributes its part: the brisk circulation of the animal spirits occasioned by acute pain, continues after the pain is gone, and produceth a very pleasant emotion. Sickness hath not that effect, because it is always attended with a depression of spirits.

Hence it is, that the gradual diminution of acute pain, occasions a mixt emotion, partly pleasant, partly painful: the partial diminution produceth joy in proportion; but the remaining pain balanceth the joy. This mixt emotion, however, hath no long endurance; for the joy that ariseth upon the diminution of pain, soon vanisheth, and leaveth in the undisturbed possession, that degree of pain which remains.

What is above observed about bodily pain, is equally applicable to the distresses of the mind; and accordingly it is a common artifice, to pre-<61>pare us for the reception of good news by alarming our fears.

SECTION IV

Sympathetic Emotion of Virtue, and its cause.

One feeling there is that merits a deliberate view, for its singularity as well as utility. Whether to call it an emotion or a passion, seems uncertain: the former it can scarce be, because it involves desire; the latter it can scarce be, because it has no object. But this feeling, and its nature, will be best un-

---

Venice Preserved, 1682, to which Kames refers, were successful blank verse plays. The punctuation varies between editions of Otway.

derstood from examples. A signal act of gratitude produceth in the spectator or reader, not only love or esteem for the author, but also a separate feeling, being a vague feeling of gratitude without an object; a feeling, however, that disposes the spectator or reader to acts of gratitude, more than upon an ordinary occasion. This feeling is overlooked by writers upon ethics; but a man may be convinced of its reality, by attentively watching his own heart when he thinks warmly of any signal act of gratitude: he will be conscious of the feeling, as distinct from the esteem or admiration he has for the grateful person. The feeling is singular in the following respect, that it is accompanied with a desire to perform acts of gratitude, without having any object; though in <62> that state, the mind, wonderfully bent on an object, neglects no opportunity to vent itself: any act of kindness or good-will that would pass unregarded upon another occasion, is greedily seized; and the vague feeling is converted into a real passion of gratitude: in such a state, favours are returned double.

In like manner, a courageous action produceth in a spectator the passion of admiration directed to the author: and beside this well-known passion, a separate feeling is raised in the spectator; which may be called *an emotion of courage;* because, while under its influence, he is conscious of a boldness and intrepidity beyond what is usual, and longs for proper objects upon which to exert this emotion:

> Spumantemque dari, pecora inter inertia, votis
> Optat aprum, aut fulvum descendere monte leonem.
> *Aeneid.* iv. 158.[10]

> Non altramente il tauro, oue l'irriti
> Geloso amor con stimoli pungenti,
> Horribilmente mugge, e co'muggiti
> Gli spirti in se risueglia, e l'ire ardenti:
> E'l corno aguzza a i tronchi, e par ch' inuiti

---

10. And rather wou'd the tusky Boar attend,
    Or see the tawny Lyon downward bend.
        (Dryden, 4.228)

Con vani colpi a'la battaglia i venti.   *Tasso, canto 7. st. 55.*[11]

So full of valour that they smote the air
For breathing in their faces.   *Tempest, act 4. sc. 4.*[12] <63>

The emotions raised by music independent of words, must be all of this nature: courage roused by martial music performed upon instruments without a voice, cannot be directed to any object; nor can grief or pity raised by melancholy music of the same kind have an object.

For another example, let us figure some grand and heroic action, highly agreeable to the spectator: beside veneration for the author, the spectator feels in himself an unusual dignity of character, which disposeth him to great and noble actions: and herein chiefly consists the extreme delight every one hath in the histories of conquerors and heroes.

This singular feeling, which may be termed *the sympathetic emotion of virtue,* resembles, in one respect, the well-known appetites that lead to the propagation and preservation of the species. The appetites of hunger, thirst, and animal love, arise in the mind before they are directed to any object; and in no case whatever is the mind more solicitous for a proper object, than when under the influence of any of these appetites.

The feeling I have endeavoured to unfold, may well be termed *the sympathetic emotion of virtue;* for it is raised in a spectator, or in a reader, by virtuous actions of every kind, and by no other sort. When we contemplate

---

11. Torquato Tasso (1544–95): Italian courtier and author of the epic poem *Gerusalemme Liberata,* 1576–81, partly translated into English by Richard Carew in 1594 as *Jerusalem Delivered.* Lully, Handel, Haydn, Gluck, and Rossini were among the many composers who used the epic as a libretto for their operas.

Like as a bull when prickt with iealousie,
He spies the riuall of his hot desire,
Through all the fields doth bellow, rore and vrie,
And with his thund'ring voice augments his ire,
And threat'ning battaile to the emptie skie,
Tears with his horne, each tree, plant, bush and brire.
                              (trans. Edward Fairfax)

12. Act 4, sc. 1.

a virtuous action, which fails not to prompt our love for the <64> author, our propensity at the same time to such actions is so much enlivened, as to become for a time an actual emotion. But no man hath a propensity to vice as such: on the contrary, a wicked deed disgusts him, and makes him abhor the author; and this abhorrence is a strong antidote against vice, as long as any impression remains of the wicked action.

In a rough road, a halt to view a fine country is refreshing; and here a delightful prospect opens upon us. It is indeed wonderful to observe what incitements there are to virtue in the human frame: justice is perceived to be our duty; and it is guarded by natural punishments, from which the guilty never escape: to perform noble and generous actions, a warm sense of their dignity and superior excellence is a most efficacious incitement.* And to leave virtue in no quarter unsupported, here is unfolded an admirable contrivance, by which good example commands the heart, and adds to virtue the force of habit. We approve every virtuous action, and bestow our affection on the author; but if virtuous actions produced no other effect upon us, good example would not have great influence: the sympathetic emotion under consideration bestows upon good example the utmost influence, by prompting us <65> to imitate what we admire. This singular emotion will readily find an object to exert itself upon: and at any rate, it never exists without producing some effect; because virtuous emotions of that sort, are in some degree an exercise of virtue; they are a mental exercise at least, if they appear not externally. And every exercise of virtue, internal and external, leads to habit; for a disposition or propensity of the mind, like a limb of the body, becomes stronger by exercise. Proper means, at the same time, being ever at hand to raise this sympathetic emotion, its frequent reiteration may, in a good measure, supply the want of a more complete exercise. Thus, by proper discipline, every person may acquire a settled habit of virtue: intercourse with men of worth, histories of generous and disinterested actions, and frequent meditation upon them, keep the sympathetic emotion in constant exercise, which by degrees introduceth a habit, and confirms the authority of virtue: with respect to education in

* See *Essays on morality and natural religion,* part 1. ess. 2. ch. 4. [By Henry Home, Edinburgh, 1751.]

particular, what a spacious and commodious avenue to the heart of a young person is here opened! <66>

SECTION V

In many instances one Emotion is productive of another.
The same of Passions.

In the first chapter it is observed, that the relations by which things are connected, have a remarkable influence on the train of our ideas. I here add, that they have an influence, no less remarkable, in the production of emotions and passions. Beginning with the former, an agreeable object makes every thing connected with it appear agreeable; for the mind gliding sweetly and easily through related objects, carries along the agreeable properties it meets with in its passage, and bestows them on the present object, which thereby appears more agreeable than when considered apart.* This reason may appear obscure and meta-<67>physical, but the fact is beyond all dispute. No relation is more intimate than that between a being and its qualities: and accordingly, every quality in a hero, even the slightest, makes a greater figure than more substantial qualities in others. The propensity of carrying along agreeable properties from one object to another, is some-

---

* Such proneness has the mind to this communication of properties, that we often find a property ascribed to a related object, of which naturally it is not susceptible. Sir Richard Grenville in a single ship, being surprised by the Spanish fleet, was advised to retire. He utterly refused to turn from the enemy; declaring, "he would rather die, than dishonour himself, his country, and her Majesty's ship." *Hakluyt, vol. 2. part 2. p. 169.* [Richard Hakluyt (1552–1616), *The Principal Navigations, Voyages, Traffiques and Discoveries of the English Nation,* 1599–1600. He was a clergyman and the English ambassador to Paris, 1583–88.] To aid the communication of properties in instances like the present, there always must be a momentary personification: a ship must be imagined a sensible being, to make it susceptible of honour or dishonour. In the battle of Mantinea, Epaminondas being mortally wounded, was carried to his tent in a manner dead: recovering his senses, the first thing he inquired about was his shield: which being brought, he kissed it as the companion of his valour and glory. It must be remarked, that among the Greeks and Romans it was deemed infamous for a soldier to return from battle without his shield. [The Theban general Epaminondas used an oblique form of attack at the Battle of Mantineia (362 B.C.), which became a model both for Alexander and, much later, for Frederick the Great.]

times so vigorous as to convert defects into properties: the wry neck of Alexander was imitated by his courtiers as a real beauty, without intention to flatter: Lady Piercy, speaking of her husband Hotspur,

———— ———— By his light
Did all the chivalry of England move,
To do brave acts. He was indeed the glass,
Wherein the noble youths did dress themselves.
He had no legs that practis'd not his gait:
And speaking thick, which Nature made his blemish,
Became the accents of the valiant:
For those who could speak slow and tardily,
Would turn their own perfection to abuse,
To seem like him.   *Second part, Henry* IV. *act* 2. *sc.* 6.[13]

The same communication of passion obtains in the relation of principal and accessory. Pride, of <68> which self is the object, expands itself upon a house, a garden, servants, equipage, and every accessory. A lover address-eth his mistress's glove in the following terms,

Sweet ornament that decks a thing divine.[14]

Veneration for relicks has the same natural foundation; and that foun-dation with the superstructure of superstition, has occasioned much blind devotion to the most ridiculous objects, to the supposed milk, for example, of the Virgin Mary, or the supposed blood of St. Janivarius.*[15] A temple is in a proper sense an accessory of the deity to which it is dedicated: Diana is chaste, and not only her temple, but the very isicle which hangs on it, must partake of that property:

* But why worship the cross which is supposed to be that upon which our Saviour suffered? That cross ought to be the object of hatred, not of veneration. If it be urged, that as an instrument of Christ's suffering it was salutary to mankind, I answer, Why is not also Pontius Pilate reverenced, Cajaphas the high priest, and Judas Iscariot?

13. Act 2, sc. 3.
14. *Two Gentlemen of Verona,* act 2, sc. 1.
15. Patron saint of Naples, capital of the Kingdom of the Sicilies.

> The noble sister of Poplicola,
> The moon of Rome; chaste as the isicle
> That's curdled by the frost from purest snow,
> And hangs on Dian's temple.   *Coriolanus, act* 5. *sc.* 3.

Thus it is, that the respect and esteem, which the great, the powerful, the opulent, naturally < 69 > command, are in some measure communicated to their dress, to their manners, and to all their connections: and it is this communication of properties, which, prevailing even over the natural taste of beauty, helps to give currency to what is called *the fashion.*

By means of the same easiness of communication, every bad quality in an enemy is spread upon all his connections. The sentence pronounced against Ravaillac[16] for the assassination of Henry IV. of France, ordains, that the house in which he was born should be razed to the ground, and that no other building should ever be erected on that spot. Enmity will extend passion to objects still less connected. The Swiss suffer no peacocks to live, because the Duke of Austria, their ancient enemy, wears a peacock's tail in his crest. A relation more slight and transitory than that of enmity, may have the same effect: thus the bearer of bad tidings becomes an object of aversion:

> Fellow, begone; I cannot brook thy sight;
> This news hath made thee a most ugly man.
>
>   *King John, act* 3. *sc.* 1.

> Yet the first bringer of unwelcome news
> Hath but a losing office: and his tongue
> Sounds ever after, as a sullen bell
> Remember'd, tolling a departed friend.
>
>   *Second part, Henry* IV. *act* 1. *sc.* 3.[17] <70>

In borrowing thus properties from one object to bestow them on another, it is not any object indifferently that will answer. The object from

---

16. François Ravaillac (1578–1610), lawyer and schoolmaster, was hung for assassinating Henry IV of France (1553–1610).

17. Act 1, sc. 1.

which properties are borrowed, must be such as to warm the mind and enliven the imagination. Thus the beauty of a mistress, which inflames the imagination, is readily communicated to a glove, as above mentioned; but the greatest beauty a glove is susceptible of, touches the mind so little, as to be entirely dropped in passing from it to the owner. In general it may be observed, that any dress upon a fine woman is becoming; but that ornaments upon one who is homely, must be elegant indeed to have any remarkable effect in mending her appearance.*

The emotions produced as above may properly be termed *secondary*, being occasioned either by antecedent emotions or antecedent passions, which in that respect may be termed *primary*. And to complete the present theory, I must add, that a secondary emotion may readily swell into a passion <71> for the accessory object, provided the accessory be a proper object for desire. Thus it happens that one passion is often productive of another: examples are without number; the sole difficulty is a proper choice. I begin with self-love, and the power it hath to generate love to children. Every man, beside making part of a greater system, like a comet, a planet, or satellite only, hath a less system of his own, in the centre of which he represents the sun darting his fire and heat all around; especially upon his nearest connections: the connection between a man and his children, fundamentally that of cause and effect, becomes, by the addition of other circumstances, the completest that can be among individuals; and therefore self-love, the most vigorous of all passions, is readily expanded upon children. The secondary emotion they produce by means of their connection, is sufficiently strong to move desire even from the beginning; and the new passion swells by degrees, till it rival in some measure self-love, the primary passion. To demonstrate the truth of this theory, I urge the following argument. Remorse for betraying a friend, or murdering an enemy in cold blood, makes a man even hate himself: in that state, he is not conscious of

* A house and gardens surrounded with pleasant fields, all in good order, bestow greater lustre upon the owner than at first will be imagined. The beauties of the former are, by intimacy of connection, readily communicated to the latter; and if it have been done at the expence of the owner himself, we naturally transfer to him whatever of design, art, or taste, appears in the performance. Should not this be a strong motive with proprietors to embellish and improve their fields?

affection to his children, but rather of disgust or ill will. What cause can be assigned for that change, other than the hatred he has to himself, which is expanded upon his children? And if <72> so, may we not with equal reason derive from self-love, some part at least of the affection a man generally has to them?

The affection a man bears to his blood-relations, depends partly on the same principle: self-love is also expanded upon them; and the communicated passion is more or less vigorous in proportion to the degree of connection. Nor doth self-love rest here: it is, by the force of connection, communicated even to things inanimate: and hence the affection a man bears to his property, and to every thing he calls his own.

Friendship, less vigorous than self-love, is, for that reason, less apt to communicate itself to the friend's children, or other relations. Instances however are not wanting of such communicated passion, arising from friendship when it is strong. Friendship may go higher in the matrimonial state than in any other condition; and Otway, in *Venice preserv'd*, takes advantage of that circumstance: in the scene where Belvidera sues to her father for pardon, she is represented as pleading her mother's merit, and the resemblance she bore to her mother:

> *Priuli.* My daughter!
> *Belvidera.* Yes, your daughter, by a mother
> Virtuous and noble, faithful to your honour,
> Obedient to your will, kind to your wishes,
> Dear to your arms. By all the joys she gave you <73>
> When in her blooming years she was your treasure,
> Look kindly on me; in my face behold
> The lineaments of hers y'have kiss'd so often,
> Pleading the cause of your poor cast-off child.

And again,

> *Belvidera.* Lay me, I beg you, lay me
> By the dear ashes of my tender mother:
> She would have pitied me, had fate yet spar'd her.
>
> *Act* 5. *sc.* 1.

This explains why any meritorious action or any illustrious qualification in my son or my friend, is apt to make me overvalue myself: if I value my friend's wife or son upon account of their connection with him, it is still more natural that I should value myself upon account of my connection with him.

Friendship, or any other social affection, may, by changing the object, produce opposite effects. Pity, by interesting us strongly for the person in distress, must of consequence inflame our resentment against the author of the distress: for, in general, the affection we have for any man, generates in us good-will to his friends, and ill-will to his enemies. Shakespear shows great art in the funeral oration pronounced by Antony over the body of Caesar. He first endeavours to excite grief in the hearers, by dwelling upon the deplorable loss of so great a man: this passion, in-<74>teresting them strongly in Caesar's fate, could not fail to produce a lively sense of the treachery and cruelty of the conspirators; an infallible method to inflame the resentment of the people beyond all bounds:

> *Antony.* If you have tears, prepare to shed them now.
> You all do know this mantle; I remember
> The first time ever Caesar put it on,
> 'Twas on a summer's evening in his tent,
> That day he overcame the Nervii—
> Look! in this place ran Cassius's dagger through;—
> See what a rent the envious Casca made.—
> Through this the well-beloved Brutus stabb'd;
> And as he pluck'd his cursed steel away,
> Mark how the blood of Caesar follow'd it!
> As rushing out of doors, to be resolv'd,
> If Brutus so unkindly knock'd, or no:
> For Brutus, as you know, was Caesar's angel.
> Judge, oh you gods! how dearly Caesar lov'd him;
> This, this, was the unkindest cut of all;
> For when the noble Caesar saw him stab,
> Ingratitude, more strong than traitor's arms,
> Quite vanquish'd him; then burst his mighty heart;
> And, in his mantle muffling up his face,
> Which all the while ran blood, great Caesar fell,
> Even at the base of Pompey's statue.
> O what a fall was there, my countrymen!
> Then I and you, and all of us fell down,

Whilst bloody treason flourish'd over us.
O, now you weep; and I perceive you feel
The dint of pity; these are gracious drops.
Kind souls! what! weep you when you but behold <75>
Our Caesar's vesture wounded? look you here!
Here is himself, marr'd, as you see, by traitors.

Julius Caesar, act 3. *sc.* 6.[18]

Had Antony endeavoured to excite his audience to vengeance, without paving the way by raising their grief, his speech would not have made the same
impression.

Hatred, and other dissocial passions, produce effects directly opposite
to those above mentioned. If I hate a man, his children, his relations, nay
his property, become to me objects of aversion: his enemies, on the other
hand, I am disposed to esteem.

The more slight and transitory relations are not favourable to the communication of passion. Anger, when sudden and violent, is one exception;
for if the person who did the injury be removed out of reach, that passion
will vent itself against any related object, however slight the relation be. Another exception makes a greater figure: a group of beings or things, becomes
often the object of a communicated passion, even where the relation of the
individuals to the percipient is but slight. Thus though I put no value upon
a single man for living in the same town with myself; my townsmen, however,
considered in a body, are preferred before others. This is still more remarkable
with respect to my countrymen in general: the grandeur of the complex object swells <76> the passion of self-love by the relation I have to my native
country; and every passion, when it swells beyond its ordinary bounds, hath
a peculiar tendency to expand itself along related objects. In fact, instances
are not rare, of persons, who upon all occasions are willing to sacrifice their
lives and fortunes for their country. Such influence upon the mind of man
hath a complex object, or, more properly speaking, a general term.*

The sense of order hath influence in the communication of passion. It
is a common observation, that a man's affection to his parents is less vig-

* See *Essays on morality and natural religion,* part 1. ess. 2. ch. 5.
18. Act 3, sc. 2.

orous than to his children: the order of nature in descending to children, aids the transition of the affection: the ascent to a parent, contrary to that order, makes the transition more difficult. Gratitude to a benefactor is readily extended to his children; but not so readily to his parents. The difference however between the natural and inverted order, is not so considerable, but that it may be balanced by other circumstances. Pliny* gives an account of a woman of rank condemned to die for a crime; and, to avoid public shame, detained in prison to die of hunger: her life being prolonged beyond expectation, it was disco-<77>vered, that she was nourished by sucking milk from the breasts of her daughter. This instance of filial piety, which aided the transition, and made ascent no less easy than descent is commonly, procured a pardon to the mother, and a pension to both. The story of Androcles and the lion† may be accounted for in the same manner: the admiration, of which the lion was the object for his kindness and gratitude to Androcles, produced good-will to Androcles, and a pardon of his crime.

And this leads to other observations upon communicated passions. I love my daughter less after she is married, and my mother less after a second marriage: the marriage of my son or of my father diminishes not my affection so remarkably. The same observation holds with respect to friendship, gratitude, and other passions: the love I bear my friend, is but faintly extended to his married daughter: the resentment I have against a man, is readily extended against children who make part of his family; not so readily against children who are forisfamiliated,[19] especially by marriage. This difference is also more remarkable in daughters than in sons. These are curious facts; and in order to discover the cause, we must examine minutely that operation of the mind by which a passion is extended to a related

---

* Lib. 7. cap. 36. [Gaius Plinius Caecilius Secundus (ca. A.D. 61–112) was the nephew of Pliny the Elder, who was killed during the volcanic destruction of Herculaneum A.D. 79; he was a lawyer, prominent member of the Roman Senate, and friend of Tacitus, the historian.]

† Aulus Gellius, lib. 5. cap. 14. [Aulus Gellius, second-century Latin grammarian and author of a miscellany of reflections and extracts written during winter nights in Athens, *Noctes Atticae*. The story of Androcles and the lion was often retold and was popular among Renaissance painters.]

19. In Scots law, a son who has been emancipated from his family by receipt of part of his inheritance.

object. In consi-<78>dering two things as related, the mind is not stationary, but passeth and repasseth from the one to the other, viewing the relation
from each of them perhaps oftener than once; which holds more especially
in considering a relation between things of unequal rank, as between the
cause and the effect, or between a principal and an accessory: in contemplating, for example, the relation between a building and its ornaments,
the mind is not satisfied with a single transition from the former to the
latter; it must also view the relation, beginning at the latter, and passing
from it to the former. This vibration of the mind in passing and repassing
between things related, explains the facts above mentioned: the mind passeth easily from the father to the daughter; but where the daughter is married, this new relation attracts the mind, and obstructs, in some measure,
the return from the daughter to the father; and any circumstance that obstructs the mind in passing and repassing between its objects, occasions a
like obstruction in the communication of passion. The marriage of a male
obstructs less the easiness of transition; because a male is less sunk by the
relation of marriage than a female.

The foregoing instances are of passion communicated from one object
to another. But one passion may be generated by another, without change
of object. It in general is observable, that a passion paves the way to others
similar in their <79> tone, whether directed to the same or to a different
object; for the mind heated by any passion, is, in that state, more susceptible
of a new impression in a similar tone, than when cool and quiescent. It is
a common observation, that pity generally produceth friendship for a person in distress. One reason is, that pity interests us in its object, and recommends all its virtuous qualities: female beauty accordingly shows best in
distress; being more apt to inspire love, than upon an ordinary occasion.
But the chief reason is, that pity, warming and melting the spectator, prepares him for the reception of other tender affections; and pity is readily
improved into love or friendship, by a certain tenderness and concern for
the object, which is the tone of both passions. The aptitude of pity to produce love, is beautifully illustrated by Shakespear:

> *Othello.* Her father lov'd me; oft invited me;
> Still question'd me the story of my life,
> From year to year; the battles, sieges, fortunes,

That I have past.
I ran it through, e'en from my boyish days,
To th' very moment that he bade me tell it:
Wherein I spoke of most disast'rous chances,
Of moving accidents by flood and field;
Of hair-breadth 'scapes in th' imminent deadly breach;
Of being taken by the insolent foe,
And sold to slavery; of my redemption thence,
And with it all my travel's history.
——— ——— All these to hear <80>
Would Desdemona seriously incline;
But still the house-affairs would draw her thence,
Which ever as she could with haste dispatch,
She'd come again, and with a greedy ear
Devour up my discourse: which I observing,
Took once a pliant hour, and found good means
To draw from her a prayer of earnest heart,
That I would all my pilgrimage dilate,
Whereof by parcels she had something heard,
But not distinctively. I did consent,
And often did beguile her of her tears,
When I did speak of some distressful stroke,
That my youth suffer'd. My story being done,
She gave me for my pains a world of sighs:
She swore, in faith, 'twas strange, 'twas passing strange—
'Twas pitiful, 'twas wondrous pitiful—
She wish'd she had not heard it:——yet she wish'd,
That Heaven had made her such a man:—she thank'd me,
And bade me, if I had a friend that lov'd her,
I should but teach him how to tell my story,
And that would woo her. On this hint I spake:
She lov'd me for the dangers I had past,
And I lov'd her, that she did pity them:
This only is the witchcraft I have us'd.

Othello, act I. *sc.* 8.[20]

20. Act I, sc. 3.

In this instance it will be observed that admiration concurred with pity to produce love. <81>

SECTION VI

Causes of the Passions of Fear and Anger.

Fear and anger, to answer the purposes of nature, are happily so contrived as to operate sometimes instinctively sometimes deliberately, according to circumstances. As far as deliberate, they fall in with the general system, and require no particular explanation: if any object have a threatening appearance, reason suggests means to avoid the danger: if a man be injured, the first thing he thinks of, is what revenge he shall take, and what means he shall employ. These particulars are no less obvious than natural. But as the passions of fear and anger in their instinctive state, are less familiar to us, it may be acceptable to the reader to have them accurately delineated. He may also possibly be glad of an opportunity to have the nature of instinctive passions more fully explained, than there was formerly opportunity to do. I begin with fear.

Self-preservation is a matter of too great importance to be left entirely to the conduct of reason. Nature hath acted here with her usual foresight. Fear and anger are passions that move us to act, sometimes deliberately sometimes instinctively, according to circumstances; and by operating in <82> the latter manner, they frequently afford security when the slower operations of deliberate reason would be too late: we take nourishment commonly, not by the direction of reason, but by the impulse of hunger and thirst; and in the same manner, we avoid danger by the impulse of fear, which often, before there is time for reflection, placeth us in safety. Here we have an illustrious instance of wisdom in the formation of man; for it is not within the reach of fancy, to conceive any thing more artfully contrived to answer its purpose, than the instinctive passion of fear, which, upon the first surmise of danger, operates instantaneously. So little doth the passion, in such instances, depend on reason, that it frequently operates in contradiction to it: a man who is not upon his guard, cannot avoid shrinking at a blow, tho' he knows it to be aimed in sport; nor avoid closing his eyes at the approach of what may hurt them, tho' conscious that he is in no danger. And it also operates by impelling us to act even where we are conscious that our interposition can be of no service: if a passage-boat in a brisk gale bear much to one side, I cannot avoid applying the whole force of my shoulders to set it upright; and if my horse stumble, my hands and knees are instantly at work to prevent him from falling.

Fear provides for self-preservation by flying from harm; anger, by repelling it. Nothing indeed can be better contrived to repel or prevent injury, <83> than anger or resentment: destitute of that passion, men, like defenceless lambs, would lie constantly open to mischief.* Deliberate anger caused by a voluntary injury, is too well known to require any explanation: if my desire be to resent an affront, I must use means; and these means must be discovered by reflection: deliberation is here requisite; and in that case the passion seldom exceeds just bounds. But where anger impels one suddenly to return a blow, even without thinking of doing mischief, the passion is instinctive; and it is chiefly in such a case that it is rash and ungovernable, because it operates blindly, without affording time for deliberation or foresight.

Instinctive anger is frequently raised by bodily pain, by a stroke for example on a tender part, which, ruffling the temper and unhinging the mind, is in its tone similar to anger: and when a man is thus beforehand disposed to anger, he is not nice nor scrupulous about an object; the person who gave the stroke, however accidentally, is by an inflammable temper held a proper object, merely for having occasioned the pain. It is still more remarkable, that a stock or a stone by which I am <84> hurt, becomes an object for my resentment: I am violently incited to crush it to atoms. The passion indeed in that case can be but a single flash; for being entirely irrational, it must vanish with the first reflection. Nor is that irrational effect confined to bodily pain: internal distress, when excessive, may be the occasion of effects

---

* Brasidas being bit by a mouse he had catched, let it slip out of his fingers: "No creature (says he) is so contemptible, but what may provide for its own safety, if it have courage." *Plutarch. Apothegmata.*
[Plutarch (ca. A.D. 50–120): biographer and moral philosopher. His *Parallel Lives* of Greek and Roman leaders, often translated, was a major source of Shakespeare's plots. *Apothegmata* is a collection of brief essays.]

equally irrational: perturbation of mind occasioned by the apprehension of having lost a dear friend, will, in a fiery temper, produce momentary sparks of anger against that very friend, however innocent: thus Shakespear, in the *Tempest*,

> *Alonzo.* ——— Sit down and rest.
> Ev'n here I will put off my hope, and keep it
> No longer for my flatterer; he is drown'd
> Whom thus we stray to find, and the sea mocks
> Our frustrate search on land. Well, let him go.
>
> *Act 3. sc. 3.*

The final words, *Well, let him go,* are an expression of impatience and anger at Ferdinand, whose absence greatly distressed his father, dreading that he was lost in the storm. This nice operation of the human mind, is by Shakespear exhibited upon another occasion, and finely painted. In the tragedy of *Othello,* Iago, by dark hints and suspicious circumstances, had roused Othello's jealousy; which, however, appeared too slightly founded to be vented upon Desdemona, its proper <85> object. The perturbation and distress of mind thereby occasioned, produced a momentary resentment against Iago, considered as occasioning the jealousy, though innocent:

> *Othello.* Villain, be sure thou prove my love a whore;
> Be sure of it: give me the ocular proof,
> Or by the wrath of man's eternal soul
> Thou hadst been better have been born a dog,
> Than answer my wak'd wrath.
>   *Iago.* Is't come to this?
>   *Othello.* Make me see't; or, at the least, so prove it,
> That the probation bear no hinge or loop
> To hang a doubt on: or wo upon thy life!
>   *Iago.* My Noble Lord—
>   *Othello.* If thou dost slander her, and torture me,
> Never pray more; abandon all remorse;
> On horrors head horrors accumulate;
> Do deeds to make heav'n weep, all earth amaz'd:
> For nothing canst thou to damnation add
> Greater than that.
>
> *Othello, act 3. sc. 3.*

This blind and absurd effect of anger, is more gaily illustrated by Addison, in a story, the *dramatis personae* of which are, a cardinal, and a spy retained in pay for intelligence. The cardinal is represented as minuting down the particulars. The spy begins with a low voice, "Such an one the advocate whispered to one of his friends within my hearing, that your Eminence was a very great poltroon"; and after having given his <86> patron time to take it down, adds, "That another called him a mercenary rascal in a public conversation." The cardinal replies, "Very well," and bids him go on. The spy proceeds, and loads him with reports of the same nature, till the cardinal rises in a fury, calls him an impudent scoundrel, and kicks him out of the room.*

We meet with instances every day of resentment raised by loss at play, and wreaked on the cards or dice. But anger, a furious passion, is satisfied with a connection still slighter than that of cause and effect; of which Congreve, in the *Mourning Bride,* gives one beautiful example:

> *Gonsalez.* Have comfort.
> *Almeria.* Curs'd be that tongue that bids me be of comfort,
> Curs'd my own tongue that could not move his pity,
> Curs'd these weak hands that could not hold him here,
> For he is gone to doom Alphonso's death.
>
> *Act. 4. sc. 8.*

I have chosen to exhibit anger in its more rare appearances, for in these we can best trace its nature and extent. In the examples above given, it appears to be an absurd passion, and altogether ir-<87>rational. But we ought to consider, that it is not the intention of nature to subject this passion, in every instance, to reason and reflection: it was given us to prevent or to repel injuries; and, like fear, it often operates blindly and instinctively, without the least view to consequences: the very first apprehension of harm, sets it in motion to repel injury by punishment. Were it more cool and deliberate, it would lose its threatening appearance, and be insufficient to guard us against violence. When such is and ought to be the nature of the

---

* *Spectator,* No. 439. [*The Spectator,* no. 439, 1712. Joseph Addison (1672–1719): classical scholar, author, dramatist, member of parliament, and secretary of state in 1706, and chief secretary in Ireland in 1709 and 1715. With Richard Steele (1672–1729), he ran the *Spectator* from 1711 to 1712. Read "in Great Wrath" for "in a fury."]

passion, it is not wonderful to find it exerted irregularly and capriciously, as it sometimes is where the mischief is sudden and unforeseen. All the harm that can be done by the passion in that state, is instantaneous; for the shortest delay sets all to rights; and circumstances are seldom so unlucky as to put it in the power of a passionate man to do much harm in an instant.

Social passions, like the selfish, sometimes drop their character, and become instinctive. It is not unusual to find anger and fear respecting others so excessive, as to operate blindly and impetuously, precisely as where they are selfish. <88>

SECTION VII

Emotions caused by Fiction.

The attentive reader will observe, that hitherto no fiction hath been assigned as the cause of any passion or emotion: whether it be a being, action, or quality, that moveth us, it is supposed to be really existing. This observation shows that we have not yet completed our task; because passions, as all the world know, are moved by fiction as well as by truth. In judging beforehand of man, so remarkably addicted to truth and reality, one should little dream that fiction can have any effect upon him: but man's intellectual faculties are not sufficiently perfect to dive far even into his own nature. I shall take occasion afterward to show, that the power of fiction to generate passion is an admirable contrivance, subservient to excellent purposes: in the mean time, we must try to unfold the means that give fiction such influence over the mind.

That the objects of our external senses really exist in the way and manner we perceive, is a branch of intuitive knowledge: when I see a man walking, a tree growing, or cattle grasing, I cannot doubt but that these objects are really what they appear to be: if I be a spectator of any trans-<89>action or event, I have a conviction of the real existence of the persons engaged, of their words, and of their actions. Nature determines us to rely on the veracity of our senses; for otherwise they could not in any degree answer their end, that of laying open things existing and passing around us.

By the power of memory, a thing formerly seen may be recalled to the mind with different degrees of accuracy. We commonly are satisfied with a slight recollection of the capital circumstances; and, in such recollection, the thing is not figured as in our view, nor any image formed: we retain the consciousness of our present situation, and barely remember that formerly we saw that thing. But with respect to an interesting object or event that made a strong impression, I am not satisfied with a cursory review, but must dwell upon every circumstance. I am imperceptibly converted into a spectator, and perceive every particular passing in my presence, as when I was in reality a spectator. For example, I saw yesterday a beautiful woman in tears for the loss of an only child, and was greatly moved with her distress: not satisfied with a slight recollection or bare remembrance, I ponder upon the melancholy scene: conceiving myself to be in the place where I was an eye-witness, every circumstance appears to me as at first: I think I see the woman in tears, and hear her moans. Hence it may be justly said, that in a complete idea of memory there is no past <90> nor future: a thing recalled to the mind with the accuracy I have been describing, is perceived as in our view, and consequently as existing at present. Past time makes part of an incomplete idea only: I remember or reflect, that some years ago I was at Oxford, and saw the first stone laid of the Ratcliff library;[21] and I remember that at a still greater distance of time, I heard a debate in the House of Commons about a standing army.[22]

Lamentable is the imperfection of language, almost in every particular that falls not under external sense. I am talking of a matter exceedingly clear in the perception: and yet I find no small difficulty to express it clearly in words; for it is not accurate, to talk of incidents long past as passing in our sight, nor of hearing at present what we really heard yesterday or at a more distant time. And yet the want of proper words to describe ideal presence, and to distinguish it from real presence, makes this inaccuracy unavoidable. When I recall any thing to my mind in a manner so distinct as

21. Radcliffe Library, Oxford, designed by James Gibbs, was begun in 1737.

22. Annual parliamentary debates over the army estimates, followed by a division, were held between 1727 and 1742, with the exception of 1738. Kames was in London and in Oxford in 1737 for the trial in Westminster of Provost Wilson of Edinburgh, concerning the Porteous riots in Edinburgh of the previous year. (He had also been an attorney for John Porteous in 1736.)

to form an idea or image of it as present, I have not words to describe that act, but that I perceive the thing as a spectator, and as existing in my presence; which means not that I am really a spectator, but only that I conceive myself to be a spectator, and have a perception of the object similar to what a real spectator hath.

As many rules of criticism depend on ideal presence, the reader, it is hoped, will take some pains <91> to form an exact notion of it, as distinguished on the one hand from real presence, and on the other from a superficial or reflective remembrance. In contradistinction to real presence, ideal presence may properly be termed *a waking dream;* because, like a dream, it vanisheth the moment we reflect upon our present situation: real presence, on the contrary, vouched by eye-sight, commands our belief, not only during the direct perception, but in reflecting afterward on the object. To distinguish ideal presence from reflective remembrance, I give the following illustration: when I think of an event as past, without forming any image, it is barely reflecting or remembering that I was an eye-witness: but when I recall the event so distinctly as to form a complete image of it, I perceive it as passing in my presence; and this perception is an act of intuition, into which reflection enters not, more than into an act of sight.

Tho' ideal presence is thus distinguished from real presence on the one side, and from reflective remembrance on the other, it is however variable without any precise limits; rising sometimes toward the former, and often sinking toward the latter. In a vigorous exertion of memory, ideal presence is extremely distinct: thus, when a man, entirely occupied with some event that made a deep impression, forgets himself, he perceives every thing as passing before him, and hath a consciousness of presence similar to that of a <92> spectator; with no difference but that in the former the perception of presence is less firm and clear than in the latter. But such vigorous exertion of memory is rare: ideal presence is oftener faint, and the image so obscure as not to differ widely from reflective remembrance.

Hitherto of an idea of memory. I proceed to consider the idea of a thing I never saw, raised in me by speech, by writing, or by painting. That idea, with respect to the present subject, is of the same nature with an idea of memory, being either complete or incomplete. A lively and accurate description of an important event, raises in me ideas no less distinct than if

I had been originally an eye-witness: I am insensibly transformed into a spectator; and have an impression that every incident is passing in my presence. On the other hand, a slight or superficial narrative produceth but a faint and incomplete idea, of which ideal presence makes no part. Past time is a circumstance that enters into this idea, as it doth into an incomplete idea of memory: I believe that Scipio existed about 2000 years ago, and that he overcame Hannibal in the famous battle of Zama.[23] When I reflect so slightly upon that memorable event, I consider it as long past. But let it be spread out in a lively and beautiful description, I am insensibly transformed into a spectator: I perceive these two heroes in act to engage: I perceive them brandishing their swords, and chearing their <93> troops; and in that manner I attend them through the battle, every incident of which appears to be passing in my sight.

I have had occasion to observe,* that ideas both of memory and of speech, produce emotions of the same kind with what are produced by an immediate view of the object; only fainter, in proportion as an idea is fainter than an original perception. The insight we have now got, unfolds that mystery: ideal presence supplies the want of real presence; and in idea we perceive persons acting and suffering, precisely as in an original survey: if our sympathy be engaged by the latter, it must also in some degree be engaged by the former, especially if the distinctness of ideal presence approach to that of real presence. Hence the pleasure of a reverie, where a man, forgetting himself, is totally occupied with the ideas passing in his mind, the objects of which he conceives to be really existing in his presence. The power of language to raise emotions, depends entirely on the raising such lively and distinct images as are here described: the reader's passions are never sensibly moved, till he be thrown into a kind of reverie; in which state, forgetting that he is reading, he conceives every incident as passing in his presence, precisely as if he were an eye-witness. A general or reflective remembrance cannot <94> warm us into any emotion: it may be agreeable in some slight degree; but its ideas are too faint and obscure to raise any

---

* Part I. sect. I. of the present chapter.

23. Scipio defeated Hannibal at the battle of Zama in 202 B.C., leading to the surrender of Carthage and the end of the Punic Wars between Rome and Carthage for mastery of the Mediterranean.

thing like an emotion; and were they ever so lively, they pass with too much precipitation to have that effect: our emotions are never instantaneous; even such as come the soonest to their height, have different periods of birth and increment; and to give opportunity for these different periods, it is necessary that the cause of every emotion be present to the mind a due time; for an emotion is not carried to its height but by reiterated impressions. We know that to be the case of emotions arising from objects of sight; a quick succession, even of the most beautiful objects, scarce making any impression; and if this hold in the succession of original perceptions, how much more in the succession of ideas?

Tho' all this while I have been only describing what passeth in the mind of every one, and what every one must be conscious of, it was necessary to enlarge upon the subject; because, however clear in the internal conception, it is far from being so when described in words. Ideal presence, tho' of general importance, hath scarce ever been touched by any writer; and however difficult the explication, it could not be avoided in accounting for the effects produced by fiction. Upon that point, the reader, I guess, has prevented me: it already must have occurred to him, that if, in reading, <95> ideal presence be the means by which our passions are moved, it makes no difference whether the subject be a fable or a true history: when ideal presence is complete, we perceive every object as in our sight; and the mind, totally occupied with an interesting event, finds no leisure for reflection. This reasoning is confirmed by constant and universal experience. Let us take under consideration the meeting of Hector and Andromache in the sixth book of the Iliad, or some of the passionate scenes in King Lear: these pictures of human life, when we are sufficiently engaged, give an impression of reality not less distinct than that given by Tacitus describing the death of Otho:[24] we never once reflect whether the story be true or feigned; reflection comes afterward, when we have the scene no longer before our eyes. This reasoning will appear in a still clearer light, by opposing ideal presence

---

24. Publius Cornelius Tacitus (ca. A.D. 56–118): Roman historian, who held several public offices including, finally, proconsulship of Asia. He was the son-in-law of Gnaeus Iulius Agricola, governor of Britain (A.D. 78–85), whose biography he published in the same year as *De moribus Germanorum* (A.D. 98). He was a friend of the Younger Pliny. Otho's suicide is described in *Historiae* (*The Histories*), bk. 2, chap. 49.

to ideas raised by a cursory narrative; which ideas being faint, obscure, and imperfect, leave a vacuity in the mind, which solicits reflection. And accordingly, a curt narrative of feigned incidents is never relished: any slight pleasure it affords, is more than counterbalanced by the disgust it inspires for want of truth.

To support the foregoing theory, I add what I reckon a decisive argument; which is, that even genuine history has no command over our passions but by ideal presence only; and consequently that in this respect it stands upon the same footing with <96> fable. To me it appears clear, that in neither can our sympathy hold firm against reflection: for if the reflection that a story is a pure fiction prevent our sympathy, so will equally the reflection that the persons described are no longer existing. What effect, for example, can the belief of the rape of Lucretia[25] have to raise our sympathy, when she died above 2000 years ago, and hath at present no painful feeling of the injury done her? The effect of history in point of instruction, depends in some measure upon its veracity. But history cannot reach the heart, while we indulge any reflection upon the facts: such reflection, if it engage our belief, never fails at the same time to poison our pleasure, by convincing us that our sympathy for those who are dead and gone is absurd. And if reflection be laid aside, history stands upon the same footing with fable: what effect either may have to raise our sympathy, depends on the vivacity of the ideas they raise; and with respect to that circumstance, fable is generally more successful than history.

Of all the means for making an impression of ideal presence, theatrical representation is the most powerful. That words independent of action have the same power in a less degree, every one of sensibility must have felt: a good tragedy will extort tears in private, though not so forcibly as upon the stage. That power belongs also to painting: a good historical picture makes a deeper impression <97> than words can, tho' not equal to that of theatrical action. Painting seems to possess a middle place between

25. Wife of Tarquinius Collatinus, who was raped by Sextus, son of Tarquin, king of Rome. After urging her father and husband to seek revenge, Lucretia committed suicide; the Tarquins were expelled from Rome, enabling the introduction of republican government.

reading and acting: in making an impression of ideal presence, it is not less superior to the former than inferior to the latter.

It must not however be thought, that our passions can be raised by painting to such a height as by words: a picture is confined to a single instant of time, and cannot take in a succession of incidents: its impression indeed is the deepest that can be made instantaneously; but seldom is a passion raised to any height in an instant, or by a single impression: it was observed above, that our passions, those especially of the sympathetic kind, require a succession of impressions; and for that reason, reading and acting have greatly the advantage, by reiterating impressions without end.

Upon the whole, it is by means of ideal presence that our passions are excited; and till words produce that charm, they avail nothing: even real events intitled to our belief, must be conceived present and passing in our sight, before they can move us. And this theory serves to explain several phenomena otherwise unaccountable. A misfortune happening to a stranger, makes a less impression than happening to a man we know, even where we are no way interested in him: our acquaintance with this man, however slight, aids the conception of his suffering in our presence. For the same reason, we are little moved by any di-<98>stant event; because we have more difficulty to conceive it present, than an event that happened in our neighbourhood.

Every one is sensible, that describing a past event as present, has a fine effect in language: for what other reason than that it aids the conception of ideal presence? Take the following example.

> And now with shouts the shocking armies clos'd,
> To lances lances, shields to shields oppos'd;
> Host against host the shadowy legions drew,
> The sounding darts, an iron tempest, flew;
> Victors and vanquish'd join promiscuous cries,
> Triumphing shouts and dying groans arise,
> With streaming blood the slipp'ry field is dy'd,
> And slaughter'd heroes swell the dreadful tide.[26]

26. Kames always used the translations of *The Iliad* by Alexander Pope (1688–1744). A major literary figure of the century, as poet, critic, and satirist, his free translations

In this passage we may observe how the writer, inflamed with the subject, insensibly advances from the past time to the present; led to that form of narration by conceiving every circumstance as passing in his own sight: which at the same time has a fine effect upon the reader, by presenting things to him as a spectator. But change from the past to the present requires some preparation; and is not sweet where there is no stop in the sense; witness the following passage.

> Thy fate was next, O Phaestus! doom'd to feel
> The great Idomeneus' protended steel; <99>
> Whom Borus sent (his son and only joy)
> From fruitful Tarne to the fields of Troy.
> The Cretan jav'lin reach'd him from afar,
> And pierc'd his shoulder as he *mounts* his car. *Iliad,* v. 57.

It is still worse to fall back to the past in the same period; for that is an anticlimax in description:

> Through breaking ranks his furious course he bends,
> And at the goddess his broad lance extends;
> Through her bright veil the daring weapon drove,
> Th' ambrosial veil, which all the graces wove:
> Her snowy hand the razing steel profan'd,
> And the transparent skin with crimson stain'd.
>
> *Iliad,* v. 415.

Again, describing the shield of Jupiter,

> Here all the terrors of grim War appear,
> Here rages Force, here tremble Flight and Fear,
> Here storm'd Centention, and here Fury frown'd,
> And the dire orb portentous Gorgon crown'd.
>
> *Iliad,* v. 914.

Nor is it pleasant to be carried backward and forward alternately in a rapid succession:

---

were celebrated as independent triumphs of English poetry. Kames inaccurately transcribes Pope's words from IV.508.

Then dy'd Scamandrius, expert in the chace,
In woods and wilds to wound the savage race;
Diana taught him all her sylvan arts,
To bend the bow and aim unerring darts:
But vainly here Diana's arts he tries,
The fatal lance arrests him as he flies; <100>
From Menelaus' arm the weapon sent,
Through his broad back and heaving bosom went:
Down sinks the warrior with a thund'ring sound,
His brazen armour rings against the ground.   *Iliad,* v. 65.

It is wonderful to observe, upon what slight foundations nature erects some of her most solid and magnificent works. In appearance at least, what can be more slight than ideal presence? and yet from it is derived that extensive influence which language hath over the heart; an influence, which, more than any other means, strengthens the bond of society, and attracts individuals from their private system to perform acts of generosity and benevolence. Matters of fact, it is true, and truth in general, may be inculcated without taking advantage of ideal presence; but without it, the finest speaker or writer would in vain attempt to move any passion: our sympathy would be confined to objects that are really present; and language would lose entirely its signal power of making us sympathize with beings removed at the greatest distance of time as well as of place. Nor is the influence of language, by means of ideal presence, confined to the heart: it reacheth also the understanding, and contributes to belief. For when events are related in a lively manner, and every circumstance appears as passing before us, we suffer not patiently the truth of the facts to be <101> questioned. An historian accordingly who hath a genius for narration, seldom fails to engage our belief. The same facts related in a manner cold and indistinct, are not suffered to pass without examination: a thing ill described is like an object seen at a distance, or through a mist; we doubt whether it be a reality or a fiction. Cicero says, that to relate the manner in which an event passed, not only enlivens the story, but makes it appear more credible.* For that reason,

---

* *De oratore,* lib. 2. sect. 81. [Marcus Tullius Cicero (106–43 B.C.), sometimes called Tully: lawyer and philosopher, who achieved fame and political power as a pleader. His

a poet who can warm and animate his reader, may employ bolder fictions
than ought to be ventured by an inferior genius: the reader, once thoroughly
engaged, is susceptible of the strongest impressions:

> Veraque constituunt, quae belle tangere possunt
> Aureis, et lepido quae sunt fucata sonore.
>
> *Lucretius, lib.* 1. *l.* 644.[27]

A masterly painting has the same effect: Le Brun[28] is no small support to
Quintus Curtius: and among the vulgar in Italy, the belief of scripture-
history is perhaps founded as much upon the authority of Raphael, Michael
Angelo, and other celebrated painters, as upon that of the sacred writers.*
<102>

---

writings on rhetoric and earlier Greek thinkers greatly influenced the eighteenth century.
The modern reference is *De Oratore* II.80.328.]

* At quae Polycleto defuerunt, Phidiae atque Alcameni dantur. Phidias tamen diis
quam hominibus efficiendis melior artifex traditur: in ebore vero longe citra aemulum,
vel si nihil nisi Minervam Athenis, aut Olympium in Elide Jovem fecisset, cujus pul-
chritudo adjecisse aliquid etiam receptae religioni videtur; adeo majestas operis Deum
aequavit. *Quintilian, lib.* 12. *cap.* 10. § 1. [Marcus Fabius Quintilianus (ca. A.D. 35–100):
Roman rhetorician who, with Cicero, much influenced eighteenth-century writers.

> But the qualities lacking in Polyclitus are allowed to have been possessed by Phid-
> ias and Alcamenes. On the other hand, Phidias is regarded as more gifted in his
> representation of gods than of men, and indeed for chryselephantine statues he
> is without a peer, as he would in truth be, even if he had produced nothing in
> this material beyond his Minerva at Athens and his Jupiter at Olympia in Elis,
> whose beauty is such that it is said to have added something even to the awe with
> which the god was already regarded. (bk. 12, chap. 10)]

27. Titus Lucretius Carus (ca. 99–55 B.C.): Roman poet, chiefly known for a philosophic poem in which the atomism of Epicurus (371–270 B.C.) is expounded, *De Rerum
Natura* (*On the Nature of Things*); the work was popular in the eighteenth century. The
1682 translation (bk. 1, line 672) by Thomas Creech reads:

> . . . For only Fools regard
> What seems obscure, and intricate, and hard
> Take that for Truth, whose Phrases smooth appear.

28. Charles Le Brun (1619–90), French painter to Louis XIV, was commissioned in
1661 to paint for display in the Palace of Versailles the first of a series of subjects from
the history of Alexander, "The Tent of Darius."

The foregoing theory must have fatigued the reader with much dry reasoning: but his labour will not be fruitless; because from that theory are derived many useful rules in criticism, which shall be mentioned in their proper places. One specimen shall be our present entertainment. Events that surprise by being unexpected, and yet are natural, enliven greatly an epic poem: but in such a poem, if it pretend to copy human manners and actions, no improbable incident ought to be admitted; that is, no incident contrary to the order and course of nature. A chain of imagined incidents linked together according to the order of nature, finds easy admittance into the mind; and a lively narrative of such incidents, occasions complete images, or in other words ideal presence: but our judgement revolts against an improbable incident; and if we once begin to doubt of its reality, farewell relish and concern—an unhappy effect; for it will require more than an ordinary effort, to restore the waking dream, and to make the reader conceive even the more probable incidents as passing in his presence.

I never was an admirer of machinery in an epic poem, and I now find my taste justified by reason; <103> the foregoing argument concluding still more strongly against imaginary beings, than against improbable facts: fictions of that nature may amuse by their novelty and singularity; but they never move the sympathetic passions, because they cannot impose on the mind any perception of reality. I appeal to the discerning reader, whether that observation be not applicable to the machinery of Tasso and of Voltaire:[29] such machinery is not only in itself cold and uninteresting, but gives an air of fiction to the whole composition. A burlesque poem, such as the Lutrin or the Dispensary,[30] may employ machinery with success; for these poems, tho' they assume the air of history, give entertainment chiefly by their pleasant and ludicrous pictures, to which machinery contributes: it is not the aim of such a poem, to raise our sympathy; and for that reason, a strict imitation of nature is not required. A poem professedly ludicrous,

29. Voltaire: François Marie Arouet (1694–1778). French political philosopher, poet, dramatist, and historian, who was offended by Kames's criticisms. Kames apologized for the unintended offense (vol. 2, <390n>).

30. *The Dispensary,* 1699, a burlesque poem by Sir Samuel Garth (1661–1719). Garth was a physician and a member of the Whig club and the Kit-Kat Club (named after the owner of their meeting house, Christopher Katt), whose members included Addison, Congreve, and Vanbrugh.

may employ machinery to great advantage; and the more extravagant the better.

Having assigned the means by which fiction commands our passions; what only remains for accomplishing our present task, is to assign the final cause. I have already mentioned, that fiction, by means of language, has the command of our sympathy for the good of others. By the same means, our sympathy may also be raised for our own good. In the fourth section of the present chapter, it is observed, that examples both of virtue and of vice <104> raise virtuous emotions; which becoming stronger by exercise, tend to make us virtuous by habit as well as by principle. I now further observe, that examples confined to real events are not so frequent as without other means to produce a habit of virtue: if they be, they are not recorded by historians. It therefore shows great wisdom, to form us in such a manner, as to be susceptible of the same improvement from fable that we receive from genuine history. By that contrivance, examples to improve us in virtue may be multiplied without end: no other sort of discipline contributes more to make virtue habitual, and no other sort is so agreeable in the application. I add another final cause with thorough satisfaction; because it shows, that the author of our nature is not less kindly provident for the happiness of his creatures, than for the regularity of their conduct: the power that fiction hath over the mind affords an endless variety of refined amusements, always at hand to employ a vacant hour: such amusements are a fine resource in solitude; and by chearing and sweetening the mind, contribute mightily to social happiness.[31] <105>

PART II

Emotions and Passions as pleasant and painful, agreeable and disagreeable. Modifications of these Qualities.

It will naturally occur at first, that a discourse upon the passions ought to commence with explaining the qualities now mentioned: but upon trial, I

---

31. The first edition reads: "by sweetening the temper, improves society."

found that this explanation could not be made distinctly, till the difference should first be ascertained between an emotion and a passion, and their causes unfolded.

Great obscurity may be observed among writers with regard to the present point: particularly no care is taken to distinguish agreeable from pleasant, disagreeable from painful; or rather these terms are deemed synonymous. This is an error not at all venial in the science of ethics; as instances can and shall be given, of painful passions that are agreeable, and of pleasant passions that are disagreeable. These terms, it is true, are used indifferently in familiar conversation, and in compositions for amusement; but more accuracy is required from those who profess to explain the passions. In writing upon the critical art, I would avoid every refinement that may seem more curious than <106> useful: but the proper meaning of the terms under consideration must be ascertained, in order to understand the passions, and some of their effects that are intimately connected with criticism.

I shall endeavour to explain these terms by familiar examples. Viewing a fine garden, I perceive it to be beautiful or agreeable; and I consider the beauty or agreeableness as belonging to the object, or as one of its qualities. When I turn my attention from the garden to what passes in my mind, I am conscious of a pleasant emotion, of which the garden is the cause: the pleasure here is felt, as a quality, not of the garden, but of the emotion produced by it. I give an opposite example. A rotten carcass is disagreeable, and raises in the spectator a painful emotion: the disagreeableness is a quality of the object; the pain is a quality of the emotion produced by it. In a word, agreeable and disagreeable are qualities of the objects we *perceive;* pleasant and painful are qualities of the emotions we *feel:* the former qualities are perceived as adhering to objects; the latter are felt as existing within us.

But a passion or emotion, beside being felt, is frequently made an object of thought or reflection: we examine it; we enquire into its nature, its cause, and its effects. In that view, like other objects, it is either agreeable or disagreeable. Hence clearly appear the different significations of the terms under consideration, as applied to pas-<107>sion: when a passion is termed *pleasant* or *painful,* we refer to the actual feeling; when termed *agreeable* or *disagreeable,* we refer to it as an object of thought or reflection; a passion is pleasant or painful to the person in whom it exists; it is agreeable or disagreeable to the person who makes it a subject of contemplation.

In the description of emotions and passions, these terms do not always coincide: to make which evident, we must endeavour to ascertain, first, what passions and emotions are pleasant what painful; and next, what are agreeable what disagreeable. With respect to both, there are general rules, which, if I can trust to induction, admit not a single exception. The nature of an emotion or passion as pleasant or painful, depends entirely on its cause: the emotion produced by an agreeable object is invariably pleasant; and the emotion produced by a disagreeable object is invariably painful.* Thus a lofty oak, a generous action, a valuable discovery in art or science, are agreeable objects that invariably produce pleasant emotions. A stinking puddle, a treacherous action, an irregular ill-contrived edifice, being disagreeable objects, produce painful emotions. Selfish passions are pleasant; for they arise from self, an agreeable object or cause. A social passion directed upon an agreeable object is always pleasant; <108> directed upon an object in distress, is painful.† Lastly, all dissocial passions, such as envy, resentment, malice, being caused by disagreeable objects, cannot fail to be painful.

A general rule for the agreeableness or disagreeableness of emotions and passions is a more difficult enterprise: it must be attempted however. We have a sense of a common nature in every species of animals, particularly in our own; and we have a conviction that this common nature is *right,* or *perfect,* and that individuals *ought* to be made conformable to it.‡ To every faculty, to every passion, and to every bodily member, is assigned a proper office and a due proportion: if one limb be longer than the other, or be disproportioned to the whole, it is wrong and disagreeable: if a passion deviate from the common nature, by being too strong or too weak, it is also wrong and disagreeable: but as far as conformable to common nature, every emotion and every passion is perceived by us to be right, and as it ought to be; and upon that account it must appear agreeable. That this holds true

* See part 7. of this chapter.
† See part 7. of this chapter.
‡ See this doctrine fully explained, chap. 25. Standard of Taste.

in pleasant emotions and passions, will readily be admitted: but the painful are no less natural than the other; and therefore ought not to be an exception. Thus the pain-<109>ful emotion raised by a monstrous birth or brutal action, is no less agreeable upon reflection, than the pleasant emotion raised by a flowing river or a lofty dome: and the painful passions of grief and pity are agreeable, and applauded by all the world.

Another rule more simple and direct for ascertaining the agreeableness or disagreeableness of a passion as opposed to an emotion, is derived from the desire that accompanies it. If the desire be to perform a right action in order to produce a good effect, the passion is agreeable: if the desire be, to do a wrong action in order to produce an ill effect, the passion is disagreeable. Thus, passions as well as actions are governed by the moral sense. These rules by the wisdom of Providence coincide: a passion that is conformable to our common nature must tend to good; and a passion that deviates from our common nature must tend to ill.

This deduction may be carried a great way farther: but to avoid intricacy and obscurity, I make but one other step. A passion which, as aforesaid, becomes an object of thought to a spectator, may have the effect to produce a passion or emotion in him; for it is natural, that a social being should be affected with the passions of others. Passions or emotions thus generated, submit, in common with others, to the general law above mentioned, namely, that an agreeable object produces a pleasant <110> emotion, and a disagreeable object a painful emotion. Thus the passion of gratitude, being to a spectator an agreeable object, produceth in him the pleasant passion of love to the grateful person: and malice, being to a spectator a disagreeable object, produceth in him the painful passion of hatred to the malicious person.

We are now prepared for examples of pleasant passions that are disagreeable, and of painful passions that are agreeable. Self-love, as long as confined within just bounds, is a passion both pleasant and agreeable: in excess it is disagreeable, tho' it continues to be still pleasant. Our appetites are precisely in the same condition. Resentment, on the other hand, is, in every stage of the passion, painful; but is not disagreeable unless in excess. Pity is always painful, yet always agreeable. Vanity, on the contrary, is always pleasant, yet always disagreeable. But however distinct these qualities are, they coincide, I acknowledge, in one class of passions: all vicious passions tending to the hurt of others, are equally painful and disagreeable.

The foregoing qualities of pleasant and painful, may be sufficient for ordinary subjects: but with respect to the science of criticism, it is necessary, that we also be made acquainted with the several modifications of these qualities, with the modifications at least that make the greatest figure. Even at first view one is sensible, that the pleasure or <111> pain of one passion differs from that of another: how distant the pleasure of revenge gratified from that of love? So distant, as that we cannot without reluctance admit them to be any way related. That the same quality of pleasure should be so differently modified in different passions, will not be surprising, when we reflect on the boundless variety of agreeable sounds, tastes, and smells, daily perceived. Our discernment reaches differences still more minute, in objects even of the same sense: we have no difficulty to distinguish different sweets, different sours, and different bitters; honey is sweet, so is sugar, and yet the one never is mistaken for the other: our sense of smelling is sufficiently acute, to distinguish varieties in sweet-smelling flowers without end. With respect to passions and emotions, their differences as to pleasant and painful have no limits; tho' we want acuteness of feeling for the more delicate modifications. There is here an analogy between our internal and external senses: the latter are sufficiently acute for all the useful purposes of life, and so are the former. Some persons indeed, Nature's favourites, have a wonderful acuteness of sense, which to them unfolds many a delightful scene totally hid from vulgar eyes. But if such refined pleasure be confined to a small number, it is however wisely ordered that others are not sensible of the defect; nor detracts it from their happiness that others secretly are more happy. With <112> relation to the fine arts only, that qualification seems essential; and there it is termed *delicacy of taste*.[32]

Should an author of such a taste attempt to describe all those varieties in pleasant and painful emotions which he himself feels, he would soon meet an invincible obstacle in the poverty of language: a people must be thoroughly refined, before they invent words for expressing the more deli-

---

32. A favorite term in French criticism of the seventeenth century, it was the title of the opening essay in David Hume, *Essays Moral, Political and Literary*, 1740–41.

cate feelings; and for that reason, no known tongue hitherto has reached that perfection. We must therefore rest satisfied with an explanation of the more obvious modifications.

In forming a comparison between pleasant passions of different kinds, we conceive some of them to be *gross,* some refined. Those pleasures of external sense that are felt as at the organ of sense, are conceived to be corporeal, or gross:* the pleasures of the eye and the ear are felt to be internal; and for that reason are conceived to be more pure and refined.

The social affections are conceived by all to be more refined than the selfish. Sympathy and humanity are universally esteemed the finest temper of mind; and for that reason, the prevalence of the social affections in the progress of society, is held to be a refinement in our nature. A savage knows little of social affection, and therefore is not <113> qualified to compare selfish and social pleasure; but a man, after acquiring a high relish for the latter, loses not thereby a taste for the former: he is qualified to judge, and he will give preference to social pleasures as more sweet and refined. In fact they maintain that character, not only in the direct feeling, but also when we make them the subject of reflection: the social passions are far more agreeable than the selfish, and rise much higher in our esteem.

There are differences not less remarkable among the painful passions. Some are voluntary, some involuntary: the pain of the gout is an example of the latter; grief, of the former, which in some cases is so voluntary as to reject all consolation. One pain softens the temper, pity is an instance; one tends to render us savage and cruel, which is the case of revenge. I value myself upon sympathy: I hate and despise myself for envy.

Social affections have an advantage over the selfish, not only with respect to pleasure as above explained, but also with respect to pain. The pain of an affront, the pain of want, the pain of disappointment, and a thousand other selfish pains, are cruciating and tormenting, and tend to a habit of peevishness and discontent. Social pains have a very different tendency: the pain of sympathy, for example, is not only voluntary, but softens my temper, and raises me in my own esteem.

Refined manners, and polite behaviour, must <114> not be deemed al-

---

* See the Introduction.

together artificial: men who, inured to the sweets of society, cultivate humanity, find an elegant pleasure in preferring others, and making them happy, of which the proud, the selfish, scarce have a conception.

Ridicule, which chiefly arises from pride, a selfish passion, is at best but a gross pleasure: a people, it is true, must have emerged out of barbarity before they can have a taste for ridicule; but it is too rough an entertainment for the polished and refined. Cicero[33] discovers in Plautus a happy talent for ridicule, and a peculiar delicacy of wit: but Horace, who made a figure in the court of Augustus, where taste was considerably purified, declares against the lowness and roughness of that author's raillery. Ridicule is banished [in] France, and is losing ground in England.

Other modifications of pleasant passions will be occasionally mentioned hereafter. Particularly, the modifications of *high* and *low* are to be handled in the chapter of grandeur and sublimity; and the modifications of *dignified* and *mean,* in the chapter of dignity and grace. <115>

PART III

Interrupted Existence of Emotions and Passions. —Their Growth and Decay.

Were it the nature of an emotion to continue, like colour and figure, in its present state till varied by some operating cause, the condition of man would be deplorable: it is ordered wisely, that emotions should more resemble another attribute of matter, namely, motion, which requires the constant exertion of an operating cause, and ceases when the cause is withdrawn. An emotion may subsist while its cause is present; and when its cause is removed, may subsist by means of an idea, though in a fainter manner: but the moment another thought breaks in and engrosses the mind, the emotion is gone, and is no longer felt: if it return with its cause, or an idea of its cause, it again vanisheth with them when other thoughts crowd in.

---

33. Cicero on Plautus: *De Oratore* III.12.45. Horace frequently refers to the topic in his *Odes.* Ridicule had been a commonplace topic for moralists and writers on the arts in France and Britain since the seventeenth century. See the editor's Introduction.

The reason is, that an emotion or passion is connected with the perception or idea of its cause, so intimately as not to have any independent existence: a strong passion, it is true, hath a mighty influence to detain its cause in the mind; but not so as to detain it for ever, because a succession of perceptions or ideas is unavoidable.* Further, even while a <116> passion subsists, it seldom continues long in the same tone, but is successively vigorous and faint: the vigour of a passion depends on the impression made by its cause; and a cause makes its deepest impression, when, happening to be the single interesting object, it attracts our whole attention:† its impression is slighter when our attention is divided between it and other objects; and at that time the passion is fainter in proportion.

When emotions and passions are felt thus by intervals and have not a continued existence, it may be thought a nice problem to determine when they are the same, when different. In a strict philosophic view, every single impression made even by the same object, is distinguishable from what have gone before, and from what succeed: neither is an emotion raised by an idea, the same with what is raised by a sight of the object. But such accuracy not being found in common apprehension, is not necessary in common language: the emotions raised by a fine landscape in its successive appearances are not distinguishable from each other, nor even from those raised by successive ideas of the object; all of them being held to be the same: a passion also is always reckoned the same as long as it is fixed upon the same object; and thus love and hatred are said to continue the same for life. Nay, <117> so loose are we in that way of thinking, that many passions are reckoned the same even after a change of object; which is the case of all passions that proceed from some peculiar propensity: envy, for example, is considered to be the same passion, not only while it is directed to the same person, but even where it comprehends many persons at once: pride and malice are examples of the same. So much was necessary to be said upon the identity of a passion and emotion, in order to prepare for examining their growth and decay.

* See this point explained afterward, chap. 9.
† See the Appendix, containing definitions, and explanation of terms, sect. 33.

The growth and decay of passions and emotions, traced through all their mazes, is a subject too extensive for an undertaking like the present: I pretend only to give a cursory view of it, such as may be necessary for the purposes of criticism. Some emotions are produced in their utmost perfection, and have a very short endurance; which is the case of surprise, of wonder, and sometimes of terror. Emotions raised by inanimate objects, trees, rivers, buildings, pictures, arrive at perfection almost instantaneously; and they have a long endurance, a second view producing nearly the same pleasure with the first. Love, hatred, and some other passions, swell gradually to a certain pitch; after which they decay gradually. Envy, malice, pride, scarce ever decay. Some passions, such as gratitude and revenge, are often exhausted by a single act of gratification: other passions, such as pride, malice, envy, love, hatred, are not so <118> exhausted; but having a long continuance, demand frequent gratification.

To handle every single passion and emotion with a view to these differences, would be an endless work: we must be satisfied at present with some general views. And with respect to emotions, which are quiescent because not productive of desire, their growth and decay are easily explained: an emotion caused by an inanimate object, cannot naturally take longer time to arrive at maturity, than is necessary for a leisurely survey: such emotion also must continue long stationary, without any sensible decay; a second or third view of the object being nearly as agreeable as the first: this is the case of an emotion produced by a fine prospect, an impetuous river, or a towering hill; while a man remains the same, such objects ought to have the same effect upon him. Familiarity, however, hath an influence here, as it hath every where: frequency of view, after short intervals especially, weans the mind gradually from the object, which at last loses all relish: the noblest object in the material world, a clear and serene sky, is quite disregarded, unless perhaps after a course of bad weather. An emotion raised by human virtues, qualities, or actions, may, by reiterated views of the object, swell imperceptibly till it become so vigorous as to generate desire: in that condition it must be handled as a passion.

As to passion, I observe, first, that when na-<119>ture requires a passion to be sudden, it is commonly produced in perfection; which is the case of fear and of anger. Wonder and surprise are always produced in perfection: reiterated impressions made by their cause, exhaust these passions instead of inflaming them. This will be explained afterward.*

In the next place, when a passion hath for its foundation an original propensity peculiar to some men, it generally comes soon to maturity: the propensity, upon presenting a proper object, is immediately enlivened into a passion; which is the case of pride, of envy, and of malice.

In the third place, the growth of love and of hatred is slow or quick according to circumstances: the good qualities of a person raise in me a pleasant emotion; which, by reiterated views, is swelled into a passion involving desire of that person's happiness: this desire, being freely indulged, works gradually a change internally, and at last produceth in me a settled habit of affection for that person, now my friend. Affection thus produced operates precisely like an original propensity; for to enliven it into a passion, no more is required but the real or ideal presence of the object. The habit of aversion or of hatred is brought on in the same manner. And here I must observe by the way, that love and hatred signify commonly <120> affection and aversion, not passion. The bulk of our passions are indeed affection or aversion inflamed into a passion by different circumstances: the affection I bear to my son, is inflamed into the passion of fear when he is in danger; becomes hope when he hath a prospect of good fortune; becomes admiration when he performs a laudable action; and shame when he commits any wrong: aversion becomes fear when there is a prospect of good fortune to my enemy; becomes hope when he is in danger; becomes joy when he is in distress; and sorrow when a laudable action is performed by him.

Fourthly,[34] passions generally have a tendency to excess, occasioned by the following means. The mind affected by any passion, is not in a proper state for distinct perception, nor for cool reflection: it hath always a strong bias to the object of an agreeable passion, and a bias no less strong against the object of a disagreeable passion. The object of love, for example, however indifferent to others, is to the lover's conviction a paragon; and of hatred, is vice itself without alloy. What less can such delusion operate, than

---

* Chap. 6.
34. This paragraph did not appear in the first edition.

to swell the passion beyond what it was at first? for if the seeing or conversing with a fine woman, have had the effect to carry me from indifference to love; how much stronger must her influence be, when now to my conviction she is an angel? and hatred as well as other passions must run the same course. <121> Thus between a passion and its object there is a natural operation, resembling action and reaction in physics: a passion acting upon its object, magnifies it greatly in appearance; and this magnified object reacting upon the passion, swells and inflames it mightily.

Fifthly, the growth of some passions depends often on occasional circumstances: obstacles to gratification, for example, never fail to augment and inflame a passion; because a constant endeavour to remove an obstacle, preserves the object of the passion ever in view, which swells the passion by impressions frequently reiterated: thus the restraint of conscience, when an obstacle to love, agitates the mind and inflames the passion:

> Quod licet, ingratum est: quod non licet, acrius urit.
> Si nunquam Danaën habuisset ahenea turris,
> Non esset Danaë de Jove facta parens.
> *Ovid, Amor. l.* 2.[35]

At the same time, the mind, distressed with the obstacle, becomes impatient for gratification, and consequently more desirous of it. Shakespear expresses this observation finely:

> All impediments in fancy's course,
> Are motives of more fancy.[36]

We need no better example than a lover who hath many rivals. Even the caprices of a mistress have <122> the effect to inflame love; these occasioning uncertainty of success, tend naturally to make the anxious lover overvalue the happiness of fruition.

---

35. Publius Ovidius Naso (43 B.C.–A.D. 18): Roman poet; much favored in the Middle Ages, he wrote extensively on love.

> What one may do freely has no charm; what one may not do pricks more keenly on. . . . Had Danae never been mewed in the brazen tower, Danae would never have been made mother by Jove.   (*Amores* II.xix.2, 27–28)

36. *All's Well That Ends Well*, act 5, sc. 3. The first line begins "As all . . ."

So much upon the growth of passions: their continuance and decay come next under consideration. And, first, it is a general law of nature, That things sudden in their growth are equally sudden in their decay. This is commonly the case of anger. And with respect to wonder and surprise, which also suddenly decay, another reason concurs, that their causes are of short duration: novelty soon degenerates into familiarity; and the unexpectedness of an object, is soon sunk in the pleasure that the object affords. Fear, which is a passion of greater importance as tending to self-preservation, is often instantaneous; and yet is of equal duration with its cause: nay, it frequently subsists after the cause is removed.

In the next place, a passion founded on a peculiar propensity, subsists generally for ever; which is the case of pride, envy, and malice: objects are never wanting to inflame the propensity into a passion.

Thirdly, it may be laid down as a general law of nature, That every passion ceases upon attaining its ultimate end. To explain that law, we must distinguish between a particular and a general end. I call a particular end what may be accomplished by a single act: a general end, on the contrary, admits acts without number; because it <123> cannot be said, that a general end is ever fully accomplished, while the object of the passion subsists. Gratitude and revenge are examples of the first kind: the ends they aim at may be accomplished by a single act; and when that act is performed, the passions are necessarily at an end. Love and hatred are examples of the other kind; desire of doing good or of doing mischief to an individual, is a general end, which admits acts without number, and which seldom is fully accomplished: therefore these passions have frequently the same duration with their objects.

Lastly, it will afford us another general view, to consider the difference between an original propensity, and affection or aversion produced by custom. The former adheres too close to the constitution ever to be eradicated; and for that reason, the passions to which it gives birth, continue during life with no remarkable diminution. The latter, which owe their birth and increment to time, owe their decay to the same cause: affection and aversion decay gradually as they grow; and accordingly hatred as well as love are extinguished by long absence. Affection decays more gradually between persons who, living together, have daily occasion to testify mutually their good-will and kindness: and when affection is decay'd, habit supplies its place; for it makes these persons necessary to each other, by the pain of separa-<124>tion.* Affection to children hath a long endurance, longer perhaps than any other affection: its growth keeps pace with that of its objects: they display new beauties and qualifications daily, to feed and augment the affection. But whenever the affection becomes stationary, it must begin to decay; with a slow pace indeed, in proportion to its increment. In short, man with respect to this life is a temporary being: he grows, becomes stationary, decays; and so must all his powers and passions.

PART IV

Coexistent Emotions and Passions.

For a thorough knowledge of the human passions and emotions, it is not sufficient that they be examined singly and separately: as a plurality of them are sometimes felt at the same instant, the manner of their coexistence, and the effects thereby produced, ought also to be examined. This subject is extensive, and it will be difficult to trace all the laws that govern its endless variety of cases: if such an undertaking can be brought to perfection, it must be by degrees. The following hints may suffice for a first attempt. <125>

We begin with emotions raised by different sounds, as the simplest case. Two sounds that mix, and, as it were, incorporate before they reach the ear, are said to be concordant. That each of the two sounds, even after their union, produceth an emotion of its own, must be admitted: but these emotions, like the sounds that produce them, mix so intimately, as to be rather one complex emotion than two emotions in conjunction. Two sounds that refuse incorporation or mixture, are said to be discordant: and when heard at the same instant, the emotions produced by them are unpleasant in conjunction, however pleasant separately.

Similar to the emotion raised by mixed sounds, is the emotion raised by an object of sight with its several qualities: a tree, for example, with its

* See chap. 14.

qualities of colour, figure, size, &c. is perceived to be one object; and the emotion it produceth is rather one complex emotion than different emotions combined.

With respect to coexistent emotions produced by different objects of sight, it must be observed, that however intimately connected such objects may be, there cannot be a concordance among them like what is perceived in some sounds. Different objects of sight, meaning objects that can exist each of them independent of the others, never mix nor incorporate in the act of vision: each object is perceived as it exists, separately from <126> others; and each raiseth an emotion different from that raised by the other. And the same holds in all the causes of emotion or passion that can exist independent of each other, sounds only excepted.

To explain the manner in which such emotions exist, similar emotions must be distinguished from those that are dissimilar. Two emotions are said to be similar, when they tend each of them to produce the same tone of mind: chearful emotions, however different their causes may be, are similar; and so are those which are melancholy. Dissimilar emotions are easily explained by their opposition to what are similar: pride and humility, gaiety and gloominess, are dissimilar emotions.

Emotions perfectly similar, readily combine and unite,* so as in a manner to become one complex emotion; witness the emotions produced by a number of flowers in a parterre, or of trees in a wood. Emotions that are opposite, or extremely dissimilar, never combine or unite: the mind cannot simultaneously take on opposite tones; it cannot at the same instant be both joyful and sad, an-<127>gry and satisfied, proud and humble: dissimilar emotions may succeed each other with rapidity, but they cannot exist simultaneously.

Between these two extremes, emotions unite more or less, in proportion to the degree of their resemblance, and the degree in which their causes are connected. Thus the emotions produced by a fine landscape and the singing

---

* It is easier to conceive the manner of coexistence of similar emotions, than to describe it. They cannot be said to mix or incorporate, like concordant sounds: their union is rather of agreement or concord; and therefore I have chosen the words in the text, not as sufficient to express clearly the manner of their coexistence, but only as less liable to exception than any other I can find.

of birds, being similar in a considerable degree, readily unite, tho' their causes are little connected. And the same happens where the causes are intimately connected, tho' the emotions themselves have little resemblance to each other: an example of which is a mistress in distress, whose beauty gives pleasure, and her distress pain: these two emotions, proceeding from different views of the object, have very little resemblance to each other; and yet so intimately connected are their causes, as to force them into a sort of complex emotion, partly pleasant partly painful. This clearly explains some expressions common in poetry, *a sweet distress, a pleasant pain.*

It was necessary to describe, with some accuracy, in what manner similar and dissimilar emotions coexist in the mind, in order to explain their different effects, both internal and external. This subject, tho' obscure, is capable to be set in a clear light; and it merits attention, not only for its extensive use in criticism, but for the nobler purpose of deciphering many intricacies in the actions of <128> men. Beginning with internal effects, I discover two, clearly distinguishable from each other, both of them produced by pleasant emotions that are similar; of which, the one may be represented by addition in numbers, the other by harmony in sounds. Two pleasant emotions that are similar, readily unite when they are coexistent; and the pleasure felt in the union, is the sum of the two pleasures: the same emotions in succession, are far from making the same figure; because the mind at no instant of the succession is conscious of more than a single emotion. This doctrine may aptly be illustrated by a landscape comprehending hills, vallies, plains, rivers, trees, &c: the emotions produced by these several objects, being similar in a high degree as falling in easily and sweetly with the same tone of mind, are in conjunction extremely pleasant. This multiplied effect is felt from objects even of different senses, as where a landscape is conjoined with the music of birds and odor of flowers; and results partly from the resemblance of the emotions and partly from the connection of their causes: whence it follows, that the effect must be the greatest, where the causes are intimately connected and the emotions perfectly similar. The same rule is obviously applicable to painful emotions that are similar and coexistent.

The other pleasure arising from pleasant emotions similar and coexistent, cannot be better explained than by the foregoing example of a land-

<129>scape, where the sight, hearing, and smelling, are employed: beside the accumulated pleasure above mentioned of so many different similar emotions, a pleasure of a different kind is felt from the concord of these emotions. As that pleasure resembles greatly the pleasure of concordant sounds, it may be termed the *Harmony of Emotions.* This harmony is felt in the different emotions occasioned by the visible objects; but it is felt still more sensibly in the emotions occasioned by the objects of different senses, as where the emotions of the eye are combined with those of the ear. The former pleasure comes under the rule of addition: this comes under a different rule. It is directly in proportion to the degree of resemblance between the emotions, and inversely in proportion to the degree of connection between the causes: to feel this pleasure in perfection, the resemblance between the emotions cannot be too strong, nor the connection between their causes too slight. The former condition is self-evident; and the reason of the latter is, that the pleasure of harmony is felt from various similar emotions, distinct from each other, and yet sweetly combining in the mind; which excludes causes intimately connected, for the emotions produced by them are forced into one complex emotion. This pleasure of concord or harmony, which is the result of pleasant emotions, and cannot have place with respect to those that are painful, will be further illustrated, when <130> the emotions produced by the sound of words and their meaning are taken under consideration.*

The pleasure of concord from conjoined emotions, is felt even where the emotions are not perfectly similar. Tho' love be a pleasant passion, yet by its softness and tenderness it resembles in a considerable degree the painful passion of pity or of grief; and for that reason, love accords better with these passions than with what are gay and sprightly. I give the following example from Catullus, where the concord between love and grief has a fine effect even in so slight a subject as the death of a sparrow.

> Lugete, ô Veneres, Cupidinesque,
> Et quantum est hominum venustiorum!
> Passer mortuus est meae puellae,
> Quem plus illa oculis suis amabat.

* Chap. 18. sect. 3.

Nam mellitus erat, suamque norat
Ipsam tam bene, quam puella matrem:
Nec sese a gremio illius movebat;
Sed circumsiliens modo huc, modo illuc,
Ad solam dominam usque pipilabat.
Qui nunc it per iter tenebricosum,
Illuc, unde negant redire quemquam.
At vobis male fit, malae tenebrae
Orci, quae omnia bella devoratis;
Tam bellum mihi passerem abstulistis.
O factum male, ô miselle passer.
Tua nunc opera, meae puellae
Flendo turgiduli rubent ocelli. [37] <131>

Next as to the effects of dissimilar emotions, which we may guess will
be opposite to what are above described. Dissimilar coexistent emotions,
as said above, never fail to distress the mind by the difference of their tones;
from which situation a feeling of harmony never can proceed; and this
holds whether the causes be connected or not. But it holds more remarkably

37. Gaius Valerius Catullus (ca. 84–54 B.C.): Roman poet who turned away from the
ideals of Rome toward earlier Hellenistic culture:

Mourn all ye Belles and Beaux, and all
Ye Toasts, the Town does Beauties call;
For Lesbia's Sparrow's dead, a Bird
Which to her Eyes my Girl prefer'd;
Grown so familiar, it would stand
And court her Bosom, or her hand;
And with its Fondness make such pother,
As Lesbia did for her own Mother.
'Twould chirp and hop from Knee to Knee,
But with none else it would be Free.
Who now is gone to Shades below,
Where those, can ne'er return, that go.
Curst be those Shades malicious Power,
Which all our pretty things Devour.
O cruel Death! curst be thy Arrow,
For killing Lesbia's pretty Sparrow;
Poor little Wretch! it is for thee
Her Eyes from Tears are never free.
                    (anon. trans., London, 1730)

where the causes are connected; for in that case the dissimilar emotions being forc'd into an unnatural union, produce an actual feeling of discord. In the next place, if we would estimate the force of dissimilar emotions coexistent, we must distinguish between their causes as connected or unconnected: and in order to compute their force in the former case, subtraction must be used instead of addition; which will be evident from what follows. Dissimilar emotions forc'd into union by the connection of their causes, are felt obscurely and imperfectly; for each tends to vary the tone of mind that is suited to the other; and the mind thus distracted between two objects, is at no instant in a condition to receive a deep impression from either. Dissimilar emotions proceeding from unconnected causes, are in a very different condition; for as there is nothing to force them into union, they are never felt but in succession; by which means, each hath an opportunity to make a complete impression.

This curious theory requires to be illustrated by examples. In reading the description of the dis-<132>mal waste, book I. of *Paradise lost,*[38] we are sensible of a confused feeling, arising from dissimilar emotions forc'd into union, to wit, the beauty of the description, and the horror of the object described:

> Seest thou yon dreary plain, forlorn and wild,
> The seat of desolation, void of light,
> Save what the glimmering of these livid flames
> Casts pale and dreadful?

And with respect to this and many similar passages in *Paradise lost,* we are sensible, that the emotions being obscured by each other, make neither of them that figure they would make separately. For the same reason, ascending smoke in a calm morning, which inspires stillness and tranquillity, is improper in a picture full of violent action. A parterre, partly ornamented partly in disorder, produces a mixt feeling of the same sort. Two great armies in act to engage, mix the dissimilar emotions of grandeur and of terror:

---

38. John Milton (1608–74), *Paradise Lost* I.180, published in 1667 although completed earlier.

Sembra d'alberi densi alta foresta
L'un campo, e l'altro; di tant' aste abbonda.
Son tesi gli archi, e son le lance in resta:
Vibransi i dardi, e rotasi ogni fionda.
Ogni cavallo in guerra anco s'appresta,
Gli odii, e'l furor del suo signor seconda:
Raspa, batte, nitrisce, e si raggira,
Gonfia le nari; e fumo, e fuoco spira. <133>

Bello in sì bella vista anco è l'orrore:
E di mezzo la tema esce il diletto.
Ne men le trombe orribili e canore,
Sono a gli orecchi, lieto e fero oggetto.
Pur il campo fedel, benchè minore,
Par di suon più mirabile, e d'aspeto.
E canta in più guerriero e chiaro carme
Ogni sua tromba, e maggior luce han l'arme.

Gerusalemme liberata, cant. 20. *st.* 29. *& 30.*[39]

Suppose a virtuous man has drawn on himself a great misfortune, by a fault incident to human nature, and therefore venial: the remorse he feels aggravates his distress, and consequently raises our pity to a high pitch: we at the same time blame the man; and the indignation raised by the fault he

---

39. Of drie topt Oakes, they seemd two forests thicke:
　　So did each hoste with speares and pikes abound,
　　Bent were their bowes, in rests their launces sticke,
　　Their hands shooke swords, their slings held cobles round:
　　Each stead to runne was readie, prest and quicke
　　At this commaunders spurre, his hand, his sound;
　　He chafes, he stampes, careers, and turnes about,
　　He fomes, snorts, neies, and fire and smoake breaths out.

　　Horrour, it selfe in that faire sight seem'd faire,
　　And pleasure flew amid sad dreed and feare:
　　The trumpets shrill, that thundred in the aire,
　　Were musicke milde and sweete to euerie eare:
　　The faithfull campe (though lesse) yet seem'd more raire
　　In that strange noice, more warlike, shrill and cleare,
　　In notes more sweete, the Pagan trumpets iarre,
　　These sung, their armours shin'd, these glistred farre.
　　　　(*Gerusalemme liberata,* trans. Edward Fairfax)

has committed, is dissimilar to pity: these two passions, however, proceeding from the same object, are forc'd into a sort of union; but the indignation is so slight, as scarce to be felt in the mixture with pity. Subjects of this kind are of all the fittest for tragedy; but of that afterward.*

Opposite emotions are so dissimilar as not to admit any sort of union, even where they proceed from causes the most intimately connected. Love to a mistress, and resentment for her infidelity, are of that nature: they cannot exist otherwise than in succession, which by the connection of their <134> causes is commonly rapid; and these emotions will govern alternately, till one of them obtain the ascendant, or both be spent. A succession opens to me by the death of a worthy man, who was my friend as well as my kinsman: when I think of my friend I am griev'd; but the succession gives me joy. These two causes are intimately connected; for the succession is the direct consequence of my friend's death: the emotions however being opposite, do not mix; they prevail alternately, perhaps for a course of time, till grief for my friend's death be banished by the pleasures of opulence. A virtuous man suffering unjustly, is an example of the same kind: I pity him, and have great indignation at the author of the wrong. These emotions proceed from causes nearly connected; but being directed to different objects, they are not forc'd into union: their opposition preserves them distinct: and accordingly they are found to prevail alternately.

I proceed to examples of dissimilar emotions arising from unconnected causes. Good and bad news of equal importance arriving at the same instant from different quarters, produce opposite emotions, the discordance of which is not felt, because they are not forc'd into union: they govern alternately, commonly in a quick succession, till their force be spent:

Shylock. How now, Tubal, what news from Genoa? hast thou found my daughter? <135>

Tubal. I often came where I did hear of her, but cannot find her.

Shy. Why there, there, there, there! a diamond gone, cost me two thousand ducats in Francfort? the curse never fell upon our nation till now, I never felt it till now; two thousand ducats in that, and other precious, precious jewels! I would my daughter were dead at my foot, and the jewels

* Chap. 22.

in her ear; O would she were hers'd at my foot, and the ducats in her coffin. No news of them; why, so! and I know not what's spent in the search: why, thou loss upon loss! the thief gone with so much, and so much to find the thief; and no satisfaction, no revenge, nor no ill luck stirring but what lights o'my shoulders; no sighs but o' my breathing, no tears but o' my shedding.

Tub. Yes, other men have ill luck too; Anthonio, as I heard in Genoa—

Shy. What, what, what? ill luck, ill luck?

Tub. Hath an Argosie cast away, coming from Tripolis.

Shy. I thank God, I thank God; is it true? is it true?

Tub. I spoke with some of the sailors that escaped the wreck.

Shy. I thank thee, good Tubal; good news, good news, ha, ha: where? in Genoa?

Tub. Your daughter spent in Genoa, as I heard, one night, fourscore ducats.

Shy. Thou stick'st a dagger in me; I shall never see my gold again; fourscore ducats at a sitting, fourscore ducats!

Tub. There came divers of Anthonio's creditors in my company to Venice, that swear he cannot chuse but break. <136>

Shy. I am glad of it, I'll plague him, I'll torture him; I am glad of it.

Tub. One of them shew'd me a ring, that he had of your daughter for a monkey.

Shy. Out upon her! thou torturest me, Tubal; it was my Turquoise; I had it of Leah when I was a bachelor; I would not have given it for a wilderness of monkies.

Tub. But Anthonio is certainly undone.

Shy. Nay, that's true, that's very true; go fee me an officer, bespeak him a fortnight before. I will have the heart of him, if he forfeit; for were he out of Venice, I can make what merchandise I will. Go, go, Tubal, and meet me at our synagogue; go, good Tubal; at our synagogue, Tubal.

Merchant of Venice, act 3. sc. 1.

In the same manner, good news arriving to a man labouring under distress, occasions a vibration in his mind from the one to the other:

> *Osmyn.* By Heav'n thou'st rous'd me from my lethargy.
> The spirit which was deaf to my own wrongs,

And the loud cries of my dead father's blood,
Deaf to revenge—nay, which refus'd to hear
The piercing sighs and murmurs of my love
Yet unenjoy'd; what not Almeria could
Revive, or raise, my people's voice has waken'd.
O my Antonio, I am all on fire,
My soul is up in arms, ready to charge
And bear amidst the foe with conqu'ring troops.
I hear 'em call to lead 'em on to liberty, <137>
To victory; their shouts and clamours rend
My ears, and reach the heav'ns: where is the king?
Where is Alphonso? ha! where! where indeed?
O I could tear and burst the strings of life,
To break these chains. Off, off, ye stains of royalty!
Off, slavery! O curse, that I alone
Can beat and flutter in my cage, when I
Would soar, and stoop at victory beneath!

Mourning Bride, act 3. *sc.* 2.

If the emotions be unequal in force, the stronger after a conflict will extinguish the weaker. Thus the loss of a house by fire, or of a sum of money by bankruptcy, will make no figure in opposition to the birth of a long-expected son, who is to inherit an opulent fortune: after some slight vibrations, the mind settles in joy, and the loss is forgot.

The foregoing[40] observations will be found of great use in the fine arts. Many practical rules are derived from them, which shall afterward be mentioned; but for instant gratification in part, the reader will accept the following specimen, being an application of these observations to music. It must be premised, that no disagreeable combination of sounds is entitled to the name of music: for all music is resolvable into melody and harmony, which imply agreeableness in their very conception.* Secondly, the agree-

---

* Sounds may be so contrived as to produce horror, and several other painful feelings, which in a tragedy, or in an opera, may be introduced with advantage to accompany the representation of a dissocial or disagreeable passion. But such sounds must in themselves be disagreeable; and upon that account cannot be dignified with the name of music.

40. This and the following paragraphs are revised versions of the text in the first edition.

ableness of vocal <138> music differs from that of instrumental: the former, being intended to accompany words, ought to be expressive of the sentiment that they convey; but the latter having no connection with words, may be agreeable without relation to any sentiment: harmony properly so called, though delightful when in perfection, hath no relation to sentiment; and we often find melody without the least tincture of it.* Thirdly, in vocal music, the intimate connection of sense and sound rejects dissimilar emotions, those especially that are opposite. Similar emotions produced by the sense and the sound, go naturally into union; and at the same time are concordant or harmonious: but dissimilar emotions, forc'd into union by these causes intimately connected, obscure each other, and are also unpleasant by discordance.

These premises make it easy to determine what sort of poetical compositions are fitted for music. In general, as music in all its various tones ought <139> to be agreeable, it never can be concordant with any composition in language expressing a disagreeable passion, or describing a disagreeable object: for here the emotions raised by the sense and by the sound, are not only dissimilar but opposite; and such emotions forc'd into union produce always an unpleasant mixture. Music accordingly is a very improper companion for sentiments of malice, cruelty, envy, peevishness, or of any other dissocial passion; witness among a thousand King John's speech in Shakespear, soliciting Hubert to murder Prince Arthur, which even in the most cursory view will appear incompatible with any sort of music.[41] Music is a companion no less improper for the description of any disagreeable object, such as that of Polyphemus in the third book of the *Aeneid,* or that of Sin in the second book of *Paradise lost:* the horror of the object described and the pleasure of the music, would be highly discordant.

With regard to vocal music, there is an additional reason against associating it with disagreeable passions. The external signs of such passions

---

* It is beyond the power of music to raise a passion or a sentiment: but it is in the power of music to raise emotions similar to what are raised by sentiments expressed in words pronounced with propriety and grace; and such music may justly be termed *sentimental.*

41. *King John,* act 3, sc. 3.

are painful; the looks and gestures to the eye, and the tone of pronunciation to the ear: such tones therefore can never be expressed musically, for music must be pleasant, or it is not music.

On the other hand, music associates finely with poems that tend to inspire pleasant emotions: music for example in a chearful tone, is perfectly con-<140>cordant with every emotion in the same tone; and hence our taste for airs expressive of mirth and jollity. Sympathetic joy associates finely with chearful music; and sympathetic pain no less finely with music that is tender and melancholy. All the different emotions of love, namely, tenderness, concern, anxiety, pain of absence, hope, fear, accord delightfully with music: and accordingly, a person in love, even when unkindly treated, is soothed by music; for the tenderness of love still prevailing, accords with a melancholy strain. This is finely exemplified by Shakespear in the fourth act of *Othello,* where Desdemona calls for a song expressive of her distress. Wonderful is the delicacy of that writer's taste, which fails him not even in the most refined emotions of human nature. Melancholy music is suited to slight grief, which requires or admits consolation: but deep grief, which refuses all consolation, rejects for that reason even melancholy music.

Where the same person is both the actor and the singer, as in an opera, there is a separate reason why music should not be associated with the sentiments of any disagreeable passion, nor the description of any disagreeable object; which is, that such association is altogether unnatural: the pain, for example, that a man feels who is agitated with malice or unjust revenge, disqualifies him for relishing music, or any thing that is pleasing; and therefore to represent such a man, contrary to <141> nature, expressing his sentiments in a song, cannot be agreeable to any audience of taste.

For a different reason, music is improper for accompanying pleasant emotions of the more important kind; because these totally ingross the mind, and leave no place for music, nor for any sort of amusement: in a perilous enterprise to dethrone a tyrant, music would be impertinent, even where hope prevails, and the prospect of success is great: Alexander attacking the Indian town, and mounting the wall, had certainly no impulse to exert his prowess in a song.[42]

---

42. The reference is to act 1 of Handel's opera *Alessandro,* which opened at the King's Theatre, Haymarket, in 1726. Kames refers to it again below, 2.443.

It is true, that not the least regard is paid to these rules either in the French or Italian opera; and the attachment we have to operas, may at first be considered as an argument against the foregoing doctrine. But the general taste for operas is no argument: in these compositions the passions are so imperfectly expressed, as to leave the mind free for relishing music of any sort indifferently; and it cannot be disguised, that the pleasure of an opera is derived chiefly from the music, and scarce at all from the sentiments: a happy concordance of the emotions raised by the song and by the music, is extremely rare; and I venture to affirm, that there is no example of it, unless where the emotion raised by the former is agreeable as well as that raised by the latter.* <142>

The subject we have run through, appears not a little entertaining. It is extremely curious to observe, in many instances, a plurality of causes producing in conjunction a great pleasure: in other instances, no less frequent, no conjunction, but each cause acting in opposition. To enter bluntly upon a subject of such intricacy, might gravel an acute philosopher; but taking matters in a train, the intricacy vanisheth.

Next in order, according to the method proposed, come external effects; which lead us to passions as the causes of external effects. Two coexistent passions that have the same tendency, must be similar: they accordingly readily unite, and in conjunction have double force. This is verified by experience; from which we learn, that the mind receives not impulses alternately from such passions, but one strong impulse from the whole in conjunction; and indeed it is not easy to conceive what should bar the union of passions that have all of them the same tendency.

Two passions having opposite tendencies, may proceed from the same cause considered in differ-<143>ent views. Thus a mistress may at once be the cause both of love and of resentment: her beauty inflames the passion

---

* A censure of the same kind is pleasantly applied to the French ballettes by a celebrated writer: "Si le Prince est joyeux, on prend part à sa joye, et l'on danse: s'il est triste, on veut l'égayer, et l'on danse. Mais il y a bien d'autres sujets de danses; les plus graves actions de la vie se font en dansant. Les prêtres dansent, les soldats dansent, les dieux dansent, les diables dansent, on danse jusques dans les enterremens, et tout danse à propos de tout." ["If the Prince is happy, we're all happy, and we dance. If he's sad, we want to make him happy, so we dance. But there are other occasions for dancing: the most serious events in life can be an occasion for dancing. Priests dance, soldiers dance, Gods dance, Devils dance, one dances even at interments: anything can be an occasion for dancing."]

of love; her cruelty or inconstancy causes resentment. When two such passions coexist in the same breast, the opposition of their aim prevents any sort of union; and accordingly, they are not felt otherwise than in succession: the consequence of which must be, either that the passions will balance each other and prevent external action, or that one of them will prevail and accomplish its end. Guarini, in his *Pastor Fido,* describes beautifully the struggle between love and resentment directed to the same object:

> *Corisea.* Chi vide mai, chi mai udi più strana
> E più folle, e più fera, e più importuna
> Passione amorosa? amore, ed odio
> Con sì mirabil tempre in un cor misti,
> Che l'un par l'altro (e non so ben dir come)
> E si strugge, e s'avanza, e nasce, e more.
> S' i' miro alle bellezze di Mirtillo
> Dal piè leggiadro al grazioso volto,
> Il vago portamento, il bel sembiante,
> Gli atti, i costumi, e le parole, e 'l guardo;
> M'affale Amore con sì possente foco
> Ch' i' ardo tutta, e par, ch' ogn' altro affetto
> Da questo sol sia superato, e vinto:
> Ma se poi penso all' ostinato amore,
> Ch' ei porta ad altra donna, e che per lei
> Di me non cura, e sprezza (il vo' pur dire)
> La mia famosa, e da mill' alme, e mille, <144>
> Inchinata beltà, bramata grazia;
> L' odio così, così l'aborro, e schivo,
> Che impossibil mi par, ch'unqua per lui
> Mi s'accendesse al cor fiamma amorosa.
> Tallor meco ragiono: o s'io potessi
> Gioir del mio dolcissimo Mirtillo,
> Sicche fosse mio tutto, e ch' altra mai
> Posseder no 'l potesse, o più d' ogn' altra
> Beata, e felicissima Corisca!
> Ed in quel punto in me sorge un talento
> Verso di luisì dolce, e sì gentile,
> Che di seguirlo, e di pregarlo ancora,

E di scoprirgli il cor prendo consiglio.
Che più? così mi stimola il desio,
Che se potessi allor l' adorerei.
Dall' altra parte i' mi risento, e dico,
Un ritroso? uno schifo? un che non degna?
Un, che può d'altra donna esser amante?
Un, ch'ardisce mirarmi, e non m'adora?
E dal mio volto si difende in guisa,
Che per amor non more? ed io, che lui
Dovrei veder, come molti altri i' veggio
Supplice, e lagrimoso a' piedi miei,
Supplice, e lagrimoso a' piedi suoi
Sosterro di cadere? ah non fia mai.
Ed in questo pensier tant' ira accoglio
Contra di lui, contra di me, che volsi
A seguirlo il pensier, gli occhi a mirarlo,
Che 'l nome di Mirtillo, e l' amor mio
Odio più che la morte; e lui vorrei
Veder il più dolente, il più infelice
Pastor, che viva; e se potessi allora,
Con le mie proprie man l'anciderei.
Così sdegno, desire, odio, ed amore <145>
Mi fanno guerra, ed io, che stata sono
Sempre fin qui di mille cor la fiamma,
Di mill' alme il tormento, ardo, e languisco:
E provo nel mio mal le pene altrui.   *Act* I. *sc.* 3.[43]

43. Giovanni Battista Guarini (1537–1612): Italian poet whose pastoral drama *Il Pastor Fido*, 1585, was repeatedly translated into English and was also acted in Latin. Handel used the text for his opera *Il Pastor Fido*, 1712 (rev. 1734).

Who ever saw, what heart did ever prove
So strange, fond, impotent a Passion? Love
And cold Disdain (a miracle to me
Two contraries should in one subject be
Both in extremes!) I know not how, each other
Destroy, and generate; enflame, and smother.
When I behold Mirtillo's every grace,
From his neat foot to his bewitching face,
His unaffected carriage, sweet aspect,

Words, actions, looks and manners, they eject
Such flames of love that every passion
Besides seems to be conquerd by this one.
But when I think how dotingly he prizes
Another woman, and for her despises
My almost peerless face (although I say't)
On which a thousand eyes for alms do wait,
Then do I scorn, abhor, and loath him more
Then ever I did value him before,
And scarce can think it possible that he
Had ever any interest in me.
O if my sweet Mirtillo were mine own,
So that I had him to my self alone!
(These are my thoughts sometimes) no mortall wight
More blisse could boast of then Corisca might!
And then I feel such kindly flames, so sweet
A vapour rise, that I could almost meet
His love half way; yea, follow him, adore
His very steps, and aid from him implore:
Nay, I do love him so, I could expire
His sacrifice in such a pleasing fire.
Then I'm my self again: And what (say I)
A proud disdainfull boy! one that doth fly
From me, and love another! That can look
Upon this face of mine, and not be strook!
But guard himself so well as not to dye
For love! Shall I, that should behold him lye
Trembling and weeping at these feet of mine
(As many better men have done) incline
Trembling and weeping at his feet? O no!
And with this thought into such a rage I grow
Against my self, and him, that sounding straight
Unto my eyes and fancy a retreat,
Mirtillo's name worser then death I seem
To hate, and mine own self for loving him;
Whom I would see the miserablest swain,
The most despised thing that doth remain
Upon the earth; and if I had my will,
With mine own hands I could the villain kill.
Thus like two seas encountring, Hate and Love,
Desire and Scorn in me dire battell move:
And I (the flame of thousand hearts, the rack
Of thousand souls) languish, and burn, and lack
That pitie I deny'd to others.
(*Il Pastor Fido,* I.iii, trans. Sir Richard Fanshawe, 1608–66)

Ovid paints in lively colours the vibration of mind between two opposite passions directed to the same object. Althea had two brothers much beloved, who were unjustly put to death by her son Meleager in a fit of passion: she was strongly impelled to revenge; but the criminal was her own son. This ought to have with-held her hand; but the story is more interesting, by the violence of the struggle between resentment and maternal love:

> Dona Deûm templis nato victore ferebat;
> Cum videt extinctos fratres Althaea referri.
> Quae plangore dato, moestis ululatibus urbem
> Implet; et auratis mutavit vestibus atras.
> At simul est auctor necis editus; excidit omnis
> Luctus: et a lacrymis in poenae versus amorem est.
> Stipes erat, quem, cum partus enixa jaceret
> Thestias, in flammam triplices posuêre sorores;
> Staminaque impresso fatalia pollici nentes,
> Tempora, dixerunt, eadem lignoque, tibique,
> O modo nate, damus. Quo postquam carmine dicto
> Excessere deae; flagrantem mater ab igne
> Eripuit torrem: sparsitque liquentibus undis.
> Ille diu fuerat penetralibus abditus imis;
> Servatusque, tuos, juvenis, servaverat annos.
> Protulit hunc genitrix, taedasque in fragmina poni <146>
> Imperat; et positis inimicos admovet ignes.
> Tum conata quater flammis imponere ramum,
> Coepta quater tenuit. Pugnat materque, sororque,
> Et diversa trahunt unum duo nomina pectus.
> Saepe metu sceleris pallebant ora futuri:
> Saepe suum fervens oculis dabat ira ruborem,
> Et modo nescio quid similis crudele minanti
> Vultus erat; modo quem misereri credere posses:
> Cumque ferus lacrymas animi siccaverat ardor;
> Inveniebantur lacrymae tamen. Utque carina,

There are some minor variations between the Italian text used by Kames and modern versions: for line 6 read "e nasce, e muore"; for line 25 read "nol potesse godere, oh più d'ogna'altra."

Quam ventus, ventoque rapit contrarius aestus,
Vim geminam sentit, paretque incerta duobus:
Thestias haud aliter dubiis affectibus errat,
Inque vices ponit, positamque resuscitat iram.
Incipit esse tamen melior germana parente;
Et, consanguineas ut sanguine leniat umbras,
Impietate pia est. Nam postquam pestifer ignis
Convaluit; Rogus iste cremet mea viscera, dixit.
Utque manu dirâ lignum fatale tenebat;
Ante sepulchrales infelix adstitit aras.
Poenarumque deae triplices, furialibus, inquit,
Eumenides, sacris, vultus advertite vestros.
Ulciscor, facioque nefas. Mors morte pianda est;
In scelus addendum scelus est, in funera funus;
Per coacervatos pereat domus impia luctus.
An felix Oeneus nato victore fruetur,
Thestius orbus erit? melius lugebitis ambo.
Vos modo, fraterni manes, animaeque recentes,
Officium sentite meum; magnoque paratas
Accipite inferias, uteri mala pignora nostri.
Hei mihi! quo rapior? fratres ignoscite matri.
Deficiunt ad coepta manus. Meruisse fatemur
Illum, cur pereat: mortis mihi displicet auctor. <147>
Ergo impune feret; vivusque, et victor, et ipso
Successu tumidus regnum Calydonis habebit?
Vos cinis exiguus, gelidaeque jacebitis umbrae?
Haud equidem patiar. Pereat sceleratus; et ille
Spemque patris, regnique trahat, patriaeque ruinam,
Mens ubi materna est; ubi sunt pia jura parentum?
Et, quos sustinui, bis mensûm quinque labores?
O utinam primis arsisses ignibus infans;
Idque ego passa forem! vixisti munere nostro:
Nunc merito moriere tuo. Cape praemia facti;
Bisque datam, primum partu, mox stipite rapto,
Redde animam; vel me fraternis adde sepulchris.
Et cupio, et nequeo. Quid agam? modo vulnera fratrum
Ante oculos mihi sunt, et tantae caedis imago;

Nunc animum pietas, maternaque nomina frangunt.

Me miseram! male vincetis, sed vincite, fratres;

Dummodo, quae dedero vobis solatia, vosque

Ipsa sequar, dixit: dextraque aversa trementi

Funereum torrem medios conjecit in ignes.

Aut dedit, aut visus gemitus est ille dedisse,

Stipes; et invitis correptus ab ignibus arsit.

Metamorph. lib. 8. *l.* 445.[44]

44. "Althaea had been told of her son's victory, and was already carrying offerings to the temple of the gods, when she saw her brothers being brought home dead. The city was filled with her wailing, as she gave vent to her clamorous grief: she beat her breast, and changed the gold-embroidered robes she wore for black clothing. However, when she heard who had killed her brothers, she forgot her grief, and turned from tears to concentrate on revenge. There was a log, which the three sister goddesses had placed on the fire, at the time when this Althaea, Thestius' daughter, was lying in bed with her baby newly born. As they spun the threads of destiny, holding them firmly under their thumbs, they said: 'To the log and to the new-born child we assign the same span of years.' As soon as the goddesses had recited their verses and left the house, the mother snatched the blazing log from the fire, and flung cold water on it. For long it had been hidden away in the depths of the house, and its preservation had kept the young hero safe too. Now his mother brought it out, called for chips of pine wood and shavings, and when these had been piled up, kindled the flames that were to be her son's undoing. Then four times she tried to throw the log on the flames, and four times she stopped herself. Her affection for her son fought against her feelings for her brothers, and divided loyalty tore her heart in opposite directions. Often her face grew pale with fear at the thought of such a crime, often blazing anger made her eyes sparkle with fire. At times her expression was cruel and threatening, at others it could have been thought to be full of compassion. The heat of her fierce rage dried up her tears, yet still the tears welled up, and like a ship which feels the double pull as wind and tides draw it in different directions, as it sways uncertainly with both, so Thestius' daughter was swayed by her shifting emotions, and her anger alternately died away and flared up again. However, her sisterly affection began to get the better of her feelings as a mother, and in order to satisfy her brothers' ghosts with blood, by a guilty deed she saved herself from guilt. When the deadly flames were burning steadily: 'Let this funeral pyre consume the child I bore!' she cried. Then taking the fateful log in her murderous hands, the wretched woman stood before the funeral altars and prayed; 'Goddesses three, who reside over punishments, Furies, behold this unnatural sacrifice, by which I am at once avenging and committing crime. Death must atone for death, wickedness be piled on wickedness, slaughter upon slaughter, till this accursed household perish under its accumulation of woe. Shall Oeneus continue to enjoy the company of his victorious son, while Thestius is deprived of his? Better that both should have cause to mourn! Only do you, my broth-

In cases of this kind, one circumstance always augments the fluctuation: after balancing between two actions, a resolution to prefer one of them is an inchoated gratification of the prevailing passion, which moderates it in some degree; and that circumstance tends to give a superiority to the opposite passion: another circumstance also concurs, that this opposite passion has by restraint acquired in the interim some additional force. <148>

Love and jealousy connected by a common object, occupy the mind alternately: when the object is considered as beautiful, love prevails; when considered as possibly unfaithful, jealousy prevails. A situation of that kind affords great scope for fluctuation of passion; which is painted to the life by several masterly hands in words as well as in colours. Shakespear handles the same subject, but in a manner uncommon, and peculiar to himself: in Othello's soliloquy before putting his wife to death, love and jealousy are represented, each exerting its whole force, but without any struggle: Othello

---

ers, ghosts but recently descended to the shades, recognise my devotion, and welcome this offering provided at such a cost, the child of my womb, born to my sorrow!

'Alas, where do I rush so fast? O my brothers, forgive a mother! My hands cannot carry out their purpose: I confess my son has deserved to die, but I cannot bear that I should be the author of his death. Will he then go unpunished? Will he live, a victorious hero, exulting in this very exploit, ruling the kingdom of Calydon, while you lie dead, nothing but chill ghosts and a few ashes? No, that I cannot endure. Let the guilty wretch perish too, and carry with him to the grave his father's hopes, his kingdom, and his ruined country. But where is the affection a mother should feel for her son? Where are the loving ties that ought to bind parents to their children. Where the anguish I endured through ten long months? O my son, how much better had I allowed you to burn in those flames, when you were a baby! You received your life from my hands, but now you will die the death you have deserved! Accept the reward for what you have done: give me back the life I have twice bestowed on you, once when you were born, and again when I snatched the log from the fire. Either that, or send me to join my brothers in the tomb!

'I want to, yet I cannot! What am I to do? At one moment I see before my eyes my brother's wounds, and a vision of their dreadful murder: the next, my love for my son, the name of mother, break my resolution. Poor wretch that I am! It will be an evil thing, my brothers, if you triumph—yet triumph, none the less, provided that I too may follow you to the shades, you and the son I sacrifice to solace you!' With these words she flung the fatal log, with unsteady hands, into the heart of the flames, turning her face away as she did so. The very wood groaned, or seemed to groan, as it was kindled and set alight by the unwilling fire."

(*The Metamorphoses of Ovid,* trans. Mary M. Innes, Harmondsworth, Middlesex, England: Penguin Books, 1955)

was naturally inflexible; and the tenderest love could not divert him from a purpose he approved as right, not even for a moment: but every thing consistent with such a character is done to reconcile the two opposite passions; he is resolved to put her to death, but he will not shed her blood, nor so much as ruffle her skin:

> *Othello.* It is the cause, it is the cause, my soul;—
> Let me not name it to you, you chaste stars!
> It is the cause.—Yet I'll not shed her blood,
> Nor scar that whiter skin of hers than snow,
> And smooth as monumental alabastar.
>   [*Lays down the sword.*
> Yet she must die; else she'll betray more men.
> Put out the light, and then—Put out the light!—
> If I quench thee, thou flaming minister,
> I can again, thy former light restore,
> Should I repent: but once put out *thy* light, <149>
> Thou cunning'st pattern of excelling nature,
> I know not where is that Promethean heat
> That can thy light relumine.—   [*Sets down the taper.*
> When I have pluck'd thy rose,
> I cannot give it vital growth again;
> It needs must wither.—I'll smell thee on the tree:
>   [*Kissing her.*
> Oh balmy breath, that dost almost persuade
> Justice to break her sword!—One more; one more;
> Be thus when thou art dead, and I will kill thee,
> And love thee after.—One more, that's the last;
> So sweet was ne'er so fatal! I must weep,
> But they are cruel tears! this sorrow's heav'nly;
> It strikes where it doth love.—   *Act* 5. *sc.* 6.[45]

In Otway's *Orphan,* we have an illustrious example of the address employ'd to gratify opposite passions directed to the same object. Castalio and Polydore, brothers and rivals, had sworn mutual confidence: Castalio broke

45. Act 5, sc. 2.

his faith by a private marriage; which unwarily betray'd Polydore into a dismal deed, that of polluting his brother's bed. Thus he had injured his brother, and was injured by him: justice prompted him to make full atonement by his own death; resentment against his brother, required a full atonement to be made to himself. In coexistent passions so contradictory, one of them commonly prevails after a struggle: but here happily an expedient occurred to Polydore for gratifying both; which was, that he should provoke his brother to put him to death. Poly-<150>dore's crime in his own opinion merited that punishment; and justice was satisfied when he fell by the hand of the man he had injured: he wanted at the same time to punish his brother for breach of faith; and he could not punish more effectually than by betraying his brother to be his executioner.

If difference of aim prevent the union of two passions, tho' having the same object; much more will it prevent their union, when their objects are also different: in both cases there is a fluctuation; but in the latter the fluctuation is slower than in the former. A beautiful situation of that kind is exhibited in the *Cid* of Corneille.[46] Don Diegue, an old soldier worn out with age, having received a mortal affront from the Count, father to Chimene, employs his son Don Rodrigue, Chimene's lover, to demand satisfaction. This situation occasions in the breast of Don Rodrigue a cruel struggle between love and honour, one of which must be sacrificed. The scene is finely conducted, chiefly by making love in some degree take part with honour, Don Rodrigue reflecting, that if he lost his honour he could not deserve his mistress: honour triumphs; and the Count, provoked to a single combat, falls by the hand of Don Rodrigue.

This produceth another beautiful situation respecting Chimene, which, making part of the same story, is placed here, tho' it properly be-<151>longs to the foregoing head. It became the duty of that lady to demand justice against her lover, for whose preservation, in other circumstances, she chearfully would have sacrificed her own life. The struggle between these opposite passions directed to the same object is finely expressed in the third scene of the third act:

46. Corneille (1606–84), *The Cid,* 1636.

Elvire. Il vous prive d'un pére, et vous l'aimez encore!
Chimene. C'est peu de dire aimer, Elvire, je l'adore;
Ma passion s'oppose à mon resentiment,
Dedans mon ennemi je trouve mon amant,
Et je sens qu'en depit de toute ma colere,
Rodrigue dans mon cœur combat encore mon pére.
Il l'attaque, il le presse, il céde, il se défend,
Tantôt fort, tantôt foible, et tantôt triomphant;
Mais en ce dur combat de colére et de flame,
Il déchire mon cœur sans partager mon ame,
Et quoique mon amour ait sur moi de pouvoir,
Je ne consulte point pour suivre mon devoir.
Je cours sans balancer où mon honneur m'oblige;
Rodrigue m'est bien cher, son interêt m'afflige,
Mon cœur prend son parti; mais malgré son effort,
Je sai que je suis, et que mon pére est mort.[47]

Not less when the objects are different than when the same, are means some-times afforded to gratify both passions; and such means are greedily em-

---

47. Ibid., act 3, sc. 3:

[Elvira]
You love him still, he who unfathered you?

[Ximena]
I love, Elvira, nay, I worship him.
My passion and my anger are at odds.
I find my sweetheart in my enemy,
And still I feel in spite of all my wrath
Rodrigo fights my father in my heart,
Attacks, strikes home, gives ground, defends himself,
Now strong, now weak and now triumphantly;
But, in this combat between love and wrath,
He rends my heart, but does not bend my will.
Whatever power my love has over me,
I will not shrink from doing what is right.
I go unwavering where my duty calls.
Rodrigo's dear to me. Would he were not!
Despite my passion which takes sides with him,
I am the daughter of the man he killed.
                         (trans. John Cairncross)

braced. In Tasso's *Gerusalemme,* Edward and Gildippe, husband and wife, are introduced fighting gallantly against the Saracens: Gildippe receives <152> a mortal wound by the hand of Soliman: Edward inflamed with revenge, as well as concern for Gildippe, is agitated between the two different objects. The poet* describes him endeavouring to gratify both at once, applying his right hand against Soliman, the object of his resentment, and his left hand to support his wife, the object of his love.

PART V

Influence of Passion with respect to our Perceptions, Opinions, and Belief.

Considering how intimately our perceptions, passions, and actions, are mutually connected, it would be wonderful if they should have no mutual influence. That our actions are too much influenced by passion, is a known truth; but it is not less certain, tho' not so well known, that passion hath also an influence upon our perceptions, opinions, and belief. For example, the opinions we form of men and things, are generally directed by affection: an advice given by a man of figure, hath great weight; the same advice from one in a low condition, is despised or neglected: a man of <153> courage under-rates danger; and to the indolent the slightest obstacle appears unsurmountable.

This doctrine is of great use in logic; and of still greater use in criticism, by serving to explain several principles of the fine arts that will be unfolded in the course of this work. A few general observations shall at present suffice; leaving the subject to be prosecuted more particularly afterward when occasion offers.

There is no truth more universally known,[48] than that tranquillity and sedateness are the proper state of mind for accurate perception and cool deliberation; and for that reason, we never regard the opinion even of the wisest man, when we discover prejudice or passion behind the curtain. Pas-

---

* Canto 20. st. 97.

48. This and the following paragraphs are revisions of the text in the first edition.

sion, as observed above,* hath such influence over us, as to give a false light to all its objects. Agreeable passions prepossess the mind in favour of their objects, and disagreeable passions, no less against their objects: a woman is all perfection in her lover's opinion, while in the eye of a rival-beauty she is aukward and disagreeable: when the passion of love is gone, beauty vanishes with it,—nothing left of that genteel motion, that sprightly conversation, those numberless graces, which formerly, in the lover's opinion, charmed all hearts. To a zealot every one of his own sect is a saint, while the most upright of a different sect are to <154> him children of perdition: the talent of speaking in a friend, is more regarded than prudent conduct in any other. Nor will this surprise one acquainted with the world: our opinions, the result frequently of various and complicated views, are commonly so slight and wavering, as readily to be susceptible of a bias from passion.

With that natural bias another circumstance concurs, to give passion an undue influence on our opinions and belief; and that is a strong tendency in our nature to justify our passions as well as our actions, not to others only, but even to ourselves. That tendency is peculiarly remarkable with respect to disagreeable passions: by its influence, objects are magnified or lessened, circumstances supplied or suppressed, every thing coloured and disguised, to answer the end of justification. Hence the foundation of self-deceit, where a man imposes upon himself innocently, and even without suspicion of a bias.

There are subordinate means that contribute to pervert the judgement, and to make us form opinions contrary to truth; of which I shall mention two. First, It was formerly observed,† that tho' ideas seldom start up in the mind without connection, yet that ideas suited to the present tone of mind are readily suggested by any slight connection: the arguments for a favourite <155> opinion are always at hand, while we often search in vain for those that cross our inclination. Second, The mind taking delight in agreeable circumstances or arguments, is deeply impressed with them; while those that are disagreeable are hurried over so as scarce to make any impression:

* Page 120.
† Chap. 1.

the same argument, by being relished or not relished, weighs so differently, as in truth to make conviction depend more on passion than on reasoning. This observation is fully justified by experience: to confine myself to a single instance, the numberless absurd religious tenets that at different times have pestered the world, would be altogether unaccountable but for that irregular bias of passion.

We proceed to a more pleasant task, which is, to illustrate the foregoing observations by proper examples. Gratitude, when warm, is often exerted upon the children of the benefactor; especially where he is removed out of reach by death or absence.* The passion in this case being exerted for the sake of the benefactor, requires no peculiar excellence in his children: but the practice of doing good to these children produces affection for them, which never fails to advance them in our esteem. By such means, strong connections of affection are often formed among in-<156>dividuals, upon the slight foundation now mentioned.

Envy is a passion, which, being altogether unjustifiable, cannot be excused but by disguising it under some plausible name. At the same time, no passion is more eager than envy, to give its object a disagreeable appearance: it magnifies every bad quality, and fixes on the most humbling circumstances:

> *Cassius.* I cannot tell what you and other men
> Think of this life; but for my single self,
> I had as lief not be, as live to be
> In awe of such a thing as I myself.
> I was born free as Caesar, so were you;
> We both have fed as well; and we can both
> Endure the winter's cold as well as he.
> For once, upon a raw and gusty day,
> The troubled Tyber chafing with his shores,
> Caesar says to me, Dar'st thou, Cassius, now
> Leap in with me into this angry flood,
> And swim to yonder point?—Upon the word,
> Accoutred as I was, I plunged in,

---

* See part I. sect. 1. of the present chapter.

And bid him follow; so indeed he did.
The torrent roar'd, and we did buffet it
With lusty sinews; throwing it aside,
And stemming it with hearts of controversy.
But ere we could arrive the point propos'd,
Caesar cry'd, Help me, Cassius, or I sink.
I, as Aeneas, our great ancestor,
Did from the flames of Troy upon his shoulder
The old Anchises bear; so from the waves of Tyber <157>
Did I the tired Caesar: and this man
Is now become a god, and Cassius is
A wretched creature; and must bend his body,
If Caesar carelessly but nod on him.
He had a fever when he was in Spain,
And when the fit was on him, I did mark
How he did shake. 'Tis true, this god did shake;
His coward lips did from their colour fly,
And that same eye whose bend doth awe the world,
Did lose its lustre; I did hear him grone;
Ay, and that tongue of his, that bade the Romans
Mark him, and write his speeches in their books,
Alas! it cry'd—Give me some drink, Titinius,—
As a sick girl. Ye gods, it doth amaze me,
A man of such a feeble temper should
So get the start of the majestic world,
And bear the palm alone.   *Julius Caesar, act* 1. *sc.* 3.[49]

Glo'ster inflamed with resentment against his son Edgar, could even force himself into a momentary conviction that they were not related:

O strange fasten'd villain!
Would he deny his letter?—I never got him.

                                King Lear, act 2. *sc.* 3.[50]

49. Act 1, sc. 2.
50. Act 2, sc. 1.

When by great sensibility of heart, or other means, grief becomes immoderate, the mind, in order to justify itself, is prone to magnify the cause:
and if the real cause admit not of being <158> magnified, the mind seeks
a cause for its grief in imagined future events:

> *Bushy.* Madam, your Majesty is much too sad:
> You promis'd, when you parted with the King,
> To lay aside self-harming heaviness,
> And entertain a chearful disposition.
>   *Queen.* To please the King, I did; to please myself,
> I cannot do it. Yet I know no cause
> Why I should welcome such a guest as grief;
> Save bidding farewell to so sweet a guest
> As my sweet Richard: yet again, methinks,
> Some unborn sorrow, ripe in Fortune's womb,
> Is coming tow'rd me; and my inward soul
> With something trembles, yet at nothing grieves,
> More than with parting from my lord the King.
>   *Richard* II. *act* 2. *sc.* 5.[51]

Resentment at first is vented on the relations of the offender, in order
to punish him: but as resentment, when so outrageous, is contrary to conscience, the mind, to justify its passion, is disposed to paint these relations
in the blackest colours; and it comes at last to be convinced, that they ought
to be punished for their own demerits.

Anger raised by an accidental stroke upon a tender part of the body, is
sometimes vented upon the undesigning cause. But as the passion in that
case is absurd, and as there can be no solid gratification in punishing the
innocent; the mind, prone to justify as well as to gratify its passion, de-
<159>ludes itself into a conviction of the action's being voluntary. The
conviction however is but momentary: the first reflection shows it to be
erroneous; and the passion vanisheth almost instantaneously with the conviction. But anger, the most violent of all passions, has still greater influence: it sometimes forces the mind to personify a stock or a stone if it happen to occasion bodily pain, and even to believe it a voluntary agent, in

---

51. Act 2, sc. 2.

order to be a proper object of resentment. And that we have really a momentary conviction of its being a voluntary agent, must be evident from considering, that without such conviction the passion can neither be justified nor gratified: the imagination can give no aid; for a stock or a stone imagined sensible, cannot be an object of punishment, if the mind be conscious that it is an imagination merely without any reality. Of such personification, involving a conviction of reality, there is one illustrious instance: when the first bridge of boats over the Hellespont was destroyed by a storm, Xerxes fell into a transport of rage, so excessive, that he commanded the sea to be punished with 300 stripes; and a pair of fetters to be thrown into it, enjoining the following words to be pronounced: "O thou salt and bitter water! thy master hath condemned thee to this punishment for offending him without cause; and is resolved to pass over thee in despite of thy insolence: with reason all men neglect to sacrifice to thee, <160> because thou art both disagreeable and treacherous."*

Shakespear exhibits beautiful examples of the irregular influence of passion in making us believe things to be otherwise than they are. King Lear, in his distress, personifies the rain, wind, and thunder; and in order to justify his resentment, believes them to be taking part with his daughters:

> *Lear.* Rumble thy belly-full, spit fire, spout rain!
> Nor rain, wind, thunder, fire, are my daughters.
> I tax not you, you elements, with unkindness;
> I never gave you kingdoms, call'd you children;
> You owe me no subscription. Then let fall
> Your horrible pleasure.—Here I stand, your brave;
> A poor, infirm, weak, and despis'd old man!
> But yet I call you servile ministers,
> That have with two pernicious daughters join'd
> Your high-engender'd battles, 'gainst a head
> So old and white as this. Oh! oh! 'tis foul!   *Act* 3. *sc.* 2.

King Richard, full of indignation against his favourite horse for carrying Bolingbroke, is led into the conviction of his being rational:

* Herodotus, book 7. [Herodotus (ca. 480–425 B.C.): Greek historian who traveled widely in Europe, Asia, and Africa and is regarded as the father of history.]

> *Groom.* O, how it yearn'd my heart, when I beheld
> In London streets, that coronation-day,
> When Bolingbroke rode on Roan Barbary,
> That horse that thou so often hast bestrid,
> That horse that I so carefully have dressed. <161>
>   *K. Rich.* Rode he on Barbary? tell me, gentle friend,
> How went he under him.
>   *Groom.* So proudly as he had disdain'd the ground.
>   *K. Rich.* So proud that Bolingbroke was on his back!
> That jade had eat bread from my royal hand.
> This hand hath made him proud with clapping him.
> Would he not stumble? would he not fall down,
> (Since pride must have a fall), and break the neck
> Of that proud man that did usurp his back?
>
> > *Richard* II. *act* 5. *sc.* II.[52]

Hamlet, swelled with indignation at his mother's second marriage, was strongly inclined to lessen the time of her widowhood, the shortness of the time being a violent circumstance against her; and he deludes himself by degrees into the opinion of an interval shorter than the real one:

> *Hamlet.* ——— That it should come to this!
> But two months dead! nay, not so much; not two;—
> So excellent a king, that was, to this,
> Hyperion to a satyr: so loving to my mother,
> That he permitted not the winds of heav'n
> Visit her face too roughly. Heav'n and earth!
> Must I remember—why, she would hang on him,
> As if increase of appetite had grown
> By what it fed on; yet, within a month—
> Let me not think—Frailty, thy name is *Woman!*
> A little month! or ere those shoes were old,
> With which she follow'd my poor father's body,
> Like Niobe, all tears—Why she, ev'n she—
> (O heav'n! a beast that wants discourse of reason, <162>
> Would have mourn'd longer—) married with mine uncle,

---

52. Act 5, sc. 5.

My father's brother; but no more like my father,
Than I to Hercules. Within a month!—
Ere yet the salt of most unrighteous tears
Had left the flushing in her gauled eyes,
She married—Oh, most wicked speed, to post
With such dexterity to incestuous sheets!
It is not, nor it cannot come to good.
But break, my heart, for I must hold my tongue.

Act I. *sc.* 3.[53]

The power of passion to falsify the computation of time is remarkable in this instance; because time, which hath an accurate measure, is less obsequious to our desires and wishes, than objects which have no precise standard of less or more.

Good news are greedily swallowed upon very slender evidence: our wishes magnify the probability of the event, as well as the veracity of the relater; and we believe as certain, what at best is doubtful:

Quel, che l'huom vede, amor li fa invisible
E l'invisibil fa veder amore.
Questo creduto fu, che 'l miser suole
Dar facile credenza a' quel, che vuole.

Orland. Furios. cant. I. *st.* 56.[54]

For the same reason, bad news gain also credit upon the slightest evidence: fear, if once alarm-<163>ed, has the same effect with hope, to magnify every circumstance that tends to conviction. Shakespear, who shows more knowledge of human nature than any of our philosophers, hath in his *Cymbeline** represented this bias of the mind; for he makes the person who alone was

---

* Act 2. sc. 6. [Act 2, sc. 4.]

53. Act 1, sc. 2.

54. Lodovico Ariosto (1474–1533) of Ferrara served Duke Alfonso d'Este: he wrote *Orlando Furioso* (1532), exalting the house of Este.

Since Love, who sees without one guiding gleam,
Spies in broad day but that which likes him best:
For one sign of the afflicted man's disease
Is to give ready faith to things which please
(trans. W. S. Rose, 1775–1843)

affected with the bad news, yield to evidence that did not convince any of his companions. And Othello* is convinced of his wife's infidelity from circumstances too slight to move any person less interested.

If the news interest us in so low a degree as to give place to reason, the effect will not be altogether the same: judging of the probability or improbability of the story, the mind settles in a rational conviction either that it is true or not. But even in that case, the mind is not allow'd to rest in that degree of conviction which is produced by rational evidence: if the news be in any degree favourable, our belief is raised by hope to an improper height; and if unfavourable, by fear.

This observation holds equally with respect to future events: if a future event be either much wished or dreaded, the mind never fails to augment the probability beyond truth.

That easiness of belief with respect to wonders and prodigies, even the most absurd and ridiculous, is a strange phenomenon; because nothing <164> can be more evident than the following proposition, That the more singular any event is, the more evidence is required to produce belief: a familiar event daily occurring, being in itself extremely probable, finds ready credit, and therefore is vouched by the slightest evidence; but to overcome the improbability of a strange and rare event, contrary to the course of nature, the very strongest evidence is required. It is certain, however, that wonders and prodigies are swallowed by the vulgar, upon evidence that would not be sufficient to ascertain the most familiar occurrence. It has been reckoned difficult to explain that irregular bias of mind; but we are now made acquainted with the influence of passion upon opinion and belief: a story of ghosts or fairies, told with an air of gravity and truth, raiseth an emotion of wonder, and perhaps of dread; and these emotions imposing upon a weak mind, impress upon it a thorough conviction contrary to reason.

Opinion and belief are influenced by propensity as well as by passion. An innate propensity is all we have to convince us, that the operations of nature are uniform: influenced by that propensity, we often rashly think, that good or bad weather will never have an end; and in natural philosophy,

---

* Act 3. sc. 8. [Act 3, sc. 4.]

writers, influenced by the same propensity, stretch commonly their ana-
logical reasonings beyond just bounds.

Opinion and belief are influenced by affection <165> as well as by propensity. The noted story of a fine lady and a curate viewing the moon
through a telescope, is a pleasant illustration: I perceive, says the lady, two
shadows inclining to each other; they are certainly two happy lovers: Not
at all, replies the curate, they are two steeples of a cathedral.

APPENDIX TO PART V

Methods that Nature hath afforded for computing
Time and Space.

This subject is introduced, because it affords several curious examples of
the influence of passion to bias the mind in its conceptions and opinions;
a lesson that cannot be too frequently inculcated, as there is not perhaps
another bias in human nature that hath an influence so universal to make
us wander from truth as well as from justice.

I begin with time; and the question is, What was the measure of time
before artificial measures were invented; and what is the measure at present
when these are not at hand? I speak not of months and days, which are
computed by the moon and sun; but of hours, or in general of the time
that passes between any two occurrences <166> when there is not access to
the sun. The only natural measure, is the succession of our thoughts; for
we always judge the time to be long or short, in proportion to the number
of perceptions and ideas that have passed during that interval. This measure
is indeed far from being accurate; because in a quick and in a slow succession, it must evidently produce different computations of the same time:
but however inaccurate, it is the only measure by which we naturally cal-
culate time; and that measure is applied on all occasions, without regard to
any casual variation in the rate of succession.

That measure would however be tolerable, did it labour under no other
imperfection beside that mentioned: but in many instances it is much more
fallacious; in order to explain which distinctly, an analysis will be necessary.
Time is computed at two different periods; one while it is passing, another

after it is past: these computations shall be considered separately, with the errors to which each of them is liable. Beginning with computation of time while it is passing, it is a common and trite observation, That to lovers absence appears immeasurably long, every minute an hour, and every day a year: the same computation is made in every case where we long for a distant event; as where one is in expectation of good news, or where a profligate heir watches for the death of an old rich miser. Opposite to these are instances not <167> fewer in number: to a criminal the interval between sentence and execution appears wofully short: and the same holds in every case where one dreads an approaching event; of which even a schoolboy can bear witness: the hour allowed him for play, moves, in his apprehension, with a very swift pace; before he is thoroughly engaged, the hour is gone. A computation founded on the number of ideas, will never produce estimates so regularly opposite to each other; for our wishes do not produce a slow succession of ideas, nor our fears a quick succession. What then moves nature, in the cases mentioned, to desert her ordinary measure for one very different? I know not that this question ever has been resolved; the false estimates I have suggested being so common and familiar that no writer has thought of their cause. And indeed, to enter upon this matter without preparation, might occasion some difficulty; to encounter which, we luckily are prepared, by what is said upon the power of passion to bias the mind in its perceptions and opinions. Among the circumstances that terrify a condemned criminal, the short time he has to live is one; which time, by the influence of terror, is made to appear still shorter than it is in reality. In the same manner, among the distresses of an absent lover, the time of separation is a capital circumstance, which for that reason is greatly magnified by his anxiety and impatience: he imagines that the time of meeting <168> comes on very slow, or rather that it will never come: every minute is thought of an intolerable length. Here is a fair, and I hope satisfactory, reason, why time is thought to be tedious when we long for a future event, and not less fleet when we dread the event. The reason is confirmed by other instances. Bodily pain, fixt to one part, produceth a slow train of perceptions, which, according to the common measure of time, ought to make it appear short: yet we know, that in such a state time has the opposite appearance; and the reason is, that bodily pain is always attended with a degree of impatience, which makes us think every minute to be an hour. The same holds where the pain shifts from place to place; but not so remarkably, because such a pain is not attended with the same degree of impatience. The impatience a man hath in travelling through a barren country, or in a bad road, makes him think, during the journey, that time goes on with a very slow pace. We shall see afterward, that a very different computation is made when the journey is over.

How ought it to stand with a person who apprehends bad news? It will probably be thought, that the case of this person resembles that of a criminal, who, terrified at his approaching execution, believes every hour to be but a minute: yet the computation is directly opposite. Reflecting upon the difficulty, there appears one capital dis-<169>tinguishing circumstance: the fate of the criminal is determined; in the case under consideration, the person is still in suspense. Every one has felt the distress that accompanies suspense: we wish to get rid of it at any rate, even at the expence of bad news. This case therefore, upon a more narrow inspection, resembles that of bodily pain: the present distress in both cases, makes the time appear extremely tedious.

The reader probably will not be displeased, to have this branch of the subject illustrated, by an author who is acquainted with every maze of the human heart, and who bestows ineffable grace and ornament upon every subject he handles:

Rosalinda. I pray you, what is't a-clock?

Orlando. You should ask me, what time o'day; there's no clock in the forest.

Ros. Then there is no true lover in the forest; else, sighing every minute, and groning every hour, would detect the lazy foot of Time, as well as a clock.

Orla. Why not the swift foot of Time? Had not that been as proper?

Ros. By no means, Sir. Time travels in diverse paces with diverse persons. I'll tell you who Time ambles withal, who Time trots withal, who Time gallops withal, and who he stands still withal.

Orla. I pr'ythee whom doth he trot withal?

Ros. Marry, he trots hard with a young maid between the contract of her marriage and the day it is <170> solemnized: if the interim be but a se'ennight, Time's pace is so hard that it seems the length of seven years.

Orla. Who ambles Time withal?

Ros. With a priest that lacks Latin, and a rich man that hath not the gout: for the one sleeps easily, because he cannot study; and the other lives merrily, because he feels no pain: the one lacking the burden of lean and wasteful learning; the other knowing no burthen of heavy tedious penury. These Time ambles withal.

Orla. Whom doth he gallop withal?

Ros. With a thief to the gallows: for tho' he go as softly as foot can fall, he thinks himself too soon there.

Orla. Whom stays it still withal?

Ros. With lawyers in the vacation: for they sleep between term and term, and then they perceive not how Time moves.

As you like it, act 3. *sc.* 8.[55]

The natural method of computing present time, shows how far from truth we may be led by the irregular influence of passion: nor are our eyes immediately opened when the scene is past; for the deception continues while there remain any traces of the passion. But looking back upon past time when the joy or distress is no longer remembered, the computation is very different: in that condition, we coolly and deliberately make use of the ordinary measure, namely, the course of our perceptions. And I shall now proceed to the errors that this measure is subjected to. Here we must distinguish between a train of perceptions, <171> and a train of ideas: real objects make a strong impression, and are faithfully remembered: ideas, on the contrary, however entertaining at the time, are apt to escape a subsequent recollection. Hence it is, that in retrospection, the time that was employ'd upon real objects, appears longer than that employ'd upon ideas: the former are more accurately recollected than the latter; and we measure the time by the number that is recollected. This doctrine shall be illustrated by

55. Act 3, sc. 2.

examples. After finishing a journey through a populous country, the frequency of agreeable objects distinctly recollected by the traveller, makes the time spent in the journey appear to him longer than it was in reality; which is chiefly remarkable in the first journey, when every object is new, and makes a strong impression. On the other hand, after finishing a journey through a barren country thinly peopled, the time appears short, being measured by the number of objects, which were few, and far from interesting. Here in both instances a computation is made, directly opposite to that made during the journey. And this, by the way, serves to account for what may appear singular, that in a barren country, a computed mile is always longer, than near the capital where the country is rich and populous: the traveller has no natural measure of the miles he has travelled, other than the time bestow'd upon the journey; nor any natural measure of the time, other than the num-<172>ber of his perceptions: now these, being few from the paucity of objects in a waste country, lead him to compute that the time has been short, and consequently that the miles have been few: by the same method of computation, the great number of perceptions from the quantity of objects in a populous country, make the traveller conjecture that the time has been long, and the miles many. The last step of the computation is obvious: in estimating the distance of one place from another, if the miles be reckoned few in number, each mile must of course be long; if many in number, each must be short.

Again, the travelling with an agreeable companion, produceth a short computation both of the road and of time; especially if there be few objects that demand attention, or if the objects be familiar: and the case is the same of young people at a ball, or of a joyous company over a bottle: the ideas with which they have been entertained, being transitory, escape the memory; after the journey and the entertainment are over, they reflect that they have been much diverted, but scarce can say about what.

When one is totally occupied with any agreeable work that admits not many objects, time runs on without observation: and upon a subsequent recollection, must appear short, in proportion to the paucity of objects. This is still more remarkable in close contemplation and in deep thinking, <173> where the train, composed wholly of ideas, proceeds with an extreme slow pace: not only are the ideas few in number, but are apt to escape an after reckoning. The like false reckoning of time, may proceed from an opposite state of mind: in a reverie, where ideas float at random without making any impression, time goes on unheeded, and the reckoning is lost. A reverie may be so profound as to prevent the recollection of any one idea: that the mind was busied in a train of thinking, may in general be remembered; but what was the subject, has quite escaped the memory. In such a case, we are altogether at a loss about the time, having no *data* for making a computation. No cause produceth so false a reckoning of time, as immoderate grief: the mind, in that state, is violently attached to a single object, and admits not a different thought: any other object breaking in, is instantly banished, so as scarce to give an appearance of succession. In a reverie, we are uncertain of the time that is past; but in the example now given, there is an appearance of certainty, that the time must have been short, when the perceptions are so few in number.

The natural measure of space, appears more obscure than that of time. I venture however to mention it, leaving it to be further prosecuted, if it be thought of any importance.

The space marked out for a house, appears considerably larger after it is divided into its proper <174> parts. A piece of ground appears larger after it is surrounded with a fence; and still larger when it is made a garden and divided into different compartments.

On the contrary, a large plain looks less after it is divided into parts. The sea must be excepted, which looks less from that very circumstance of not being divided into parts.

A room of a moderate size appears larger when properly furnished. But when a very large room is furnished, I doubt whether it be not lessened in appearance.

A room of a moderate size looks less by having a ceiling lower than in proportion. The same low ceiling makes a very large room look larger than it is in reality.

These experiments are by far too small a stock for a general theory: but they are all that occur at present; and instead of a regular system, I have nothing for the reader's instruction but a few conjectures.

The largest angle of vision seems to be the natural measure of space: the eye is the only judge; and in examining with it the size of any plain, or the length of any line, the most accurate method that can be taken is, to run over the object in parts: the largest part that can be seen with one stedfast look, determines the largest angle of vision; and when that angle is given, one may in-<175>stitute a calculation by trying with the eye how many of these parts are in the whole.

Whether this angle be the same in all men, I know not: the smallest angle of vision is ascertained; and to ascertain the largest, would not be less curious.

But supposing it known, it would be a very imperfect measure; perhaps more so than the natural measure of time: for it requires great steadiness of eye to measure a line with any accuracy, by applying to it the largest angle of distinct vision. And supposing that steadiness to be acquired by practice, the measure will be imperfect from other circumstances. The space comprehended under this angle, will be different according to the distance, and also according to the situation of the object: of a perpendicular this angle will comprehend the smallest space; the space will be larger in looking upon an inclined plain; and will be larger or less in proportion to the degree of inclination.

This measure of space, like the measure of time, is liable to several errors from certain operations of the mind, which will account for some of the erroneous judgements above mentioned. The space marked out for a dwelling-house, where the eye is at any reasonable distance, is seldom greater than can be seen at once without moving the head: divide that space into two or three equal parts, and none of these parts will appear much less than what can be comprehended at one distinct <176> look; consequently each of them will appear equal, or nearly equal, to what the whole did before the division. If, on the other hand, the whole be very small, so as scarce to fill the eye at one look, its divisions into parts will, I conjecture, make it appear still less: the minuteness of the parts is, by an easy transition of ideas, transferred to the whole; and we pass the same judgement on the latter that we do on the former.

The space marked out for a small garden, is survey'd almost at one view; and requires a motion of the eye so slight, as to pass for an object that can be comprehended under the largest angle of distinct vision: if not divided into too many parts, we are apt to form the same judgement of each part;

and consequently to magnify the garden in proportion to the number of its parts.

A very large plain without protuberances, is an object no less rare than beautiful; and in those who see it for the first time, it must produce an emotion of wonder. That emotion, however slight, imposes on the mind, and makes it judge that the plain is larger than it is in reality. Divide the plain into parts, and our wonder ceases: it is no longer considered as one great plain, but as so many different fields or inclosures.

The first time one beholds the sea, it appears to be large beyond all bounds. When it becomes familiar, and ceases to raise our wonder, it appears less than it is in reality. In a storm it appears large, <177> being distinguishable by the rolling waves into a number of great parts. Islands scattered at considerable distances, add in appearance to its size: each intercepted part looks extremely large, and we insensibly apply arithmetic to increase the appearance of the whole. Many islands scattered at hand, give a diminutive appearance to the sea, by its connection with its diminutive parts: the Lomond lake would undoubtedly look larger without its islands.[56]

Furniture increaseth in appearance the size of a small room, for the same reason that divisions increase in appearance the size of a garden.[57] The emotion of wonder which is raised by a very large room without furniture, makes it look larger than it is in reality: if completely furnished, we view it in parts, and our wonder is not raised.

A low ceiling hath a diminutive appearance, which, by an easy transition of ideas, is communicated to the length and breadth, provided they bear any proportion to the height. If they be out of all proportion, the opposition seizes the mind, and raises some degree of wonder, which makes the difference appear greater than it really is. <178>

---

56. As a circuit judge, Kames's legal tours in Argyll took him to Inverary by way of Loch Lomond.

57. The impact of the styles and placing of furniture was widely debated in France by architects and writers on architecture under the headings of *distribution* and *convenance*.

PART VI

The Resemblance of Emotions to their Causes.

That many emotions have some resemblance to their causes, is a truth that can be made clear by induction; tho', as far as I know, the observation has not been made by any writer. Motion, in its different circumstances, is productive of feelings that resemble it: sluggish motion, for example, causeth a languid unpleasant feeling; slow uniform motion, a feeling calm and pleasant; and brisk motion, a lively feeling that rouses the spirits and promotes activity. A fall of water through rocks, raises in the mind a tumultuous confused agitation, extremely similar to its cause. When force is exerted with any effort, the spectator feels a similar effort, as of force exerted within his mind. A large object swells the heart. An elevated object makes the spectator stand erect.

Sounds also produce emotions or feelings that resemble them. A sound in a low key, brings down the mind: such a sound in a full tone, hath a certain solemnity, which it communicates to the feeling produced by it. A sound in a high key, chears the mind by raising it: such a sound in a full tone, both elevates and swells the mind. <179>

Again, a wall or pillar that declines from the perpendicular, produceth a painful feeling, as of a tottering and falling within the mind: and a feeling somewhat similar is produced by a tall pillar that stands so ticklish as to look like falling.* A column with a base looks more firm and stable than upon the naked ground; and for that reason is more agreeable: and tho' the cylinder is a more beautiful figure, yet the cube for a base is preferred; its angles being extended to a greater distance from the centre than the cir-

---

* Sunt enim Tempe saltus transitu difficilis: nam praeter angustias per quinque millia, quâ exiguum jumento onusto iter est, rupes utrinque ita abscissae sunt, ut despici vix sine vertigine quadam simul oculorum animique possit. *Titus Livius, lib.* 44. *sect.* 6. [Titus Livius (59 B.C.–A.D. 17), Roman historian, only part of whose history of Rome survives: "{For even without the opposition of an enemy} Tempe is a defile difficult of passage; for besides five miles of narrows through which the road is cramped for a loaded animal, the cliffs on either side are so sheer that one can hardly look down without some dizziness of eye or brain." Kames omits the phrase in braces.]

cumference of a cylinder. This excludes not a different reason, that the base, the shaft, and the capital, of a pillar, ought, for the sake of variety, to differ from each other: if the shaft be round, the base and capital ought to be square.[58]

A constrained posture, uneasy to the man himself, is disagreeable to the spectator; whence a rule in painting, that the drapery ought not to adhere to the body, but hang loose, that the figures may appear easy and free in their movements. The constrained posture of a French dancing-master in one of Hogarth's pieces, is for that reason disagreeable; and it is also ridiculous, because the constraint is assumed as a grace.[59] <180>

The foregoing observation is not confined to emotions or feelings raised by still life: it holds also in what are raised by the qualities, actions, and passions, of a sensible being. Love inspired by a fine woman, assumes her qualities: it is sublime, soft, tender, severe, or gay, according to its cause. This is still more remarkable in emotions raised by human actions: it hath already been remarked,* that any signal instance of gratitude, beside procuring esteem for the author, raiseth in the spectator a vague emotion of gratitude, which disposeth him to be grateful; and I now further remark, that this vague emotion hath a strong resemblance to its cause, namely, the passion that produced the grateful action: courage exerted inspires the reader as well as the spectator with a like emotion of courage, a just action fortifies our love of justice, and a generous action rouses our generosity. In short, with respect to all virtuous actions, it will be found by induction, that they lead us to imitation by inspiring emotions resembling the passions that produced these actions. And hence the advantage of choice books and choice company.

Grief as well as joy are infectious: the emotions they raise in a spectator resemble them perfectly. Fear is equally infectious: and hence in an army, a few taking fright, even without cause, <181> spread the infection till it

---

* Part I. of this chapter, sect. 4.

58. The reference is to debate in the Edinburgh Society for the Encouragement of Arts, Sciences, Manufactures, and Agriculture (1755–56). See the editor's Introduction.

59. William Hogarth (1697–1764): painter, engraver, political caricaturist, and author of *The Analysis of Beauty* (1753). The reference is to plate 2 of *The Rake's Progress*, published in 1735.

becomes an universal panic. Pity is similar to its cause: a parting scene between lovers or friends, produceth in the spectator a sort of pity, which is tender like the distress: the anguish of remorse, produceth pity of a harsh kind; and if the remorse be extreme, the pity hath a mixture of horror. Anger I think is singular; for even where it is moderate, and causeth no disgust, it disposes not the spectator to anger in any degree.* Covetousness, cruelty, treachery, and other vicious passions, are so far from raising any emotion similar to themselves, to incite a spectator to imitation, that they have an opposite effect: they raise abhorrence, and fortify the spectator in his aversion to such actions. When anger is immoderate, it cannot fail to produce the same effect.

PART VII

Final Causes of the more frequent Emotions and Passions.

It is a law in our nature, that we never act but by the impulse of desire; which in other words is saying, that passion, by the desire included in <182> it, is what determines the will. Hence in the conduct of life, it is of the utmost importance, that our passions be directed to proper objects, tend to just and rational ends, and with relation to each other be duly balanced. The beauty of contrivance, so conspicuous in the human frame, is not confined to the rational part of our nature, but is visible over the whole. Concerning the passions in particular, however irregular, headstrong, and perverse, in a slight view, they may appear, I hope to demonstrate, that they are by nature modelled and tempered with perfect wisdom, for the good of society as well as for private good. The subject, treated at large, would be too extensive for the present work: all there is room for are a few general observations upon the sensitive part of our nature, without regarding that strange irregularity of passion discovered in some individuals. Such topical irregularities, if I may use the term, cannot fairly be held an objection to

* Aristotle, Poet. cap. 18. § 3. says, that anger raiseth in the spectator a similar emotion of anger. [The modern reference is part II, chap. xvii.]

the present theory: we are frequently, it is true, misled by inordinate passion; but we are also, and perhaps no less frequently, misled by wrong judgement.

In order to fulfil my engagement, it must be premised, that an agreeable cause produceth always a pleasant emotion; and a disagreeable cause, a painful emotion. This is a general law of nature, which admits not a single exception: agreeableness in the cause, is indeed so essentially con- <183>nected with pleasure in the emotion, its effect, that an agreeable cause cannot be better defined, than by its power of producing a pleasant emotion: and disagreeableness in the cause, has the same necessary connection with pain in the emotion produced by it.

From this preliminary it appears, that in order to know for what end an emotion is made pleasant or painful, we must begin with inquiring for what end its cause is made agreeable or disagreeable. And with respect to inanimate objects, considered as the causes of emotions, many of them are made agreeable in order to promote our happiness; and it proves invincibly the benignity of the Deity, that we are placed in the midst of objects for the most part agreeable. But that is not all: the bulk of such objects, being of real use in life, are made agreeable in order to excite our industry; witness a large tree, a well-dressed fallow, a rich field of grain, and others that may be named without end. On the other hand, it is not easy to specify a disagreeable object that is not at the same time hurtful: some things are made disagreeable, such as a rotten carcase, because they are noxious: others, a dirty marsh, for example, or a barren heath, are made disagreeable in order, as above, to excite our industry. And with respect to the few things that are neither agreeable nor disagreeable, it will be made evident, that their being left indifferent is not a work of chance <184> but of wisdom: of such I shall have occasion to give several instances.

Because inanimate objects that are agreeable fix our attention and draw us to them, they in that respect are termed *attractive:* such objects inspire pleasant emotions, which are gratified by adhering to the objects, and enjoying them. Because disagreeable objects of the same kind repel us from them, they in that respect are termed *repulsive:* and the painful emotions raised by such objects, are gratified by flying from them. Thus in general, with respect to things inanimate, the tendency of every pleasant emotion is to prolong the pleasure; and the tendency of every painful emotion is to end the pain.

Sensible beings considered as objects of passion, lead into a more complex theory. A sensible being that is agreeable by its attributes, inspires us with a pleasant emotion accompanied with desire; and the question is, What is naturally the gratification of that desire? Were man altogether selfish, his nature would lead him to indulge the pleasant emotion, without making any acknowledgement to the person who gives him pleasure, more than to a pure air or temperate clime: but as man is endued with a principle of benevolence as well as of selfishness, he is prompted by his nature, to desire the good of every sensible being that gives him pleasure; and the happiness of that being, is the gratification of his desire. The final <185> cause of desire so directed is illustrious: it contributes to a man's own happiness, by affording him means of gratification beyond what selfishness can afford; and at the same time, it tends eminently to advance the happiness of others. This lays open a beautiful theory in the nature of man: a selfish action can only benefit myself: a benevolent action benefits myself as much as it benefits others. In a word, benevolence may not improperly be said to be the most refined selfishness; which, by the way, ought to silence certain shallow philosophers, who, ignorant of human nature, teach a disgustful doctrine, That to serve others, unless with a view to our own happiness, is weakness and folly; as if self-love only, and not benevolence, contributed to our happiness. The hand of God is too visible in the human frame to permit us to think seriously, that there ever can be any jarring or inconsistency among natural principles, those especially of self-love and benevolence, which govern the bulk of our actions.* <186>

---

* With shallow thinkers the selfish system naturally prevails in theory, I do not say in practice. During infancy our desires center mostly in ourselves: every one perceives intuitively the comfort of food and raiment, of a snug dwelling, and of every convenience. But that the doing good to others will make us happy, is not so evident; feeding the hungry, for example, or clothing the naked. This truth is seen but obscurely by the gross of mankind, if at all seen: the superior pleasure that accompanies the exercise of benevolence, of friendship, and of every social principle, is not clearly understood till it be frequently felt. To perceive the social principle in its triumphant state, a man must

Next in order come sensible beings that are in distress. A person in distress, being so far a disagreeable object, must raise in the spectator a painful passion; and were man purely a selfish being, he would desire to be relieved from that pain, by turning from the object. But the principle of benevolence gives an opposite direction to his desire: it makes him desire to afford relief; and by relieving the person from distress, his passion is gratified. The painful passion thus directed, is termed *sympathy;* which, tho' painful, is yet in its nature attractive. And with respect to its final cause, we can be at no loss: it not only tends to relieve a fellow-creature from distress, but in its gratification is greatly more pleasant than if it were repulsive.

We in the last place bring under consideration persons hateful by vice or wickedness. Imagine a <187> wretch who has lately perpetrated some horrid crime: he is disagreeable to every spectator; and consequently raiseth in every spectator a painful passion. What is the natural gratification of that passion? I must here again observe, that supposing man to be entirely a selfish being, he would be prompted by his nature to relieve himself from the pain, by averting his eye, and banishing the criminal from his thoughts. But man is not so constituted: he is composed of many principles, which, tho' seemingly contradictory, are perfectly concordant. His actions are influenced by the principle of benevolence, as well as by that of selfishness: and in order to answer the foregoing question, I must introduce a third principle, no less remarkable in its influence than either of these mentioned; it is that principle, common to all, which prompts us to punish those who do wrong. An envious, a malicious, or a cruel action, being disagreeable, raiseth in the spectator the painful emotion of resentment, which frequently swells into a passion; and the natural gratification of the desire included in that passion is to punish the guilty person: I must chastise the wretch by indignation at least and hatred, if not more severely. Here the final cause is self-evident.

An injury done to myself, touching me more than when done to others,

---

forget himself, and turn his thoughts upon the character and conduct of his fellow-creatures: he will feel a secret charm in every passion that tends to the good of others, and a secret aversion against every unfeeling heart that is indifferent to the happiness and distress of others. In a word, it is but too common for men to indulge selfishness in themselves; but all men abhor it in others.

raises my resentment to a higher degree. The desire accordingly included in this passion, is not satisfied with so slight a <188> punishment as indignation or hatred: it is not fully gratified without retaliation; and the author must by my hand suffer mischief, as great at least as he has done to me. Neither can we be at any loss about the final cause of that higher degree of resentment: the whole vigour of the passion is required to secure individuals from the injustice and oppression of others.*

A wicked or disgraceful action is disagreeable not only to others, but even to the delinquent himself; and raises in both a painful emotion including a desire of punishment. The painful emotion felt by the delinquent, is distinguished by the name of *remorse;* which naturally excites him to punish himself. There cannot be imagined a better contrivance to deter us from vice; for remorse itself is a severe punishment. That passion, and the desire of self-punishment derived from it, are touched delicately by Terence:

> *Menedemus.* Ubi comperi ex iis, qui ei fuere conscii,
> Domum revortor moestus, atque animo fere
> Perturbato, atque incerto prae aegritudine:
> Adsido, adcurrunt servi, soccos detrahunt:
> Video alios festinare, lectos sternere,
> Coenam adparare: pro se quisque sedulo
> Faciebat, quo illam mihi lenirent miseriam.
> Ubi video haec, coepi cogitare: Hem! tot mea
> Solius solliciti sint causa, ut me unum expleant? <189>
> Ancillae tot me vestiant? sumptus domi
> Tantos ego solus faciam? sed gnatum unicum,
> Quem pariter uti his decuit, aut etiam amplius,
> Quod illa aetas magis ad haec utenda idonea 'st,
> Eum ego hinc ejici miserum injustitia mea.
> Malo quidem me dignum quovis deputem,
> Si id faciam: nam usque dum ille vitam illam colet
> Inopem, carens patria ob meas injurias,
> Interea usque illi de me supplicium dabo:
> Laborans, quaerens, parcens, illi serviens.
> Ita facio prorsus: nihil relinquo in aedibus,

---

* See *Historical Law-Tracts,* Tract 1. [Henry Home, Lord Kames.]

Nec vas, nec vestimentum: conrasi omnia,
Ancillas, servos, nisi eos, qui opere rustico
Faciundo facile sumptum exercerent suum:
Omnes produxi ac vendidi: inscripsi illico
Aedes mercede: quasi talenta ad quindecim
Coëgi: agrum hunc mercatus sum: hic me exerceo.
Decrevi tantisper me minus injuriae,
Chreme, meo gnato facere, dum fiam miser:
Nec fas esse ulla me voluptate hic frui,
Nisi ubi ille huc salvos redierit meus particeps.

Heautontimorumenos, act I. *sc.* I.[60]

Otway reaches the same sentiment:

Monimia. Let mischiefs multiply! let ev'ry hour
Of my loath'd life yield me increase of horror!

---

60. Publius Terentius Afer (ca. 190–159 B.C.): born in Carthage, he later went to Rome, where he became a freed slave and a comic poet. The Latin text used by Kames differs in many minor details from modern editions.

When I found out from those who were in his confidence, I returned home, sad, pretty upset, and uncertain what to do in my distress. I sat down, and slaves ran up and took off my shoes. I saw others bustling about, setting the table, preparing the dinner, every one of them doing his very best to soothe my grief. When I saw them, I began to think: "What! So many people taking all this trouble just for my sake, to satisfy one man's needs? Should I have so many maids to dress me? Should I be so extravagant when I'm living at home alone? And my only son, who should be enjoying these things as much—or indeed more, since he's at a more suitable age to enjoy them—I've driven him out of here, poor boy, by my unjust treatment. I should regard myself as deserving any misfortune you care to name, if I carried on like this. So long as he lives a life of poverty and exile through my injustice, I shall punish myself on his behalf, toiling, scraping, earning my living, slaving away for him." I'm doing exactly that. I've left nothing in the house, no silver plate, no fine clothing; I collected it all up. All my maids and slaves, except those who could readily earn their keep by working on the farm, I put on the market and sold. I advertised my house for sale on the spot, and raised about fifteen talents. I bought this piece of land, and here I keep myself busy. I've decided, Chremes, that I'll be doing my son less injustice so long as I make myself miserable; it is not right for me to enjoy any pleasure here, until he comes safe home to share it with me.

(*The Self-Tormentor,* act 1, l. 121ff)

Oh let the sun to these unhappy eyes
Ne'er shine again, but be eclips'd for ever!
May every thing I look on seem a prodigy,
To fill my soul with terror, till I quite
Forget I ever had humanity,
And grow a curser of the works of nature!

Orphan, act 4. <190>

In the cases mentioned, benevolence alone, or desire of punishment alone, governs without a rival; and it was necessary to handle these cases separately, in order to elucidate a subject which by writers is left in great obscurity. But neither of these principles operates always without rivalship: cases may be figured, and cases actually exist, where the same person is an object both of sympathy, and of punishment. Thus the sight of a profligate in the venereal disease, over-run with botches and sores, puts both principles in motion: while his distress fixes my attention, sympathy prevails; but as soon as I think of his profligacy, hatred prevails, accompanied sometimes with a desire to punish. This in general is the case of distress occasioned by immoral actions that are not highly criminal: and if the distress and the immoral action make impressions equal or nearly so, sympathy and hatred counterbalancing each other, will not suffer me either to afford relief or to inflict punishment. What then will be the result? The principle of self-love solves the question: abhorring an object so loathsome, I naturally avert my eye, and walk off as fast as I can, in order to be relieved from the pain.

The present subject gives birth to several other observations, for which I could not find room above, without relaxing more from the strictness of order and connection, than with safety could be indulged in discoursing upon an intricate subject. <191> These observations I shall throw out loosely as they occur.

No action, right nor wrong, is indifferent even to a mere spectator: if right, it inspires esteem; disgust, if wrong. But it is remarkable, that these emotions seldom are accompanied with desire: the abilities of man are limited, and he finds sufficient employment, in relieving the distressed, in requiting his benefactors, and in punishing those who wrong him, without moving out of his sphere for the benefit or chastisement of those with whom he has no connection.

If the good qualities of others raise my esteem, the same qualities in myself must produce a similar effect in a superior degree, upon account of the natural partiality every man hath for himself: and this increases self-love. If these qualities be of a high rank, they produce a conviction of superiority, which excites me to assume some sort of government over others. Mean qualities, on the other hand, produce in me a conviction of inferiority, which makes me submit to others. These convictions, distributed among individuals by measure and proportion, may justly be esteemed the solid basis of government; because upon them depend the natural submission of the many to the few, without which even the mildest government would be in a violent state, and have a constant tendency to dissolution.

No other branch of the human constitution <192> shows more visibly our destination for society, nor tends more to our improvement, than appetite for fame or esteem: for as the whole conveniencies of life, are derived from mutual aid and support in society; it ought to be a capital aim, to secure these conveniencies by gaining the esteem and affection of others. Reason indeed dictates that lesson: but reason alone is not sufficient in a matter of such importance; and the appetite mentioned is a motive more powerful than reason, to be active in gaining esteem and affection. That appetite, at the same time, is finely adjusted to the moral branch of our constitution, by promoting all the moral virtues: for what means are there to attract love and esteem, so effectual as a virtuous course of life? if a man be just and beneficent, if he be temperate, modest, and prudent, he will infallibly gain the esteem and love of all who know him.

Communication of passion to related objects, is an illustrious instance of the care of Providence, to extend social connections as far as the limited nature of man can admit. That communication is so far hurtful, as to spread the malevolent passions beyond their natural bounds: but let it be remarked, that this unhappy effect regards savages only, who give way to malevolent passions; for under the discipline of society, these passions being subdued, are in a good measure eradicated; and in their place succeed the kindly affections, which, <193> meeting with all encouragement, take possession of the mind, and govern all our actions. In that condition, the progress of passion along related objects, by spreading the kindly affections through a multitude of individuals, hath a glorious effect.

Nothing can be more entertaining to a rational mind, than the economy of the human passions, of which I have attempted to give some faint notion. It must however be acknowledged, that our passions, when they happen to swell beyond proper limits, take on a less regular appearance: reason may proclaim our duty, but the will, influenced by passion, makes gratification always welcome. Hence the power of passion, which, when in excess, cannot be resisted but by the utmost fortitude of mind: it is bent upon gratification; and where proper objects are wanting, it clings to any object at hand without distinction. Thus joy inspired by a fortunate event, is diffused upon every person around by acts of benevolence; and resentment for an atrocious injury done by one out of reach, seizes the first object that occurs to vent itself upon. Those who believe in prophecies, even wish the accomplishment; and a weak mind is disposed voluntarily to fulfil a prophecy, in order to gratify its wish. Shakespear, whom no particle of human nature hath escaped, however remote from common observation, describes that weakness: <194>

> *K. Henry.* Doth any name particular belong
> Unto that lodging where I first did swoon?
> *Warwick.* 'Tis call'd *Jerusalem,* my Noble Lord.
> *K. Henry.* Laud be to God! ev'n there my life must end,
> It hath been prophesy'd to me many years,
> I should not die but in Jerusalem,
> Which vainly I suppos'd the holy land.
> But bear me to that chamber, there I'll lie:
> In that Jerusalem shall Henry die.
> *Second part, Henry* IV. *act* 4. *sc. last.*[61]

I could not deny myself the amusement of the foregoing observation, tho' it doth not properly come under my plan. The irregularities of passion

---

61. Act 4, sc. 5.

proceeding from peculiar weaknesses and biasses, I do not undertake to justify; and of these we have had many examples.* It is sufficient that passions common to all, are made subservient to beneficial purposes. I shall only observe, that in a polished society, instances of irregular passions are rare, and that their mischief doth not extend far. <195>

* Part 5. of the present chapter.

❧ CHAPTER III ❧

Beauty

Having discoursed in general of emotions and passions, I proceed to a more narrow inspection of such of them as serve to unfold the principles of the fine arts. It is the province of a writer upon ethics, to give a full enumeration of all the passions; and of each separately to assign the nature, the cause, the gratification, and the effects. But a treatise of ethics is not my province: I carry my view no farther than to the elements of criticism, in order to show, that the fine arts are a subject of reasoning as well as of taste. An extensive work would ill suit a design so limited; and to confine this work within moderate bounds, the following plan may contribute. The observation made above, that things are the causes of emotions, by means of their properties and attributes,* furnisheth a hint for distribution. Instead of a painful and tedious examination of the several passions and emotions, I purpose to confine my inquiries to such attributes, relations, and circumstances, as in the fine arts are chiefly employ'd to raise agreeable emotions. <196> Attributes of single objects, as the most simple, shall take the lead; to be followed with particulars, which, depending on relations, are not found in single objects. Dispatching next some coincident matters, I proceed to my chief aim; which is, to establish practical rules for the fine arts, derived from principles previously established. This is a general view of the intended method; reserving however a privilege to vary it in particular instances, where a deviation may be more commodious. I begin with beauty, the most noted of all the qualities that belong to single objects.

The term *beauty,* in its native signification, is appropriated to objects of

---

* Chap. 2. part 1. sect. 1. first note.

sight: objects of the other senses may be agreeable, such as the sounds of musical instruments, the smoothness and softness of some surfaces; but the agreeableness denominated *beauty* belongs to objects of sight.

Of all the objects of external sense, an object of sight is the most complex: in the very simplest, colour is perceived, figure, and length, breadth, and thickness. A tree is composed of a trunk, branches, and leaves; it has colour, figure, size, and sometimes motion: by means of each of these particulars, separately considered, it appears beautiful; how much more so, when they are all united together? The beauty of the human figure is extraordinary, being a composition of numberless beauties arising from the parts and qualities of <197> the object, various colours, various motions, figures, size, &c.; all united in one complex object, and striking the eye with combined force. Hence it is, that beauty, a quality so remarkable in visible objects, lends its name to express every thing that is eminently agreeable: thus, by a figure of speech, we say a beautiful sound, a beautiful thought or expression, a beautiful theorem, a beautiful event, a beautiful discovery in art or science. But as figurative expression is the subject of a following chapter, this chapter is confined to beauty in its proper signification.

It is natural to suppose, that a perception so various as that of beauty, comprehending sometimes many particulars, sometimes few, should occasion emotions equally various: and yet all the various emotions of beauty maintain one common character, that of sweetness and gaiety.

Considering attentively the beauty of visible objects, we discover two kinds.[1] The first may be termed *intrinsic* beauty, because it is discovered in a single object viewed apart without relation to any other: the examples above given are of that kind. The other may be termed *relative* beauty, being founded on the relation of objects. The purposed distribution would lead me to handle these beauties separately; but they are frequently so intimately connected, that, for the sake of connection, I am forc'd in this instance to vary from the plan, and to bring them both into the same <198> chapter. Intrinsic beauty is an object of sense merely: to perceive the beauty of a spreading oak or of a flowing river, no more is required but singly an act

---

1. Kames's references to intrinsic and relative beauty, and the beauty of utility, allude to contemporary debate: see the editor's Introduction.

of vision. The perception of relative beauty is accompanied with an act of understanding and reflection; for of a fine instrument or engine, we perceive not the relative beauty, until we be made acquainted with its use and destination. In a word, intrinsic beauty is ultimate: relative beauty is that of means relating to some good end or purpose. These different beauties agree in one capital circumstance, that both are equally perceived as belonging to the object. This is evident with respect to intrinsic beauty; but will not be so readily admitted with respect to the other: the utility of the plough, for example, may make it an object of admiration or of desire; but why should utility make it appear beautiful? A natural propensity mentioned above,* will explain that doubt: the beauty of the effect, by an easy transition of ideas, is transferred to the cause; and is perceived as one of the qualities of the cause. Thus a subject void of intrinsic beauty, appears beautiful from its utility; an old Gothic tower, that has no beauty in itself, appears beautiful, considered as proper to defend against an enemy; a dwelling-house void of all regularity, is however beautiful in the view of convenience; and the <199> want of form or symmetry in a tree, will not prevent its appearing beautiful, if it be known to produce good fruit.

When these two beauties coincide in any object, it appears delightful: every member of the human body possesses both in a high degree: the fine proportions and slender make of a horse destined for running, please every eye; partly from symmetry, and partly from utility.

The beauty of utility, being proportioned accurately to the degree of utility, requires no illustration; but intrinsic beauty, so complex as I have said, cannot be handled distinctly without being analysed into its constituent parts. If a tree be beautiful by means of its colour, its figure, its size, its motion, it is in reality possessed of so many different beauties, which ought to be examined separately, in order to have a clear notion of them when combined. The beauty of colour is too familiar to need explanation. Do not the bright and chearful colours of gold and silver contribute to preserve these metals in high estimation? The beauty of figure, arising from various circumstances and different views, is more complex: for example, viewing any body as a whole, the beauty of its figure arises from regularity

---

* Chap. 2. part 1. sect. 5.

and simplicity; viewing the parts with relation to each other, uniformity, proportion, and order, contribute to its beauty. The beauty of motion deserves a chapter by itself; and another chapter is destined <200> for grandeur being distinguishable from beauty in its proper sense. For a description of regularity, uniformity, proportion, and order, if thought necessary, I remit my reader to the Appendix at the end of the book. Upon simplicity I must make a few cursory observations, such as may be of use in examining the beauty of single objects.

A multitude of objects crowding into the mind at once, disturb the attention, and pass without making any impression, or any distinct impression: in a group, no single object makes the figure it would do apart, when it occupies the whole attention.* For the same reason, the impression made by an object that divides the attention by the multiplicity of its parts, equals not that of a more simple object comprehended in a single view: parts extremely complex must be considered in portions successively; and a number of impressions in succession, which cannot unite because not simultaneous, never touch the mind like one entire impression made as it were at one stroke. This justifies simplicity in works of art, as opposed to complicated circumstances and crowded ornaments. There is an additional reason for simplicity, in works of dignity or elevation; which is, that the mind attached to beauties of a high rank, cannot descend to inferior beauties. The best artists accordingly have in all ages been go-<201>verned by a taste for simplicity. How comes it then that we find profuse decoration prevailing in works of art? The reason plainly is, that authors and architects who cannot reach the higher beauties, endeavour to supply want of genius by multiplying those that are inferior.

These things premised, I proceed to examine the beauty of figure as arising from the above-mentioned particulars, namely, regularity, uniformity, proportion, order, and simplicity. To exhaust this subject, would require a volume; and I have not even a whole chapter to spare. To inquire why an object, by means of the particulars mentioned, appears beautiful, would, I am afraid, be a vain attempt: it seems the most probable opinion, that the nature of man was originally framed with a relish for them, in order to

* See the Appendix, containing definitions, and explanation of terms, § 33.

answer wise and good purposes. To explain these purposes or final causes, tho' a subject of great importance, has scarce been attempted by any writer. One thing is evident, that our relish for the particulars mentioned, adds much beauty to the objects that surround us; which of course tends to our happiness: and the Author of our nature has given many signal proofs, that this final cause is not below his care. We may be confirmed in this thought upon reflecting, that our taste for these particulars is not accidental, but uniform and universal, making a branch of our nature. At the same time it ought not to be overlooked, <202> that regularity, uniformity, order, and simplicity, contribute each of them to readiness of apprehension; enabling us to form more distinct images of objects, than can be done with the utmost attention where these particulars are not found. With respect to proportion, it is in some instances connected with a useful end, as in animals, where the best proportioned are the strongest and most active: but instances are still more numerous, where the proportions we relish have no connection with utility. Writers on architecture[2] insist much on the proportions of a column, and assign different proportions to the Doric, Ionic, and Corinthian: but no architect will maintain, that the most accurate proportions contribute more to use, than several that are less accurate and less agreeable; neither will it be maintained, that the length, breadth and height of rooms assigned as the most beautiful proportions, tend also to make them the more commodious. With respect then to the final cause of proportion, I see not more to be made of it but to rest upon the final cause first mentioned, namely, its contributing to our happiness, by increasing the beauty of visible objects.

And now with respect to the beauty of figure as far as it depends on the other circumstances mentioned; as to which, having room only for a slight specimen, I confine myself to the simplest figures. A circle and a square are each of them perfectly regular, being equally confined to a pre-<203>cise form, which admits not the slightest variation: a square however is less beautiful than a circle. And the reason seems to be, that the attention is divided

2. The reference is to the Edinburgh discussion of Claude Perrault's views. See the notes for <179> and <400> in volume 1, <465> in volume 2, and the editor's Introduction.

among the sides and angles of a square; whereas the circumference of a circle, being a single object, makes one entire impression. And thus simplicity contributes to beauty: which may be illustrated by another example: a square, tho' not more regular than a hexagon or octagon, is more beautiful than either; for what other reason, but that a square is more simple, and the attention less divided? This reasoning will appear still more conclusive, when we consider any regular polygon of very many sides; for of this figure the mind can never have any distinct perception.

A square is more regular than a parallelogram, and its parts more uniform; and for these reasons, it is more beautiful. But that holds with respect to intrinsic beauty only; for in many instances, utility turns the scale on the side of the parallelogram: this figure for the doors and windows of a dwelling-house, is preferred because of utility; and here we find the beauty of utility, prevailing over that of regularity and uniformity.

A parallelogram again depends, for its beauty, on the proportion of its sides: a great inequality of sides annihilates its beauty: approximation toward equality hath the same effect; for proportion there degenerates into imperfect uniformity, and the figure appears an unsuccessful attempt to-<204>ward a square. And thus proportion contributes to beauty.

An equilateral triangle yields not to a square in regularity, nor in uniformity of parts, and it is more simple. But an equilateral triangle is less beautiful than a square; which must be owing to inferiority of order in the position of its parts: the sides of an equilateral triangle incline to each other in the same angle, being the most perfect order they are susceptible of; but this order is obscure, and far from being so perfect as the parallelism of the sides of a square. Thus order contributes to the beauty of visible objects, no less than simplicity, regularity, or proportion.

A parallelogram exceeds an equilateral triangle in the orderly disposition of its parts; but being inferior in uniformity and simplicity, it is less beautiful.

Uniformity is singular in one capital circumstance, that it is apt to disgust by excess: a number of things destined for the same use, such as windows, chairs, spoons, buttons, cannot be too uniform; for supposing their figure to be good, utility requires uniformity: but a scrupulous uniformity of parts in a large garden or field, is far from being agreeable. Uniformity among connected objects, belongs not to the present subject: it is handled in the chapter of uniformity and variety.

In all the works of nature, simplicity makes an <205> illustrious figure. It also makes a figure in works of art: profuse ornament in painting, gardening, or architecture, as well as in dress or in language, shows a mean or corrupted taste:

> Poets, like painters, thus unskill'd to trace
> The naked nature and the living grace,
> With gold and jewels cover ev'ry part,
> And hide with ornaments their want of art.
>
> *Pope's Essay on Criticism.*[3]

No single property recommends a machine more than its simplicity; not solely for better answering its purpose, but by appearing in itself more beautiful. Simplicity in behaviour and manners has an enchanting effect, and never fails to gain our affection: very different are the artificial manners of modern times. General theorems, abstracting from their importance, are delightful by their simplicity, and by the easiness of their application to variety of cases. We take equal delight in the laws of motion, which, with the greatest simplicity, are boundless in their operations.

A gradual progress from simplicity to complex forms and profuse ornament, seems to be the fate of all the fine arts: in that progress these arts resemble behaviour, which, from original candor and simplicity, has degenerated into artificial refinements. At present, literary productions are crowded with words, epithets, figures: in music, <206> sentiment is neglected for the luxury of harmony, and for difficult movement: in *taste* properly so called, poignant sauces with complicated mixtures of different savours, prevail among people of condition: the French, accustomed to artificial red on a female cheek, think the modest colouring of nature altogether insipid.

The same tendency is discovered in the progress of the fine arts among the ancients. Some vestiges of the old Grecian buildings prove them to be of the Doric order: the Ionic succeeded, and seems to have been the fa-

3. Lines 293–96.

vourite order, while architecture was in its height of glory: the Corinthian came next in vogue; and in Greece, the buildings of that order, appear mostly to have been erected after the Romans got footing there. At last came the Composite with all its extravagancies, where simplicity is sacrificed to finery and crowded ornament.

But what taste is to prevail next? for fashion is in a continual flux, and taste must vary with it. After rich and profuse ornaments become familiar, simplicity appears lifeless and insipid; which would be an unsurmountable obstruction, should any person of genius and taste endeavour to restore ancient simplicity.*[4] <207>

The distinction between primary and secondary qualities in matter, seems now fully established. Heat and cold, smell and taste, though seeming to exist in bodies, are discovered to be effects caused by these bodies in a sensitive being: colour, which appears to the eye as spread upon a substance, has no existence but in the mind of the spectator. Qualities of that kind, which owe their existence to the percipient as much as to the object, are termed *secondary* qualities; and are distinguished from figure, extension, solidity, which in contradistinction to the former are termed *primary* qualities, because they inhere in subjects whether perceived or not. This distinction suggests a curious inquiry, Whether beauty be a primary or only a secondary quality of objects? The question is easily determined with respect to the beauty of colour; for if colour be a secondary quality, existing no where but in the mind of the spectator, its beauty must exist there also. This conclusion equally holds with respect to the beauty of utility, which is plainly a conception of the mind, arising not from sight, but from reflecting that the thing is fitted for some good end or purpose. The question is more intricate with respect to the beauty of regularity; for if regularity be a primary quality, why not also its beauty? That <208> this is not a good inference, will appear from considering, that beauty, in its very conception, refers to a percipient; for an object is said to be beautiful, for no other reason but that it appears so to a spectator: the same piece of matter that to a man

* A sprightly writer observes, "that the noble simplicity of the Augustan age was driven out by false taste; that the gigantic, the puerile, the quaint, and at last the barbarous and the monkish, had each their successive admirers; that music has become a science of tricks and slight of hand," &c.

4. Kames here omits three pages from the first edition.

appears beautiful, may possibly appear ugly to a being of a different species. Beauty therefore, which for its existence depends on the percipient as much as on the object perceived, cannot be an inherent property in either. And hence it is wittily observed by the poet, that beauty is not in the person beloved, but in the lover's eye. This reasoning is solid; and the only cause of doubt or hesitation is, that we are taught a different lesson by sense: a singular determination of nature makes us perceive both beauty and colour as belonging to the object, and, like figure or extension, as inherent properties. This mechanism is uncommon; and when nature to fulfil her intention prefers any singular method of operation, we may be certain of some final cause that cannot be reached by ordinary means. For the beauty of some objects we are indebted entirely to nature; but with respect to the endless variety of objects that owe their beauty to art and culture, the perception of beauty greatly promotes industry; being to us a strong additional incitement to enrich our fields and improve our manufactures. These however are but slight effects, compared with the connections that are formed among indi-<209>viduals in society by means of this singular mechanism: the qualifications of the head and heart, form undoubtedly the most solid and most permanent connections; but external beauty, which lies more in view, has a more extensive influence in forming these connections: at any rate, it concurs in an eminent degree with mental qualifications, to produce social intercourse, mutual goodwill, and consequently mutual aid and support, which are the life of society.

It must not however be overlooked, that the perception of beauty doth not, when immoderate, tend to advance the interests of society. Love in particular arising from a perception of beauty, loses, when excessive, its sociable character: the appetite for gratification prevailing over affection for the beloved object, is ungovernable; and tends violently to its end, regardless of the misery that must follow. Love in that state is no longer a sweet agreeable passion: it becomes painful, like hunger or thirst; and produceth no happiness but in the instant of fruition. This discovery suggests a most important lesson, That moderation in our desires and appetites, which fits us for doing our duty, contributes at the same time the most to happiness: even social passions, when moderate, are more pleasant than when they swell beyond proper bounds. <210>

Grandeur and Sublimity

Nature hath not more remarkably distinguished us from other animals by an erect posture, than by a capacious and aspiring mind, attaching us to things great and elevated. The ocean, the sky, seize the attention, and make a deep impression:* robes of state are made large and full to draw respect: we admire an elephant for its magnitude, notwithstanding its unwieldiness.[1]

The elevation of an object affects us no less than its magnitude: a high place is chosen for the statue of a deity or hero: a tree growing on the brink of a precipice, looks charming when viewed from the plain below: a throne is erected for the chief magistrate; and a chair with a high seat for the president of a court. Among all nations, heaven is placed far above us, hell far below us. <211>

In some objects, greatness and elevation concur to make a complicated impression: the Alps and the Peak of Teneriff are proper examples; with

---

* Longinus observes, that nature inclines us to admire, not a small rivulet, however clear and transparent, but the Nile, the Ister, the Rhine, or still more the ocean. The sight of a small fire produceth no emotion; but we are struck with the boiling furnaces of Aetna, pouring out whole rivers of liquid flame. *Treatise of the Sublime, chap.* 29. [Longinus: in the eighteenth century he was mistakenly thought to be a third-century A.D. statesman and critic. Scholars now agree that his treatise was written in Greek, in the first century A.D., by a writer with both Roman and Jewish contacts. The reference is chapter 35. In spite of English translations available from 1712, Kames was typical of many eighteenth-century readers who used the French translation and commentary by Boileau (1674)—see the note for <224>.]

1. The next eight paragraphs are revisions of the text in the first edition.

the following difference, that in the former greatness seems to prevail, elevation in the latter.

The emotions raised by great and by elevated objects, are clearly distinguishable, not only in the internal feeling, but even in their external expressions. A great object makes the spectator endeavour to enlarge his bulk; which is remarkable in plain people who give way to nature without reserve; in describing a great object, they naturally expand themselves by drawing in air with all their force. An elevated object produces a different expression: it makes the spectator stretch upward, and stand a-tiptoe.

Great and elevated objects considered with relation to the emotions produced by them, are termed *grand* and *sublime*. *Grandeur* and *sublimity* have a double signification: they commonly signify the quality or circumstance in objects by which the emotions of grandeur and sublimity are produced; sometimes the emotions themselves.

In handling the present subject, it is necessary that the impression made on the mind by the magnitude of an object, abstracting from its other qualities, should be ascertained. And because abstraction is a mental operation of some difficulty, the safest method for judging is, to chuse a plain <212> object that is neither beautiful nor deformed, if such a one can be found. The plainest that occurs, is a huge mass of rubbish, the ruins perhaps of some extensive building, or a large heap of stones, such as are collected together for keeping in memory a battle or other remarkable event. Such an object, which in miniature would be perfectly indifferent, makes an impression by its magnitude, and appears agreeable. And supposing it so large, as to fill the eye, and to prevent the attention from wandering upon other objects, the impression it makes will be so much the deeper.*

But tho' a plain object of that kind be agreeable, it is not termed *grand:* it is not intitled to that character, unless, together with its size, it be possessed of other qualities that contribute to beauty, such as regularity, proportion, order, or colour: and according to the number of such qualities combined with magnitude, it is more or less grand. Thus St. Peter's church at Rome, the great pyramid of Egypt, the Alps towering above the clouds, a great arm of the sea, and above all a clear and serene sky, are grand, be-

---

* See Appendix, Terms defined, § 33.

cause, beside their size, they are beautiful in an eminent degree. On the other hand, an overgrown whale, having a disagreeable appearance, is not grand. A large building agreeable by its regularity and proportions, is grand, and yet a much larger building <213> destitute of regularity, has not the least tincture of grandeur. A single regiment in battle-array, makes a grand appearance; which the surrounding crowd does not, tho' perhaps ten for one in number. And a regiment where the men are all in one livery and the horses of one colour, makes a grander appearance, and consequently strikes more terror, than where there is confusion of colours and of dress. Thus greatness or magnitude is the circumstance that distinguishes grandeur from beauty: agreeableness is the genus, of which beauty and grandeur are species.

The emotion of grandeur, duly examined, will be found an additional proof of the foregoing doctrine. That this emotion is pleasant in a high degree, requires no other evidence but once to have seen a grand object; and if an emotion of grandeur be pleasant, its cause or object, as observed above, must infallibly be agreeable in proportion.

The qualities of grandeur and beauty are not more distinct, than the emotions are which these qualities produce in a spectator. It is observed in the chapter immediately foregoing, that all the various emotions of beauty have one common character, that of sweetness and gaiety. The emotion of grandeur has a different character: a large object that is agreeable, occupies the whole attention, and swells the heart into a vivid emotion, which, tho' extremely pleasant, is rather serious than gay. And this affords a good reason for distinguishing in <214> language these different emotions. The emotions raised by colour, by regularity, by proportion, and by order, have such a resemblance to each other, as readily to come under one general term, *viz. the emotion of beauty;* but the emotion of grandeur is so different from these mentioned, as to merit a peculiar name.

Tho' regularity, proportion, order, and colour, contribute to grandeur as well as to beauty, yet these qualities are not by far so essential to the former as to the latter. To make out that proposition, some preliminaries are requisite. In the first place, the mind, not being totally occupied with a small object, can give its attention at the same time to every minute part; but in a great or extensive object, the mind being totally occupied with the capital and striking parts, has no attention left for those that are little or indifferent. In the next place, two similar objects appear not similar when viewed at different distances: the similar parts of a very large object, cannot be seen but at different distances; and for that reason, its regularity, and the proportion of its parts, are in some measure lost to the eye; neither are the irregularities of a very large object so conspicuous as of one that is small. Hence it is, that a large object is not so agreeable by its regularity, as a small object; nor so disagreeable by its irregularities.

These considerations make it evident, that gran-<215>deur is satisfied with a less degree of regularity and of the other qualities mentioned, than is requisite for beauty; which may be illustrated by the following experiment. Approaching to a small conical hill, we take an accurate survey of every part, and are sensible of the slightest deviation from regularity and proportion. Supposing the hill to be considerably enlarged, so as to make us less sensible of its regularity, it will upon that account appear less beautiful. It will not however appear less agreeable, because some slight emotion of grandeur comes in place of what is lost in beauty. And at last, when the hill is enlarged to a great mountain, the small degree of beauty that is left, is sunk in its grandeur. Hence it is, that a towering hill is delightful, if it have but the slightest resemblance of a cone; and a chain of mountains no less so, tho' deficient in the accuracy of order and proportion. We require a small surface to be smooth; but in an extensive plain, considerable inequalities are overlooked. In a word, regularity, proportion, order, and colour, contribute to grandeur as well as to beauty; but with a remarkable difference, that in passing from small to great, they are not required in the same degree of perfection. This remark serves to explain the extreme delight we have in viewing the face of nature, when sufficiently enriched and diversified with objects. The bulk of the objects in a natural landscape are beautiful, and some of them grand: a <216> flowing river, a spreading oak, a round hill, an extended plain, are delightful; and even a rugged rock or barren heath, tho' in themselves disagreeable, contribute by contrast to the beauty of the whole: joining to these, the verdure of the fields, the mixture of light and shade, and the sublime canopy spread over all; it will not appear wonderful, that so extensive a group of splendid objects, should swell the heart to its utmost bounds, and raise the strongest emotion of grandeur.

The spectator is conscious of an enthusiasm, which cannot bear confinement, nor the strictness of regularity and order: he loves to range at large; and is so enchanted with magnificent objects, as to overlook slight beauties or deformities.

The same observation is applicable in some measure to works of art: in a small building, the slightest irregularity is disagreeable; but in a magnificent palace, or a large Gothic church, irregularities are less regarded: in an epic poem we pardon many negligences that would not be permitted in a sonnet or epigram. Notwithstanding such exceptions, it may be justly laid down for a rule, That in works of art, order and regularity ought to be governing principles: and hence the observation of Longinus,* "In works of art we have regard to exact proportion; in those of nature, to grandeur and magnificence." <217>

The same reflections are in a good measure applicable to sublimity; particularly, that, like grandeur, it is a species of agreeableness; that a beautiful object placed high, appearing more agreeable than formerly, produces in the spectator a new emotion, termed *the emotion of sublimity;* and that the perfection of order, regularity, and proportion, is less required in objects placed high, or at a distance, than at hand.

The pleasant emotion raised by large objects, has not escaped the poets:

> ———— He doth bestride the narrow world
> Like a Colossus; and we petty men
> Walk under his huge legs.   *Julius Caesar, act* I. *sc.* 3.[2]

> *Cleopatra.* I dreamt there was an Emp'ror Antony;
> Oh such another sleep, that I might see
> But such another man!
> His face was as the heavens: and therein stuck

* Chap. 30. [Chap. 36.]
2. Act I, sc. 2.

A sun and moon, which kept their course, and lighted
The little O o' th' earth.
His legs bestrid the ocean, his rear'd arm
Crested the world.　　　*Antony and Cleopatra, act* 5. *sc.* 3.[3]

———— Majesty
Dies not alone, but, like a gulf, doth draw
What's near it with it. It's a massy wheel
Fix'd on the summit of the highest mount; <218>
To whose huge spokes, ten thousand lesser things
Are mortis'd and adjoin'd; which when it falls,
Each small annexment, petty consequence,
Attends the boist'rous ruin.　　　*Hamlet, act* 3. *sc.* 8.[4]

The poets have also made good use of the emotion produced by the elevated situation of an object:

Quod si me lyricis vatibus inseres,
Sublimi feriam sidera vertice.　　　*Horat. Carm. l.* 1. *ode* 1.[5]

Oh thou! the earthly author of my blood,
Whose youthful spirit, in me regenerate,
Doth with a twofold vigour lift me up,
To reach at victory above my head.
　　　　　　　　　Richard II. *act* 1. *sc.* 4.[6]

Northumberland, thou ladder wherewithal
The mounting Bolingbroke ascends my throne.
　　　　　　　　　Richard II. *act* 5. *sc.* 2.[7]

3. Act 5, sc. 3.
4. Act 3, sc. 3.
5. "But if you rank me among lyric bards, I shall touch the stars with my exalted head."
6. Act 1, sc. 3.
7. Act 5, sc. 1.

> *Anthony.* Why was I rais'd the meteor of the world,
> Hung in the skies, and blazing as I travell'd,
> Till all my fires were spent; and then cast downward
> To be trod out by Caesar?   *Dryden, All for love, act* 1.

The description of Paradise in the fourth book <219> of *Paradise lost,* is a fine illustration of the impression made by elevated objects:

> So on he fares, and to the border comes
> Of Eden, where delicious Paradise,
> Now nearer, crowns with her inclosure green,
> As with a rural mound, the champain head
> Of a steep wilderness; whose hairy sides
> With thicket overgrown, grotesque and wild,
> Access deny'd; and over head up grew
> Insuperable height of loftiest shade,
> Cedar, and pine, and fir, and branching palm,
> A sylvan scene; and as the ranks ascend,
> Shade above shade, a woody theatre
> Of stateliest view. Yet higher than their tops
> The verd'rous wall of Paradise up sprung;
> Which to our general fire gave prospect large
> Into his nether empire neighb'ring round.
> And higher than that wall a circling row
> Of goodliest trees, loaden with fairest fruit,
> Blossoms and fruits at once of golden hue,
> Appear'd, with gay enamell'd colours mix'd.   *B.* 4. *l.* 131.

Tho' a grand object is agreeable, we must not infer that a little object is disagreeable; which would be unhappy for man, considering that he is surrounded with so many objects of that kind. The same holds with respect to place: a body placed high is agreeable; but the same body placed low, is not by that circumstance rendered dis-<220>agreeable. Littleness and lowness of place are precisely similar in the following particular, that they neither give pleasure nor pain. And in this may visibly be discovered peculiar attention in fitting the internal constitution of man to his external circumstances: were littleness and lowness of place agreeable, greatness and elevation could not be so: were littleness and lowness of place disagreeable, they would occasion perpetual uneasiness.

The difference between great and little with respect to agreeableness, is remarkably felt in a series when we pass gradually from the one extreme to the other. A mental progress from the capital to the kingdom, from that to Europe—to the whole earth—to the planetary system—to the universe, is extremely pleasant: the heart swells, and the mind is dilated, at every step. The returning in an opposite direction is not positively painful, tho' our pleasure lessens at every step, till it vanish into indifference: such a progress may sometimes produce pleasure of a different sort, which arises from taking a narrower and narrower inspection. The same observation holds in a progress upward and downward. Ascent is pleasant because it elevates us: but descent is never painful; it is for the most part pleasant from a different cause, that it is according to the order of nature. The fall of a stone from any height, is extremely agreeable by its accelerated motion. I feel it pleasant to descend from a mountain, because the de-<221>scent is natural and easy. Neither is looking downward painful; on the contrary, to look down upon objects, makes part of the pleasure of elevation: looking down becomes then only painful when the object is so far below as to create dizziness; and even when that is the case, we feel a sort of pleasure mixt with the pain, witness Shakespear's description of Dover cliffs:

> ———— ———— How fearful
> And dizzy 'tis, to cast one's eye so low!
> The crows and choughs, that wing the midway-air,
> Shew scarce so gross as beetles. Half-way down
> Hangs one that gathers samphire; dreadful trade!
> Methinks he seems no bigger than his head.
> The fishermen that walk upon the beach,
> Appear like mice; and yon tall anchoring bark
> Diminish'd to her cock; her cock, a buoy
> Almost too small for sight. The murmuring surge,
> That on th' unnumber'd idle pebbles chafes,
> Cannot be heard so high. I'll look no more,

Lest my brain turn, and the deficient sight
Topple down headlong.   *King Lear, act* 4. *sc.* 6.

A remark is made above, that the emotions of grandeur and sublimity are nearly allied. And hence it is, that the one term is frequently put for the other: an increasing series of numbers, for example, producing an emotion similar to that of mounting upward, is commonly termed *an ascend-* <222>*ing series:* a series of numbers gradually decreasing, producing an emotion similar to that of going downward, is commonly termed *a descending series:* we talk familiarly of going *up* to the capital, and of going *down* to the country: from a lesser kingdom we talk of going *up* to a greater; whence the *anabasis* in the Greek language, when one travels from Greece to Persia. We discover the same way of speaking in the language even of Japan;* and its universality proves it the offspring of a natural feeling.

The foregoing observation leads us to consider grandeur and sublimity in a figurative sense, and as applicable to the fine arts. Hitherto these terms have been taken in their proper sense, as applicable to objects of sight only: and it was of importance to bestow some pains upon that article; because, generally speaking, the figurative sense of a word is derived from its proper sense, which holds remarkably at present. Beauty in its original signification, is confined to objects of sight; but as many other objects, intellectual as well as moral, raise emotions resembling that of beauty, the resemblance of the effects prompts us to extend the term *beauty* to these objects. This equally accounts for the terms *grandeur* and *sublimity* taken in a figurative sense. Every emotion, from whatever cause proceeding, that resembles <223> an emotion of grandeur or elevation, is called by the same name: thus generosity is said to be an *elevated* emotion, as well as great courage; and that firmness of soul which is superior to misfortunes, obtains the peculiar name of *magnanimity.* On the other hand, every emotion that contracts the mind, and fixeth it upon things trivial or of no importance, is

* Kempfer's *history of Japan,* b. 5. ch. 2. [Engelbert Kaempfer (1651–1716): *The History of Japan,* London, 1727 (*Histoire naturelle, civile, et ecclesiastique de l'empire du Japon,* La Haye, 1729).]

termed *low*, by its resemblance to an emotion produced by a little or low object of sight: thus an appetite for trifling amusements, is called *a low taste*. The same terms are applied to characters and actions: we talk familiarly of an *elevated* genius, of a *great* man, and equally so of *littleness* of mind: some actions are *great* and *elevated*, and others are *little* and *groveling*. Sentiments, and even expressions, are characterised in the same manner: an expression or sentiment that raises the mind, is denominated *great* or *elevated*; and hence the SUBLIME* in poetry. <224> In such figurative terms, we lose the distinction between *great* and *elevated* in their proper sense; for the resemblance is not so entire, as to preserve these terms distinct in their figurative application. We carry this figure still farther. Elevation in its proper sense, imports superiority of place; and lowness, inferiority of place: and hence a man of *superior* talents, of *superior* rank, of *inferior* parts, of *inferior* taste, and such like. The veneration we have for our ancestors, and for the ancients in general, being similar to the emotion produced by an elevated object of sight, justifies the figurative expression, of the ancients being *raised* above us, or possessing a *superior* place. And we may remark in passing, that as words are intimately connected with ideas, many, by this form of expression, are led to conceive their ancestors as really above them in place, and their posterity below them:

---

* Longinus gives a description of the sublime that is not amiss, tho' far from being just in every circumstance, "That the mind is elevated by it, and so sensibly affected as to swell in transport and inward pride, as if what is only heard or read, were its own invention." But he adheres not to this description: in his 6th chapter he justly observes, that many passions have nothing of the grand, such as grief, fear, pity, which depress the mind instead of raising it; and yet in chapter 8. he mentions Sappho's ode upon love as sublime: beautiful it is undoubtedly, but it cannot be sublime, because it really depresses the mind instead of raising it. His translator Boileaux is not more successful in his instances: in his 10th reflection he cites a passage from Demosthenes and another from Herodotus as sublime, which have not the least tincture of that quality. [Longinus: chaps. 7, 8, 10. Boileau's first nine *Réflexions Critiques sur quelques Passages du Rheteur Longin* were published in 1694. *Réflexions X,* published posthumously in 1713, was in part a reply to Pierre Daniel Huet, whose private letter of 1683 had been published without permission as "Examen du sentiment de Longin, sur ce passage de la Genese, etc.," *Bibliothèque Choisie* x, 1706, and Jean Le Clerc, "Remarques sur la X Réflexion sur Longin," *ibid.* xxvi, 1713. Kames refers to both Boileau and Huet <242> below.]

A grandam's name is little less in love,
Than is the doting title of a mother:
They are as children but one step below.

Richard III. *act* 4. *sc.* 5.[8] <225>

The notes of the gamut,[9] proceeding regularly from the blunter or grosser
sounds to the more acute and piercing, produce in the hearer a feeling somewhat similar to what is produced by mounting upward; and this gives occasion to the figurative expressions, *a high note, a low note.*

Such is the resemblance in feeling between real and figurative grandeur,
that among the nations on the east coast of Afric, who are directed purely
by nature, the officers of state are, with respect to rank, distinguished by
the length of the batoon each carries in his hand: and in Japan, princes and
great lords shew their rank by the length and size of their sedan-poles.*
Again, it is a rule in painting, that figures of a small size are proper for
grotesque pieces; but that an historical subject, grand and important, requires figures as great as the life. The resemblance of these feelings is in
reality so strong, that elevation in a figurative sense is observed to have the
same effect, even externally, with real elevation:

K. Henry. This day is call'd the feast of Crispian.
He that outlives this day, and comes safe home,
Will stand a-tiptoe when this day is nam'd,
And rouse him at the name of Crispian.

Henry V. *act* 4. *sc.* 8.[10]

The resemblance in feeling between real and <226> figurative grandeur,
is humorously illustrated by Addison in criticising upon English tragedy:
"The ordinary method of making an hero, is to clap a huge plume of feathers upon his head, which rises so high, that there is often a greater length
from his chin to the top of his head, than to the sole of his foot. One would

---

* Kempfer's *history of Japan.*
8. Act 4, sc. 4.
9. The lowest note in the medieval scale, corresponding to the modern bottom G of
the base stave.
10. Act 4, sc. 3.

believe, that we thought a great man and a tall man the same thing. As these superfluous ornaments upon the head, make a great man; a princess generally receives her grandeur, from those additional incumbrances that fall into her tail: I mean the broad sweeping train, that follows her in all her motions; and finds constant employment for a boy, who stands behind her to open and spread it to advantage."* The Scythians, impressed with the fame of Alexander, were astonished when they found him a little man.

A gradual progress from small to great, is no less remarkable in figurative, than in real grandeur or elevation. Every one must have observed the delightful effect of a number of thoughts or sentiments, artfully disposed like an ascending series, and making impressions deeper and deeper: such disposition of members in a period, is termed a *climax*.

Within certain limits grandeur and sublimity <227> produce their strongest effects, which lessen by excess as well as by defect. This is remarkable in grandeur and sublimity taken in their proper sense: the grandest emotion that can be raised by a visible object is where the object can be taken in at one view; if so immense as not to be comprehended but in parts, it tends rather to distract than satisfy the mind:† in like manner, the strongest emotion produced by elevation, is where the object is seen distinctly; a greater elevation lessens in appearance the object, till it vanish out of sight with its pleasant emotion. The same is equally remarkable in figurative grandeur and elevation, which shall be handled together, because, as observed above, they are scarce distinguishable. Sentiments may be so strained, as to become obscure, or to exceed the capacity of the human mind: against such licence of imagination, every good writer will be upon his guard. And therefore it is of greater importance to observe, that even the true sublime may be carried beyond that pitch which produces the highest entertainment: <228> we are undoubtedly susceptible of a greater

---

* *Spectator,* No. 42.

† It is justly observed by Addison, that perhaps a man would have been more astonished with the majestic air that appeared in one of Lysippus's statues of Alexander, tho' no bigger than the life, than he might have been with Mount Athos, had it been cut into the figure of the hero, according to the proposal of Phidias, with a river in one hand and a city in the other. *Spectator,* No. 415.

elevation than can be inspired by human actions, the most heroic and mag-
nanimous; witness what we feel from Milton's description of superior
beings: yet every man must be sensible of a more constant and sweet elevation, when the history of his own species is the subject; he enjoys an
elevation equal to that of the greatest hero, of an Alexander, or a Caesar,
of a Brutus, or an Epaminondas; he accompanies these heroes in their sub-
limest sentiments and most hazardous exploits, with a magnanimity equal
to theirs; and finds it no stretch, to preserve the same tone of mind for
hours together, without sinking. The case is not the same in describing the
actions or qualities of superior beings: the reader's imagination cannot keep
pace with that of the poet; the mind, unable to support itself in a strained
elevation, falls as from a height; and the fall is immoderate like the elevation:
where that effect is not felt, it must be prevented by some obscurity in the
conception, which frequently attends the description of unknown objects.
Hence the St. Francises, St. Dominics, and other tutelary saints among the
Roman Catholics. A mind unable to raise itself to the Supreme Being self-
existent and eternal, or to support itself in a strained elevation, finds itself
more at ease in using the intercession of some saint whose piety and penances while on earth are supposed to have made him a favourite in heaven.
< 229 >

A strained elevation is attended with another inconvenience, that the
author is apt to fall suddenly as well as the reader; because it is not a little
difficult, to descend sweetly and easily from such elevation, to the ordinary
tone of the subject. The following passage is a good illustration of that
observation:

> Saepe etiam immensum coelo venit agmen aquarum,
> Et foedam glomerant tempestatem imbribus atris
> Conlectae ex alto nubes. Ruit arduus aether,
> Et pluvia ingenti sata laeta boumque labores
> Diluit. Inplentur fossae, et cava flumina crescunt
> Cum sonitu, fervetque fretis spirantibus aequor.
> Ipse Pater, media nimborum in nocte, coruscâ
> Fulmina molitur dextra. Quo maxima motu
> Terra tremit: fugêre ferae! et mortalia corda
> Per gentes humilis stravit pavor. Ille flagranti

Aut Atho, aut Rhodopen, aut alta Ceraunia telo
Dejicit: *ingeminant austri, et densissimus imber.*

Virg. Georg. l. 1.[11]

In the description of a storm, to figure Jupiter throwing down huge mountains with his thunderbolts, is hyperbolically sublime, if I may use the expression: the tone of mind produced by that image, is so distant from the tone produced by a thick shower of rain, that the sudden transition must be unpleasant.

Objects of sight that are not remarkably great nor high, scarce raise any emotion of grandeur or of sublimity: and the same holds in other objects; <230> for we often find the mind roused and animated, without being carried to that height. This difference may be discerned in many sorts of music, as well as in some musical instruments: a kettledrum rouses, and a hautboy[12] is animating; but neither of them inspires an emotion of sublimity: revenge animates the mind in a considerable degree; but I think it never produceth an emotion that can be termed *grand* or *sublime;* and I

---

11. And oft whole sheets descend of slucy Rain,
   Suck'd by the spongy Clouds from off the Main:
   The lofty Skies at once come pouring down,
   The promis'd Crop and golden Labours drown.
   The Dykes are fill'd, and with a roaring sound
   The rising Rivers float the nether Ground;
   And Rocks the bellowing Voice of boiling Seas rebound.
   The Father of the Gods his Glory shrouds,
   Involv'd in Tempests, and a Night of Clouds.
   And from the middle Darkness flashing out,
   By fits he deals his fiery Bolts about.
   Earth feels the Motions of her angry God,
   Her entrails tremble, and her Mountains nod;
   And flying Beasts in Forests seek Abode:
   Deep Horror seizes evr'y Humane Breast,
   Their Pride is humbled, and their Fear confess'd:
   While he from high his rowling Thunder throws,
   And fires the Mountains with repeated Blows:
   The Rocks are from their old Foundations rent;
   The Winds redouble, and the Rains augment.
                         (Dryden, 1.437ff)

12. Oboe.

shall have occasion afterward to observe, that no disagreeable passion ever has that effect. I am willing to put this to the test, by placing before my reader a most spirited picture of revenge: it is a speech of Antony wailing over the body of Caesar:

> Wo to the hand that shed this costly blood!
> Over thy wounds now do I prophesy,
> (Which, like dumb mouths, do ope their ruby lips,
> To beg the voice and utterance of my tongue),
> A curse shall light upon the kind of men;
> Domestic fury, and fierce civil strife,
> Shall cumber all the parts of Italy;
> Blood and destruction shall be so in use,
> And dreadful objects so familiar,
> That mothers shall but smile, when they behold
> Their infants quarter'd by the hands of war,
> All pity chok'd with custom of fell deeds,
> And Caesar's spirit, ranging for revenge,
> With *Atè* by his side come hot from hell,
> Shall in these confines, with a monarch's voice,
> Cry, *Havock!* and let slip the dogs of war.
>
> *Julius Caesar, act* 3. *sc.* 4.[13] <231>

No desire is more universal than to be exalted and honoured; and upon that account chiefly, are we ambitious of power, riches, titles, fame, which would suddenly lose their relish did they not raise us above others, and command submission and deference:* and it may be thought, that our at-

---

* Honestum per se esse expetendum indicant pueri, in quibus, ut in speculis, natura cernitur. Quanta studia decertantium sunt! Quanta ipsa certamina! Ut illi efferuntur laetitia, cum vicerunt! Ut pudet victos! Ut se accusari nolunt! Ut cupiunt laudari! Quos illi labores non perferunt, ut aequalium principes sint! *Cicero de finibus.* [V.22. "This Morality to which I allude is an object of our desire, {not only because of our love of self, but also} intrinsically and for its own sake. A hint of this is given by children, in whom nature is discerned as in a mirror. How hotly they pursue their rivalries! How fierce their contests and competitions! What exultation they feel when they win, and what shame when they are beaten! How they dislike blame! How they covet praise! What toils do they not undergo to stand first among their companions!" Kames omits the passage in braces.]

13. Act 3, sc. 1.

tachment to things grand and lofty, proceeds from their connection with our favourite passion. This connection has undoubtedly an effect; but that the preference given to things grand and lofty must have a deeper root in human nature, will appear from considering, that many bestow their time upon low and trifling amusements, without having the least tincture of this favourite passion: yet these very persons talk the same language with the rest of mankind; and prefer the more elevated pleasures: they acknowledge a more refined taste, and are ashamed of their own as low and groveling. This sentiment, constant and universal, must be the work of nature; and it plainly indicates an original attachment in human nature to every object that elevates the mind: some men may have a greater relish for an object <232> not of the highest rank; but they are conscious of the preference given by mankind in general to things grand and sublime; and they are sensible, that their peculiar taste ought to yield to the general taste.

What is said above suggests a capital rule for reaching the sublime in such works of art as are susceptible of it; and that is, to present those parts or circumstances only which make the greatest figure, keeping out of view every thing low or trivial; for the mind, elevated by an important object, cannot, without reluctance, be forc'd down to bestow any share of its attention upon trifles. Such judicious selection of capital circumstances, is by an eminent critic styled *grandeur of manner*.* In none of the fine arts is there so great scope for that rule as in poetry; which, by that means, enjoys a remarkable power of bestowing upon objects and events an air of grandeur: when we are spectators, every minute object presents itself in its order; but in describing at second hand, these are laid aside, and the capital objects are brought close together. A judicious taste in thus selecting the most interesting incidents, to give them an united force, accounts for a fact that may appear surprising; which is, that we are more moved by a spirited narrative at second hand, <233> than by being spectators of the event itself, in all its circumstances.

---

* *Spectator*, No. 415. [Addison was citing John Evelyn's 1664 translation of Roland Fréart, *Parallèle de l'Architecture antique et de la moderne* (1650).]

Longinus exemplifies the foregoing rule by a comparison of two passages.* The first, from Aristaeus, is thus translated:

Ye pow'rs, what madness! how on ships so frail
(Tremendous thought!) can thoughtless mortals sail?
For stormy seas they quit the pleasing plain,
Plant woods in waves, and dwell amidst the main.
Far o'er the deep (a trackless path) they go,
And wander oceans in pursuit of wo.
No ease their hearts, no rest their eyes can find,
On heaven their looks, and on the waves their mind,
Sunk are their spirits, while their arms they rear,
And gods are wearied with their fruitless prayer.

The other, from Homer, I shall give in Pope's translation:

Burst as a wave that from the cloud impends,
And swell'd with tempests on the ship descends.
White are the decks with foam: the winds aloud
Howl o'er the masts, and sing through every shroud.
Pale, trembling, tir'd, the sailors freeze with fears,
And instant death on every wave appears.[14]

In the latter passage, the most striking circumstances are selected to fill the mind with terror and astonishment. The former is a collection of mi-<234>nute and low circumstances, which scatter the thought and make no impression: it is at the same time full of verbal antitheses and low conceit, extremely improper in a scene of distress. But this last observation belongs to another head.

The following description of a battle is remarkably sublime, by collecting together in the fewest words, those circumstances which make the greatest figure.

Like Autumn's dark storms pouring from two echoing hills, toward each
other approached the heroes: as two dark streams from high rocks meet

---

* Chap. 8. of the Sublime. [Chap. 10. The lines are from a lost poem of the seventh century B.C. attributed to Aristeas of Proconnesus.]
14. Pope's translation of *The Iliad:* xv.752ff.

and roar on the plain, loud, rough, and dark in battle, meet Lochlin and Inisfail. Chief mixes his strokes with chief, and man with man: steel sounds on steel, and helmets are cleft on high: blood bursts and smokes around: strings murmur on the polish'd yew: darts rush along the sky: spears fall like sparks of flame that gild the stormy face of night.

As the noise of the troubled ocean when roll the waves on high, as the last peal of thundering heaven, such is the noise of battle. Tho' Cormac's hundred bards were there, feeble were the voice of a hundred bards to send the deaths to future times; for many were the deaths of the heroes, and wide poured the blood of the valiant. *Fingal*.[15]

The following passage in the 4th book of the Iliad is a description of a battle, wonderfully ardent. "When now gathered on either side, the <235> hosts plunged together in fight; shield is harshly laid to shield; spears crash on the brazen corslets; bossy buckler with buckler meets; loud tumult rages over all; groans are mixed with boasts of men; the slain and slayer join in noise; the earth is floating round with blood. As when two rushing streams from two mountains come roaring down, and throw together their rapid waters below, they roar along the gulphy vale. The startled shepherd hears the sound, as he stalks o'er the distant hills; so, as they mixed in fight, from both armies clamour with loud terror arose."[16] But such general descriptions are not frequent in Homer. Even his single combats are rare. The fifth book is the longest account of a battle that is in the Iliad; and yet contains nothing but a long catalogue of chiefs killing chiefs, not in single combat neither, but at a distance with an arrow or a javelin; and these chiefs named for the first time and the last. The same scene is continued through a great part of the sixth book. There is at the same time a minute description of every wound, which for accuracy may do honour to an anatomist, but in an epic poem is tiresome and fatiguing. There is no relief from horrid languor but the beautiful Greek language and melody of Homer's versification.

---

15. *Fingal: An Ancient Epic Poem, in six books,* 1762. Translated from the Gaelic by James Macpherson (1736–96). Although admired by fellow Scots and by German poets such as Goethe and Hölderlin, Dr. Johnson challenged its authenticity. Modern scholars judge Macpherson to have blended the translation of traditional Gaelic ballads with adaptation and invention.

16. Bk. 4, line 508ff. Kames used Pope's version at <98> above.

In the twenty-first book of the Odyssey, there is a passage which deviates widely from the rule above laid down: it concerns that part of the
hi-<236>story of Penelope and her suitors, in which she is made to declare
in favour of him who should prove the most dextrous in shooting with the
bow of Ulysses:

> Now gently winding up the fair ascent,
> By many an easy step, the matron went:
> Then o'er the pavement glides with grace divine,
> (With polish'd oak the level pavements shine);
> The folding gates a dazzling light display'd,
> With pomp of various architrave o'erlay'd.
> The bolt, obedient to the silken string,
> Forsakes the staple as she pulls the ring;
> The wards respondent to the key turn'd round;
> The bars fall back; the flying valves resound.
> Loud as a bull makes hill and valley ring;
> So roar'd the lock when it releas'd the spring.
> She moves majestic through the wealthy room
> Where treasur'd garments cast a rich perfume;
> There from the column where aloft it hung,
> Reach'd, in its splendid case, the bow unstrung.[17]

Virgil sometimes errs against this rule: in the following passages minute
circumstances are brought into full view; and what is still worse, they are
described with all the pomp of poetical diction, *Aeneid, L.* 1. *l.* 214. *to* 219.
L. 6. *l.* 176. *to* 182. *L.* 6. *l.* 212. *to* 231.: and the last, which describes a funeral,
is the less excusable, as the man whose funeral it is makes no figure in the
poem. <237>

The speech of Clytemnestra, descending from her chariot in the Iphigenia of Euripides,* is stuffed with a number of common and trivial circumstances.

---

* Beginning of act 3. [Euripides (480–406 B.C.): Greek tragedian, younger than Aes-
chylus and Sophocles. About twenty of his ninety works survive, including *Iphigenia in
Tauris* and *Alcestis.*]

17. Pope's translation of *Odyssey*, bk. XXI, line 41ff.

But of all writers, Lucan[18] as to this article is the most injudicious: the sea-fight between the Romans and Massilians,* is described so much in detail, without exhibiting any grand or total view, that the reader is fatigued with endless circumstances, without ever feeling any degree of elevation; and yet there are some fine incidents, those for example of the two brothers, and of the old man and his son, which, taken separately, would affect us greatly. But Lucan, once engaged in a description, knows no end. See other passages of the same kind, *L. 4. l. 292. to 337. L. 4. l. 750. to 765.* The episode of the sorceress Erictho, end of book 6. is intolerably minute and prolix.

To these I venture to oppose a passage from an old historical ballad:

Go, little page, tell Hardiknute
  That lives on hill so high,†
To draw his sword, the dread of faes,
  And haste to follow me. <238>
The little page flew swift as dart
  Flung by his master's arm.
"Come down, come down, Lord Hardiknute,
  And rid your king from harm."[19]

This rule is also applicable to other fine arts. In painting it is established, that the principal figure must be put in the strongest light; that the beauty of attitude consists in placing the nobler parts most in view, and in suppressing the smaller parts as much as possible; that the folds of the drapery must be few and large; that foreshortenings are bad, because they make the parts appear little; and that the muscles ought to be kept as entire as possible, without being divided into small sections. Every one at present subscribes to that rule as applied to gardening, in opposition to parterres split into a

---

* Lib. 3. beginning at line 567.

† *High,* in the old Scotch language, is pronounced *hee.*

18. Marcus Annaeus Lucan (A.D. 39–65): Roman poet, born in Spain, and nephew of Seneca (ca. 4 B.C.–A.D. 65). *Pharsalia* (*The Civil War*) describes the conflict between Caesar and Pompey.

19. Imitation ballad by Elizabeth, Lady Wardlaw (1677–1727), published anonymously in 1719; a tune for it was published in Oswald's *Curious Collection,* 1742.

thousand small parts in the stiffest regularity of figure.[20] The most eminent architects have governed themselves by the same rule in all their works.

Another rule chiefly regards the sublime, tho' it is applicable to every sort of literary performance intended for amusement; and that is, to avoid as much as possible abstract and general terms. Such terms, similar to mathematical signs, are contrived to express our thoughts in a concise manner; but images, which are the life of poetry, cannot be raised in any perfection but by introducing particular objects. General terms that comprehend <239> a number of individuals, must be excepted from that rule: our kindred, our clan, our country, and words of the like import, tho' they scarce raise any image, have however a wonderful power over our passions: the greatness of the complex object overbalances the obscurity of the image.

Grandeur, being an extreme vivid emotion, is not readily produced in perfection but by reiterated impressions. The effect of a single impression can be but momentary; and if one feel suddenly somewhat like a swelling or exaltation of mind, the emotion vanisheth as soon as felt. Single thoughts or sentiments, I know, are often cited as examples of the sublime; but their effect is far inferior to that of a grand subject display'd in its capital parts. I shall give a few examples, that the reader may judge for himself. In the famous action of Thermopylae, where Leonidas the Spartan king, with his chosen band, fighting for their country, were cut off to the last man, a saying is reported of Dieneces, one of the band, which, expressing chearful and undisturbed bravery, is well entitled to the first place in examples of that kind. Respecting the number of their enemies, it was observed, that the arrows shot by such a multitude would intercept the light of the sun. So much the better, says he, for we shall then fight in the shade.* <240>

> *Somerset.* Ah! Warwick, Warwick, wert thou as we are,
> We might recover all our loss again.
> The Queen from France hath brought a puissant power,

---

* Herodotus, book 7.

20. The reference is to a dispute over French and Dutch influence, countered by Charles Bridgeman (1680–1738): see the note for <302> below.

Ev'n now we heard the news. Ah! couldst thou fly!
Warwick. Why, then I would not fly.

Third part, Henry VI. *act* 5. *sc.* 3.[21]

Such a sentiment from a man expiring of his wounds, is truly heroic; and must elevate the mind to the greatest height that can be done by a single expression: it will not suffer in a comparison with the famous sentiment *Qu'il mourut* of Corneille:[22] the latter is a sentiment of indignation merely, the former of firm and chearful courage.

To cite in opposition many a sublime passage, enriched with the finest images, and dressed in the most nervous expressions, would scarce be fair: I shall produce but one instance, from Shakespear, which sets a few objects before the eye, without much pomp of language: it operates its effect by representing these objects in a climax, raising the mind higher and higher till it feel the emotion of grandeur in perfection:

> The cloud-capt tow'rs, the gorgeous palaces,
> The solemn temples, the great globe itself,
> Yea all which it inherit, shall dissolve, &c.

The cloud-capt tow'rs produce an elevating emotion, heightened by the *gorgeous palaces;* and <241> the mind is carried still higher and higher by the images that follow. Successive images, making thus deeper and deeper impressions, must elevate more than any single image can do.

As, on the one hand, no means directly apply'd have more influence to raise the mind than grandeur and sublimity; so, on the other, no means indirectly apply'd have more influence to sink and depress it: for in a state

21. Act 5, sc. 2.
22. "That he may die." An English commentator of 1759 explains: "A messenger arrives to inform old Horatius, that two of his sons were killed, and that the third was flying from the three Curiatii. The venerable old man is filled with indignation at the conduct of his remaining son. The messenger to excuse him asks what other option he had. 'A glorious death' replies the old Horatius." The quotation is from the last act of Corneille's tragedy *Horace* (1640), which Boileau discusses in *Réflexions X,* published posthumously in French and in an English translation, in 1713. D'Alembert also discussed it in his essay on taste in volume 7 of *l'Encyclopédie* (1757), translated into English in 1759, together with essays by Voltaire and Montesquieu, and published with Alexander Gerard's *Essay on Taste.*

of elevation, the artful introduction of an humbling object, makes the fall great in proportion to the elevation. Of this observation Shakespear gives a beautiful example, in the passage last quoted:

> The cloud-capt tow'rs, the gorgeous palaces,
> The solemn temples, the great globe itself,
> Yea all which it inherit, shall dissolve,
> And like the baseless fabric of a vision
> Leave not a rack behind.—   *Tempest, act* 4. *sc.* 4.[23]

The elevation of the mind in the former part of this beautiful passage, makes the fall great in proportion, when the most humbling of all images is introduced, that of an utter dissolution of the earth and its inhabitants. The mind, when warmed, is more susceptible of impressions than in a cool state; and a depressing or melancholy object listened to, makes the strongest impression when it reaches the mind in its highest state of elevation or chearfulness. <242>

But a humbling image is not always necessary to produce that effect: a remark is made above, that in describing superior beings, the reader's imagination, unable to support itself in a strained elevation, falls often as from a height, and sinks even below its ordinary tone. The following instance comes luckily in view; for a better cannot be given: "God said, Let there be light, and there was light." Longinus quotes this passage from Moses as a shining example of the sublime; and it is scarce possible, in fewer words, to convey so clear an image of the infinite power of the Deity: but then it belongs to the present subject to remark, that the emotion of sublimity raised by this image is but momentary; and that the mind, unable to support itself in an elevation so much above nature, immediately sinks down into humility and veneration for a being so far exalted above groveling mortals. Every one is acquainted with a dispute about that passage between two French critics,* the one positively affirming it to be sublime, the other as positively denying. What I have remarked shows that both of them have

---

* Boileau and Huet. [See the note for <223> above.]
23. Act 4, sc. 1.

reached the truth, but neither of them the whole truth: the primary effect of the passage is undoubtedly an emotion of grandeur; which so far justifies Boileau: but then every one must be sensible, that the emotion is merely a flash, which, <243> vanishing instantaneously, gives way to humility and veneration. That indirect effect of sublimity justifies Huet, who being a man of true piety, and probably not much carried by imagination, felt the humbling passion more sensibly than his antagonist did. And laying aside difference of character, Huet's opinion may, I think, be defended as the more solid; because in such images, the depressing emotions are the more sensibly felt, and have the longer endurance.

The straining an elevated subject beyond due bounds, is a vice not so frequent as to require the correction of criticism. But false sublime is a rock that writers of more fire than judgement commonly split on; and therefore a collection of examples may be of use as a beacon to future adventurers. One species of false sublime, known by the name of *bombast*, is common among writers of a mean genius: it is a serious endeavour, by strained description, to raise a low or familiar subject above its rank; which, instead of being sublime, becomes ridiculous. I am extremely sensible how prone the mind is, in some animating passions, to magnify its objects beyond natural bounds: but such hyperbolical description has its limits; and when carried beyond the impulse of the propensity, it degenerates into burlesque. Take the following examples. <244>

> *Sejanus.* ——— Great and high
> The world knows only two, that's Rome and I.
> My roof receives me not; 'tis air I tread,
> And at each step I feel my advanc'd head
> Knock out a star in heav'n.
>
> *Sejanus, Ben Johnson, act* 5.[24]

A writer who has no natural elevation of mind, deviates readily into bombast: he strains above his natural powers; and the violent effort carries him beyond the bounds of propriety. Boileau expresses this happily:

24. Ben Jonson (1572–1637): soldier, actor, poet, and playwright for the court. Shakespeare performed in at least two of his early works, and his company at the Globe launched Jonson's *Sejanus* in 1603. *Catiline* was first performed in 1611.

L'autre à peur de ramper, il se perd dans la nue.*

The same author, Ben Johnson, abounds in the bombast:

——— The mother,
Th' expulsed Apicata, finds them there;
Whom when she saw lie spread on the degrees,
After a world of fury on herself,
Tearing her hair, defacing of her face,
Beating her breasts and womb, kneeling amaz'd,
Crying to heav'n, then to them; at last
Her drowned voice got up above her woes:
And with such black and bitter execrations,
(As might affright the gods, and force the sun
Run backward to the east; nay, make the old
Deformed chaos rise again t' o'erwhelm <245>
Them, us, and all the world), she fills the air,
Upbraids the heavens with their partial dooms,
Defies their tyrannous powers, and demands
What she and those poor innocents have transgress'd,
That they must suffer such a share in vengeance.

                              Sejanus, act 5. sc. last.

——— Lentulus, the man,
If all our fire were out, would fetch down new,
Out of the hand of Jove; and rivet him,
To Caucasus, should he but frown; and let
His own gaunt eagle fly at him to tire.   *Catiline, act 3.*

Can these, or such, be any aid to us?
Look they as they were built to shake the world,
Or be a moment to our enterprise?
A thousand, such as they are, could not make
One atom of our souls. They should be men
Worth heaven's fear, that looking up, but thus,

---

* L'art poet. chant. 1. l. 68. ["The other is afraid to crawl, and loses himself in the clouds."]

Would make Jove stand upon his guard, and draw
Himself within his thunder; which, amaz'd,
He should discharge in vain, and they unhurt.
Or, if they were, like Capaneus at Thebes,
They should hang dead upon the highest spires,
And ask the second bolt to be thrown down.
Why Lentulus talk you so long? This time
Had been enough t' have scatter'd all the stars,
T' have quench'd the sun and moon, and made the world
Despair of day, or any light but ours.

Catiline, act 4. <246>

This is the language of a madman:

Guildford. Give way, and let the gushing torrent come,
Behold the tears we bring to swell the deluge,
Till the flood rise upon the guilty world
And make the ruin common.

Lady Jane Gray, act 4. near the end.[25]

I am sorry to observe that the following bombast stuff dropt from the pen of Dryden.[26]

To see this fleet upon the ocean move,
    Angels drew wide the curtains of the skies;
And heaven, as if there wanted lights above,
    For tapers made two glaring comets rise.

Another species of false sublime, is still more faulty than bombast; and that is, to force elevation by introducing imaginary beings without preserving any propriety in their actions; as if it were lawful to ascribe every extravagance and inconsistence to beings of the poet's creation. No writers are more licentious in that article than Johnson and Dryden:

25. *Lady Jane Gray,* 1715, by Nicholas Rowe (1674–1718): barrister, translator of Lucan, and the first systematic editor of Shakespeare's works. Kames frequently refers both to this play and to *The Fair Penitent* (1703) and *Jane Shore* (1714).
26. Dryden, "Annus Mirabilis," 1.16.

Methinks I see Death and the furies waiting
What we will do, and all the heaven at leisure
For the great spectacle. Draw then your swords:
And if our destiny envy our virtue
The honour of the day, yet let us care
To sell ourselves at such a price, as may
Undo the world to buy us, and make Fate,
While she tempts ours, to fear her own estate.

Catiline, act 5. <247>

———— The Furies stood on hill
Circling the place, and trembled to see men
Do more than they: whilst Piety left the field,
Griev'd for that side, that in so bad a cause
They knew not what a crime their valour was.
The Sun stood still, and was, behind the cloud
The battle made, seen sweating to drive up
His frighted horse, whom still the noise drove backward.

Ibid. act 5.

    Osmyn. While we indulge our common happiness,
He is forgot by whom we all possess,
The brave Almanzor, to whose arms we owe
All that we did, and all that we shall do;
Who like a tempest that outrides the wind,
Made a just battle ere the bodies join'd.
    Abdalla. His victories we scarce could keep in view,
Or polish 'em so fast as he rough drew.
    Abdemelech. Fate after him below with pain did move,
And victory could scarce keep pace above.
Death did at length so many slain forget,
And lost the tale, and took 'em by the great.

Conquest of Granada, act 2. *at beginning.*

The gods of Rome fight for ye; loud Fame calls ye,
Pitch'd on the topless Apenine, and blows
To all the under world, all nations,

The seas, and unfrequented deserts, where the snow dwells,
Wakens the ruin'd monuments, and there
Where nothing but eternal death and sleep is,
Informs again the dead bones.
Beaumont and Fletcher, Bonduca, act 3. sc. 3.[27] <248>

An actor on the stage may be guilty of bombast as well as an author in his closet: a certain manner of acting, which is grand when supported by dignity in the sentiment and force in the expression, is ridiculous where the sentiment is mean and the expression flat.

This chapter shall be closed with some observations. When the sublime is carried to its due height and circumscribed within proper bounds, it enchants the mind, and raises the most delightful of all emotions: the reader, engrossed by a sublime object, feels himself raised as it were to a higher rank. Considering that effect, it is not wonderful, that the history of conquerors and heroes, should be universally the favourite entertainment. And this fairly accounts for what I once erroneously suspected to be a wrong bias originally in human nature; which is, that the grossest acts of oppression and injustice scarce blemish the character of a great conqueror: we, nevertheless, warmly espouse his interest, accompany him in his exploits, and are anxious for his success: the splendor and enthusiasm of the hero transfused into the readers, elevate their minds far above the rules of justice, and render them in a great measure insensible of the wrongs that are committed:

For in those days might only shall be admir'd,
And valour and heroic virtue call'd;
To overcome in battle, and subdue
Nations, and bring home spoils with infinite <249>
Manslaughter, shall be held the highest pitch
Of human glory, and for glory done
Of triumph, to be styl'd great conquerors,
Patrons of mankind, gods, and sons of gods;
Destroyers rightlier call'd, and plagues of men.

27. Francis Beaumont (1584–1616) and John Fletcher (1579–1625): authors and producers. *Bonduca* was first performed in 1614.

Thus fame shall be atchiev'd, renown on earth,
And what most merits fame in silence hid.

Milton, b. 11.[28]

The irregular influence of grandeur reaches also to other matters: however good, honest, or useful, a man may be, he is not so much respected as is one of a more elevated character, tho' of less integrity; nor do the misfortunes of the former affect us so much as those of the latter. And I add, because it cannot be disguised, that the remorse which attends breach of engagement, is in a great measure proportioned to the figure that the injured person makes: the vows and protestations of lovers are an illustrious example; for these commonly are little regarded when made to women of inferior rank. <250>

---

28. *Paradise Lost,* bk. 11, line 693.

Motion and Force

That motion is agreeable to the eye without relation to purpose or design, may appear from the amusement it gives to infants: juvenile exercises are relished chiefly on that account.

If a body in motion be agreeable, one will be apt to conclude that at rest it must be disagreeable: but we learn from experience, that this would be a rash conclusion. Rest is one of those circumstances that are neither agreeable nor disagreeable, being view'd with perfect indifferency. And happy is it for mankind to have the matter so ordered: if rest were agreeable, it would disincline us to motion, by which all things are performed: if it were disagreeable, it would be a source of perpetual uneasiness; for the bulk of the things we see appear to be at rest. A similar instance of designing wisdom I have had occasion to explain, in opposing grandeur to littleness, and elevation to lowness of place.* Even in the simplest matters, the finger of God is conspicuous: the happy adjustment of the internal na-<251>ture of man to his external circumstances, display'd in the instances here given, is indeed admirable.

Motion is agreeable in all its varieties of quickness and slowness; but motion long continued admits some exceptions. That degree of continued motion which corresponds to the natural course of our perceptions, is the most agreeable. The quickest motion is for an instant delightful; but soon appears to be too rapid: it becomes painful by forcibly accelerating the course of our perceptions. Slow continued motion becomes disagreeable

---

* See chap. 4.

from an opposite cause, that it retards the natural course of our perceptions.*

There are other varieties in motion, beside quickness and slowness, that make it more or less agreeable: regular motion is preferred before what is irregular; witness the motion of the planets in orbits nearly circular: the motion of the comets in orbits less regular, is less agreeable.

Motion uniformly accelerated, resembling an ascending series of numbers, is more agreeable than when uniformly retarded: motion upward is agreeable by tendency to elevation. What then shall we say of downward motion regularly accelerated by the force of gravity, compared with upward motion regularly retarded by the same <252> force? Which of these is the most agreeable? This question is not easily solved.

Motion in a straight line is agreeable: but we prefer undulating motion, as of waves, of a flame, of a ship under sail; such motion is more free, and also more natural. Hence the beauty of a serpentine river.[1]

The easy and sliding motion of a fluid, from the lubricity of its parts, is agreeable upon that account: but the agreeableness chiefly depends on the following circumstance, that the motion is perceived, not as of one body, but as of an endless number moving together with order and regularity. Poets struck with that beauty, draw more images from fluids in motion than from solids.

Force is of two kinds; one quiescent, and one exerted in motion. The former, dead weight for example, must be laid aside; for a body at rest is not by that circumstance either agreeable or disagreeable. Moving force only is my province; and tho' it is not separable from motion, yet by the power of abstraction, either of them may be considered independent of the other. Both of them are agreeable, because both of them include activity. It is agreeable to see a thing move: to see it moved, as when it is dragged or pushed along, is neither agreeable nor disagreeable, more than when at rest. It is agreeable to see a thing exert force; but it makes not the thing either agreeable or disagreeable, to see force exerted upon it. <253>

Tho' motion and force are each of them agreeable, the impressions they

---

* This will be explained more fully afterward, ch. 9.
1. The reference is to William Hogarth, *The Analysis of Beauty.*

make are different. This difference, clearly felt, is not easily described. All we can say is, that the emotion raised by a moving body, resembling its cause, is felt as if the mind were carried along: the emotion raised by force exerted, resembling also its cause, is felt as if force were exerted within the mind.

To illustrate that difference, I give the following examples. It has been explained why smoke ascending in a calm day, suppose from a cottage in a wood, is an agreeable object;* so remarkably agreeable, that landscape-painters introduce it upon all occasions. The ascent being natural, and without effort, is pleasant in a calm state of mind: it resembles a gently-flowing river, but is more agreeable, because ascent is more to our taste than descent. A fire-work or a *jet d'eau*[2] rouses the mind more; because the beauty of force visibly exerted, is superadded to that of upward motion. To a man reclining indolently upon a bank of flowers, ascending smoke in a still morning is charming; but a fire-work or a *jet d'eau* rouses him from that supine posture, and puts him in motion.

A *jet d'eau* makes an impression distinguishable from that of a water-fall. Downward motion being natural and without effort, tends rather to quiet the mind than to rouse it: upward motion, <254> on the contrary, overcoming the resistance of gravity, makes an impression of a great effort, and thereby rouses and enlivens the mind.

The public games of the Greeks and Romans, which gave so much entertainment to the spectators, consisted chiefly in exerting force, wrestling, leaping, throwing great stones, and such-like trials of strength. When great force is exerted, the effort felt internally is animating. The effort may be such, as in some measure to over-power the mind: thus the explosion of gun-powder, the violence of a torrent, the weight of a mountain, and the crush of an earthquake, create astonishment rather than pleasure.

No quality nor circumstance contributes more to grandeur than force, especially where exerted by sensible beings. I cannot make the observation more evident than by the following quotations.

* Chap. 1.
2. Fountain.

———— ———— Him the almighty power
Hurl'd headlong flaming from th' ethereal sky,
With hideous ruin and combustion, down
To bottomless perdition, there to dwell
In adamantine chains and penal fire,
Who durst defy th' Omnipotent to arms.

Paradise lost, book 1.

———— ———— Now storming fury rose,
And clamour such as heard in heaven till now
Was never; arms on armour clashing bray'd <255>
Horrible discord, and the madding wheels
Of brazen chariots rag'd; dire was the noise
Of conflict; over head the dismal hiss
Of fiery darts in flaming vollies flew,
And flying vaulted either host with fire.
So under fiery cope together rush'd
Both battles main, with ruinous assault
And inextinguishable rage; all heaven
Resounded; and had earth been then, all earth
Had to her centre shook.   *Ibid. book* 6.

They ended parle, and both address'd for fight
Unspeakable; for who, though with the tongue
Of angels, can relate, or to what things
Liken on earth conspicuous, that may lift
Human imagination to such height
Of godlike pow'r? for likest gods they seem'd,
Stood they or mov'd, in stature, motion, arms,
Fit to decide the empire of great Heav'n.
Now wav'd their fiery swords, and in the air
Made horrid circles: two broad suns their shields
Blaz'd opposite, while Expectation stood
In horror: from each hand with speed retir'd,
Where erst was thickest fight, th' angelic throng,
And left large field, unsafe within the wind
Of such commotion; such as, to set forth

Great things by small, if Nature's concord broke,
Among the constellations war were sprung,
Two planets, rushing from aspect malign
Of fiercest opposition, in mid sky
Should combat, and their jarring spheres confound.

Ibid. book 6. <256>

We shall next consider the effect of motion and force in conjunction. In contemplating the planetary system, what strikes us the most, is the spherical figures of the planets, and their regular motions; the conception we have of their activity and enormous bulk being more obscure: the beauty accordingly of that system, raises a more lively emotion than its grandeur. But if we could comprehend the whole system at one view, the activity and irresistible force of these immense bodies would fill us with amazement: nature cannot furnish another scene so grand.

Motion and force, agreeable in themselves, are also agreeable by their utility when employ'd as means to accomplish some beneficial end. Hence the superior beauty of some machines, where force and motion concur to perform the work of numberless hands. Hence the beautiful motions, firm and regular, of a horse trained for war: every single step is the fittest that can be, for obtaining the purposed end. But the grace of motion is visible chiefly in man, not only for the reasons mentioned, but because every gesture is significant. The power however of agreeable motion is not a common talent: every limb of the human body has an agreeable and disagreeable motion; some motions being extremely graceful, others plain and vulgar; some expressing dignity, others meanness. But the pleasure here, arising, not singly from the beauty of motion, but from indicating <257> character and sentiment, belongs to different chapters.*

I should conclude with the final cause of the relish we have for motion and force, were it not so evident as to require no explanation. We are placed here in such circumstances as to make industry essential to our well-being; for without industry the plainest necessaries of life are not obtained. When our situation therefore in this world requires activity and a constant exertion

---

* Chap. 11. and 15.

of motion and force, Providence indulgently provides for our welfare by making these agreeable to us: it would be a gross imperfection in our nature, to make any thing disagreeable that we depend on for existence; and even indifference would slacken greatly that degree of activity which is indispensable. <258>

CHAPTER VI

Novelty, and the Unexpected
Appearance of Objects

Of all the circumstances that raise emotions, not excepting beauty, nor even greatness, novelty hath the most powerful influence. A new object produceth instantaneously an emotion termed *wonder,* which totally occupies the mind, and for a time excludes all other objects. Conversation among the vulgar never is more interesting than when it turns upon strange objects and extraordinary events. Men tear themselves from their native country in search of things rare and new; and novelty converts into a pleasure, the fatigues and even perils of travelling. To what cause shall we ascribe these singular appearances? To curiosity undoubtedly, a principle implanted in human nature for a purpose extremely beneficial, that of acquiring knowledge; and the emotion of wonder, raised by new and strange objects, inflames our curiosity to know more of them. This emotion is different from *admiration:* novelty where ever found, whether in a quality or action, is the cause of wonder; admiration is directed to the person who performs any thing wonderful. <259>

During infancy, every new object is probably the occasion of wonder, in some degree; because, during infancy, every object at first sight is strange as well as new: but as objects are rendered familiar by custom, we cease by degrees to wonder at new appearances, if they have any resemblance to what we are acquainted with; for a thing must be singular as well as new, to raise our wonder. To save multiplying words, I would be understood to comprehend both circumstances when I hereafter talk of novelty.

In an ordinary train of perceptions where one thing introduces another, not a single object makes its appearance unexpectedly:* the mind thus prepared for the reception of its objects, admits them one after another without perturbation. But when a thing breaks in unexpectedly, and without the preparation of any connection, it raises an emotion, known by the name of *surprise*. That emotion may be produced by the most familiar object, as when one unexpectedly meets a friend who was reported to be dead; or a man in high life, lately a beggar. On the other hand, a new object, however strange, will not produce the emotion, if the spectator be prepared for the sight: an elephant in India will not surprise a traveller who goes to see one; and yet its novelty will raise his wonder: an Indian in Britain would <260> be much surprised to stumble upon an elephant feeding at large in the open fields: but the creature itself, to which he was accustomed, would not raise his wonder.

Surprise thus in several respects differs from wonder: unexpectedness is the cause of the former emotion; novelty is the cause of the latter. Nor differ they less in their nature and circumstances, as will be explained by and by. With relation to one circumstance they perfectly agree; which is, the shortness of their duration: the instantaneous production of these emotions in perfection, may contribute to that effect, in conformity to a general law, That things soon decay which soon come to perfection: the violence of the emotions may also contribute; for an ardent emotion, which is not susceptible of increase, cannot have a long course. But their short duration is occasioned chiefly by that of their causes: we are soon reconciled to an object, however unexpected; and novelty soon degenerates into familiarity.

Whether these emotions be pleasant or painful, is not a clear point. It may appear strange, that our own feelings and their capital qualities, should afford any matter for a doubt: but when we are engrossed by any emotion, there is no place for speculation; and when sufficiently calm for speculation, it is not easy to recal the emotion with accuracy. New objects are sometimes terrible, <261> sometimes delightful: the terror which a tyger inspires is greatest at first, and wears off gradually by familiarity: on the other hand, even women will acknowledge that it is novelty which pleases the most in a new fashion. It would be rash however to conclude, that wonder is in

* See chap. I.

itself neither pleasant nor painful, but that it assumes either quality according to circumstances. An object, it is true, that hath a threatening appearance, adds to our terror by its novelty: but from that experiment it doth not follow, that novelty is in itself disagreeable; for it is perfectly consistent, that we be delighted with an object in one view, and terrified with it in another: a river in flood swelling over its banks, is a grand and delightful object; and yet it may produce no small degree of fear when we attempt to cross it: courage and magnanimity are agreeable; and yet, when we view these qualities in an enemy, they serve to increase our terror. In the same manner, novelty may produce two effects clearly distinguishable from each other: it may, directly and in itself, be agreeable; and it may have an opposite effect indirectly, which is, to inspire terror; for when a new object appears in any degree dangerous, our ignorance of its powers and qualities, affords ample scope for the imagination to dress it in the most frightful colours.* The first sight of a lion, for <262> example, may at the same instant produce two opposite feelings, the pleasant emotion of wonder, and the painful passion of terror: the novelty of the object, produces the former directly, and contributes to the latter indirectly. Thus, when the subject is analysed, we find, that the power which novelty hath indirectly to inflame terror, is perfectly consistent with its being in every circumstance agreeable. The matter may be put in the clearest light, by adding the following circumstances. If a lion be first seen from a place of safety, the spectacle is altogether agreeable without the least mixture of terror. If again the first sight puts us within reach of that dangerous animal, our terror may be so great as quite to exclude any sense of novelty. But this fact proves not that wonder is painful: it proves only, that wonder may be excluded by a more powerful passion. Every man may be made certain from his own experience, that wonder raised by a new object which is inoffensive, is always pleasant; and with respect to offensive objects, it appears from the foregoing deduction, that the same must hold as long as the spectator can attend to the novelty.

Whether surprise be in itself pleasant or painful, is a question no less intricate than the former. It is certain that surprise inflames our joy when unexpectedly we meet with an old friend, and our terror when we stumble

---

* *Essays on the Principles of Morality and Natural Religion,* part 2. ess. 6.

upon any thing noxious. To clear that question, the first thing to <263> be remarked is, that in some instances an unexpected object overpowers the mind, so as to produce a momentary stupefaction: where the object is dangerous, or appears so, the sudden alarm it gives, without preparation, is apt totally to unhinge the mind, and for a moment to suspend all its faculties, even thought itself;* in which state a man is quite helpless; and if he move at all, is as like to run upon the danger as from it. Surprise carried to such a height, cannot be either pleasant or painful; because the mind, during such momentary stupefaction, is in a good measure, if not totally, insensible.

If we then enquire for the character of this emotion, it must be where the unexpected object or event produceth less violent effects. And while the mind remains sensible of pleasure and pain, is it not natural to suppose, that surprise, like wonder, should have an invariable character? I am inclined however to think, that surprise has no invariable character, but assumes that of the object which raises it. Wonder being an emotion invariably raised by novelty, and being distinguishable from all other emotions, ought naturally to possess one constant character. The unexpected appearance of an object, seems not equally intitled to produce an emotion distinguishable from that <264> which is produced by the object in its ordinary appearance: the effect it ought naturally to have, is only to swell that emotion, by making it more pleasant or more painful than it commonly is. And that conjecture is confirmed by experience, as well as by language, which is built upon experience: when a man meets a friend unexpectedly, he is said to be agreeably surprised; and when he meets an enemy unexpectedly, he is said to be disagreeably surprised. It appears, then, that the sole effect of surprise is to swell the emotion raised by the object. And that effect can be clearly explained: a tide of connected perceptions, glide gently into the mind, and produce no perturbation; but an object breaking in unexpectedly, sounds an alarm, rouses the mind out of its calm state, and directs its whole attention to the object, which, if agreeable, becomes doubly so. Several circumstances concur to produce that effect: on the one hand, the agitation of the mind, and its keen attention, prepare it in the

---

* Hence the Latin names for surprise, *torpor, animi stupor.*

most effectual manner for receiving a deep impression: on the other hand, the object, by its sudden and unforeseen appearance, makes an impression, not gradually as expected objects do, but as at one stroke with its whole force. The circumstances are precisely similar where the object is in itself disagreeable.* <265>

The pleasure of novelty is easily distinguished from that of variety: to produce the latter, a plurality of objects is necessary; the former arises from a circumstance found in a single object. A-<266>gain, where objects, whether coexistent or in succession, are sufficiently diversified, the pleasure of variety is complete, tho' every single object of the train be familiar: but the pleasure of novelty, directly opposite to familiarity, requires no diversification.

There are different degrees of novelty, and its effects are in proportion.

* What the Mareschal Saxe terms *le cœur humain* is no other than fear occasion'd by surprise. It is owing to that cause that an ambush is generally so destructive: intelligence of it beforehand renders it harmless. The Mareschal gives from Caesar's Commentaries two examples of what he calls *le cœur humain*. At the siege of Amiens by the Gauls, Caesar came up with his army, which did not exceed 7000 men, and began to intrench himself in such hurry, that the barbarians, judging him to be afraid, attacked his intrenchments with great spirit. During the time they were filling up the ditch, he issued out with his cohorts; and, by attacking them unexpectedly, struck a panic that made them fly with precipitation, not a single man offering to make a stand. At the siege of Alesia, the Gauls, infinitely superior in number, attacked the Roman lines of circumvallation, in order to raise the siege. Caesar ordered a body of his men to march out silently, and to attack them on the one flank, while he with another body did the same on the other flank. The surprise of being attacked when they expected a defence only, put the Gauls into disorder, and gave an easy victory to Caesar.
A third may be added no less memorable. In the year 846 an obstinate battle was fought between Xamire King of Leon and Abdoulrahman the Moorish King of Spain. After a very long conflict, the night only prevented the Arabians from obtaining a complete victory. The King of Leon, taking advantage of the darkness, retreated to a neighbouring hill, leaving the Arabians masters of the field of battle. Next morning, perceiving that he could not maintain his place for want of provisions, nor be able to draw off his men in the face of a victorious army, he ranged his men in order of battle, and, without losing a moment, march'd to attack the enemy, resolving to conquer or die. The Arabians, astonish'd to be attacked by those who were conquered the night before, lost all heart: fear succeeded to astonishment, the panic was universal, and they all turned their backs without almost drawing a sword. [Maurice, Comte de Saxe (1696–1750): marshal of France and author of *Les Rêveries ou Mémoires sur l'Art de la Guerre*, 1756 (English trans. 1757).]

The lowest degree is found in objects surveyed a second time after a long interval; and that in this case an object takes on some appearance of novelty, is certain from experience: a large building of many parts variously adorned, or an extensive field embellished with trees, lakes, temples, statues, and other ornaments, will appear new oftener than once: the memory of an object so complex is soon lost, of its parts at least, or of their arrangement. But experience teaches, that even without any decay of remembrance, absence alone will give an air of novelty to a once familiar object; which is not surprising, because familiarity wears off gradually by absence: thus a person with whom we have been <267> intimate, returning after a long interval, appears like a new acquaintance: and distance of place contributes to this appearance, no less than distance of time: a friend, for example, after a short absence in a remote country, has the same air of novelty as if he had returned after a longer interval from a place nearer home: the mind forms a connection between him and the remote country, and bestows upon him the singularity of the objects he has seen. For the same reason, when two things equally new and singular are presented, the spectator balances between them; but when told that one of them is the product of a distant quarter of the world, he no longer hesitates, but clings to it as the more singular. Hence the preference given to foreign luxuries, and to foreign curiosities, which appear rare in proportion to their original distance.

The next degree of novelty, mounting upward, is found in objects of which we have some information at second hand; for description, tho' it contribute to familiarity, cannot altogether remove the appearance of novelty when the object itself is presented: the first sight of a lion occasions some wonder, after a thorough acquaintance with the correctest pictures and statues of that animal.

A new object that bears some distant resemblance to a known species, is an instance of a third degree of novelty: a strong resemblance among <268> individuals of the same species, prevents almost entirely the effect of novelty, unless distance of place or some other circumstance concur; but where the resemblance is faint, some degree of wonder is felt, and the emotion rises in proportion to the faintness of the resemblance.

The highest degree of wonder ariseth from unknown objects that have no analogy to any species we are acquainted with. Shakespear in a simile introduces that species of novelty:

As glorious to the sight
As is a winged messenger from heaven
Unto the white up-turned wond'ring eye
Of mortals, that fall back to gaze on him
When he bestrides the lazy-pacing clouds,
And sails upon the bosom of the air.   *Romeo and Juliet.*[1]

One example of that species of novelty deserves peculiar attention; and that is, when an object altogether new is seen by one person only, and but once. These circumstances heighten remarkably the emotion: the singularity of the spectator concurs with the singularity of the object, to inflame wonder to its highest pitch.

In explaining the effects of novelty, the place a being occupies in the scale of existence, is a circumstance that must not be omitted. Novelty in the individuals of a low class is perceived with in-<269>difference, or with a very slight emotion: thus a pebble, however singular in its appearance, scarce moves our wonder. The emotion rises with the rank of the object; and, other circumstances being equal, is strongest in the highest order of existence: a strange insect affects us more than a strange vegetable; and a strange quadruped more than a strange insect.

However natural novelty may be, it is a matter of experience, that those who relish it the most are careful to conceal its influence. Love of novelty, it is true, prevails in children, in idlers, and in men of shallow understanding: and yet, after all, why should one be ashamed of indulging a natural propensity? A distinction will afford a satisfactory answer. No man is ashamed of curiosity when it is indulged in order to acquire knowledge. But to prefer any thing merely because it is new, shows a mean taste, which one ought to be ashamed of: vanity is commonly at the bottom, which leads those who are deficient in taste to prefer things odd, rare, or singular, in order to distinguish themselves from others. And in fact, that appetite, as above mentioned, reigns chiefly among persons of a mean taste, who are ignorant of refined and elegant pleasures.

One final cause of wonder, hinted above, is, that this emotion is intended to stimulate our curiosity. Another, somewhat different, is, to pre-

1. Act 2, sc. 2. Read "of heaven" for "from heaven."

pare the mind for receiving deep impressions of <270> new objects. An acquaintance with the various things that may affect us and with their properties, is essential to our well-being: nor will a slight or superficial acquaintance be sufficient; they ought to be so deeply engraved on the mind, as to be ready for use upon every occasion. Now, in order to a deep impression, it is wisely contrived, that things should be introduced to our acquaintance with a certain pomp and solemnity productive of a vivid emotion. When the impression is once fairly made, the emotion of novelty, being no longer necessary, vanisheth almost instantaneously; never to return, unless where the impression happens to be obliterated by length of time or other means; in which case, the second introduction hath nearly the same solemnity with the first.

Designing wisdom is no where more legible than in this part of the human frame. If new objects did not affect us in a very peculiar manner, their impressions would be so slight as scarce to be of any use in life: on the other hand, did objects continue to affect us as deeply as at first, the mind would be totally engrossed with them, and have no room left either for action or reflection.

The final cause of surprise is still more evident than of novelty. Self-love makes us vigilantly attentive to self-preservation; but self-love, which operates by means of reason and reflection, and impels not the mind to any particular object or from it, is a principle too cool for a sudden emergency: <271> an object breaking in unexpectedly, affords no time for deliberation; and, in that case, the agitation of surprise comes in seasonably to rouse self-love into action: surprise gives the alarm; and if there be any appearance of danger, our whole force is instantly summoned up to shun or to prevent it. <272>

Risible Objects

Such is the nature of man, that his powers and faculties are soon blunted by exercise. The returns of sleep, suspending all activity, are not alone sufficient to preserve him in vigor: during his walking hours, amusement by intervals is requisite to unbend his mind from serious occupation. To that end, nature hath kindly made a provision of many objects, which may be distinguished by the epithet of *risible,* because they raise in us a peculiar emotion expressed externally by *laughter:* that emotion is pleasant; and being also mirthful, it most successfully unbends the mind, and recruits the spirits. Imagination contributes a part by multiplying such objects without end.

Ludicrous is a general term, signifying, as may appear from its derivation, what is playsome, sportive, or jocular. *Ludicrous* therefore seems the genus, of which *risible* is a species, limited as above to what makes us laugh.

However easy it may be, concerning any particular object, to say whether it be risible or not, it seems difficult, if at all practicable, to establish <273> any general character, by which objects of that kind may be distinguished from others. Nor is that a singular case; for upon a review, we find the same difficulty in most of the articles already handled. There is nothing more easy, viewing a particular object, than to pronounce that it is beautiful or ugly, grand or little: but were we to attempt general rules for ranging objects under different classes, according to these qualities, we should be much gravelled. A separate cause increases the difficulty of distinguishing risible objects by a general character: all men are not equally affected by risible objects: nor the same man at all times; for in high spirits a thing will make him laugh outright, which scarce provokes a smile in a grave mood. Risible

objects however are circumscribed within certain limits; which I shall suggest, without pretending to accuracy. And, in the first place, I observe, that
no object is risible but what appears slight, little, or trivial; for we laugh at
nothing that is of importance to our own interest, or to that of others. A
real distress raises pity, and therefore cannot be risible; but a slight or imaginary distress, which moves not pity, is risible. The adventure of the fulling-
mills[1] in Don Quixote,[2] is extremely risible; so is the scene where Sancho,
in a dark night, tumbling into a pit, and attaching himself to the side by
hand and foot, hangs there in terrible dismay till the morning, when he
discovers himself <274> to be within a foot of the bottom. A nose remarkably long or short, is risible; but to want it altogether, far from pro-
voking laughter, raises horror in the spectator. Secondly, With respect to
works both of nature and of art, none of them are risible but what are out
of rule, some remarkable defect or excess; a very long visage, for example,
or a very short one. Hence nothing just, proper, decent, beautiful, proportioned, or grand, is risible.

Even from this slight sketch it will readily be conjectured, that the emotion raised by a risible object is of a nature so singular, as scarce to find place
while the mind is occupied with any other passion or emotion: and the
conjecture is verified by experience; for we scarce ever find that emotion
blended with any other. One emotion I must except; and that is, contempt
raised by certain improprieties: every improper act inspires us with some
degree of contempt for the author; and if an improper act be at the same
time risible to provoke laughter, of which blunders and absurdities are
noted instances, the two emotions of contempt and of laughter unite intimately in the mind, and produce externally what is termed *a laugh of
derision* or *of scorn*. Hence objects that cause laughter may be distinguished
into two kinds: they are either *risible* or *ridiculous*. A risible object is mirthful only: a ridiculous object is both mirthful and contemptible. The first
<275> raises an emotion of laughter that is altogether pleasant: the pleasant
emotion of laughter raised by the other, is blended with the painful emotion
of contempt; and the mixed emotion is termed *the emotion of ridicule*. The

1. Cloth mills.
2. Miguel de Cervantes Saavedra (1547–1616), *Don Quixote* (1605), bk. 1, chap. 8.

pain a ridiculous object gives me, is resented and punished by a laugh of
derision. A risible object, on the other hand, gives me no pain: it is altogether pleasant by a certain sort of titillation, which is expressed externally
by mirthful laughter. Ridicule will be more fully explained afterward: the
present chapter is appropriated to the other emotion.

Risible objects are so common, and so well understood, that it is unnecessary to consume paper or time upon them. Take the few following
examples.

> *Falstaff.* I do remember him at Clement's inn, like a man made after
> supper of a cheese-paring. When he was naked, he was for all the world
> like a forked radish, with a head fantastically carved upon it with a knife.
>   *Second part, Henry* IV. *act* 3. *sc.* 5.[3]

The foregoing is of disproportion. The following examples are of slight
or imaginary misfortunes.

> *Falstaff.* Go fetch me a quart of sack; put a toast in't. Have I liv'd to be
> carried in a basket, like a barrow of butcher's offal, and to be thrown into
> the <276> Thames! Well, if I be served such another trick, I'll have my
> brains ta'en out and butter'd, and give them to a dog for a new-year's gift.
> The rogues slighted me into the river with as little remorse as they would
> have drown'd a bitch's blind puppies, fifteen i' th' litter; and you may know
> by my size, that I have a kind of alacrity in sinking: if the bottom were as
> deep as hell, I should down. I had been drown'd, but that the shore was
> shelvy and shallow; a death that I abhor; for the water swells a man: and
> what a thing should I have been when I had been swell'd? I should have
> been a mountain of mummy.
>   *Merry Wives of Windsor, act* 3. *sc.* 15.

> *Falstaff.* Nay, You shall hear, Master Brook, what I have suffer'd to bring
> this woman to evil for your good. Being thus cramm'd in the basket, a
> couple of Ford's knaves, his hinds, were call'd forth by their mistress, to
> carry me in the name of foul cloaths to Datchet-lane. They took me on
> their shoulders, met the jealous knave their master in the door, who ask'd
> them once or twice what they had in their basket. I quak'd for fear, lest

3. Act 3, sc. 2.

the lunatic knave would have search'd it; but Fate, ordaining he should
be a cuckold, held his hand. Well, on went he for a search, and away went
I for foul cloaths. But mark the sequel, Master Brook. I suffer'd the pangs
of three egregious deaths: first, an intolerable fright, to be detected by a
jealous rotten bell-weather; next, to be compass'd like a good bilbo,[4] in
the circumference of a peck,[5] hilt to point, heel to head; and then to be
stopt in, like a strong distillation, with stinking cloaths that fretted in their
own grease. Think of that, a <277> man of my kidney; think of that, that
am as subject to heat as butter; a man of continual dissolution and thaw;
it was a miracle to 'scape suffocation. And in the height of this bath, when
I was more than half stew'd in grease, like a Dutch dish, to be thrown into
the Thames, and cool'd glowing hot, in that surge, like a horse shoe; think
of that; hissing hot; think of that, Master Brook.

Merry Wives of Windsor, act 3. *sc.* 17.[6] <278>

4. Bilbo: a bar locked to the floor of a prison cell.
5. Peck: a two-gallon vessel.
6. Act 3, sc. 5—both quotations.

‫‪∞‬‬ CHAPTER VIII ‫‪∞‬‬

Resemblance and Dissimilitude[1]

Having discussed those qualities and circumstances of single objects that seem peculiarly connected with criticism, we proceed, according to the method proposed in the chapter of beauty, to the relations of objects, beginning with the relations of resemblance and dissimilitude.

The connection that man hath with the beings around him, requires some acquaintance with their nature, their powers, and their qualities, for regulating his conduct. For acquiring a branch of knowledge so essential to our well-being, motives alone of reason and interest are not sufficient: nature hath providently superadded curiosity, a vigorous propensity, which never is at rest. This propensity attaches us to every new object;* and incites us to compare objects, in order to discover their differences and resemblances.

Resemblance among objects of the same kind, and dissimilitude among objects of different kinds, are too obvious and familiar to gratify our curio-<279>sity in any degree: its gratification lies in discovering differences among things where resemblance prevails, and resemblances where difference prevails. Thus a difference in individuals of the same kind of plants or animals, is deemed a discovery; while the many particulars in which they agree, are neglected: and in different kinds, any resemblance is greedily remarked, without attending to the many particulars in which they differ.

A comparison however may be too far stretched. When differences or resemblances are carried beyond certain bounds, they appear slight and triv-

---

* See chap. 6.
1. "Contrast" in first edition.

ial; and for that reason, will not be relished by a man of taste: yet such propensity is there to gratify passion, curiosity in particular, that even among good writers, we find many comparisons too slight to afford satisfaction. Hence the frequent instances among logicians, of distinctions without any solid difference: and hence the frequent instances among poets and orators, of similes without any just resemblance. With regard to the latter, I shall confine myself to one instance, which will probably amuse the reader, being a quotation, not from a poet nor orator, but from a grave author writing an institute of law. "Our student shall observe, that the knowledge of the law is like a deep well, out of which each man draweth according to the strength of his understanding. He that reacheth deepest, seeth the amiable and admirable secrets of the law, <280> wherein I assure you the sages of the law in former times have had the deepest reach. And as the bucket in the depth is easily drawn to the uppermost part of the water, (for *nullum elementum in suo proprio loco est grave*), but take it from the water, it cannot be drawn up but with a great difficulty; so, albeit beginnings of this study seem difficult, yet when the professor of the law can dive into the depth, it is delightful, easy, and without any heavy burden, so long as he keep himself in his own proper element."* Shakespear with uncommon humour ridicules such disposition to simile-making, by putting in the mouth of a weak man, a resemblance much of a piece with that now mentioned:

> *Fluellen.* I think it is in Macedon where Alexander is porn: I tell you, Captain, if you look in the maps of the orld, I warrant that you sall find, in the comparisons between Macedon and Monmouth, that the situasions, look you, is both alike. There is a river in Macedon, there is also moreover a river in Monmouth: it is called *Wye* at Monmouth, but it is out of my prains what is the name of the other river; but it is all one, 'tis as like as my fingers to my fingers, and there is salmons in both. If you mark Alexander's life well, Harry of Monmouth's life is come after it indifferent well; for there is figures in all things, Alexander, God knows, and you know, in his rages, <281> and his furies, and his wraths, and his chol-

* *Coke upon Lyttleton*, p. 71. [Sir Edward Coke, *The First Part of the Institutes of the Lawes of England; Or, a Commentary upon Littleton*, 1639.]

ers, and his moods, and his displeasures, and his indignations; and also being a little intoxicates in his prains, did, in his ales and his angers, look you, kill his pest friend Clytus.

Gower. Our King is not like him in that; he never kill'd any of his friends.

Fluellen. It is not well done, mark you now, to take the tales out of my mouth, ere it is made and finished. I speak but in figures, and comparisons of it: As Alexander kill'd his friend Clytus, being in his ales and his cups; so also Harry Monmouth, being in his right wits and his good judgements, turn'd away the fat knight with the great belly doublet; he was full of jests, and gypes, and knaveries, and mocks: I have forgot his name.

Gower. Sir John Falstaff.

Fluellen. That is he: I tell you there is good men porn at Monmouth.

K. Henry V. *act* 4. *sc.* 13.[2]

Instruction, no doubt, is the chief end of comparison; but that it is not the only end, will be evident from considering, that a comparison may be employ'd with success to put a subject in a strong point of view. A lively idea is formed of a man's courage, by likening it to that of a lion; and eloquence is exalted in our imagination, by comparing it to a river overflowing its banks, and involving all in its impetuous course. The same effect is produced by contrast: a man in prosperity, becomes more sensible of his happiness by oppo-<282>sing his condition to that of a person in want of bread. Thus, comparison is subservient to poetry as well as to philosophy; and with respect to both, the foregoing observation holds equally, that resemblance among objects of the same kind, and dissimilitude among objects of different kinds, have no effect: such a comparison neither tends to gratify our curiosity, nor to set the objects compared in a stronger light: two apartments in a palace, similar in shape, size, and furniture, make separately as good a figure as when compared; and the same observation is applicable to two similar copartments in a garden: on the other hand, oppose a regular building to a fall of water, or a good picture to a towering hill, or even a little dog to a large horse, and the contrast will produce no effect. But a resemblance between objects of different kinds, and a difference between

2. Act 4, sc. 7.

objects of the same kind, have remarkably an enlivening effect. The poets, such of them as have a just taste, draw all their similes from things that in the main differ widely from the principal subject; and they never attempt a contrast, but where the things have a common genus and a resemblance in the capital circumstances: place together a large and a small sized animal of the same species, the one will appear greater, the other less, than when viewed separately: when we oppose beauty to deformity, each makes a greater figure by the comparison. We compare the dress of <283> different nations with curiosity, but without surprise; because they have no such resemblance in the capital parts as to please us by contrasting the smaller parts. But a new cut of a sleeve or of a pocket enchants by its novelty, and in opposition to the former fashion raises some degree of surprise.

That resemblance and dissimilitude have an enlivening effect upon objects of sight, is made sufficiently evident; and that they have the same effect upon objects of the other senses, is also certain. Nor is that law confined to the external senses; for characters contrasted make a greater figure by the opposition: Iago, in the tragedy of *Othello*,[3] says,

> He hath a daily beauty in his life,
> That makes me ugly.

The character of a fop, and of a rough warrior, are no where more successfully contrasted than in Shakespear:

> *Hotspur.* My liege, I did deny no prisoners;
> But I remember, when the fight was done,
> When I was dry with rage, and extreme toil,
> Breathless and faint, leaning upon my sword;
> Came there a certain Lord, neat, trimly dress'd,
> Fresh as a bridegroom; and his chin, new-reap'd,
> Shew'd like a stubble-land at harvest-home.
> He was perfumed like a milliner;
> And 'twixt his finger and his thumb he held <284>
> A pouncet-box, which ever and anon
> He gave his nose;—and still he smil'd, and talk'd;

3. Act 5, sc. 1.

And as the soldiers bare dead bodies by,
He call'd them untaught knaves, unmannerly,
To bring a slovenly, unhandsome corse!
Betwixt the wind and his nobility.
With many holiday and lady terms
He question'd me: among the rest, demanded
My pris'ners, in your Majesty's behalf.
I then all smarting with my wounds; being gall'd
To be so pester'd with a popinjay,
Out of my grief, and my impatience,
Answer'd, neglectingly, I know not what:
He should, or should not; for he made me mad,
To see him shine so brisk, and smell so sweet,
And talk so like a waiting gentlewoman,
Of guns, and drums, and wounds; (God save the mark!)
And telling me, the sovereign'st thing on earth
Was parmacity, for an inward bruise;
And that it was great pity, so it was,
This villanous saltpetre should be digg'd,
Out of the bowels of the harmless earth,
Which many a good, tall fellow had destroy'd
So cowardly: and but for these vile guns,
He would himself have been a soldier.—

First part, Henry IV. *act* I. *sc.* 4.[4]

Passions and emotions are also inflamed by comparison. A man of high rank humbles the bystanders, even to annihilate them in their own opinion: Caesar, beholding the statue of Alexander, was greatly mortified, that now at the age of thir-<285>ty-two when Alexander died, he had not performed one memorable action.

Our opinions also are much influenced by comparison. A man whose opulence exceeds the ordinary standard, is reputed richer than he is in reality; and wisdom or weakness, if at all remarkable in an individual, is generally carried beyond the truth.

4. Act I, sc. 3.

The opinion a man forms of his present distress is heightened by contrasting it with his former happiness:

> Could I forget
> What I have been, I might the better bear
> What I am destin'd to. I'm not the first
> That have been wretched: but to think how much
> I have been happier.   *Southern's Innocent adultery, act* 2.[5]

The distress of a long journey makes even an indifferent inn agreeable: and in travelling, when the road is good and the horseman well covered, a bad day may be agreeable by making him sensible how snug he is.

The same effect is equally remarkable, when a man opposes his condition to that of others. A ship tossed about in a storm, makes the spectator reflect upon his own ease and security, and puts these in the strongest light:

> Suave, mari magno turbantibus aequora ventis,
> E terra magnum alterius spectare laborem; <286>
> Non quia vexari quemquam est jucunda voluptas,
> Sed quibus ipse malis careas, quia cernere suave est.
>
> > *Lucret. l.* 2. *principio.*[6]

A man in grief cannot bear mirth: it gives him a more lively notion of his unhappiness, and of course makes him more unhappy. Satan contemplating the beauties of the terrestrial paradise, has the following exclamation.

> With what delight could I have walk'd thee round,
> If I could joy in ought, sweet interchange
> Of hill and valley, rivers, woods, and plains,
> Now land, now sea, and shores with forest crown'd,
> Rocks, dens, and caves! but I in none of these

---

5. Thomas Southern (1659–1746): author and friend of Dryden. *The Fatal Marriage, or the Innocent Adultery* was produced in 1694, with music by Purcell, and in a new version by Garrick, under the title *Isabella, or the Fatal Marriage.*
   6. Tis pleasant, safely to behold from shore
   The Rolling ship, and hear the tempest roar;
   Not that another's pain is our delight,
   But pains unfelt produce the pleasing sight.
   (trans. Dryden)

Find place or refuge; and the more I see
Pleasures about me, so much more I feel
Torment within me, as from the hateful siege
Of contraries: all good to me becomes
Bane, and in heav'n much worse would be my state.

Paradise lost, book 9. *l.* 114.

    Gaunt. All places that the eye of heaven visits,
Are to a wise man ports and happy havens.
Teach thy necessity to reason thus:
There is no virtue like necessity.
Think not the King did banish thee;
But thou the King. Wo doth the heavier sit,
Where it perceives it is but faintly borne.
Go say, I sent thee forth to purchase honour;
And not, the King exil'd thee. Or suppose,
Devouring pestilence hangs in our air,
And thou art flying to a fresher clime, <287>
Look what thy soul holds dear, imagine it
To lie that way thou go'st, not whence thou com'st.
Suppose the singing birds, musicians;
The grass whereon thou tread'st, the presence-floor;
The flow'rs, fair ladies; and thy steps, no more
Than a delightful measure, or a dance.
For gnarling Sorrow hath less power to bite
The man that mocks at it, and sets it light.
    Bolingbroke. Oh, who can hold a fire in his hand,
By thinking on the frosty Caucasus?
Or cloy the hungry edge of Appetite,
By bare imagination of a feast?
Or wallow naked in December snow,
By thinking on fantastic summer's heat?
Oh, no! the apprehension of the good
Gives but the greater feeling to the worse.

King Richard II. *act* 1. *sc.* 6.[7]

7. Act 1, sc. 3.

The appearance of danger gives sometimes pleasure, sometimes pain. A timorous person upon the battlements of a high tower, is seized with fear, which even the consciousness of security cannot dissipate. But upon one of a firm head, this situation has a contrary effect: the appearance of danger heightens, by opposition, the consciousness of security, and consequently, the satisfaction that arises from security: here the feeling resembles that above mentioned, occasioned by a ship labouring in a storm.

The effect of magnifying or lessening objects by means of comparison, is so familiar, that no philo-<288>sopher has thought of searching for a cause.* The obscurity of the subject may possibly have contributed to their silence; but luckily, we discover the cause to be a principle unfolded above, which is the influence of passion over our opinions.† We have had occasion to see many illustrious effects of that singular power of passion; and that the magnifying or diminishing objects by means of comparison, proceeds from the same cause, will evidently appear, by reflecting in what manner a spectator is affected, when a very large animal is for the first time placed beside a very small one of the same species. The first thing that strikes the mind, is the difference between the two animals, which is so great as to occasion surprise; and this, like other emotions, magnifying its object, makes us conceive the difference to be the greatest that can be: we see, or seem to see, the one animal extremely little, and the other extremely large. The emotion of surprise arising from any unusual resemblance, serves equally to explain, why at first view we are apt to think such <289> resemblance more entire than it is in reality. And it must not escape observation, that the circumstances of more and less, which are the proper subjects of

---

* Practical writers upon the fine arts will attempt any thing, being blind both to the difficulty and danger. De Piles, accounting why contrast is agreeable, says, "That it is a sort of war, which puts the opposite parties in motion." Thus, to account for an effect of which there is no doubt, any cause, however foolish, is made welcome. [Roger de Piles (1635–1709) studied philosophy, theology, and painting; he became secretary to the French ambassador in Venice, whom he had earlier taken on the Grand Tour, undertook diplomatic missions for Louis XIV, and became the leading art theorist of his day. *Abrégé de la vie des peintures* was published in 1699, and in English as *The Art of Painting,* 1706. The reference is to bk. 1: Introduction.]

† Chap. 2. part 5.

comparison, raise a perception so indistinct and vague as to facilitate the effect described: we have no mental standard of great and little, nor of the several degrees of any attribute; and the mind thus unrestrained, is naturally disposed to indulge its surprise to the utmost extent.

In exploring the operations of the mind, some of which are extremely nice and slippery, it is necessary to proceed with the utmost caution: and after all, seldom it happens that speculations of that kind afford any satisfaction. Luckily, in the present case, our speculations are supported by facts and solid argument. First, a small object of one species opposed to a great object of another, produces not, in any degree, that deception which is so remarkable when both objects are of the same species. The greatest disparity between objects of different kinds, is so common as to be observed with perfect indifference; but such disparity between objects of the same kind, being uncommon, never fails to produce surprise: and may we not fairly conclude, that surprise, in the latter case, is what occasions the deception, when we find no deception in the former? In the next place, if surprise be the sole cause of the deception, it follows necessarily, that the deception will vanish as soon as the objects compared become familiar. <290> This holds so unerringly, as to leave no reasonable doubt that surprise is the prime mover: our surprise is great the first time a small lapdog is seen with a large mastiff; but when two such animals are constantly together, there is no surprise, and it makes no difference whether they be viewed separately or in company: we set no bounds to the riches of a man who has recently made his fortune, the surprising disproportion between his present and his past situation being carried to an extreme; but with regard to a family that for many generations hath enjoy'd great wealth, the same false reckoning is not made: it is equally remarkable, that a trite simile has no effect; a lover compared to a moth scorching itself at the flame of a candle, originally a sprightly simile, has by frequent use lost all force; love cannot now be compared to fire, without some degree of disgust: it has been justly objected against Homer, that the lion is too often introduced into his similes; all the variety he is able to throw into them, not being sufficient to keep alive the reader's surprise.

To explain the influence of comparison upon the mind, I have chosen the simplest case, to wit, the first sight of two animals of the same kind, differing in size only; but to complete the theory, other circumstances must be taken in. And the next supposition I make, is where both animals, separately familiar to the spectator, are brought together for the first time. In that case, the ef-<291>fect of magnifying and diminishing, is found remarkably greater than in that first mentioned; and the reason will appear upon analysing the operation: the first feeling we have is of surprise at the uncommon difference of two creatures of the same species: we are next sensible, that the one appears less, the other larger, than they did formerly; and that new circumstance, increasing our surprise, makes us imagine a still greater opposition between the animals than if we had formed no notion of them beforehand.

I shall confine myself to one other supposition; That the spectator was acquainted beforehand with one of the animals only, the lapdog for example. This new circumstance will vary the effect; for instead of widening the natural difference, by enlarging in appearance the one animal, and diminishing the other in proportion, the whole apparent alteration will rest upon the lapdog: the surprise to find it less than it appeared formerly, directs to it our whole attention, and makes us conceive it to be a most diminutive creature: the mastiff in the mean time is quite overlooked. I am able to illustrate this effect by a familiar example. Take a piece of paper or of linen tolerably white, and compare it with a pure white of the same kind: the judgement we formed of the first object is instantly varied; and the surprise occasioned by finding it less white than was thought, produceth a <292> hasty conviction that it is much less white than it is in reality: withdrawing now the pure white, and putting in its place a deep black, the surprise occasioned by that new circumstance carries us to the other extreme, and makes us conceive the object first mentioned to be a pure white: and thus experience compels us to acknowledge, that our emotions have an influence even upon our eye-sight. This experiment leads to a general observation, That whatever is found more strange or beautiful than was expected, is judged to be more strange or beautiful than it is in reality. Hence a common artifice, to depreciate beforehand what we wish to make a figure in the opinion of others.

The comparisons employ'd by poets and orators, are of the kind last mentioned; for it is always a known object that is to be magnified or lessened. The former is effected by likening it to some grand object, or by contrasting it with one of an opposite character. To effectuate the latter, the method must be reversed: the object must be contrasted with something superior to it, or likened to something inferior. The whole effect is produced upon the principal object, which by that means is elevated above its rank, or depressed below it.

In accounting for the effect that any unusual resemblance or dissimilitude hath upon the mind, no cause has been mentioned but surprise; and to <293> prevent confusion, it was proper to discuss that cause first. But surprise is not the only cause of the effect described: another concurs, which operates perhaps not less powerfully, namely, a principle in human nature that lies still in obscurity, not having been unfolded by any writer, tho' its effects are extensive; and as it is not distinguished by a proper name, the reader must be satisfied with the following description. Every man who studies himself or others, must be sensible of a tendency or propensity in the mind, to complete every work that is begun, and to carry things to their full perfection. There is little opportunity to display that propensity upon natural operations, which are seldom left imperfect; but in the operations of art, it hath great scope: it impels us to persevere in our own work, and to wish for the completion of what another is doing: we feel a sensible pleasure when the work is brought to perfection; and our pain is no less sensible when we are disappointed. Hence our uneasiness, when an interesting story is broke off in the middle, when a piece of music ends without a close, or when a building or garden is left unfinished. The same propensity operates in making collections, such as the whole works good and bad of any author. A certain person attempted to collect prints of all the capital paintings, and succeeded except as to a few. La Bruyere remarks,[8] that an

---

8. Jean de La Bruyère (1645–96): French author, critic, and moralist. The reference is to Les Caractères, "De la Mode" ("Of Fashion").

anxious search was <294> made for these; not for their value, but to complete the set.* <295>

The final cause of the propensity is an additional proof of its existence: human works are of no significancy till they be completed; and reason is not always a sufficient counterbalance to indolence: some principle over and above is necessary, to excite our industry, and to prevent our stopping short in the middle of the course.

We need not lose time to describe the co-operation of the foregoing propensity with surprise, in producing the effect that follows any unusual

---

* The examples above given, are of things that can be carried to an end or conclusion. But the same uneasiness is perceptible with respect to things that admit not any conclusion; witness a series that has no end, commonly called *an infinite series*. The mind moving along such a series, begins soon to feel an uneasiness, which becomes more and more sensible, in continuing its progress without hope of an end.

An unbounded prospect doth not long continue agreeable: we soon feel a slight uneasiness, which increases with the time we bestow upon the prospect. An avenue without a terminating object, is one instance of an unbounded prospect; and we might hope to find the cause of its disagreeableness, if it resembled an infinite series. The eye indeed promises no resemblance; for the sharpest eye commands but a certain length of space, and there it is bounded, however obscurely. But the mind perceives things as they exist; and the line is carried on in idea without end; in which respect an unbounded prospect is similar to an infinite series. In fact, the uneasiness of an unbounded prospect, differs very little in its feeling from that of an infinite series; and therefore we may reasonably presume, that both proceed from the same cause.

We next consider a prospect unbounded every way, as, for example, a great plain or the ocean, viewed from an eminence. We feel here an uneasiness occasioned by the want of an end or termination, precisely as in the other cases. A prospect unbounded every way, is indeed so far singular, as at first to be more pleasant than a prospect that is unbounded in one direction only, and afterward to be more painful. But these circumstances are easily explained, without wounding the general theory: the pleasure we feel at first, is a vivid emotion of grandeur, arising from the immense extent of the object: and to increase the pain we feel afterward for the want of a termination, there concurs a pain of a different kind, occasioned by stretching the eye to comprehend so wide a prospect; a pain that gradually increases with the repeated efforts we make to grasp the whole.

It is the same principle, if I mistake not, which operates imperceptibly with respect to quantity and number. Another's property indented into my field, gives me uneasiness; and I am eager to make the purchase; not for profit, but in order to square my field. Xerxes and his army, in their passage to Greece, were sumptuously entertained by Pythius the Lydian: Xerxes recompensed him with 7000 Darics, which he wanted to complete the sum of four millions.

resemblance or dissimilitude. Surprise first operates, and carries our opinion of the resemblance or dissimilitude beyond truth. The propensity we have been describing carries us still farther; for it forces upon the mind a conviction, that the re-<296>semblance or dissimilitude is complete. We need no better illustration, than the resemblance that is fancied in some pebbles to a tree or an insect; which resemblance, however faint in reality, is conceived to be wonderfully perfect. The tendency to complete a resemblance acting jointly with surprise, carries the mind sometimes so far, as even to presume upon future events. In the Greek tragedy entitled *Phineides,* those unhappy women, seeing the place where it was intended they should be slain, cried out with anguish, "They now saw their cruel destiny had condemned them to die in that place, being the same where they had been exposed in their infancy."*

The propensity to advance every thing to its perfection, not only co-operates with surprise to deceive the mind, but of itself is able to produce that effect. Of this we see many instances where there is no place for surprise; and the first I shall give is of resemblance. *Unumquodque eodem modo dissolvitur quo colligatum est,*[9] is a maxim in the Roman law that has no foundation in truth; for tying and loosing, building and demolishing, are acts opposite to each other, and are performed by opposite means: but when these acts are connected by their relation to the same subject, their connection leads us to imagine a sort of resemblance between them, which by the foregoing pro-<297>pensity is conceived to be as complete as possible. The next instance shall be of contrast. Addison observes,† "That the palest features look the most agreeable in white;[10] that a face which is overflushed appears to advantage in the deepest scarlet; and that a dark complexion is not a little alleviated by a black hood." The foregoing propensity serves to account for these appearances; to make which evident, one of the cases shall suffice. A complexion, however dark, never approaches to black: when these

---

* Aristotle, *poet.* cap. 17. [*Poetics* xvi.]

† *Spectator,* No. 265.

9. "Any obligation is discharged in the same manner as that in which it was constituted"—for example, a verbal obligation may be discharged verbally.

10. Addison's text reads: "in white sarsanet," and "that the darkest complexion." Sarsanet is a fine silk material.

colours appear together, their opposition strikes us; and the propensity we have to complete the opposition, makes the darkness of complexion vanish out of sight.

The operation of this propensity, even where there is no ground for surprise, is not confined to opinion or conviction: so powerful it is, as to make us sometimes proceed to action in order to complete a resemblance or dissimilitude. If this appear obscure, it will be made clear by the following instances. Upon what principle is the *lex talionis*[11] founded, other than to make the punishment resemble the mischief? Reason dictates, that there ought to be a conformity or resemblance between a crime and its punishment; and the foregoing propensity impels us to make the resemblance as complete as possible. Titus Livius, under the influence of that propensity, accounts for <298> a certain punishment by a resemblance between it and the crime, too subtile for common apprehension. Treating of Mettus Fuffetius, the Alban general, who, for treachery to the Romans his allies, was sentenced to be torn to pieces by horses, he puts the following speech in the mouth of Tullus Hostilius, who decreed the punishment. "Mette Fuffeti, inquit, si ipse discere posses fidem ac foedera servare, vivo tibi ea disciplina a me adhibita esset. Nunc, quoniam tuum insanabile ingenium est, at tu tuo supplicio doce humanum genus, ea sancta credere, quae a te violata sunt. Ut igitur paulo ante animum inter Fidenatem Romanamque rem ancipitem gessisti, ita jam corpus passim distrahendum dabis."* By the same influence, the sentence is often executed upon the very spot where the crime was committed. In the *Electra* of Sophocles, Egistheus is dragged from the theatre into an inner room of the supposed palace, to suffer death where he murdered Agamemnon. Shakespear, whose knowledge of nature is no less profound than extensive, has not overlooked this propensity:

* Lib. I. § 28. ["Mettius Fufetius, if you were capable of learning, yourself, to keep faith and abide by treaties, you should have lived that I might teach you this; as it is, since your disposition is incurable, you shall yet by your punishment teach the human race to hold sacred the obligations you have violated. Accordingly, just as a little while ago your heart was divided between the states of Fidenae and Rome, so now you shall give up your body to be torn two ways."]

11. The law of retaliation, by which a person was made to suffer, as punishment for his offence, the same injury as that which he had inflicted, or attempted to inflict, upon another.

Othello. Get me some poison, Iago, this night; I'll not expostulate with her, lest her body and her beauty unprovide my mind again; this night, Iago.

Iago. Do it not with poison; strangle her in her bed, even in the bed she hath contaminated. <299>

Othello. Good, good: The justice of it pleases; very good.

Othello, act 4. *sc.* 5.[12]

Warwick. From off the gates of York fetch down the head,
Your father's head, which Clifford placed there.
Instead whereof let his supply the room.
Measure for measure must be answered.

Third Part of Henry VI. *act* 2. *sc.* 9.[13]

Persons in their last moments are generally seized with an anxiety to be buried with their relations. In the *Amynta* of Tasso, the lover, hearing that his mistress was torn to pieces by a wolf, expresses a desire to die the same death.*

Upon the subject in general I have two remarks to add. The first concerns resemblance, which, when too entire, hath no effect, however different in kind the things compared may be. The remark is applicable to works of art only; for natural objects of different kinds, have scarce ever an entire resemblance. To give an example in a work of art, marble is a sort of matter very different from what composes an animal; and marble cut into a human figure, produces great pleasure by the resemblance: but if a marble statue be coloured like a picture, the resemblance is so entire <300> as at a distance to make the statue appear a real person: we discover the mistake when we approach; and no other emotion is raised, but surprise occasioned by the deception: the figure still appears a real person, rather than an imitation; and we must use reflection to correct the mistake. This cannot happen in a picture; for the resemblance can never be so entire as to disguise the imitation.

The other remark relates to contrast. Emotions make the greatest figure

* Act 4. sc. 2.
12. Act 4, sc. 1.
13. Act 2, sc. 6.

when contrasted in succession; but the succession ought neither to be rapid, nor immoderately slow: if too slow, the effect of contrast becomes faint by the distance of the emotions; and if rapid, no single emotion has room to expand itself to its full size, but is stifled, as it were, in the birth by a succeeding emotion. The funeral oration of the Bishop of Meaux[14] upon the Duchess of Orleans, is a perfect hodge-podge of chearful and melancholy representations following each other in the quickest succession: opposite emotions are best felt in succession; but each emotion separately should be raised to its due pitch, before another be introduced.

What is above laid down, will enable us to determine a very important question concerning emotions raised by the fine arts, namely, Whether ought similar emotions to succeed each other, or dissimilar? The emotions raised by the fine arts, are for the most part too nearly related to make <301> a figure by resemblance; and for that reason, their succession ought to be regulated as much as possible by contrast. This holds confessedly in epic and dramatic compositions; and the best writers, led perhaps by taste more than by reasoning, have generally aimed at that beauty. It holds equally in music: in the same cantata, all the variety of emotions that are within the power of music, may not only be indulged, but, to make the greatest figure, ought to be contrasted. In gardening there is an additional reason for the rule: the emotions raised by that art, are at best so faint, that every artifice should be employ'd to give them their utmost vigour: a field may be laid out in grand, sweet, gay, neat, wild, melancholy scenes; and when these are viewed in succession, grandeur ought to be contrasted with neatness, regularity with wildness, and gaiety with melancholy, so as that each emotion may succeed its opposite: nay it is an improvement to intermix in the succession rude uncultivated spots as well as unbounded views, which in themselves are disagreeable, but in succession heighten the feeling of the agreeable objects; and we have nature for our guide, which in her most beautiful landscapes often intermixes rugged rocks, dirty marshes, and barren stony heaths. The greatest masters of music have the same view in their compositions: the second part of an Italian song, seldom conveys any sentiment;

---

14. Jacques Benigne Bossuet (1627–1704): court theologian to Louis XIV and subsequently bishop of Meaux.

and, by its harshness, seems pur-<302>posely contrived to give a greater relish for the interesting parts of the composition.

A small garden comprehended under a single view, affords little opportunity for that embellishment. Dissimilar emotions require different tones of mind; and therefore in conjunction can never be pleasant:* gaiety and sweetness may be combined, or wildness and gloominess; but a composition of gaiety and gloominess is distasteful. The rude uncultivated compartment of furze and broom in Richmond garden,[15] hath a good effect in the succession of objects; but a spot of that nature would be insufferable in the midst of a polished parterre or flower-plot. A garden therefore, if not of great extent, admits not dissimilar emotions; and in ornamenting a small garden, the safest course is to confine it to a single expression. For the same reason, a landscape ought also to be confined to a single expression; and accordingly it is a rule in painting, That if the subject be gay, every figure ought to contribute to that emotion.

It follows from the foregoing train of reasoning, that a garden near a great city ought to have an air of solitude. The solitariness again of a waste country ought to be contrasted in forming a garden; no temples, no obscure walks; but *jets d'eau,* cascades, objects active, gay and splendid. Nay such a garden should in some measure avoid <303> imitating nature, by taking on an extraordinary appearance of regularity and art, to show the busy hand of man, which in a waste country has a fine effect by contrast.

It may be gathered from what is said above,† that wit and ridicule make not an agreeable mixture with grandeur. Dissimilar emotions have a fine effect in a slow succession; but in a rapid succession, which approaches to coexistence, they will not be relished: in the midst of a laboured and elevated description of a battle, Virgil introduces a ludicrous image, which is certainly out of its place:

---

* See chap. 2. part 4.

† Chap. 2. part 4.

15. The Royal Park at Richmond was designed in 1725 by Charles Bridgeman (1680–1738), who became Royal Gardener in 1728, was much involved with the gardens at Stowe from 1714 until 1738, and was greatly admired by George II and Prime Minister Robert Walpole (1676–1745). He is regarded as the first specialist English garden designer.

Obvius ambustum torrem Chorinaeus ab ara
Corripit, et venienti Ebuso plagamque ferenti
Occupat os flammis: illi ingens barba reluxit,
Nidoremque ambusta dedit.   *Aen.* xii. 298.[16]

The following image is no less ludicrous, nor less improperly placed.

Mentre fan questi i bellici stromenti
Perche debbiano tosto in uso porse,
Il gran nemico de l'humane genti
Contra i Christiani i lividi occhi torse:
E lor veggendo à le bell' opre intenti,
Ambo le labra per furor si morse; <304>
E qual tauro ferito, il suo dolore
Verso mugghiando e sospirando fuore.

Gerusal. cant. 4. *st.* 1.[17]

It would however be too austere, to banish altogether ludicrous images from an epic poem. This poem doth not always soar above the clouds: it admits great variety; and upon occasion can descend even to the ground without sinking. In its more familiar tones, a ludicrous scene may be introduced without impropriety. This is done by Virgil* in a foot-race; the

---

* *Aen.* lib. 5.

16. Priest Chorinaeus arm'd his better Hand,
    From his own Altar, with a blazing Brand;
    And, as Ebusus with a thund'ring Pace
    Advanc'd to Battel, dash'd it on his Face:
    His bristly Beard shines out with sudden Fires . . .
                        (trans. Dryden, xii.450)

17. While thus their worke went on with luckie speed,
    And reared rammes their horned fronts aduance,
    The ancient foe to man, and mortal seed,
    His wannish eies upon them bent askance;
    And when he saw their labours well succeed,
    He wept for rage, and threat'ned dire mischance,
    He chok't his curses, to himselfe he spake,
    Such noise wilde buls, that softly bellow make.
       (*Gerusalemme Liberata,* trans. Edward Fairfax)

circumstances of which, not excepting the ludicrous part, are copied from Homer.* After a fit of merriment, we are, it is true, the less disposed to the serious and sublime: but then, a ludicrous scene, by unbending the mind from severe application to more interesting subjects, may prevent fatigue, and preserve our relish entire. <305>

* *Iliad,* book 23. l. 879.

Uniformity and Variety

In attempting to explain uniformity and variety, in order to show how we are affected by these circumstances, a doubt occurs, what method ought to be followed. In adhering close to the subject, I foresee difficulties; and yet by indulging such a circuit as may be necessary for a satisfactory view, I probably shall incur the censure of wandering.—Yet the dread of censure, ought not to prevail over what is proper: beside that the intended circuit will lead to some collateral matters, that are not only curious, but of considerable importance in the science of human nature.

The necessary succession of perceptions may be examined in two different views; one with respect to order and connection, and one with respect to uniformity and variety. In the first view it is handled above:* and I now proceed to the second. The world we inhabit is replete with things no less remarkable for their variety than for their number: these, unfolded by the wonderful <306> mechanism of external sense, furnish the mind with many perceptions; which, joined with ideas of memory, of imagination, and of reflection, form a complete train that has not a gap or interval. This train of perceptions and ideas, depends very little on will. The mind, as has been observed,† is so constituted, "That it can by no effort break off the succession of its ideas, nor keep its attention long fixt upon the same object": we can arrest a perception in its course; we can shorten its natural duration, to make room for another; we can vary the succession by change

---

* Chap. 1.
† Locke, book 2. chap. 14. [*Essay Concerning Human Understanding*, II.14. This is not a direct quotation.]

of place or of amusement; and we can in some measure prevent variety, by frequently recalling the same object after short intervals: but still there must be a succession, and a change from one perception to another. By artificial means, the succession may be retarded or accelerated, may be rendered more various or more uniform, but in one shape or other is unavoidable.

The train, even when left to its ordinary course, is not always uniform in its motion: there are natural causes that accelerate or retard it considerably. The first I shall mention, is a peculiar constitution of mind. One man is distinguished from another, by no circumstance more remarkably, than his train of perceptions: to a cold languid temper belongs a slow course of perceptions, <307> which occasions dulness of apprehension and sluggishness in action: to a warm temper, on the contrary, belongs a quick course of perceptions, which occasions quickness of apprehension and activity in business. The Asiatic nations, the Chinese especially, are observed to be more cool and deliberate than the Europeans: may not the reason be, that heat enervates by exhausting the spirits? and that a certain degree of cold, as in the middle regions of Europe, bracing the fibres, rouseth the mind, and produceth a brisk circulation of thought, accompanied with vigour in action?[1] In youth is observable a quicker succession of perceptions than in old age: and hence, in youth, a remarkable avidity for variety of amusements, which in riper years give place to more uniform and more sedate occupation. This qualifies men of middle age for business, where activity is required, but with a greater proportion of uniformity than variety. In old age, a slow and languid succession makes variety unnecessary; and for that reason, the aged, in all their motions, are generally governed by an habitual uniformity. Whatever be the cause, we may venture to pronounce, that heat in the imagination and temper, is always connected with a brisk flow of perceptions.

The natural rate of succession, depends also, in some degree, upon the particular perceptions that compose the train. An agreeable object, taking

---

1. A reference to debate about Montesquieu's views in *L'Esprit des Lois,* pt. 3 (1748; English trans. *The Spirit of the Laws,* 1750). Charles de Secondat, baron de Montesquieu (1689–1755), noble landowner and parliamentary magistrate, studied law in Paris and Bordeaux and visited England, where his writings were admired, 1729–31 to study its politics.

<308> a strong hold of the mind, occasions a slower succession than when the objects are indifferent: grandeur and novelty fix the attention for a considerable time, excluding all other ideas: and the mind thus occupied is sensible of no vacuity. Some emotions, by hurrying the mind from object to object, accelerate the succession. Where the train is composed of connected perceptions or ideas, the succession is quick; for it is so ordered by nature, that the mind goes easily and sweetly along connected objects.* On the other hand, the succession must be slow, where the train is composed of unconnected perceptions or ideas, which find not ready access to the mind; and that an unconnected object is not admitted without a struggle, appears from the unsettled state of the mind for some moments after such an object is presented, wavering between it and the former train: during that short period, one or other of the former objects will intrude, perhaps oftener than once, till the attention be fixt entirely upon the new object. The same observations are applicable to ideas suggested by language: the mind can bear a quick succession of related ideas; but an unrelated idea, for which the mind is not prepared, takes time to make an impression; and therefore a train composed of such ideas, ought to proceed with a slow pace. Hence an epic poem, a play, <309> or any story connected in all its parts, may be perused in a shorter time, than a book of maxims or apothegms, of which a quick succession creates both confusion and fatigue.

Such latitude hath nature indulged in the rate of succession: what latitude it indulges with respect to uniformity, we proceed to examine. The uniformity or variety of a train, so far as composed of perceptions, depends on the particular objects that surround the percipient at the time. The present occupation must also have an influence; for one is sometimes engaged in a multiplicity of affairs, sometimes altogether vacant. A natural train of ideas of memory is more circumscribed, each object being, by some connection, linked to what precedes and to what follows it: these connections, which are many, and of different kinds, afford scope for a sufficient degree of variety; and at the same time prevent that degree which is unpleasant by excess. Temper and constitution also have an influence here, as well as upon the rate of succession: a man of a calm and sedate temper, admits not will-

* See chap. 1.

ingly any idea but what is regularly introduced by a proper connection: one of a roving disposition embraces with avidity every new idea, however slender its relation be to those that preceded it. Neither must we overlook the nature of the perceptions that compose the train; for their influence is no less with respect to uniformity and variety, than with <310> respect to the rate of succession. The mind engrossed by any passion, love or hatred, hope or fear, broods over its object, and can bear no interruption; and in such a state, the train of perceptions must not only be slow, but extremely uniform. Anger newly inflamed eagerly grasps its object, and leaves not a cranny in the mind for another thought but of revenge. In the character of Hotspur, that state of mind is represented to the life; a picture remarkable for likeness as well as for high colouring.

> *Worcester.* Peace, cousin, say no more.
> And now I will unclasp a secret book,
> And to your quick-conceiving discontents
> I'll read you matter, deep and dangerous;
> As full of peril and advent'rous spirit
> As to o'erwalk a current roaring loud,
> On the unsteadfast footing of a spear.
> *Hotspur.* If he fall in, good night. Or sink or swim,
> Send danger from the east into the west,
> So honour cross it from the north to south;
> And let them grapple. Oh! the blood more stirs
> To rouse a lion than to start a hare.
> *Worcester.* Those same Noble Scots,
> That are your prisoners—
> *Hotspur.* I'll keep them all;
> By Heav'n, he shall not have a Scot of them:
> No, if a Scot would save his soul, he shall not;
> I'll keep them, by this hand.
> *Worcester.* You start away. <311>
> And lend no ear unto my purposes;
> Those pris'ners you shall keep.
> *Hotspur.* I will, that's flat:
> He said, he would not ransom Mortimer;
> Forbade my tongue to speak of Mortimer:

But I will find him when he lies asleep,
And in his ear I'll holla *Mortimer!*
Nay, I will have a starling taught to speak
Nothing but *Mortimer,* and give it him,
To keep his anger still in motion.
   Worcester. Hear you, cousin, a word.
   Hotspur. All studies here I solemnly defy,
Save how to gall and pinch this Bolingbroke:
And that same sword-and-buckler Prince of Wales,
(But that I think his father loves him not,
And would be glad he met with some mischance),
I'd have him poison'd with a pot of ale.
   Worcester. Farewel, my kinsman, I will talk to you
When you are better temper'd to attend.

First part, Henry IV. *act* I. *sc.* 4.[2]

Having view'd a train of perceptions as directed by nature, and the variations it is susceptible of from different necessary causes, we proceed to examine how far it is subjected to will; for that this faculty hath some influence, is observed above. And first, the rate of succession may be retarded by insisting upon one object, and propelled by dismissing another before its time. But such voluntary mutations in the natural course of succession, have limits that cannot be extended by the most painful efforts: which will appear from con-<312>sidering, that the mind circumscribed in its capacity, cannot, at the same instant, admit many perceptions; and when replete, that it hath not place for new perceptions, till others are removed; consequently that a voluntary change of perceptions cannot be instantaneous, as the time it requires sets bounds to the velocity of succession. On the other hand, the power we have to arrest a flying perception, is equally limited: and the reason is, that the longer we detain any perception, the more difficulty we find in the operation; till, the difficulty becoming unsurmountable, we are forc'd to quit our hold, and to permit the train to take its usual course.

The power we have over this train as to uniformity and variety, is in some

---

2. Act I, sc. 2.

cases very great, in others very little. A train composed of perceptions of external objects, depends entirely on the place we occupy, and admits not more nor less variety but by change of place. A train composed of ideas of memory, is still less under our power; because we cannot at will call up any idea that is not connected with the train.* But a train of ideas suggested by reading, may be varied at will, provided we have books at hand.

The power that nature hath given us over our train of perceptions, may be greatly strengthened by proper discipline, and by an early application <313> to business; witness some mathematicians, who go far beyond common nature in slowness and uniformity; and still more persons devoted to religious exercises, who pass whole days in contemplation, and impose upon themselves long and severe penances. With respect to celerity and variety, it is not easily conceived what length a habit of activity in affairs will carry some men. Let a stranger, or let any person to whom the sight is not familiar, attend the chancellor of Great Britain through the labours but of one day, during a session of parliament: how great will be his astonishment! what multiplicity of law-business, what deep-thinking, and what elaborate application to matters of government! The train of perceptions must in that great man be accelerated far beyond the ordinary course of nature: yet no confusion or hurry; but in every article the greatest order and accuracy. Such is the force of habit. How happy is man, to have the command of a principle of action that can elevate him so far above the ordinary condition of humanity!†

We are now ripe for considering a train of perceptions, with respect to pleasure and pain: and to that speculation peculiar attention must be given, because it serves to explain the effects that uniformity and variety have upon the mind. A <314> man, when his perceptions flow in their natural course, feels himself free, light, and easy, especially after any forcible acceleration or retardation. On the other hand, the accelerating or retarding the natural course, excites a pain, which, tho' scarcely felt in small removes, becomes considerable toward the extremes. Aversion to fix on a single object for a

---

* See chap. 1.

† This chapter was composed in the year 1753. [The Earl of Hardwicke was lord chancellor in 1753.]

long time, or to take in a multiplicity of objects in a short time, is remarkable in children; and equally so in men unaccustomed to business: a man languishes when the succession is very slow; and, if he grow not impatient, is apt to fall asleep: during a rapid succession, he hath a feeling as if his head were turning round; he is fatigued, and his pain resembles that of weariness after bodily labour.

But a moderate course will not satisfy the mind, unless the perceptions be also diversified: number without variety is not sufficient to constitute an agreeable train. In comparing a few objects, uniformity is pleasant; but the frequent reiteration of uniform objects becomes unpleasant: one tires of a scene that is not diversified; and soon feels a sort of unnatural restraint when confined within a narrow range, whether occasioned by a retarded succession or by too great uniformity. An excess in variety is, on the other hand, fatiguing: which is felt even in a train of related perceptions; much more of unrelated perceptions, which gain not admittance without effort: the effort, it is true, <315> is scarce perceptible in a single instance; but by frequent reiteration it becomes exceedingly painful. Whatever be the cause, the fact is certain, that a man never finds himself more at ease, than when his perceptions succeed each other with a certain degree, not only of velocity, but also of variety. The pleasure that arises from a train of connected ideas, is remarkable in a reverie; especially where the imagination interposeth, and is active in coining new ideas, which is done with wonderful facility: one must be sensible, that the serenity and ease of the mind in that state, makes a great part of the enjoyment. The case is different where external objects enter into the train; for these, making their appearance without order, and without connection save that of contiguity, form a train of perceptions that may be extremely uniform or extremely diversified; which, for opposite reasons, are both of them painful.

To alter, by an act of will, that degree of variety which nature requires, is not less painful, than to alter that degree of velocity which it requires. Contemplation, when the mind is long attached to one subject, becomes painful by restraining the free range of perception: curiosity, and the prospect of useful discoveries, may fortify one to bear that pain: but it is deeply felt by the bulk of mankind, and produceth in them aversion to all abstract sciences. In any profession or calling, a train of operation that is simple and reitera-<316>ted without intermission, makes the operator languish, and lose vigour: he complains neither of too great labour, nor of too little action; but regrets the want of variety, and the being obliged to do the same thing over and over: where the operation is sufficiently varied, the mind retains its vigour, and is pleased with its condition. Actions again create uneasiness when excessive in number or variety, tho' in every other respect pleasant: thus a throng of business in law, in physic, or in traffic, distresses and distracts the mind, unless where a habit of application is acquired by long and constant exercise: the excessive variety is the distressing circumstance; and the mind suffers grievously by being kept constantly upon the stretch.

With relation to involuntary causes disturbing that degree of variety which nature requires, a slight pain affecting one part of the body without variation, becomes, by its constancy and long duration, almost insupportable: the patient, sensible that the pain is not increased in degree, complains of its constancy more than of its severity, of its engrossing his whole thoughts, and admitting no other object. A shifting pain is more tolerable, because change of place contributes to variety: and an intermitting pain, suffering other objects to intervene, still more so. Again, any single colour or sound often returning becomes unpleasant; as may be observed in viewing a train of similar <317> apartments in a great house painted with the same colour, and in hearing the prolonged tollings of a bell. Colour and sound varied within certain limits, tho' without any order, are pleasant; witness the various colours of plants and flowers in a field, and the various notes of birds in a thicket: increase the number or variety, and the feeling becomes unpleasant; thus a great variety of colours, crowded upon a small canvas or in quick succession, create an uneasy feeling, which is prevented by putting the colours at a greater distance from each other either of place or of time. A number of voices in a crowded assembly, a number of animals collected in a market, produce an unpleasant feeling; tho' a few of them together, or all of them in a moderate succession, would be pleasant. And because of the same excess in variety, a number of pains felt in different parts of the body, at the same instant or in a rapid succession, are an exquisite torture.

The pleasure or pain resulting from a train of perceptions in different circumstances, are a beautiful contrivance of nature for valuable purposes.

But being sensible, that the mind, inflamed with speculations so highly interesting, is beyond measure disposed to conviction; I shall be watchful to admit no argument nor remark, but what appears solidly founded; and with that caution I proceed to unfold these purposes. It is occasionally observed above, that persons of a phlegmatic tempera-<318>ment, having a sluggish train of perceptions, are indisposed to action; and that activity constantly accompanies a brisk flow of perceptions. To ascertain that fact, a man need not go abroad for experiments: reflecting on things passing in his own mind, he will find, that a brisk circulation of thought constantly prompts him to action; and that he is averse to action when his perceptions languish in their course. But as man by nature is formed for action, and must be active in order to be happy, nature hath kindly provided against indolence, by annexing pleasure to a moderate course of perceptions, and by making any remarkable retardation painful. A slow course of perceptions, is attended with another bad effect: man, in a few capital cases, is governed by propensity or instinct; but in matters that admit deliberation and choice, reason is assigned him for a guide: now, as reasoning requires often a great compass of ideas, their succession ought to be so quick as readily to furnish every motive that may be necessary for mature deliberation; in a languid succession, motives will often occur after action is commenced, when it is too late to retreat.

Nature hath guarded man, her favourite, against a succession too rapid, no less carefully than against one too slow: both are equally painful, tho' the pain is not the same in both. Many are the good effects of that contrivance. In the first place, as the exertion of bodily faculties is by certain pain-<319>ful sensations confined within proper limits, Nature is equally provident with respect to the nobler faculties of the mind: the pain of an accelerated course of perceptions, is Nature's admonition to relax our pace, and to admit a more gentle exertion of thought. Another valuable purpose is discovered upon reflecting in what manner objects are imprinted on the mind: to give the memory firm hold of an external object, time is required, even where attention is the greatest; and a moderate degree of attention, which is the common case, must be continued still longer to produce the same effect: a rapid succession, accordingly, must prevent objects from making an impression so deep as to be of real service in life; and Nature, for the sake of memory, has by a painful feeling guarded against a rapid succession. But a still more valuable purpose is answered by the contrivance; as, on the one hand, a sluggish course of perceptions indisposeth to action; so, on the other, a course too rapid impels to rash and precipitant action: prudent conduct is the child of deliberation and clear conception, for which there is no place in a rapid course of thought. Nature therefore, taking measures for prudent conduct, has guarded us effectually from precipitancy of thought, by making it painful.

Nature not only provides against a succession too slow or too quick, but makes the middle course extremely pleasant. Nor is that course confined <320> within narrow bounds: every man can naturally, without pain, accelerate or retard in some degree the rate of his perceptions. And he can do it in a still greater degree by the force of habit: a habit of contemplation annihilates the pain of a retarded course of perceptions; and a busy life, after long practice, makes acceleration pleasant.

Concerning the final cause of our taste for variety, it will be considered, that human affairs, complex by variety as well as number, require the distributing our attention and activity in measure and proportion. Nature therefore, to secure a just distribution corresponding to the variety of human affairs, has made too great uniformity or too great variety in the course of perceptions, equally unpleasant: and indeed, were we addicted to either extreme, our internal constitution would be ill suited to our external circumstances. At the same time, where great uniformity of operation is required as in several manufactures, or great variety as in law or physic, Nature, attentive to all our wants, hath also provided for these cases, by implanting in the breast of every person, an efficacious principle that leads to habit: an obstinate perseverance in the same occupation, relieves from the pain of excessive uniformity; and the like perseverance in a quick circulation of different occupations, relieves from the pain of excessive variety. And thus we come to take delight in several occu-<321>pations, that by nature, without habit, are not a little disgustful.

A middle rate also in the train of perceptions between uniformity and variety, is no less pleasant than between quickness and slowness. The mind of man, so framed, is wonderfully adapted to the course of human affairs, which are continually changing, but not without connection: it is equally adapted to the acquisition of knowledge, which results chiefly from discovering resemblances among differing objects, and differences among resembling objects: such occupation, even abstracting from the knowledge we acquire, is in itself delightful, by preserving a middle rate between too great uniformity and too great variety.

We are now arrived at the chief purpose of the present chapter; which is to consider uniformity and variety with relation to the fine arts, in order to discover if we can, when it is that the one ought to prevail, and when the other. And the knowledge we have obtained, will even at first view suggest a general observation, That in every work of art, it must be agreeable, to find that degree of variety which corresponds to the natural course of our perceptions; and that an excess in variety or in uniformity must be disagreeable, by varying that natural course. For that reason, works of art admit more or less variety according to the nature of the subject: in a picture of an interesting event that strongly attaches the spectator to a <322> single object, the mind relisheth not a multiplicity of figures nor of ornaments: a picture representing a gay subject, admits great variety of figures and ornaments; because these are agreeable to the mind in a chearful tone. The same observation is applicable to poetry and to music.

It must at the same time be remarked, that one can bear a greater variety of natural objects, than of objects in a picture; and a greater variety in a picture, than in a description. A real object presented to view, makes an impression more readily than when represented in colours, and much more readily than when represented in words. Hence it is, that the profuse variety of objects in some natural landscapes, neither breed confusion nor fatigue: and for the same reason, there is place for greater variety of ornament in a picture than in a poem. A picture however, like a building, ought to be so simple as to be comprehended in one view. Whether every one of Le Brun's pictures of Alexander's history will stand this test, is submitted to judges.[3]

From these general observations, I proceed to particulars. In works exposed continually to public view, variety ought to be studied. It is a rule accordingly in sculpture, to contrast the different limbs of a statue, in order

3. Le Brun's series of paintings for Versailles under the title "Battles of Alexander": see <101> above.

to give it all the variety possible. Tho' the cone in a single view, be more beautiful than the pyramid; yet a pyramidal steeple, because of its variety, is justly preferred. For the same reason, the oval is prefer-<323>red before the circle; and painters, in copying buildings or any regular work, give an air of variety, by representing the subject in an angular view: we are pleased with the variety, without losing sight of the regularity. In a landscape representing animals, those especially of the same kind, contrast ought to prevail: to draw one sleeping, another awake; one sitting, another in motion; one moving toward the spectator, another from him, is the life of such a performance.

In every sort of writing intended for amusement, variety is necessary in proportion to the length of the work. Want of variety is sensibly felt in Davila's history of the civil wars of France:[4] the events are indeed important and various; but the reader languishes by a tiresome monotony of character, every person engaged being figured a consummate politician, governed by interest only. It is hard to say, whether Ovid disgusts more by too great variety, or too great uniformity: his stories are all of the same kind, concluding invariably with the transformation of one being into another; and so far he is tiresome by excess in uniformity: he is not less fatiguing by excess in variety, hurrying his reader incessantly from story to story. Ariosto is still more fatiguing than Ovid, by exceeding the just bounds of variety: not satisfied, like Ovid, with a succession in his stories, he distracts the reader, by jumbling together a multitude of them without any connection. Nor is the Orlan-<324>do Furioso less tiresome by its uniformity than the Metamorphoses, tho' in a different manner: after a story is brought to a crisis, the reader, intent on the catastrophe, is suddenly snatch'd away to a new story, which makes no impression so long as the mind is occupied with the former. This tantalizing method, from which the author never once swerves during the course of a long work, beside its uniformity, hath another bad effect: it prevents that sympathy, which is raised by an interesting event when the reader meets with no interruption.

The emotions produced by our perceptions in a train, have been little

---

4. Enrico Caterino Davila, *Historia della guerre civili di Francia,* 1630 (trans. into English 1647).

considered, and less understood; the subject therefore required an elaborate discussion. It may surprise some readers, to find variety treated as only contributing to make a train of perceptions pleasant, when it is commonly held to be a necessary ingredient in beauty of whatever kind; according to the definition, "That beauty consists in uniformity amid variety."[5] But after the subject is explained and illustrated as above, I presume it will be evident, that this definition, however applicable to one or other species, is far from being just with respect to beauty in general: variety contributes no share to the beauty of a moral action, nor of a mathematical theorem: and numberless are the beautiful objects of sight that have little or no variety in them; a globe, the most uniform of all figures, is of all the most <325> beautiful; and a square, tho' more beautiful than a trapezium, hath less variety in its constituent parts. The foregoing definition, which at best is but obscurely expressed, is only applicable to a number of objects in a group or in succession, among which indeed a due mixture of uniformity and variety is always agreeable; provided the particular objects, separately considered, be in any degree beautiful, for uniformity amid variety among ugly objects, affords no pleasure. This circumstance is totally omitted in the definition; and indeed to have mentioned it, would at the very first glance have shown the definition to be imperfect: for to define beauty as arising from beautiful objects blended together in a due proportion of uniformity and variety, would be too gross to pass current; as nothing can be more gross, than to employ in a definition the very term that is to be explained.

5. The reference is to Francis Hutcheson, *An Inquiry into the Original of Our Ideas of Beauty and Virtue; in Two Treatises,* London, 1725, where the phrase is usually "uniformity amidst variety": for example, Treatise 1, sect. 2. Hutcheson (1694–1746) was professor of moral philosophy at Glasgow University, and Kames, like Adam Smith (1723–90) and David Hume (1711–76), was familiar with his philosophical work.

APPENDIX TO CHAPTER IX

Concerning the Works of Nature, chiefly with respect to Uniformity and Variety.

In things of Nature's workmanship, whether we regard their internal or external structure, beauty and design are equally conspicuous. We <326> shall begin with the outside of nature, as what first presents itself.

The figure of an organic body, is generally regular. The trunk of a tree, its branches, and their ramifications are nearly round, and form a series regularly decreasing from the trunk to the smallest fibre: uniformity is no where more remarkable than in the leaves, which, in the same species, have all the same colour, size, and shape: the seeds and fruits are all regular figures, approaching for the most part to the globular form. Hence a plant, especially of the larger kind, with its trunk, branches, foliage, and fruit, is a charming object.

In an animal, the trunk, which is much larger than the other parts, occupies a chief place: its shape, like that of the stem of plants, is nearly round; a figure which of all is the most agreeable: its two sides are precisely similar: several of the under parts go off in pairs; and the two individuals of each pair are accurately uniform: the single parts are placed in the middle: the limbs, bearing a certain proportion to the trunk, serve to support it, and to give it a proper elevation: upon one extremity are disposed the neck and head, in the direction of the trunk: the head being the chief part, possesses with great propriety the chief place. Hence, the beauty of the whole figure, is the result of many equal and proportional parts orderly disposed; and the smallest variation in num-<327>ber, equality, proportion, or order, never fails to produce a perception of deformity.

Nature in no particular seems more profuse of ornament, than in the beautiful colouring of her works. The flowers of plants, the furs of beasts, and the feathers of birds, vie with each other in the beauty of their colours, which in lustre as well as in harmony are beyond the power of imitation. Of all natural appearances, the colouring of the human face is the most exquisite: it is the strongest instance of the ineffable art of nature, in adapting and proportioning its colours to the magnitude, figure, and position, of the parts. In a word, colour seems to live in nature only, and to languish under the finest touches of art.

When we examine the internal structure of a plant or animal, a wonderful subtility of mechanism is display'd. Man, in his mechanical operations, is confined to the surface of bodies; but the operations of nature are exerted through the whole substance, so as to reach even the elementary parts. Thus the body of an animal, and of a plant, are composed of certain great vessels; these of smaller; and these again of still smaller, without end, as far as we can discover. This power of diffusing mechanism through the most intimate parts, is peculiar to nature; and distinguishes her operations, most remarkably, from every work of art. Such texture, continued from the grosser parts to the most minute, preserves all along the <328> strictest regularity: the fibres of plants are a bundle of cylindric canals, lying in the same direction, and parallel or nearly parallel to each other: in some instances, a most accurate arrangement of parts is discovered, as in onions, formed of concentric coats one within another to the very centre. An animal body is still more admirable, in the disposition of its internal parts, and in their order and symmetry: there is not a bone, a muscle, a bloodvessel, a nerve, that hath not one corresponding to it on the opposite side; and the same order is carried through the most minute parts: the lungs are composed of two parts, which are disposed upon the sides of the thorax; and the kidneys, in a lower situation, have a position no less orderly: as to the parts that are single, the heart is advantageously situated near the middle: the liver, stomach, and spleen, are disposed in the upper region of the abdomen, about the same height: the bladder is placed in the middle of the body; as well as the intestinal canal, which fills the whole cavity with its convolutions.

The mechanical power of nature, not confined to small bodies, reacheth equally those of the greatest size; witness the bodies that compose the solar system, which, however large, are weighed, measured, and subjected to certain laws, with the utmost accuracy. Their places round the sun, with their distances, are determined by a precise rule, corresponding to their quantity of matter. <329> The superior dignity of the central body, in respect of its bulk and lucid appearance, is suited to the place it occupies. The globular figure of these bodies, is not only in itself beautiful, but is above all others fitted for regular motion. Each planet revolves about its own axis in a given time; and each moves round the sun, in an orbit nearly circular, and in a time proportioned to its distance. Their velocities, directed by an established law, are perpetually changing by regular accelerations and retardations. In fine, the great variety of regular appearances, joined with the beauty of the system itself, cannot fail to produce the highest delight in every one who is sensible of design, power, or beauty.

Nature hath a wonderful power of connecting systems with each other, and of propagating that connection through all her works. Thus the constituent parts of a plant, the roots, the stem, the branches, the leaves, the fruit, are really different systems, united by a mutual dependence on each other: in an animal, the lymphatic and lacteal ducts, the blood-vessels and nerves, the muscles and glands, the bones and cartilages, the membranes and bowels, with the other organs, form distinct systems, which are united into one whole. There are, at the same time, other connections less intimate: every plant is joined to the earth by its roots; it requires rain and dews to furnish it with juices; and it requires heat to preserve these juices in fluidity and motion: every animal, by its <330> gravity, is connected with the earth, with the element in which it breathes, and with the sun, by deriving from it cherishing and enlivening heat: the earth furnisheth aliment to plants, these to animals, and these again to other animals, in a long train of dependence: that the earth is part of a greater system, comprehending many bodies mutually attracting each other, and gravitating all toward one common centre, is now thoroughly explored. Such a regular and uniform series of connections, propagated through so great a number of beings, and through such wide spaces, is wonderful: and our wonder must increase, when we observe these connections propagated from the minutest atoms to bodies of the most enormous size, and so widely diffused as that we can neither perceive their beginning nor their end. That these connections are not confined within our own planetary system, is certain: they are diffused over spaces still more remote, where new bodies and systems rise without end. All space is filled with the works of God, which are conducted by one plan, to answer unerringly one great end.

But the most wonderful connection of all, tho' not the most conspic-

uous, is that of our internal frame with the works of nature: man is obviously fitted for contemplating these works, because in this contemplation
he has great delight. The works of nature are remarkable in their uniformity
no less than in their variety; and the mind of <331> man is fitted to receive
pleasure equally from both. Uniformity and variety are interwoven in the
works of nature with surprising art: variety, however great, is never without
some degree of uniformity; nor the greatest uniformity without some degree of variety: there is great variety in the same plant, by the different
appearances of its stem, branches, leaves, blossoms, fruit, size, and colour;
and yet, when we trace that variety through different plants, especially of
the same kind, there is discovered a surprising uniformity: again, where
nature seems to have intended the most exact uniformity, as among individuals of the same kind, there still appears a diversity, which serves readily
to distinguish one individual from another. It is indeed admirable, that the
human visage, in which uniformity is so prevalent, should yet be so marked,
as to leave no room, among millions, for mistaking one person for another:
these marks, though clearly perceived, are generally so delicate, that words
cannot be found to describe them. A correspondence so perfect between
the human mind and the works of nature, is extremely remarkable. The
opposition between variety and uniformity is so great, that one would not
readily imagine they could both be relished by the same palate; at least not
in the same object, nor at the same time: it is however true, that the pleasures
they afford, being happily adjusted to each other, and readily mixing in in-
<332>timate union, are frequently produced by the same individual object.
Nay, further, in the objects that touch us the most, uniformity and variety
are constantly combined; witness natural objects, where this combination
is always found in perfection. Hence it is, that natural objects readily form
themselves into groups, and are agreeable in whatever manner combined:
a wood with its trees, shrubs, and herbs, is agreeable: the music of birds,
the lowing of cattle, and the murmuring of a brook, are in conjunction
delightful; tho' they strike the ear without modulation or harmony. In
short, nothing can be more happily accommodated to the inward constitution of man, than that mixture of uniformity with variety, which the eye
discovers in natural objects; and, accordingly, the mind is never more highly
gratified than in contemplating a natural landscape. <333>

ಠಠ CHAPTER X ಠಠ

Congruity and Propriety

Man is superior to the brute, not more by his rational faculties, than by his senses. With respect to external senses, brutes probably yield not to men; and they may also have some obscure perception of beauty: but the more delicate senses of regularity, order, uniformity, and congruity, being connected with morality and religion, are reserved to dignify the chief of the terrestrial creation. Upon that account, no discipline is more suitable to man, nor more *congruous* to the dignity of his nature, than that which refines his taste, and leads him to distinguish in every subject, what is regular, what is orderly, what is suitable, and what is fit and proper.* <334>

It is clear from the very conception of the terms *congruity* and *propriety,* that they are not applicable to any single object: they imply a plurality, and

---

* Nec vero illa parva vis naturae est rationisque, quod unum hoc animal sentit quid sit ordo, quid sit quod deceat in factis dictisque, qui modus. Itaque eorum ipsorum, quae aspectu sentiuntur, nullum aliud animal, pulchritudinem, venustatem, convenientiam partium sentit. Quam similitudinem natura ratioque ab oculis ad animum transferens, multo etiam magis pulchritudinem, constantiam, ordinem, in consiliis factisque conservandum putat, cavetque ne quid indecorè effeminatève faciat; tum in omnibus et opinionibus et factis ne quid libidinosè aut faciat aut cogitet. Quibus ex rebus conflatur et efficitur id, quod quaerimus, honestum. *Cicero de officiis, l.* 1. [I.iv.14: "And it is no mean manifestation of Nature and Reason that man is the only animal that has a feeling for order, for propriety, for moderation in word and deed. And so no other animal has a sense of beauty, loveliness, harmony in the visible world; and Nature and Reason, extending the analogy of this from the world of sense to the world of spirit, find that beauty, consistency, order are far more to be maintained in thought and deed, and the same Nature and Reason are careful to do nothing in an improper or unmanly fashion, and in every thought and deed to do or think nothing capriciously. It is from these elements that is forged and fashioned that moral goodness which is the subject of this inquiry."]

obviously signify a particular *relation* between different objects. Thus we say currently, that a decent garb is suitable or *proper* for a judge, modest behaviour for a young woman, and a lofty style for an epic poem: and, on the other hand, that it is unsuitable or *incongruous* to see a little woman sunk in an overgrown farthingale, a coat richly embroidered covering coarse and dirty linen, a mean subject in an elevated style, an elevated subject in a mean style, a first minister darning his wife's stocking, or a reverend prelate in lawn sleeves dancing a hornpipe.

The perception we have of this relation, which seems peculiar to man, cannot proceed from any other cause, but from a *sense* of congruity or propriety; for supposing us destitute of that sense, the terms would to us be unintelligible.* <335>

It is matter of experience, that congruity or propriety, where-ever perceived, is agreeable; and that incongruity or impropriety, where-ever perceived, is disagreeable. The only difficulty is, to ascertain what are the particular objects that in conjunction suggest these relations; for there are many objects that do not: the sea, for example, view'd in conjunction with

---

* From many things that pass current in the world without being generally condemned, one at first view would imagine, that the sense of congruity or propriety hath scarce any foundation in nature; and that it is rather an artificial refinement of those who affect to distinguish themselves from others. The fulsome panegyrics bestow'd upon the great and opulent, in epistles dedicatory and other such compositions, would incline us to think so. Did there prevail in the world, it will be said, or did nature suggest, a taste of what is suitable, decent, or proper, would any good writer deal in such compositions, or any man of sense receive them without disgust? Can it be supposed, that Lewis XIV. of France was endued by nature with any sense of propriety, when, in a dramatic performance purposely composed for his entertainment, he suffered himself, publicly and in his presence, to be styled the greatest king ever the earth produced? [All of the operas by Jean-Baptiste Lully (1632–87) at the Palais Royal from 1673 to 1686 were preceded by a prologue glorifying Louis XIV. Similarly, Molière's *Le Malade Imaginaire*, with ballet and *entractes* by Marc-Antoine Charpentier (1643–1704), ends its laudatory prologue with the words "Louis, Louis, Louis, the greatest of Kings." Followers of Jean-Philippe Rameau (1683–1764) in the 1740s fiercely rejected such features and provoked bitter rivalry between supporters of French and Italian opera.] These it is true are strong facts; but luckily they do not prove the sense of propriety to be artificial: they only prove, that the sense of propriety is at times overpowered by pride and vanity; which is no singular case, for that sometimes is the fate even of the sense of justice.

a picture, or a man view'd in conjunction with a mountain, suggest not either congruity or incongruity. It seems natural to infer, what will be found true by induction, that we never perceive congruity nor incongruity but among things that are connected by <336> some relation; such as a man and his actions, a principal and its accessories, a subject and its ornaments. We are indeed so framed by nature, as among things so connected, to require a certain suitableness or correspondence, termed *congruity* or *propriety;* and to be displeased when we find the opposite relation of *incongruity* or *impropriety.**

If things connected be the subject of congruity, it is reasonable beforehand to expect a degree of congruity proportioned to the degree of the connection. And upon examination we find our expectation to be well founded: where the relation is intimate, as between a cause and its effect, a <337> whole and its parts, we require the strictest congruity; but where the relation is slight, or accidental, as among things jumbled together, we require little or no congruity: the strictest propriety is required in behaviour and manner of living; because a man is connected with these by the relation of cause and effect: the relation between an edifice and the ground it stands upon, is of the most intimate kind, and therefore the situation of a great house ought to be lofty: its relation to neighbouring hills, rivers, plains, being that of propinquity only, demands but a small share of congruity: among members of the same club, the congruity ought to be considerable, as well as among things placed for show in the same niche: among passen-

---

* In the chapter of beauty, qualities are distinguished into primary and secondary: and to clear some obscurity that may appear in the text, it is proper to be observed, that the same distinction is applicable to relations. Resemblance, equality, uniformity, proximity, are relations that depend not on us, but exist equally whether perceived or not; and upon that account may justly be termed *primary* relations. But there are other relations, that only appear such to us, and that have not any external existence like primary relations; which is the case of congruity, incongruity, propriety, impropriety: these may be properly termed *secondary* relations. Thus it appears from what is said in the text, that the secondary relations mentioned, arise from objects connected by some primary relation. Property is an example of a secondary relation, as it exists no where but in the mind. I purchase a field or a horse: the covenant makes the primary relation; and the secondary relation built on it, is property.

gers in a stage-coach, we require very little congruity; and less still at a public spectacle.

Congruity is so nearly allied to beauty as commonly to be held a species of it; and yet they differ so essentially, as never to coincide: beauty, like colour, is placed upon a single subject; congruity upon a plurality: further, a thing beautiful in itself, may, with relation to other things, produce the strongest sense of incongruity.

Congruity and propriety are commonly reckoned synonymous terms; and hitherto in opening the subject they have been used indifferently: but they are distinguishable; and the precise meaning of each must be ascertained. Congruity is the ge-<338>nus, of which propriety is a species; for we call nothing *propriety*, but that congruity or suitableness, which ought to subsist between sensible beings and their thoughts, words, and actions.

In order to give a full view of these secondary relations, I shall trace them through some of the most considerable primary relations. The relation of a part to the whole, being extremely intimate, demands the utmost degree of congruity: even the slightest deviation is disgustful; witness the *Lutrin*, a burlesque poem, which is closed with a serious and warm panegyric on Lamoignon, one of the king's judges:

> ———— ———— Amphora coepit
> Institui; currente rota, cur urceus exit?[1]

Examples of congruity and incongruity are furnished in plenty by the relation between a subject and its ornaments. A literary performance intended merely for amusement, is susceptible of much ornament, as well as a music-room or a play-house; for in gaiety, the mind hath a peculiar relish for show and decoration. The most gorgeous apparel, however improper in tragedy, is not unsuitable to opera-actors: the truth is, an opera, in its present form, is a mighty fine thing; but as it deviates from nature in its capital circumstances, we look not for nature nor propriety in those which are accessory. On the other hand, a <339> serious and important subject

---

1. Horace *Ars Poetica* 22: "That was meant to be a wine-jar, when the wheel first turned; why has it ended up as a pitcher?"

admits not much ornament;* nor a subject that of itself is extremely beautiful: and a subject that fills the mind with its loftiness and grandeur, appears best in a dress altogether plain.

To a person of a mean appearance, gorgeous apparel is unsuitable; which, beside the incongruity, shows by contrast the meanness of appearance in the strongest light. Sweetness of look and manner requires simplicity of dress joined with the greatest elegance. A stately and majestic air requires sumptuous apparel, which ought not to be gaudy, nor crowded with little ornaments. A woman of consummate beauty can bear to be highly adorned, and yet shows best in a plain dress

———— ———— For loveliness
Needs not the foreign aid of ornament,
But is when unadorn'd, adorn'd the most.

Thomson's Autumn, 208.[2]

Congruity regulates not only the quantity of ornament, but also the kind. The decorations of a <340> dancing-room ought all of them to be gay. No picture is proper for a church, but what has religion for its subject. Every ornament upon a shield should relate to war; and Virgil, with great judgement, confines the carvings upon the shield of Aeneas, to the military history of the Romans: that beauty is overlooked by Homer; for the bulk of the sculpture upon the shield of Achilles, is of the arts of peace in general, and of joy and festivity in particular: the author[3] of Telemachus betrays the same inattention, in describing the shield of that young hero.

In judging of propriety with regard to ornaments, we must attend, not

---

* Contrary to this rule, the introduction to the third volume of the *Characteristics,* is a continued chain of metaphors: these in such profusion are too florid for the subject; and have beside the bad effect of removing our attention from the principal subject, to fix it upon splendid trifles. [Anthony Ashley Cooper, Earl of Shaftesbury (1671–1713), philosopher and moralist, critic of Hobbes, friend of Locke, and much admired by Scottish thinkers. His *Characteristics of Men, Manners, Opinions, Times* was published in 1711.]

2. James Thomson (1700–1748): poet and dramatist. Born in Scotland, he moved to London, where several of his works were set to music.

3. François de Salignac de la Mothe-Fénelon (1651–1715): theologian, author and critic, archbishop of Cambrai. *Télémaque* (1699) is a prose narrative.

only to the nature of the subject that is to be adorned, but also to the circumstances in which it is placed: the ornaments that are proper for a ball, will appear not altogether so decent at public worship: and the same person ought to dress differently for a marriage-feast and for a funeral.

Nothing is more intimately related to a man, than his sentiments, words, and actions; and therefore we require here the strictest conformity. When we find what we thus require, we have a lively sense of propriety: when we find the contrary, our sense of impropriety is no less lively. Hence the universal distaste of affectation, which consists in making a shew of greater delicacy and refinement, than is suited either to the character or circumstances of the person. Nothing in epic <341> or dramatic compositions is more disgustful than impropriety of manners. In Corneille's tragedy of *Cinna*, Aemilia, a favourite of Augustus, receives daily marks of his affection, and is loaded with benefits: yet all the while is laying plots to assassinate her benefactor, directed by no other motive but to avenge her father's death:* revenge against a benefactor, founded solely upon filial piety, cannot be directed by any principle but that of justice, and therefore never can suggest unlawful means; yet the crime here attempted, a treacherous murder, is what even a miscreant will scarce attempt against his bitterest enemy.

What is said might be thought sufficient to explain the relations of congruity and propriety. And yet the subject is not exhausted: on the contrary, the prospect enlarges upon us, when we take under view the effects these relations produce in the mind. Congruity and propriety, where-ever perceived, appear agreeable; and every agreeable object produceth in the mind a pleasant emotion: incongruity and impropriety, on the other hand, are disagreeable; and of course produce painful emotions. These emotions, whether pleasant or painful, sometimes vanish without any consequence; but more frequently occasion other emotions, to which I proceed.

When any slight incongruity is perceived in an <342> accidental combination of persons or things, as of passengers in a stage-coach, or of individuals dining at an ordinary;[4] the painful emotion of incongruity, after a momentary existence, vanisheth without producing any effect. But this

* See act I. sc. 2.
4. A tavern or eating house where public meals are provided at a fixed price.

is not the case of propriety and impropriety: voluntary acts, whether words or deeds, are imputed to the author; when proper, we reward him with our esteem; when improper, we punish him with our contempt. Let us suppose, for example, a generous action suited to the character of the author, which raises in him and in every spectator the pleasant emotion of propriety: this emotion generates in the author both self-esteem and joy; the former when he considers his relation to the action, and the latter when he considers the good opinion that others will entertain of him: the same emotion of propriety, produceth in the spectators, esteem for the author of the action; and when they think of themselves, it also produceth, by contrast, an emotion of humility. To discover the effects of an unsuitable action, we must invert each of these circumstances: the painful emotion of impropriety, generates in the author of the action both humility and shame; the former when he considers his relation to the action, and the latter when he considers what others will think of him: the same emotion of impropriety, produceth in the spectators, contempt for the author of the action; and it also produceth, by contrast when they think of <343> themselves, an emotion of self-esteem. Here then are many different emotions, derived from the same action considered in different views by different persons; a machine provided with many springs, and not a little complicated. Propriety of action, it would seem, is a favourite of nature, or of the author of nature, when such care and solicitude is bestow'd on it. It is not left to our own choice; but, like justice, is required at our hands; and, like justice, is enforced by natural rewards and punishments: a man cannot, with impunity, do any thing unbecoming or improper; he suffers the chastisement of contempt inflicted by others, and of shame inflicted by himself. An apparatus so complicated, and so singular, ought to rouse our attention: for nature doth nothing in vain; and we may conclude with certainty, that this curious branch of the human constitution is intended for some valuable purpose. To the discovery of that purpose or final cause I shall with ardour apply my thoughts, after discoursing a little more at large upon the punishment, as it may now be called, that nature hath provided for indecent and unbecoming behaviour. This, at any rate, is necessary, in order to give a full view of the subject; and who knows whether it may not, over and above, open some track that will lead us to the final cause we are in quest of?

A gross impropriety is punished with contempt and indignation, which are vented against the of-<344>fender by external expressions: nor is even the slightest impropriety suffered to pass without some degree of contempt. But there are improprieties of the slighter kind, that provoke laughter; of which we have examples without end in the blunders and absurdities of our own species: such improprieties receive a different punishment, as will appear by what follows. The emotions of contempt and of laughter occasioned by an impropriety of that kind, uniting intimately in the mind of the spectator, are expressed externally by a peculiar sort of laugh, termed *a laugh of derision* or *scorn*.* An impropriety that thus moves not only contempt but laughter, is distinguished by the epithet of *ridiculous;* and a laugh of derision or scorn is the punishment provided for it by nature. Nor ought it to escape observation, that we are so fond of inflicting that punishment, as sometimes to exert it even against creatures of an inferior species: witness a turkeycock swelling with pride, and strutting with display'd feathers, which in a gay mood is apt to provoke a laugh of derision.

We must not expect, that these different improprieties are separated by distinct boundaries: for of improprieties, from the slightest to the most gross, from the most risible to the most serious, there are degrees without end. Hence it is, that in viewing some unbecoming actions, too risible <345> for anger, and too serious for derision, the spectator feels a sort of mixt emotion, partaking both of derision and of anger; which accounts for an expression, common with respect to the impropriety of some actions, That we know not whether to laugh or be angry.

It cannot fail to be observed, that in the case of a risible impropriety, which is always slight, the contempt we have for the offender is extremely faint, tho' derision, its gratification, is extremely pleasant. This disproportion between a passion and its gratification, may seem not conformable to the analogy of nature. In looking about for a solution, I reflect upon what is laid down above, that an improper action, not only moves our contempt for the author, but also, by means of contrast, swells the good opinion we have of ourselves. This contributes, more than any other particular, to the pleasure we have in ridiculing follies and absurdities; and accordingly, it is

* See chap. 7.

well known, that those who have the greatest share of vanity, are the most prone to laugh at others. Vanity, which is a vivid passion, pleasant in itself and not less so in its gratification, would singly be sufficient to account for the pleasure of ridicule, without borrowing any aid from contempt. Hence appears the reason of a noted observation, That we are the most disposed to ridicule the blunders and absurdities of others, when we are in high spirits; <346> for in high spirits, self-conceit displays itself with more than ordinary vigour.

Having with wary steps traced an intricate road, not without danger of wandering; what remains to complete our journey, is to account for the final cause of congruity and propriety, which make so great a figure in the human constitution. One final cause, regarding congruity, is pretty obvious, that the sense of congruity, as one principle of the fine arts, contributes in a remarkable degree to our entertainment; which is the final cause assigned above for our sense of proportion,* and need not be enlarged upon here. Congruity indeed with respect to quantity, coincides with proportion: when the parts of a building are nicely adjusted to each other, it may be said indifferently, that it is agreeable by the congruity of its parts, or by the proportion of its parts. But propriety, which regards voluntary agents only, can never be the same with proportion: a very long nose is disproportioned, but cannot be termed *improper.* In some instances, it is true, impropriety coincides with disproportion in the same subject, but never in the same respect. I give for an example a very little man buckled to a long toledo:[5] considering the man and the sword with respect to size, we perceive a disproportion: considering the sword as <347> the choice of the man, we perceive an impropriety.

The sense of impropriety with respect to mistakes, blunders, and absurdities, is evidently calculated for the good of mankind. In the spectators it is productive of mirth and laughter, excellent recreation in an interval from business. But this is a trifle compared to what follows. It is painful to be the subject of ridicule; and to punish with ridicule the man who is guilty of an absurdity, tends to put him more on his guard in time coming. It is

---

* See chap. 3.

5. A sword made at Toledo, Spain.

well ordered that even the most innocent blunder is not committed with impunity; because, were errors licensed where they do no hurt, inattention would grow into habit, and be the occasion of much hurt.

The final cause of propriety as to moral duties, is of all the most illustrious. To have a just notion of it, the moral duties that respect others must be distinguished from those that respect ourselves. Fidelity, gratitude, and abstinence from injury, are examples of the first sort; temperance, modesty, firmness of mind, are examples of the other: the former are made duties by the sense of justice; the latter, by the sense of propriety. Here is a final cause of the sense of propriety, that will rouse our attention. It is undoubtedly the interest of every man, to suit his behaviour to the dignity of his nature, and to the station allotted him by Providence; for such rational conduct contributes <348> in every respect to happiness, by preserving health, by procuring plenty, by gaining the esteem of others, and, which of all is the greatest blessing, by gaining a justly-founded self-esteem. But in a matter so essential to our well-being, even self-interest is not relied on: the powerful authority of duty is superadded to the motive of interest. The God of nature, in all things essential to our happiness, hath observed one uniform method: to keep us steady in our conduct, he hath fortified us with natural laws and principles, preventive of many aberrations, which would daily happen were we totally surrendered to so fallible a guide as is human reason. Propriety cannot rightly be considered in another light, than as the natural law that regulates our conduct with respect to ourselves; as justice is the natural law that regulates our conduct with respect to others. I call propriety a law, no less than justice; because both are equally rules of conduct that *ought* to be obey'd: propriety includes that obligation; for to say an action is proper, is in other words to say, that it *ought* to be performed; and to say it is improper, is in other words to say, that it *ought* to be forborne. It is that very character of *ought* and *should* which makes justice a law to us; and the same character is applicable to propriety, tho' perhaps more faintly than to justice: but the difference is in degree only, not in kind; and we ought, without hesita-<349>tion or reluctance, to submit equally to the government of both.

But I have more to urge upon that head. To the sense of propriety as well as of justice, are annexed the sanctions of rewards and punishments;

which evidently prove the one to be a law as well as the other. The satisfaction a man hath in doing his duty, joined to the esteem and good-will of others, is the reward that belongs to both equally. The punishments also, tho' not the same, are nearly allied; and differ in degree more than in quality. Disobedience to the law of justice is punished with remorse; disobedience to the law of propriety, with shame, which is remorse in a lower degree. Every transgression of the law of justice raises indignation in the beholder; and so doth every flagrant transgression of the law of propriety. Slighter improprieties receive a milder punishment: they are always rebuked with some degree of contempt, and frequently with derision. In general, it is true, that the rewards and punishments annexed to the sense of propriety, are slighter in degree than those annexed to the sense of justice: which is wisely ordered, because duty to others is still more essential to society, than duty to ourselves: society indeed could not subsist a moment, were individuals not protected from the headstrong and turbulent passions of their neighbours.

The final cause now unfolded of the sense of propriety, must, to every discerning eye, appear <350> delightful: and yet this is but a partial view; for that sense reaches another illustrious end, which is, in conjunction with the sense of justice to enforce the performance of social duties. In fact, the sanctions visibly contrived to compel a man to be just to himself, are equally serviceable to compel him to be just to others; which will be evident from a single reflection, That an action, by being unjust, ceases not to be improper: an action never appears more eminently improper, than when it is unjust: it is obviously becoming, and suitable to human nature, that each man do his duty to others; and accordingly every transgression of duty to others, is at the same time a transgression of duty to one's self. This is a plain truth without exaggeration; and it opens a new and enchanting view in the moral landscape, the prospect being greatly enriched by the multiplication of agreeable objects. It appears now, that nothing is overlooked, nothing left undone, that can possibly contribute to the enforcing social duty; for to all the sanctions that belong to it singly, are superadded the sanctions of self-duty. A familiar example shall suffice for illustration. An act of ingratitude, considered in itself, is to the author disagreeable, as well as to every spectator: considered by the author with relation to himself, it raises self-contempt: considered by him with relation to the world, it makes him ashamed: considered by others, it raises their contempt and indignation <351> against the author. These feelings are all of them occasioned by the impropriety of the action. When the action is considered as unjust, it occasions another set of feelings: in the author it produces remorse, and a dread of merited punishment; and in others, the benefactor chiefly, indignation and hatred directed to the ungrateful person. Thus shame and remorse united in the ungrateful person, and indignation united with hatred in the hearts of others, are the punishments provided by nature for injustice. Stupid and insensible must he be, who, in a contrivance so exquisite, perceives not the benevolent hand of our Creator.[6] <352>

---

6. First edition reads: "perceives not the hand of the Sovereign Architect."

Dignity and Grace[1]

The terms *dignity* and *meanness* are applied to man in point of character, sentiment, and behaviour: we say, for example, of one man, that he hath natural dignity in his air and manner; of another, that he makes a mean figure: we perceive dignity in every action and sentiment of some persons; meanness and vulgarity in the actions and sentiments of others. With respect to the fine arts, some performances are said to be manly and suitable to the dignity of human nature; others are termed low, mean, trivial. Such expressions are common, tho' they have not always a precise meaning. With respect to the art of criticism, it must be a real acquisition to ascertain what these terms truly import; which possibly may enable us to rank every performance in the fine arts according to its dignity.

Enquiring first to what subjects the terms *dignity* and *meanness* are appropriated, we soon discover, that they are not applicable to any thing inanimate: the most magnificent palace that ever was built, may be lofty, may be grand, but it has <353> no relation to dignity: the most diminutive shrub may be little, but it is not mean. These terms must belong to sensitive beings, probably to man only; which will be evident when we advance in the enquiry.

Human actions appear in many different lights: in themselves they appear grand or little; with respect to the author, they appear proper or improper; with respect to those affected by them, just or unjust: and I now add, that they are also distinguished by dignity and meanness. If any one incline to think, that with respect to human actions, dignity coincides with

1. First edition: "Dignity and Meanness."

grandeur, and meanness with littleness, the difference will be evident upon reflecting, that an action may be grand without being virtuous, and little without being faulty; but that we never attribute dignity to any action but what is virtuous, nor meanness to any but what is faulty. Every action of dignity creates respect and esteem for the author; and a mean action draws upon him contempt. A man is admired for a grand action, but frequently is neither loved nor esteemed for it: neither is a man always contemned for a low or little action. The action of Caesar passing the Rubicon was grand; but there was no dignity in it, considering that his purpose was to enslave his country: Caesar, in a march, taking opportunity of a rivulet to quench his thirst, did a low action, but the action was not mean. <354>

As it appears to me, dignity and meanness are founded on a natural principle not hitherto mentioned. Man is endued with a SENSE of the worth and excellence of his nature: he deems it more perfect than that of the other beings around him; and he perceives, that the perfection of his nature consists in virtue, particularly in virtues of the highest rank. To express that sense, the term *dignity* is appropriated. Further, to behave with dignity, and to refrain from all mean actions, is felt to be, not a virtue only, but a duty: it is a duty every man owes to himself. By acting in that manner, he attracts love and esteem: by acting meanly, or below himself, he is disapproved and contemned.

According to the description here given of dignity and meanness, they appear to be a species of propriety and impropriety. Many actions may be proper or improper, to which dignity or meanness cannot be applied: to eat when one is hungry, is proper, but there is no dignity in that action: revenge fairly taken, if against law, is improper, but not mean. But every action of dignity is also proper, and every mean action is also improper.

This sense of the dignity of human nature, reaches even our pleasures and amusements: if they enlarge the mind by raising grand or elevated emotions, or if they humanize the mind by exercising our sympathy, they are approved as suited to the dignity of our nature: if they con-<355>tract the mind by fixing it on trivial objects, they are contemned as not suited to the dignity of our nature. Hence in general, every occupation, whether of use or amusement, that corresponds to the dignity of man, is termed *manly;* and every occupation below his nature, is termed *childish.*

To those who study human nature, there is a point which has always appeared intricate: How comes it that generosity and courage are more esteemed and bestow more dignity, than good-nature, or even justice; tho' the latter contribute more than the former to private as well as to public happiness? This question, bluntly proposed, might puzzle a cunning philosopher; but, by means of the foregoing observations, will easily be solved. Human virtues, like other objects, obtain a rank in our estimation, not from their utility, which is a subject of reflection, but from the direct impression they make on us. Justice and good-nature are a sort of negative virtues, that scarce make any impression but when they are transgressed: courage and generosity, on the contrary, producing elevated emotions, enliven greatly the sense of a man's dignity, both in himself and in others; and for that reason, courage and generosity are in higher regard than the other virtues mentioned: we describe them as grand and elevated, as of greater dignity, and more praiseworthy.

This leads us to examine more directly emotions <356> and passions with respect to the present subject: and it will not be difficult to form a scale of them, beginning with the meanest, and ascending gradually to those of the highest rank and dignity. Pleasure felt as at the organ of sense, named *corporeal pleasure,* is perceived to be low; and when indulged to excess, is perceived also to be mean: for that reason, persons of any delicacy dissemble the pleasure they take in eating and drinking. The pleasures of the eye and ear, having no organic feeling* and being free from any sense of meanness, are indulged without any shame: they even rise to a certain degree of dignity when their objects are grand or elevated. The same is the case of the sympathetic passions: a virtuous person behaving with fortitude and dignity under cruel misfortunes, makes a capital figure; and the sympathising spectator feels in himself the same dignity. Sympathetic distress at the same time never is mean: on the contrary, it is agreeable to the nature of a social being, and has general approbation. The rank that love possesses in the scale, depends in a great measure on its object: it possesses a low place when founded on external properties merely; and is mean when bestow'd on a person of inferior rank without any extraordinary qualification: but

---

* See the Introduction.

when founded on the more elevated internal properties, it assumes a con-<357>siderable degree of dignity. The same is the case of friendship. When gratitude is warm, it animates the mind; but it scarce rises to dignity. Joy bestows dignity when it proceeds from an elevated cause.

If I can depend upon induction, dignity is not a property of any disagreeable passion: one is slight, another severe; one depresses the mind, another animates it; but there is no elevation, far less dignity, in any of them. Revenge, in particular, tho' it enflame and swell the mind, is not accompanied with dignity, not even with elevation: it is not however felt as mean or groveling, unless when it takes indirect measures for gratification. Shame and remorse, tho' they sink the spirits, are not mean. Pride, a disagreeable passion, bestows no dignity in the eye of a spectator. Vanity always appears mean; and extremely so where founded, as commonly happens, on trivial qualifications.

I proceed to the pleasures of the understanding, which possess a high rank in point of dignity. Of this every one will be sensible, when he considers the important truths that have been laid open by science; such as general theorems, and the general laws that govern the material and moral worlds. The pleasures of the understanding are suited to man as a rational and contemplative being; and they tend not a little to ennoble his nature; even to the Deity he stretcheth his contemplations, <358> which, in the discovery of infinite power, wisdom, and benevolence, afford delight of the most exalted kind. Hence it appears, that the fine arts studied as a rational science, afford entertainment of great dignity; superior far to what they afford as a subject of taste merely.

But contemplation, however in itself valuable, is chiefly respected as subservient to action; for man is intended to be more an active than a contemplative being. He accordingly shows more dignity in action than in contemplation: generosity, magnanimity, heroism, raise his character to the highest pitch: these best express the dignity of his nature, and advance him nearer to divinity than any other of his attributes.

By every production that shows art and contrivance, our curiosity is excited upon two points; first, how it was made; and next, to what end. Of the two, the latter is the more important enquiry, because the means are ever subordinate to the end; and in fact, our curiosity is always more enflamed by the *final* than by the *efficient* cause. This preference is no where more visible, than in contemplating the works of nature: if in the efficient cause wisdom and power be display'd, wisdom is no less conspicuous in the final cause; and from it only can we infer benevolence, which of all the divine attributes is to man the most important. <359>

Having endeavoured to assign the efficient cause of dignity and meanness, by unfolding the principle on which they are founded, we proceed to explain the final cause of the dignity or meanness bestowed upon the several particulars above mentioned, beginning with corporeal pleasures. These, as far as useful, are, like justice, fenced with sufficient sanctions to prevent their being neglected: hunger and thirst are painful sensations; and we are incited to animal love by a vigorous propensity: were corporeal pleasures dignified over and above with a place in a high class, they would infallibly disturb the balance of the mind, by outweighing the social affections. This is a satisfactory final cause for refusing to these pleasures any degree of dignity: and the final cause is no less evident of their meanness, when they are indulged to excess. The more refined pleasures of external sense, convey'd by the eye and the ear from natural objects and from the fine arts, deserve a high place in our esteem, because of their singular and extensive utility: in some cases they rise to a considerable dignity; and the very lowest pleasures of the kind are never esteemed mean or groveling. The pleasure arising from wit, humour, ridicule, or from what is simply ludicrous, is useful, by relaxing the mind after the fatigue of more manly occupation: but the mind, when it surrenders itself to pleasure of that kind, loses its vi-<360>gor, and sinks gradually into sloth.* The place this pleasure occupies in point of dignity, is adjusted to these views: to make it useful as a relaxation, it is not branded with meanness; to prevent its usurpation, it is

---

* Neque enim ita generati à natura sumus, ut ad ludum et jocum facti esse videamur, sed ad severitatem potius et ad quaedam studia graviora atque majora. Ludo autem et joco, uti illis quidem licet sed sicut somno et quietibus caeteris, tum cum gravibus seriisque rebus satisfecerimus. *Cicero de offic. lib.* 1. [*De Officiis* I.29.103: "For Nature has not brought us into the world to act as if we were created for play and jest, but rather for earnestness and for some more serious and important pursuits. We may, of course, indulge in sport and jest, but in the same way as we enjoy sleep or other relaxations, and only when we have satisfied the claims of our earnest, serious tasks."]

removed from that place but a single degree: no man values himself for that pleasure, even during gratification; and if it have engrossed more of his time than is requisite for relaxation, he looks back with some degree of shame.

In point of dignity, the social emotions rise above the selfish, and much above those of the eye and ear: man is by his nature a social being; and to qualify him for society, it is wisely contrived, that he should value himself more for being social than selfish.*

The excellency of man is chiefly discernible in the great improvements he is susceptible of in society: these, by perseverance, may be carried on progressively above any assignable limits; and, <361> even abstracting from revelation, there is great probability, that the progress begun here will be completed in some future state. Now, as all valuable improvements proceed from the exercise of our rational faculties, the author of our nature, in order to excite us to a due use of these faculties, hath assigned a high rank to the pleasures of the understanding: their utility, with respect to this life as well as a future, intitles them to that rank.

But as action is the aim of all our improvements, virtuous actions justly possess the highest of all the ranks. These, we find, are by nature distributed into different classes, and the first in point of dignity assigned to actions that appear not the first in point of use: generosity, for example, in the sense of mankind is more respected than justice, tho' the latter is undoubtedly more essential to society; and magnanimity, heroism, undaunted courage, rise still higher in our esteem. One would readily think, that the moral virtues should be esteemed according to their importance. Nature has here deviated from her ordinary path, and great wisdom is shown in the deviation: the efficient cause is explained above, and the final cause is explained in the Essays of morality and natural religion.†

---

* For the same reason, the selfish emotions that are founded upon a social principle, rise higher in our esteem than those that are founded upon a selfish principle. As to which see above, p. 47. note.

† Part 1. essay 2. chap. 4.

We proceed[2] to analyse *grace,* which being in <362> a good measure an uncultivated field, requires more than ordinary labour.

Graceful is an attribute: *grace* and *gracefulness* express that attribute in the form of a noun.

That this attribute is agreeable, no one doubts.

As grace is display'd externally, it must be an object of one or other of our five senses. That it is an object of sight, every person of taste can bear witness; and that it is confined to that sense, appears from induction; for it is not an object of smell, nor of taste, nor of touch. Is it an object of hearing? Some music indeed is termed graceful; but that expression is metaphorical, as when we say of other music that it is beautiful: the latter metaphor, at the same time, is more sweet and easy; which shows how little applicable to music or to sound the former is, when taken in its proper sense.

That it is an attribute of man, is beyond dispute. But of what other beings is it also an attribute? We perceive at first sight that nothing inanimate is entitled to that epithet. What animal then, beside man, is entitled? Surely, not an elephant, nor even a lion. A horse may have a delicate shape with a lofty mien, and all his motions may be exquisite; but he is never said to be graceful. Beauty and grandeur are common to man with some other beings: but dignity is not apply'd to any being inferior to man; and upon <363> the strictest examination, the same appears to hold in grace.

Confining then grace to man, the next enquiry is, whether like beauty it make a constant appearance, or in some circumstances only. Does a person display this attribute at rest as well as in motion, asleep as when awake? It is undoubtedly connected with motion; for when the most graceful person is at rest, neither moving nor speaking, we lose sight of that quality as much as of colour in the dark. Grace then is an agreeable attribute, inseparable from motion as opposed to rest, and as comprehending speech, looks, gestures, and loco-motion.

As some motions are homely, the opposite to graceful, the next enquiry is, with what motions is this attribute connected? No man appears graceful in a mask; and therefore, laying aside the expressions of the countenance,

2. The text from here to the end of the chapter did not appear in the first edition.

the other motions may be genteel, may be elegant, but of themselves never are graceful. A motion adjusted in the most perfect manner to answer its end, is elegant; but still somewhat more is required to complete our idea of grace or gracefulness.

What this unknown *more* may be, is the nice point. One thing is clear from what is said, that this *more* must arise from the expressions of the countenance: and from what expressions so naturally as from those which indicate mental qualities, such as sweetness, benevolence, elevation, digni-<364>ty? This promises to be a fair analysis; because of all objects mental qualities affect us the most; and the impression made by graceful appearance upon every spectator of taste, is too deep for any cause purely corporeal.

The next step is, to examine what are the mental qualities, that in conjunction with elegance of motion, produce a graceful appearance. Sweetness, chearfulness, affability, are not separately sufficient, nor even in conjunction. As it appears to me, dignity alone with elegant motion may produce a graceful appearance; but still more graceful, with the aid of other qualities, those especially that are the most exalted.

But this is not all. The most exalted virtues may be the lot of a person whose countenance has little expression: such a person cannot be graceful. Therefore to produce this appearance, we must add another circumstance, namely, an expressive countenance, displaying to every spectator of taste, with life and energy, every thing that passes in the mind.

Collecting these circumstances together, grace may be defined, that agreeable appearance which arises from elegance of motion and from a countenance expressive of dignity. Expressions of other mental qualities, are not essential to that appearance, but they heighten it greatly.

Of all external objects, a graceful person is the most agreeable. <365>

Dancing affords great opportunity for displaying grace, and haranguing still more.

I conclude with the following reflection, That in vain will a person attempt to be graceful, who is deficient in amiable qualities. A man, it is true, may form an idea of qualities he is destitute of; and, by means of that idea, may endeavour to express these qualities by looks and gestures: but such studied expression will be too faint and obscure to be graceful. <366>

Ridicule

To define ridicule, has puzzled and vexed every critic. The definition given by Aristotle is obscure and imperfect.* Cicero handles it at great length;† but without giving any satisfaction: he wanders in the dark, and misses the distinction between risible and ridiculous. Quintilian is sensible of the distinction,‡ but has not attempted to explain it. Luckily this subject lies no longer in obscurity: a risible object produceth an emotion of laughter merely:§ a ridiculous object is improper as well as risible; and produceth a mixt emotion, which is vented by a laugh of derision or scorn.‖

Having therefore happily unravelled the knotty part, I proceed to other particulars.

Burlesque, tho' a great engine of ridicule, is not confined to that subject; for it is clearly dis-<367>tinguishable into burlesque that excites laughter merely, and burlesque that provokes derision or ridicule. A grave subject in which there is no impropriety, may be brought down by a certain colouring so as to be risible; which is the case of *Virgil Travestie;*¶ and also the case

---

* *Poet.* cap. 5. [*Poetics* I.iv.]

† L. 2. *De oratore.* [*De Oratore* II.54–71, 83.]

‡ Ideoque anceps ejus rei ratio est, quod a derisu non procul abest risus. *Lib. 6. cap.* 3. § 1. [VI.3.7: "Consequently, the cause of laughter is uncertain, since laughter is never far removed from derision" (referring to *De Oratore* II.58.236).]

§ See chap. 7.

‖ See chap. 10.

¶ Scarron. [Paul Scarron (1610–60), *La Vergile travesty en vers burlesque* (1648–53): French poet and dramatist, first husband of Mme de Maintenon (who married Louis XIV in 1685). His burlesque poems and other works were frequently translated into English from the 1690s.]

of the *Secchia Rapita:** the authors laugh first, in order to make their readers laugh. The *Lutrin* is a burlesque poem of the other sort, laying hold of a low and trifling incident, to expose the luxury, indolence, and contentious spirit of a set of monks. Boileau the author gives a ridiculous air to the subject, by dressing it in the heroic style, and affecting to consider it as of the utmost dignity and importance. In a composition of this kind, no image professedly ludicrous ought to find quarter, because such images destroy the contrast; and accordingly the author shows always the grave face, and never once betrays a smile.

Though the burlesque that aims at ridicule, produces its effect by elevating the style far above the subject, yet it has limits beyond which the elevation ought not to be carried: the poet, consulting the imagination of his readers, ought to confine himself to such images as are lively, and readily apprehended: a strained elevation, soaring above an ordinary reach of fancy, makes not a pleasant impression: the reader, fatigued with being al- <368>ways upon the stretch, is soon disgusted; and if he persevere, becomes thoughtless and indifferent. Further, a fiction gives no pleasure unless it be painted in colours so lively as to produce some perception of reality; which never can be done effectually where the images are formed with labour or difficulty. For these reasons, I cannot avoid condemning the *Batrachomuomachia,* said to be the composition of Homer: it is beyond the power of imagination to form a clear and lively image of frogs and mice, acting with the dignity of the highest of our species; nor can we form a conception of the reality of such an action, in any manner so distinct as to interest our affections even in the slightest degree.

The *Rape of the Lock*[1] is of a character clearly distinguishable from those now mentioned: it is not properly a burlesque performance, but what may rather be termed *an heroi-comical poem:* it treats a gay and familiar subject with pleasantry, and with a moderate degree of dignity: the author puts not on a mask like Boileau, nor processes to make us laugh like Tassoni. The *Rape of the Lock* is a genteel species of writing, less strained than those mentioned: and is pleasant or ludicrous without having ridicule for its chief

---

* Tassoni. [Alessandro Tassoni (1565–1635), *La Secchia rapita,* 1624.]
1. Alexander Pope, *The Rape of the Lock,* 1712.

aim; giving way however to ridicule where it arises naturally from a particular character, such as that of Sir Plume. Addison's *Spectator* upon the exercise of <369> the fan* is extremely gay and ludicrous, resembling in its subject the *Rape of the Lock.*

Humour belongs to the present chapter, because it is connected with ridicule. Congreve defines humour[2] to be "a singular and unavoidable manner of doing or saying any thing, peculiar and natural to one man only, by which his speech and actions are distinguished from those of other men." Were this definition just, a majestic and commanding air, which is a singular property, is humour; as also a natural flow of correct and commanding eloquence, which is no less singular. Nothing just or proper is denominated humour; nor any singularity of character, words, or actions, that is valued or respected. When we attend to the character of an humorist, we find that it arises from circumstances both risible and improper, and therefore that it lessens the man in our esteem, and makes him in some measure ridiculous.

Humour in writing is very different from humour in character. When an author insists upon ludicrous subjects with a professed purpose to make his readers laugh, he may be styled *a ludicrous writer;* but is scarce intitled to be styled *a writer of humour.* This quality belongs to an author, who, affecting to be grave and serious, paints his objects in such colours as to provoke mirth and laughter. A writer that is really an hu-<370>morist in character, does this without design: if not, he must affect the character in order to succeed. Swift and Fontaine[3] were humorists in character, and their writings are full of humour. Addison was not an humorist in character; and yet in his prose-writings a most delicate and refined humour prevails. Arbuthnot[4] exceeds them all in drollery and humorous painting; which shows

* No. 102.

2. *Concerning Humour in Comedy,* 1695.

3. Jean de la Fontaine (1621–95): French poet and satirist; his *Fables* appeared between 1668 and 1694. Jonathan Swift (1667–1745): cousin of Dryden, dean of St. Patrick's in Dublin, satirist, and author of numerous political works relating to Ireland and to church affairs.

4. John Arbuthnot (1667–1735): physician to Queen Anne, author and pamphleteer, and friend of Swift. His *History of John Bull* appeared in 1712.

a great genius, because, if I am not misinformed, he had nothing of that peculiarity in his character.

There remains to show by examples, the manner of treating subjects, so as to give them a ridiculous appearance.

> Il ne dit jamais, je vous donne, mais, je vous prete le bon jour.
> *Moliere.*[5]

> *Orleans.* I know him to be valiant.
> *Constable.* I was told that by one that knows him better than you.
> *Orleans.* What's he?
> *Constable.* Marry, he told me so himself; and he said, he car'd not who knew it.   *Henry* V. *Shakespear.*

He never broke any man's head but his own, and that was against a post when he was drunk.   *Ibid.*[6]

> *Millament.* Sententious Mirabell! pr'ythee don't look <371> with that violent and inflexible wise face, like Solomon at the dividing of the child in an old tapestry hanging.   *Way of the World.*

A true critic in the perusal of a book, is like a dog at a feast, whose thoughts and stomach are wholly set upon what the guests fling away, and consequently is apt to snarl most when there are the fewest bones.
> *Tale of a Tub.*[7]

In the following instances, the ridicule arises from absurd conceptions in the persons introduced.

---

5. "He never says 'I give you good day,' but always 'Allow me to bid you good day.'" Jean-Baptiste Poquelin, otherwise known as Molière (1622–73): French comic dramatist, who satirized contemporary society.

6. Act 3, sc. 7; act 3, sc. 2.

7. Jonathan Swift: *A Tale of a Tub,* 1704.

Mascarille. Te souvient-il, vicomte, de cette demi-lune, que nous emportâmes sur les ennemis au siege d'Arras?

Jodelet. Que veux tu dire avec ta demi-lune? c'étoit bien une lune tout entiere. *Moliere les Precieuses Ridicules, sc.* ii.[8]

Slender. I came yonder at Eaton to marry Mrs. Anne Page; and she's a great lubberly boy.

Page. Upon my life then you took the wrong.

Slender. What need you tell me that? I think so when I took a boy for a girl: if I had been marry'd to him, for all he was in woman's apparel, I would not have had him. *Merry Wives of Windsor.*[9]

Valentine. Your blessing, Sir.

Sir Sampson. You've had it already, Sir: I think I sent it you to-day in a bill for four thousand pound; a great deal of money, Brother Foresight.
<372>
Foresight. Ay indeed, Sir Sampson, a great deal of money for a young man; I wonder what can he do with it.

Love for Love, act 2. *sc.* 7.

Millament. I nauseate walking; 'tis a country-diversion; I lothe the country, and every thing that relates to it.

Sir Wilful. Indeed! hah! look ye, look ye, you do? nay, 'tis like you may— here are choice of pastimes here in town, as plays and the like; that must be confess'd indeed.

Millament. Ah l'etourdie! I hate the town too.

Sir Wilful. Dear heart, that's much—hah! that you should hate 'em

---

8. [Mascarille]
Vicomte, do you remember that half-moon we carried at the siege of Arras?

[Jodelet]
What do you mean with your half-moon? It was a full moon, by God!

("Half-moon" is a form of military fortification; a "full moon," if not regarded as impossible, would be a tower, and defeat the object of the defensive design.)

9. Act 5, sc. 5.

both! hah! 'tis like you may; there are some can't relish the town, and others can't away with the country—'tis like you may be one of these, Cousine.

Way of the World, act 4. *sc.* 4.

Lord Froth. I assure you, Sir Paul, I laugh at no body's jests but my own, or a lady's: I assure you, Sir Paul.

Brisk. How? how, my Lord? what, affront my wit! Let me perish, do I never say any thing worthy to be laugh'd at?

Lord Froth. O foy, don't misapprehend me, I don't say so, for I often smile at your conceptions. But there is nothing more unbecoming a man of quality, than to laugh; 'tis such a vulgar expression of the passion! every body can laugh. Then especially to laugh at the jest of an inferior person, or when any body else of the same quality does not laugh with one; ridicu-<373>lous! To be pleas'd with what pleases the crowd! Now, when I laugh I always laugh alone.   *Double Dealer,* act. 1. *sc.* 4.

So sharp-sighted is pride in blemishes, and so willing to be gratified, that it takes up with the very slightest improprieties; such as a blunder by a foreigner in speaking our language, especially if the blunder can bear a sense that reflects on the speaker:

Quickly. The young man is an honest man.

Caius. What shall de honest man do in my closet! dere is no honest man dat shall come in my closet.   *Merry Wives of Windsor.*[10]

Love-speeches are finely ridiculed in the following passage.

Quoth he, My faith as adamantine,
As chains of destiny, I'll maintain;
True as Apollo ever spoke,
Or oracle from heart of oak;
And if you'll give my flame but vent,
Now in close hugger mugger pent,
And shine upon me but benignly,
With that one, and that other pigsneye,

10. Act 1, sc. 4.

The sun and day shall sooner part,
Than love, or you, shake off my heart;
The sun, that shall no more dispense
His own, but your bright influence:
I'll carve your name on barks of trees,
With true love-knots, and flourishes; <374>
That shall infuse eternal spring,
And everlasting flourishing:
Drink ev'ry letter on't in stum,
And make it brisk champaign become.
Where-e'er you tread, your foot shall set
The primrose and the violet;
All spices, perfumes, and sweet powders,
Shall borrow from your breath their odours;
Nature her charter shall renew
And take all lives of things from you;
The world depend upon your eye,
And when you frown upon it, die.
Only our loves shall still survive,
New worlds and natures to outlive;
And, like to herald's moons, remain
All crescents, without change or wane.

Hudibras, part 2. canto 1.[11]

Irony turns things into ridicule in a peculiar manner; it consists in laughing at a man under disguise of appearing to praise or speak well of him. Swift affords us many illustrious examples of that species of ridicule. Take the following.

By these methods, in a few weeks, there starts up many a writer, capable of managing the profoundest and most universal subjects. For what though his head be empty, provided his common-place book be full! And if you will bate him but the circumstances of method, and style, and grammar, and invention; allow him but the common privileges of transcribing from <375> others, and digressing from himself, as often as he shall see

---

11. Samuel Butler (1612–80): poet and satirist, who received a stipend and pension from Charles II. *Hudibras*, 1663, 1664, 1678.

occasion; he will desire no more ingredients towards fitting up a treatise that shall make a very comely figure on a bookseller's shelf, there to be preserved neat and clean, for a long eternity, adorned with the heraldry of its title, fairly inscribed on a label; never to be thumbed or greased by students, nor bound to everlasting chains of darkness in a library; but when the fullness of time is come, shall happily undergo the trial of purgatory, in order to ascend the sky.*

I cannot but congratulate our age on this peculiar felicity, that though we have made indeed great progress in all other branches of luxury, we are not yet debauch'd with any *high relish* in poetry, but are in this one taste less *nice* than our ancestors.

If the Reverend clergy shewed more concern than others, I charitably impute it to their great charge of souls; and what confirmed me in this opinion was, that the degrees of apprehension and terror could be distinguished to be greater or less, according to their ranks and degrees in the church.†

A parody must be distinguished from every species of ridicule: it enlivens a gay subject by imitating some important incident that is serious: it <376> is ludicrous, and may be risible; but ridicule is not a necessary ingredient. Take the following examples, the first of which refers to an expression of Moses.

> The skilful nymph reviews her force with care:
> Let spades be trumps! she said, and trumps they were,
> > *Rape of the Lock, canto* iii. 45.

The next is in imitation of Achilles's oath in Homer:

> But by this lock, this sacred lock, I swear,
> (Which never more shall join its parted hair,
> Which never more its honours shall renew,
> Clip'd from the lovely head where late it grew),
> That while my nostrils draw the vital air,

---

* *Tale of a Tub,* sect. 7.

† A true and faithful narrative of what passed in London during the general consternation of all ranks and degrees of mankind. [John Arbuthnot.]

This hand, which won it, shall for ever wear.
He spoke, and speaking, in proud triumph spread
The long-contended honours of her head.

Ibid. canto iv. 133.

The following imitates the history of Agamemnon's sceptre in Homer.

Now meet thy fate, incens'd Belinda cry'd,
And drew a deadly bodkin from her side,
(The same, his ancient personage to deck,
Her great-great-grandsire wore about his neck,
In three seal-rings; which after, melted down,
Form'd a vast buckle for his widow's gown:
Her infant grandame's whistle next it grew,
The bells she jingled, and the whistle blew; <377>
Then in a bodkin grac'd her mother's hairs,
Which long she wore, and now Belinda wears.)

Ibid. canto v. 87.

Tho' ridicule, as observed above, is no necessary ingredient in a parody, yet there is no opposition between them: ridicule may be successfully employ'd in a parody: and a parody may be employ'd to promote ridicule; witness the following example with respect to the latter, in which the goddess of Dullness is addressed upon the subject of modern education:

Thou gav'st that ripeness, which so soon began,
And ceas'd so soon, he ne'er was boy nor man;
Through school and college, thy kind cloud o'ercast,
Safe and unseen the young Aeneas past;*
Thence bursting glorious, all at once let down,
Stunn'd with his giddy larum half the town.

Dunciad, b. iv. 287.

The interposition of the gods in the manner of Homer and Virgil, ought to be confined to ludicrous subjects, which are much enlivened by such interposition handled in the form of a parody; witness the cave of Spleen,

---

* *Aen.* I. I. *At Venus obscuro,* &c.

Rape of the Lock, canto 4.; the goddess of Discord, *Lutrin, canto* 1.; and the goddess of Indolence, *canto* 2.

Those who have a talent for ridicule, which is <378> seldom united with a taste for delicate and refined beauties, are quick-sighted in improprieties; and these they eagerly grasp, in order to gratify their favourite propensity. Persons galled are provoked to maintain, that ridicule is improper for grave subjects. Subjects really grave are by no means fit for ridicule: but then it is urged against them, that when it is called in question whether a certain subject be really grave, ridicule is the only means of determining the controversy. Hence a celebrated question, Whether ridicule be or be not a test of truth? I give this question a place here, because it tends to illustrate the nature of ridicule.

The question stated in accurate terms is, Whether the sense of ridicule be the proper test for distinguishing ridiculous objects, from what are not so. Taking it for granted, that ridicule is not a subject of reasoning, but of sense or taste,* I proceed thus. No person doubts but that our sense of beauty is the true test of what is beautiful; and our sense of grandeur, of what is great or sublime. Is it more doubtful whether our sense of ridicule be the true test of what is ridiculous? It is not only the true test, but indeed the only test; for this subject comes not, more than beauty or grandeur, under the province of reason. If any subject, by the influence of fashion or custom, have acquired <379> a degree of veneration to which naturally it is not intitled, what are the proper means for wiping off the artificial colouring, and displaying the subject in its true light? A man of true taste sees the subject without disguise: but if he hesitate, let him apply the test of ridicule, which separates it from its artificial connections, and exposes it naked with all its native improprieties.

But it is urged, that the gravest and most serious matters may be set in a ridiculous light. Hardly so; for where an object is neither risible nor improper, it lies not open in any quarter to an attack from ridicule. But supposing the fact, I foresee not any harmful consequence. By the same sort of reasoning, a talent for wit ought to be condemned, because it may be employ'd to burlesque a great or lofty subject. Such irregular use made of

---

* See chap. 10. compared with chap. 7.

a talent for wit or ridicule, cannot long impose upon mankind: it cannot stand the test of correct and delicate taste; and truth will at last prevail even with the vulgar. To condemn a talent for ridicule because it may be perverted to wrong purposes, is not a little ridiculous: could one forbear to smile, if a talent for reasoning were condemned because it also may be perverted? and yet the conclusion in the latter case, would be not less just than in the former: perhaps more just; for no talent is more frequently perverted than that of reason. <380>

We had best leave nature to her own operations: the most valuable talents may be abused, and so may that of ridicule: let us bring it under proper culture if we can, without endeavouring to pluck it up by the root. Were we destitute of this test of truth, I know not what might be the consequences: I see not what rule would be left us to prevent splendid trifles passing for matters of importance, show and form for substance, and superstition or enthusiasm for pure religion. <381>

CHAPTER XIII

Wit

Wit is a quality of certain thoughts and expressions: the term is never applied to an action nor to a passion, and as little to an external object.

However difficult it may be, in many instances, to distinguish a witty thought or expression from one that is not so; yet in general it may be laid down, that the term *wit* is appropriated to such thoughts and expressions as are ludicrous, and also occasion some degree of surprise by their singularity. Wit also in a figurative sense expresses a talent for inventing ludicrous thoughts or expressions: we say commonly, *a witty man,* or *a man of wit.*

Wit in its proper sense, as explained above, is distinguishable into two kinds; wit in the thought, and wit in the words or expression. Again, wit in the thought is of two kinds; ludicrous images, and ludicrous combinations of things that have little or no natural relation.

Ludicrous images that occasion surprise by their singularity, as having little or no foundation in nature, are fabricated by the imagination: and the <382> imagination is well qualified for the office; being of all our faculties the most active, and the least under restraint. Take the following example.

> *Shylock.* You knew (none so well, none so well as you) of my daughter's flight.
> *Salino.*[1] That's certain; I, for my part, knew the tailor that made the wings she flew withal.　　　　*Merchant of Venice, act* 3. *sc.* 1.

---

1. For "Salino" read "Salarino."

The image here is undoubtedly witty. It is ludicrous: and it must occasion surprise; for having no natural foundation, it is altogether unexpected.

The other branch of wit in the thought, is that only which is taken notice of by Addison, following Locke, who defines it "to lie in the assemblage of ideas; and putting those together, with quickness and variety, wherein can be found any resemblance or congruity, thereby to make up pleasant pictures and agreeable visions in the fancy."* It may be defined more concisely, and perhaps more accurately, "A junction of things by distant and fanciful relations, which surprise because they are unexpected."† The following is a proper example.

> We grant although he had much wit,
> H'was very shie of using it, <383>
> As being loth to wear it out;
> And therefore bore it not about,
> Unless on holidays, or so,
> As men their best apparel do.   *Hudibras, canto* 1.

Wit is of all the most elegant recreation: the image enters the mind with gaiety, and gives a sudden flash, which is extremely pleasant. Wit thereby gently elevates without straining, raises mirth without dissoluteness, and relaxes while it entertains.

Wit in the expression, commonly called *a play of words,* being a bastard sort of wit, is reserved for the last place. I proceed to examples of wit in the thought; and first of ludicrous images.

Falstaff, speaking of his taking Sir John Colevile of the Dale:

Here he is, and here I yield him; and I beseech your Grace, let it be book'd with the rest of this day's deeds; or, by the Lord, I will have it in a particular ballad else, with mine own picture on the top of it, Colevile kissing my foot: to the which course if I be enforc'd, if you do not all shew like gilt twopences to me; and I, in the clear sky of fame, o'ershine you as much as the full moon doth the cinders of the element, which shew like pins'

* B. 2. ch. 11. § 2. [The reference is to *The Spectator,* no. 62, 1711.]
† See chap. 1.

heads to her; believe not the word of the Noble. Therefore let me have
right, and let desert mount.

Second part, Henry IV. *act* 4. *sc.* 6.[2]

I knew, when seven justices could not take up a quar-<384>rel, but
when the parties were met themselves, one of them thought but of an *if;*
as, if you said so, then I said so; and they shook hands, and swore brothers.
Your *if* is the only peacemaker; much virtue is in *if.*

Shakespear.[3]

For there is not through all nature, another so callous, and insensible a
member, as the world's posteriors, whether you apply to it the toe or the
birch.   *Preface to a Tale of a Tub.*

The war hath introduced abundance of polysyllables, which will never be
able to live many more campaigns. Speculations, operations, preliminaries, ambassadors, palisadoes, communication, circumvallation, battalions,
as numerous as they are, if they attack us too frequently in our coffee-
houses, we shall certainly put them to flight, and cut off the rear.

Tatler, No. 230.[4]

Speaking of Discord,

She never went abroad, but she brought home such a bundle of monstrous lies, as would have amazed any mortal, but such as knew her; of a
whale that had swallowed a fleet of ships; of the lions being let out of the
tower to destroy the Protestant religion; of the Pope's being seen in a
brandyshop at Wapping, *&c.*

History of John Bull, part 1. *ch.* 16.

The other branch of wit in the thought, namely, ludicrous combinations
and oppositions, may be traced through various ramifications. And, first,
fanciful causes assigned that have no natural relation to the effects produced: <385>

2. Act 4, sc. 3.
3. *As You Like It:* act 5, sc. 4.
4. *Tatler,* 230, 1710: Swift's first letter to the fictitious Isaac Bickerstaff.

Lancaster. Fare you well, Falstaff; I, in my condition,
Shall better speak of you than you deserve. [*Exit.*

Falstaff. I would you had but the wit; 'twere better than your dukedom. Good faith, this same young sober-blooded boy doth not love me; nor a man cannot make him laugh; but that's no marvel, he drinks no wine. There's never any of these demure boys come to any proof; for thin drink doth so overcool their blood, and making many fish-meals, that they fall into a kind of male green-sickness; and then, when they marry, they get wenches. They are generally fools and cowards; which some of us should be too, but for inflammation. A good sherris-sack hath a twofold operation in it: it ascends me into the brain; dries me there all the foolish, dull, and crudy vapours which environ it; makes it apprehensive, quick, forgetive, full of nimble, fiery, and delectable shapes; which deliver'd o'er to the voice, the tongue, which is the birth, becomes excellent wit. The second property of your excellent sherris is, the warming of the blood; which before cold and settled, left the liver white and pale; which is the badge of pusillanimity and cowardice: but the sherris warms it, and makes it course from the inwards to the parts extreme; it illuminateth the face, which, as a beacon, gives warning to all the rest of this little kingdom, man, to arm; and then the vital commoners and inland petty spirits muster me all to their captain, the heart; who, great, and puff'd up with this retinue, doth any deed of courage: and thus valour comes of sherris. So that skill in the weapon is nothing without sack, for that sets it a-work; and learning a mere hoard of gold kept by a <386> devil, till sack commences it, and sets it in act and use. Hereof comes it, that Prince Harry is valiant; for the cold blood he did naturally inherit of his father, he hath, like lean, steril, and bare land, manured, husbanded, and till'd, with excellent endeavour of drinking good and good store of fertile sherris, that he is become very hot and valiant. If I had a thousand sons, the first human principle I would teach them, should be to forswear thin potations, and to addict themselves to sack. *Second part of Henry* IV. *act* 4. *sc.* 7.[5]

The trenchant blade, toledo trusty,
For want of fighting was grown rusty,

5. Act 4, sc. 3.

And ate into itself, for lack
Of some body to hew and hack.
The peaceful scabbard where it dwelt,
The rancor of its edge had felt;
For of the lower end two handful,
It had devoured, 'twas so manful;
And so much scorn'd to lurk in case,
As if it durst not shew its face.   *Hudibras, canto* 1.

Speaking of physicians,

Le bon de cette profession est, qu'il y a parmi les morts une honnêteté,
une discrétion la plus grande du monde; jamais on n'en voit se plaindre
du médicin qui l'a tué.   *Le medicin malgré lui.* [6]

> Admirez les bontez, admirez les tendresses,
> De ces vieux esclaves du sort. <387>
> Ils ne sont jamais las d'aquérir des richesses,
> Pour ceux qui souhaitent leur mort.[7]

Belinda. Lard, he has so pester'd me with flames and stuff—I think I
shan't endure the sight of a fire this twelvemonth.
                                        Old Bachelor, act 2. *sc.* 8.

To account for effects by such fantastical causes, being highly ludicrous,
is quite improper in any serious composition. Therefore the following passage from Cowley,[8] in his poem on the death of Sir Henry Wooton, is in
a bad taste.

He did the utmost bounds of knowledge find,
He found them not so large as was his mind.

---

6. Molière, *Le médecin malgré lui:* act 3, sc. 1: "The great thing about this profession
is that among the dead there is integrity, the finest sense of discretion; you never hear
them complain of the doctor who killed them."
7. "Admire the kindness, admire the tenderness of these slaves of sorcery. They never
weary of acquiring riches, for those who wish their death."
8. Abraham Cowley (1618–87): author, poet, diplomat.

But, like the brave Pellaean youth, did moan,
Because that Art had no more worlds than one.
And when he saw that he through all had past,
He dy'd, lest he should idle grow at last.

Fanciful reasoning:

Falstaff. Imbowell'd!—if thou imbowel me today, I'll give you leave to powder me, and eat me tomorrow! 'Sblood, 'twas time to counterfeit, or that hot termagant Scot had paid me scot and lot too. Counterfeit! I lie, I am no counterfeit; to die is to be a counterfeit; for he is but the counterfeit of a man, who hath not the life of a man; but to counterfeit dying, when a man thereby liveth, is to be no counterfeit, but the true and perfect image of life, indeed.   *First part, Henry* IV. *act* 1. *sc.* 10.[9] <388>

Clown. And the more pity that great folk should have countenance in this world to drown or hang themselves, more than their even Christian.
Hamlet, act 5. *sc.* 1.

Pedro. Will you have me, Lady?
Beatrice. No, my Lord, unless I might have another for working days. Your Grace is too costly to wear every day.
Much ado about nothing, act 2. *sc.* 5.[10]

Jessica. I shall be saved by my husband; he hath made me a Christian.
Launcelot. Truly the more to blame he; we were Christians enough before, e'en as many as could well live by one another: this making of Christians will raise the price of hogs; if we grow all to be pork-eaters, we shall not have a rasher on the coals for money.
Merchant of Venice, act 3. *sc.* 6.[11]

In western clime there is a town,
To those that dwell therein well known;

9. Act 5, sc. 4.
10. Act 2, sc. 1.
11. Act 3, sc. 5.

Therefore there needs no more be said here,
We unto them refer our reader:
For brevity is very good
When w' are, or are not understood.   *Hudibras, canto* 1.

But Hudibras gave him a twitch,
As quick as lightning, in the breech,
Just in the place where honour's lodg'd,
As wise philosophers have judg'd; <389>
Because a kick in that part, more
Hurts honour, than deep wounds before.   *Ibid. canto* 3.

Ludicrous junction of small things with great, as of equal importance:

This day black omens threat the brightest fair
That e'er deserv'd a watchful spirit's care:
Some dire disaster, or by force, or slight;
But what, or where, the fates have wrapt in night;
Whether the nymph shall break Diana's law;
Or some frail china jar receive a flaw;
Or stain her honour, or her new brocade;
Forget her pray'rs, or miss a masquerade;
Or lose her heart, or necklace, at a ball;
Or whether Heav'n has doom'd that Shock must fall.
                                Rape of the Lock, canto ii. 101.

One speaks the glory of the British Queen,
And one describes a charming Indian screen.
                                Ibid. canto iii. 13.

Then flash'd the living lightning from her eyes,
And screams of horror rend th' affrighted skies.
Not louder shrieks to pitying heav'n are cast,
When husbands, or when lapdogs, breathe their last;

Or when rich china vessels fall'n from high,
In glitt'ring dust and painted fragments lie!

Ibid. canto iii. 155.

Not youthful kings in battle seiz'd alive,
Not scornful virgins who their charms survive,
Not ardent lovers robb'd of all their bliss,
Not ancient ladies when refus'd a kiss, <390>
Not tyrants fierce that unrepenting die,
Not Cynthia when her manteau's pinn'd awry,
E'er felt such rage, resentment, and despair,
As thou, sad virgin! for thy ravish'd hair.

Ibid. canto iv. 3.

Joining things that in appearance are opposite. As for example, where Sir Rodger de Coverley, in the Spectator, speaking of his widow,

That he would have given her a coal-pit to have kept her in clean linen; and that her finger should have sparkled with one hundred of his richest acres.

Premisses that promise much and perform nothing. Cicero upon that article says,

Sed scitis esse notissimum ridiculi genus, cum aliud expectamus, aliud dicitur: hic nobismet ipsis noster error risum movet.*

Beatrice. ———— With a good leg and a good foot, uncle, and money enough in his purse, such a man would win any woman in the world, if he could get her good-will.

Much ado about nothing, act 2. *sc.* 1.

Beatrice. I have a good eye, uncle, I can see a church by day-light.

Ibid.

---

* *De oratore*, l. 2. cap. 63. ["You know already, however, that the most familiar of these is exemplified when we are expecting to hear a particular phrase, and something different is uttered. In this case our own mistake even makes us laugh ourselves."]

Le medicin que l'on m'indique
Sait le Latin, le Grec, l'Hebreu, <391>
Les belles lettres, la physique,
La chimie et la botanique.
Chacun lui donne son aveu:
Il auroit aussi ma pratique;
Mais je veux vivre encore un peu.[12]

Again,

Vingt fois le jour le bon Grégoire
A soin de fermer son armoire.
De quoi pensez vous qu'il a peur?
Belle demande! Qu'un voleur
Trouvant une facile proie,
Ne lui ravisse tout son bien.
Non; Grégoire a peur qu' on ne voie
Que dans son armoire il n'a rien.[13]

Again,

L'athsmatique Damon a cru que l'air des champs
Repareroit en lui le ravage des ans,
Il s'est fuit, a grands fraix, transporter en Bretagne.
Or voiez ce qu'a fait l'air natal qu'il a pris!
Damon seroit mort à Paris:
Damon est mort à la campagne.[14]

12. "The doctor of whom you told me knew Latin, Greek, Hebrew, the best literature, physic, chemistry and botany; each yielded up advice to him: he also had my own experience. But I want to live a little bit longer."

13. "Twenty times a day good old Gregory takes care to close his cupboard. What do you think he's frightened of? For goodness sake! That a burglar finding an easy prey, would carry off all his goods. No: Gregory is scared that he'll only find out that his cupboard is bare."

14. "Asthmatic Damon believed that the country air would heal the ravages of time, so he fled, to the great open spaces of Brittany. And you see what effect the fresh air had! Damon would die if he stayed in Paris; Damon died in the country."

Having discussed wit in the thought, we proceed to what is verbal only, commonly called *a play of words*. This sort of wit depends, for the most part, upon chusing a word that hath different significations: by that artifice hocus-pocus tricks are play'd in language, and thoughts plain and simple take on a very different appearance. <392> Play is necessary for man, in order to refresh him after labour; and accordingly man loves play, even so much as to relish a play of words: and it is happy for us, that words can be employ'd, not only for useful purposes, but also for our amusement. This amusement, tho' humble and low, unbends the mind; and is relished by some at all times, and by all at some times.

It is remarkable, that this low species of wit, has among all nations been a favourite entertainment in a certain stage of their progress toward refinement of taste and manners, and has gradually gone into disrepute. As soon as a language is formed into a system, and the meaning of words is ascertained with tolerable accuracy, opportunity is afforded for expressions that, by the double meaning of some words, give a familiar thought the appearance of being new; and the penetration of the reader or hearer is gratified in detecting the true sense disguised under the double meaning. That this sort of wit was in England deemed a reputable amusement, during the reigns of Elisabeth and James I. is vouched by the works of Shakespear, and even by the writings of grave divines. But it cannot have any long endurance: for as language ripens, and the meaning of words is more and more ascertained, words held to be synonymous diminish daily; and when those that remain have been more than once employ'd, the pleasure vanisheth with the novelty. <393>

I proceed to examples, which, as in the former case, shall be distributed into different classes.

A seeming resemblance from the double meaning of a word:

> Beneath this stone my wife doth lie;
> She's now at rest, and so am I.

A seeming contrast from the same cause, termed *a verbal antithesis,* which hath no despicable effect in ludicrous subjects:

> Whilst Iris his cosmetic wash would try
> To make her bloom revive, and lovers die,

Some ask for charms, and others philters chuse,
To gain Corinna, and their quartans lose.

Dispensary, canto 2.

And how frail nymphs, oft by abortion, aim
To lose a substance, to preserve a name.   *Ibid. canto* 3.

While nymphs take treats, or assignations give.

Rape of the Lock.

Other seeming connections from the same cause:

Will you employ your conqu'ring sword,
To break a fiddle and your word?   *Hudibras, canto* 2.

To whom the knight with comely grace
Put off his hat to put his case.

Hudibras, part 3. *canto* 3. <394>

Here Britain's statesmen oft the fall foredoom
Of foreign tyrants, and of nymphs at home;
Here thou, great Anna! whom three realms obey,
Dost sometimes counsel take—and sometimes tea.

Rape of the Lock, canto 3. *l.* 5.

O'er their quietus where fat judges dose,
And lull their cough and conscience to repose.

Dispensary, canto 1.

Speaking of Prince Eugene:

This general is a great taker of snuff as well as of towns.

Pope, Key to the Lock.

Exul mentisque domusque.   *Metamorphoses, l.* ix. 409.[15]

15. "Driven out of mind and home."

A seeming opposition from the same cause:

> Hic quiescit qui nunquam quievit.[16]

Again,

> Quel âge a cette Iris, dont on fait tant de bruit?
> Me demandoit Cliton n'aguere.
> Il faut, dis-je, vous satisfaire,
> Elle a vingt ans le jour, et cinquante ans la nuit.[17]

Again,

> So like the chances are of love and war,
> That they alone in this distinguish'd are; <395>
> In love the victors from the vanquish'd fly,
> They fly that wound, and they pursue that die.   *Waller.*[18]

> What new found witchcraft was in thee,
> With thine own cold to kindle me?
> Strange art; like him that should devise
> To make a burning glass of ice.   *Cowley.*[19]

Wit of this kind is unsuitable in a serious poem; witness the following line in Pope's Elegy to the memory of an unfortunate lady:

> Cold is that breast which warm'd the world before.

This sort of writing is finely burlesqued by Swift:

> Her hands the softest ever felt,
> Though cold would burn, though dry would melt.
>
> *Strephon and Chloe.*[20]

16. "Here lies he who never slept."

17. "How old is this Iris, of whom there is so much talk?" Cliton asked me recently. "If I must satisfy you," I said, "she's twenty by day, and fifty by night."

18. Edmund Waller (1606–87), member of Parliament and poet: "To a friend of the different success of their loves," in *Poems &c Written upon Several Occasions,* London, 1705.

19. "The Vain Love," 1663.

20. Jonathan Swift: *Strephon and Chloe,* 1734.

Taking a word in a different sense from what is meant, comes under wit, because it occasions some slight degree of surprise:

> *Beatrice.* I may sit in a corner, and cry *Heigh ho!* for a husband.
> *Pedro.* Lady Beatrice, I will get you one.
> *Beatrice.* I would rather have one of your father's getting. Hath your Grace ne'er a brother like you? <396> Your father got excellent husbands, if a maid could come by them.
> $\qquad\qquad\qquad$ *Much ado about nothing, act.* 2. *sc.* 5.[21]

> *Falstaff.* My honest lads, I will tell you what I am about.
> *Pistol.* Two yards and more.
> *Falstaff.* No quips now, Pistol: indeed, I am in the waste two yards about; but I am now about no waste; I am about thrift.
> $\qquad\qquad\qquad$ *Merry Wives of Windsor, act* 1. *sc.* 7.[22]

> $\quad$ *Lo. Sands.* ———— By your leave, sweet ladies,
> If I chance to talk a little wild, forgive me:
> I had it from my father.
> $\quad$ *Anne Bullen.* Was he mad, Sir?
> $\quad$ *Sands.* O, very mad, exceeding mad, in love too;
> But he would bite none ————   *K. Henry* VIII.[23]

An assertion that bears a double meaning, one right one wrong, but so introduced as to direct us to the wrong meaning, is a species of bastard wit, which is distinguished from all others by the name *pun.* For example.

> $\quad$ *Paris.* ———— Sweet Helen, I must woo you,
> To help unarm our Hector: his stubborn buckles,
> With these your white enchanting fingers touch'd,
> Shall more obey, than to the edge of steel,

21. Act 2, sc. 1.
22. Act 1, sc. 3.
23. Act 1, sc. 4.

Or force of Greekish sinews; you shall do more
Than all the island kings, disarm great Hector.

Troilus and Cressida, act 3. sc. 2.[24] <397>

The pun is in the close. The word *disarm* has a double meaning: it signifies to take off a man's armour, and also to subdue him in fight. We are directed to the latter sense by the context; but with regard to Helen, the word holds only true in the former sense. I go on with other examples:

Esse nihil dicis quicquid petis, improbe Cinna:
Si nil, Cinna, petis, nil tibi, Cinna, nego.

Martial, l. 3. epigr. 61.[25]

Jocondus geminum imposuit tibi, Sequana, pontem;
Hunc tu jure potes dicere pontificem.   *Sanazarius.*[26]

N.B. *Jocondus was a monk.*

Chief Justice. Well! the truth is, Sir John, you live in great infamy.
Falstaff. He that buckles him in my belt cannot live in less.
Chief Justice. Your means are very slender, and your waste is great.
Falstaff. I would it were otherwise: I would my means were greater, and my waste slenderer.   *Second Part, Henry* IV. *act* 1. *sc.* 5.[27]

Celia. I pray you bear with me, I can go no further.
Clown. For my part, I had rather bear with you than bear you: yet I

---

24. Act 3, sc. 1.

25. Marcus Valerius Martialis (A.D. 40–104), born in Spain, author of epigrams that illuminate Roman life: "Unconscionable Cinna, whatever you ask for, you say it's nothing. Cinna, if you ask for nothing, nothing, Cinna, do I refuse you."

26. Jacopo Sannazaro (1458–1530): Neapolitan author. His verse and prose *Arcadia,* 1504, was popular, as was *De partu virginis,* 1527. "Jocundus placed a double bridge upon you, Sequana [i.e., the Seine]; you would be right to call him 'bridgemaker.'" (The joke is in the last word, because in classical Latin *pontifex* means "high priest" but in medieval times meant "the pope.")

27. Act 1, sc. 2.

should bear no cross if I did bear you; for I think you have no money in
your purse.   *As you like it, act* 2. *sc.* 4. <398>

> He that imposes an oath makes it,
> Not he that for convenience takes it;
> Then how can any man be said,
> To break ah oath he never made?
>
> *Hudibras, part* 2. *canto* 2.

The seventh satire of the first book of Horace, is purposely contrived to
introduce at the close a most execrable pun. Talking of some infamous
wretch whose name was *Rex Rupilius,*

> Persius exclamat, Per magnos, Brute, deos te
> Oro, qui reges consueris tollere, cur non
> Hunc regem jugulas? Operum hoc, mihi crede, tu orum est.[28]

Though playing with words is a mark of a mind at ease, and disposed
to any sort of amusement, we must not thence conclude, that playing with
words is always ludicrous. Words are so intimately connected with thought,
that if the subject be really grave, it will not appear ludicrous even in that
fantastic dress. I am, however, far from recommending it in any serious
performance: on the contrary, the discordance between the thought and
expression must be disagreeable; witness the following specimen.

> He hath abandoned his physicians, Madam, under whose practices he
> hath persecuted time with hope: and <399> finds no other advantage in
> the process, but only the losing of hope by time.
>
> *All's well that ends well, act* 1. *sc.* 1.

> *K. Henry.* O my poor kingdom, sick with civil blows!
> When that my care could not with-hold thy riots,

---

28. "Perseus shouts aloud 'In the name of the gods, Brutus, I entreat you, for it is
your habit to rid us of kings, why not cut the throat of this king also? This, believe me,
is one of your proper works.'" (*Satires* I.7: trans. James Lonsdale and Samuel Lee, London, 1873.)

What wilt thou do when riot is thy care?

Second part, K. Henry IV.[29]

If any one shall observe, that there is a third species of wit, different from those mentioned, consisting in sounds merely, I am willing to give it place. And indeed it must be admitted, that many of Hudibras's double rhymes come under the definition of wit given in the beginning of this chapter: they are ludicrous, and their singularity occasions some degree of surprise. Swift is no less successful than Butler in this sort of wit; witness the following instances: *Goddess—Boddice. Pliny—Nicolini. Iscariots—Chariots. Mitre—Nitre. Dragon—Suffragan.*

A repartee may happen to be witty: but it cannot be considered as a species of wit; because there are many repartees extremely smart, and yet extremely serious. I give the following example. A certain petulant Greek, objecting to Anacharsis that he was a Scythian: True, says Anacharsis, my country disgraces me, but you disgrace your country. This fine turn gives surprise; but it is far from being ludicrous. <400>

29. Act 4, sc. 5.

∞ CHAPTER XIV ∞

Custom and Habit

Viewing man as under the influence of novelty, would one suspect that custom also should influence him? and yet our nature is equally susceptible of each; not only in different objects, but frequently in the same. When an object is new, it is enchanting: familiarity renders it indifferent; and custom, after a longer familiarity, makes it again desirable. Human nature, diversified with many and various springs of action, is wonderfully, and, indulging the expression, intricately constructed.[1]

Custom hath such influence upon many of our feelings, by warping and varying them, that we must attend to its operations if we would be acquainted with human nature. This subject, in itself obscure, has been much neglected; and a complete analysis of it would be no easy task. I pretend only to touch it cursorily; hoping, however, that what is here laid down, will dispose diligent enquirers to attempt further discoveries.

Custom respects the action, *habit* the agent. By *custom* we mean a frequent reiteration of the same act; and by *habit,* the effect that custom has on the agent. This effect may be either active, wit-<401>ness the dexterity produced by custom in performing certain exercises; or passive, as when a thing makes an impression on us different from what it did originally. The latter only, as relative to the sensitive part of our nature, comes under the present undertaking.

This subject is intricate: some pleasures are fortified by custom; and yet

---

1. See the note for <202> and the editor's Introduction.

custom begets familiarity, and consequently indifference:* in many instances, satiety and disgust are the consequences of reiteration: again, tho' custom blunts the edge of distress and of pain; yet the want of any thing to which we have been long accustomed, is a sort of torture. A clue to guide us through all the intricacies of this labyrinth, would be an acceptable present.

Whatever be the cause, it is certain that we are much influenced by custom: it hath an effect upon our pleasures, upon our actions, and even upon our thoughts and sentiments. Habit makes no figure during the vivacity of youth: in middle age it gains ground; and in old age governs without control. In that period of life, generally speaking, we eat at a certain hour, take exercise at a certain hour, go to rest at a certain hour, all by the direction of habit: nay, a particular seat, ta-<402>ble, bed, comes to be essential; and a habit in any of these cannot be controlled without uneasiness.

Any slight or moderate pleasure frequently reiterated for a long time, forms a peculiar connection between us and the thing that causes the pleasure. This connection, termed *habit,* has the effect to awaken our desire or appetite for that thing when it returns not as usual. During the course of enjoyment, the pleasure rises insensibly higher and higher till a habit be established; at which time the pleasure is at its height. It continues not however stationary: the same customary reiteration which carried it to its height, brings it down again by insensible degrees, even lower than it was at first: but of that circumstance afterward. What at present we have in view, is to prove by experiments, that those things which at first are but moderately agreeable, are the aptest to become habitual. Spirituous liquors, at first scarce agreeable, readily produce an habitual appetite: and custom prevails so far, as even to make us fond of things originally disagreeable, such as coffee, assa-foetida,[2] and tobacco; which is pleasantly illustrated by Congreve:

---

* If all the year were playing holidays,
　To sport would be as tedious as to work:
　But when they seldom come, they wish'd for come,
　And nothing pleaseth but rare accidents.
　　First part, Henry IV. *act* 1. *sc.* 3. [Act 1, sc. 2.]

2. Strongly smelling gum arabic, from Central Asia, used medicinally.

Fainall. For a passionate lover, methinks you are a man somewhat too discerning in the failings of your mistress.

Mirabell. And for a discerning man, somewhat too passionate a lover; for I like her with all her faults; nay like her for her faults. Her follies are so natural, or so artful, that they become her; and those affectations which in another woman would be odious, serve <403> but to make her more agreeable. I'll tell thee, Fainall, she once us'd me with that insolence, that in revenge I took her to pieces, sifted her, and separated her failings; I study'd 'em, and got 'em by rote. The catalogue was so large, that I was not without hopes, one day or other, to hate her heartily: to which end I so us'd myself to think of 'em, that at length, contrary to my design and expectation, they gave me every hour less and less disturbance; till in a few days, it became habitual to me to remember 'em without being displeased. They are now grown as familiar to me as my own frailties; and in all probability, in a little time longer, I shall like 'em as well.

The way of the world, act I. *sc.* 3.

A walk upon the quarter-deck, tho' intolerably confined, becomes however so agreeable by custom, that a sailor in his walk on shore, confines himself commonly within the same bounds. I knew a man who had relinquished the sea for a country-life: in the corner of his garden he reared an artificial mount with a level summit, resembling most accurately a quarter-deck, not only in shape but in size; and here he generally walked. In Minorca Governor Kane made an excellent road the whole length of the island;[3] and yet the inhabitants adhere to the old road, tho' not only longer but extremely bad.* Play or gaming, at <404> first barely amusing by the occupation it affords, becomes in time extremely agreeable; and is frequently prosecuted with avidity, as if it were the chief business of life. The same observation is applicable to the pleasures of the internal senses, those of knowledge and virtue in particular: children have scarce any sense of these pleasures; and

* Custom is a second nature. Formerly, the merchants of Bristol had no place for meeting but the street, open to every variety of weather. An exchange was erected for them with convenient piazzas. But so rivetted were they to their accustomed place, that in order to dislodge them, the magistrates were forc'd to break up the pavement, and to render the place a heap of rough stones.

3. Between 1713 and 1715 Governor Richard Kane constructed a road through Minorca, which was then under French control.

men very little who are in the state of nature without culture: our taste for virtue and knowledge improves slowly; but is capable of growing stronger than any other appetite in human nature.

To introduce an active habit, frequency of acts is not sufficient without length of time: the quickest succession of acts in a short time, is not sufficient; nor a slow succession in the longest time. The effect must be produced by a moderate soft action, and a long series of easy touches, removed from each other by short intervals. Nor are these sufficient without regularity in the time, place, and other circumstances of the action: the more uniform any operation is, the sooner it becomes habitual. And this holds equally in a passive habit; variety in any remarkable degree, prevents the effect: thus any particular food will scarce ever become habitual, where the manner of dressing is varied. The circumstances then requisite to <405> augment a moderate pleasure, and at the long-run to form a habit, are weak uniform acts, reiterated during a long course of time without any considerable interruption: every agreeable cause that operates in this manner, will grow habitual.

Affection and *aversion,* as distinguished from passion on the one hand, and on the other from original disposition, are in reality habits respecting particular objects, acquired in the manner above set forth. The pleasure of social intercourse with any person, must originally be faint, and frequently reiterated, in order to establish the habit of affection. Affection thus generated, whether it be friendship or love, seldom swells into any tumultuous or vigorous passion; but is however the strongest cement that can bind together two individuals of the human species. In like manner, a slight degree of disgust often reiterated with regularity, grows into the habit of aversion, which commonly subsists for life.

Objects of taste that are delicious, far from tending to become habitual, are apt by indulgence to produce satiety and disgust: no man contracts a habit of sugar, honey, or sweet-meats, as he doth of tobacco:

> Dulcia non ferimus; succo renovamur amaro.
>
> *Ovid. art. amand. l.* 3.[4]

---

4. *Artis Amatoriae* 3.583: "We cannot bear sweetness; let us be refreshed by bitter juices."

Insipido è quel dolce, che condito
Non è di qualche amaro, e tosto satia.

Aminta di Tasso.[5] <406>

These violent delights have violent ends,
And in their triumph die. The sweetest honey
Is loathsome in its own deliciousness,
And in the taste confounds the appetite;
Therefore love mod'rately, long love doth so;
Too swift arrives as tardy as too slow.

Romeo and Juliet, act 2. sc. 6.

The same observation holds with respect to all objects that being extremely agreeable raise violent passions: such passions are incompatible with a habit of any sort; and in particular they never produce affection nor aversion: a man who at first sight falls violently in love, has a strong desire of enjoyment, but no affection for the woman:* a <407> man who is surprised with

---

5. Tasso, *Aminta,* act 2, sc. 2: "Insipid is that sweetness, and too soon satiates when it is not seasoned with some bitterness."

* Violent love without affection is finely exemplified in the following story. When Constantinople was taken by the Turks, Irene, a young Greek of an illustrious family, fell into the hands of Mahomet II. who was at that time in the prime of youth and glory. His savage heart being subdued by her charms, he shut himself up with her, denying access even to his ministers. Love obtained such ascendant as to make him frequently abandon the army, and fly to his Irene. War relaxed, for victory was no longer the monarch's favourite passion. The soldiers, accustomed to booty, began to murmur; and the infection spread even among the commanders. The Basha Mustapha, consulting the fidelity he ow'd his master, was the first who durst acquaint him of the discourses held publicly to the prejudice of his glory.

The Sultan, after a gloomy silence, formed his resolution. He ordered Mustapha to assemble the troops next morning; and then with precipitation retired to Irene's apartment. Never before did that princess appear so charming; never before did the prince bestow so many warm caresses. To give a new lustre to her beauty, he exhorted her women next morning, to bestow their utmost art and care on her dress. He took her by the hand, led her into the middle of the army, and pulling off her vail, demanded of the Bashas with a fierce look, whether they had ever beheld such a beauty? After an awful pause, Mahomet with one hand laying hold of the young Greek by her beautiful locks, and with the other pulling out his scimitar, severed the head from the body at one stroke. Then turning to his grandees, with eyes wild and furious, "This sword," says he, "when

an unexpected favour, burns for an opportunity to exert his gratitude, without having any affection for his benefactor: neither does desire of vengeance for an atrocious injury, involve aversion.

It is perhaps not easy to say why moderate pleasures gather strength by custom: but two causes concur to prevent that effect in the more intense pleasures. These, by an original law in our nature, increase quickly to their full growth, and decay with no less precipitation;* and custom is <408> too slow in its operation to overcome that law. The other cause is no less powerful: exquisite pleasure is extremely fatiguing; occasioning, as a naturalist would say, great expence of animal spirits;† and of such the mind cannot bear so frequent gratification, as to superinduce a habit: if the thing that raises the pleasure return before the mind have recovered its tone and relish, disgust ensues instead of pleasure.

A habit never fails to admonish us of the wonted time of gratification, by raising a pain for want of the object, and a desire to have it. The pain of want is always first felt: the desire naturally follows; and upon presenting the object, both vanish instantaneously. Thus a man accustomed to tobacco, feels, at the end of the usual interval, a confused pain of want; which at first points at nothing in particular, tho' it soon settles upon its accustomed object: and the same may be observed in persons addicted to drinking, who are often in an uneasy restless state before they think of the bottle. In pleasures indulged regularly, and at equal intervals, the appetite, remarkably obsequious to custom, returns regularly with the usual time of gratification; not sooner, even tho' the object be presented. This pain of want arising <409> from habit, seems directly opposite to that of satiety;

---

it is my will, knows to cut the bands of love." However strange it may appear, we learn from experience, that desire of enjoyment may consist with the most brutal aversion, directed both to the same woman. Of this we have a noted example in the first book of Sully's memoirs; to which I chuse to refer the reader, for it is too gross to be transcribed. [Maximilien de Bethune, duc de Sully, *Mémoire des sages et royalles oeconomies d'estat, domestique* . . . , 1638. Translated into English in 1756 as *Memoirs of Maximilian de Bethune, Duke of Sully.*]

* See chap. 2. part 3.

† Lady Easy, upon her husband's reformation, expresses to her friend the following sentiment. "Be satisfy'd; Sir Charles has made me happy, even to a pain of joy." [Colly Cibber: *Careless Husband,* 1705.]

and it must appear singular, that frequency of gratification should produce effects so opposite, as are the pains of excess and of want.

The appetites that respect the preservation and propagation of our species, are attended with a pain of want similar to that occasioned by habit: hunger and thirst are uneasy sensations of want, which always precede the desire of eating or drinking; and a pain for want of carnal enjoyment, precedes the desire of an object. The pain being thus felt independent of an object, cannot be cured but by gratification. Very different is an ordinary passion, in which desire precedes the pain of want: such a passion cannot exist but while the object is in view; and therefore, by removing the object out of thought, it vanisheth, with its desire, and pain of want.*

The natural appetites above mentioned, differ from habit in the following particular: they have an undetermined direction toward all objects of gratification in general; whereas an habitual appetite is directed to a particular object: the attachment we have by habit to a particular woman, differs widely from the natural passion which comprehends the whole sex; and the habitual relish for a particular dish, is far from being the same with a vague appetite for food. That difference <410> notwithstanding, it is still remarkable, that nature hath enforc'd the gratification of certain natural appetites essential to the species, by a pain of the same sort with that which habit produceth.

The pain of habit is less under our power, than any other pain that arises from want of gratification: hunger and thirst are more easily endured, especially at first, than an unusual intermission of any habitual pleasure: persons are often heard declaring, they would forego sleep or food, rather than tobacco. We must not however conclude, that the gratification of an habitual appetite affords the same delight with the gratification of one that is natural: far from it; the pain of want only, is greater.

The flow and reiterated acts that produce a habit, strengthen the mind to enjoy the habitual pleasure in greater quantity and more frequency than originally; and by that means a habit of intemperate gratification is often formed: after unbounded acts of intemperance, the habitual relish is soon restored, and the pain for want of enjoyment returns with fresh vigor.

* See chap. 2. part 3.

The causes of the present emotions hitherto in view, are either an individual, such as a companion, a certain dwelling-place, a certain amusement; or a particular species, such as coffee, mutton, or any other food. But habit is not confined to such. A constant train of trifling diversions, may form such a habit in the mind, that it cannot <411> be easy a moment without amusement: a variety in the objects prevents a habit as to any one in particular; but as the train is uniform with respect to amusement, the habit is formed accordingly; and that sort of habit may be denominated *a generic habit,* in opposition to the former, which is a *specific habit.* A habit of a town-life, of country-sports, of solitude, of reading, or of business, where sufficiently varied, are instances of generic habits. Every specific habit hath a mixture of the generic; for the habit of any one sort of food, makes the taste agreeable, and we are fond of that taste, where-ever found. Thus a man deprived of an habitual object, takes up with what most resembles it; deprived of tobacco, any bitter herb will do, rather than want: a habit of punch, makes wine a good resource: accustomed to the sweet society and comforts of matrimony, the man, unhappily deprived of his beloved object, inclines the sooner to a second. In general, when we are deprived of a habitual object, we are fond of its qualities in any other object.

The reasons are assigned above, why the causes of intense pleasure become not readily habitual: but now we discover, that these reasons conclude only against specific habits. In the case of a weak pleasure, a habit is formed by frequency and uniformity of reiteration, which, in the case of an intense pleasure, produceth satiety and disgust. But it is remarkable, that satiety and disgust have <412> no effect, except as to that thing singly which occasions them: a surfeit of honey produceth not a loathing of sugar; and intemperance with one woman produceth no disrelish of the same pleasure with others. Hence it is easy to account for a generic habit in any intense pleasure: the delight we had in the gratification of the appetite, enflames the imagination, and makes us, with avidity, search for the same gratification in whatever other subject it can be found. And thus uniform frequency in gratifying the same passion upon different objects, produceth at length a generic habit. In this manner, one acquires an habitual delight in high and poignant sauces, rich dress, fine equipages, crowds of company, and in whatever is commonly termed *pleasure.* There concurs at the same time, to introduce this habit, a peculiarity observed above, that reiteration of acts enlarges the capacity of the mind, to admit a more plentiful gratification than originally, with regard to frequency as well as quantity.

Hence it appears, that tho' a specific habit cannot be formed but upon a moderate pleasure, a generic habit may be formed upon any sort of pleasure, moderate or immoderate, that hath variety of objects. The only difference is, that a weak pleasure runs naturally into a specific habit; whereas an intense pleasure is altogether averse to such a habit. In a word, it is only in singular cases that a moderate pleasure produces a generic habit; <413> but an intense pleasure cannot produce any other habit.

The appetites that respect the preservation and propagation of the species, are formed into habit in a peculiar manner: the time as well as measure of their gratification are much under the power of custom; which, by introducing a change upon the body, occasions a proportional change in the appetites. Thus, if the body be gradually formed to a certain quantity of food at stated times, the appetite is regulated accordingly; and the appetite is again changed, when a different habit of body is introduced by a different practice. Here it would seem, that the change is not made upon the mind, which is commonly the case in passive habits, but upon the body.

When rich food is brought down by ingredients of a plainer taste, the composition is susceptible of a specific habit. Thus the sweet taste of sugar, rendered less poignant in a mixture, may, in course of time, produce a specific habit for such mixture. As moderate pleasures, by becoming more intense, tend to generic habits; so intense pleasures, by becoming more moderate, tend to specific habits.

The beauty of the human figure, by a special recommendation of nature, appears to us supreme, amid the great variety of beauteous forms bestow'd upon animals. The various degrees in which individuals enjoy that property, render it an <414> object, sometimes of a moderate, sometimes of an intense passion. The moderate passion, admitting frequent reiteration without diminution, and occupying the mind without exhausting it, turns gradually stronger till it becomes a habit. Nay, instances are not wanting, of a face, at first disagreeable, afterward rendered indifferent by familiarity, and at length agreeable by custom. On the other hand, consummate beauty, at the very first glance, fills the mind so as to admit no increase. Enjoyment lessens the pleasure;* and if often repeated, ends commonly in satiety and disgust. The impressions made by consummate beauty, in a gradual succession from lively to faint, constitute a series opposite to that of faint impressions waxing gradually more lively, till they produce a specific habit. But the mind, when accustomed to beauty, contracts a relish for it in general, tho' often repelled from particular objects by the pain of satiety: and thus a generic habit is formed, of which inconstancy in love is the necessary consequence; for a generic habit, comprehending every beautiful object, is an invincible obstruction to a specific habit, which is confined to one.

But a matter which is of great importance to the youth of both sexes, deserves more than a cursory view. Tho' the pleasant emotion of beauty dif-<415>fers widely from the corporeal appetite, yet when both are directed to the same object, they produce a very strong complex passion:† enjoyment in that case must be exquisite; and therefore more apt to produce satiety, than in any other case whatever. This is a never-failing effect, where consummate beauty in the one party, meets with a warm imagination and great sensibility in the other. What I am here explaining, is true without exaggeration; and they must be insensible upon whom it makes no impression: it deserves well to be pondered by the young and the amorous, who in forming the matrimonial society, are too often blindly impelled by the animal pleasure merely, enflamed by beauty. It may indeed happen after the pleasure is gone, and go it must with a swift pace, that a new connection is formed upon more dignified and more lasting principles: but this is a dangerous experiment; for even supposing good sense, good temper, and internal merit of every sort, yet a new connection upon such qualifications is rarely formed: it commonly, or rather always happens, that such qualifications, the only solid foundation of an indissoluble connection, are rendered altogether invisible by satiety of enjoyment creating disgust.

One effect of custom, different from any that have been explained, must not be omitted, because <416> it makes a great figure in human nature: Tho' custom augments moderate pleasures, and lessens those that are in-

---

* See chap. 2. part 3.
† See chap. 2. part 4.

tense, it has a different effect with respect to pain; for it blunts the edge of every sort of pain and distress, faint or acute. Uninterrupted misery, therefore, is attended with one good effect: if its torments be incessant, custom hardens us to bear them.

The changes made in forming habits, are curious. Moderate pleasures are augmented gradually by reiteration, till they become habitual; and then are at their height: but they are not long stationary; for from that point they gradually decay, till they vanish altogether. The pain occasioned by want of gratification, runs a different course: it increases uniformly; and at last becomes extreme, when the pleasure of gratification is reduced to nothing:

> ———— ———— It so falls out,
> That what we have we prize not to the worth,
> While we enjoy it; but being lack'd and lost,
> Why then we rack the value; then we find,
> The virtue that possession would not shew us
> Whilst it was ours.
>
> *Much ado about nothing,* act 4. sc. 2.[6]

The effect of custom with relation to a specific habit, is display'd through all its varieties in the use of tobacco. The taste of that plant is at first extremely unpleasant: our disgust lessens gradually, till it vanish altogether; at which period the taste is <417> neither agreeable nor disagreeable: continuing the use of the plant, we begin to relish it; and our relish improves by use, till it arrive at perfection: from that period it gradually decays, while the habit is in a state of increment, and consequently the pain of want. The result is, that when the habit has acquired its greatest vigor, the relish is gone; and accordingly we often smoke and take snuff habitually, without so much as being conscious of the operation. We must except gratification after the pain of want; the pleasure of which gratification is the greatest when the habit is the most vigorous: it is of the same kind with the pleasure one feels upon being delivered from the rack, the cause of which is explained above.* This pleasure however is but occasionally the effect of

---

* Chap. 2. part I. sect. 3.
6. Act 4, sc. 1.

habit; and however exquisite, is avoided as much as possible because of the pain that precedes it.

With regard to the pain of want, I can discover no difference between a generic and a specific habit. But these habits differ widely with respect to the positive pleasure: I have had occasion to observe, that the pleasure of a specific habit decays gradually till it turn imperceptible; the pleasure of a generic habit on the contrary, being supported by variety of gratification, suffers little or no decay after it comes to its height. However it <418> may be with other generic habits, the observation, I am certain, holds with respect to the pleasures of virtue and of knowledge: the pleasure of doing good has an unbounded scope, and may be so variously gratified that it can never decay: science is equally unbounded; our appetite for knowledge having an ample range of gratification, where discoveries are recommended by novelty, by variety, by utility, or by all of them.

In this intricate enquiry, I have endeavoured, but without success, to discover by what particular means it is that custom hath influence upon us: and now nothing seems left, but to hold our nature to be so framed as to be susceptible of such influence. And supposing it purposely so framed, it will not be difficult to find out several important final causes. That the power of custom is a happy contrivance for our good, cannot have escaped any one who reflects, that business is our province, and pleasure our relaxation only. Now satiety is necessary to check exquisite pleasures, which otherwise would engross the mind and unqualify us for business. On the other hand, as business is sometimes painful and is never pleasant beyond moderation, the habitual increase of moderate pleasure, and the conversion of pain into pleasure, are admirably contrived for disappointing the malice of Fortune, and for reconciling us to whatever course of life may be our lot: <419>

> How use doth breed a habit in a man!
> This shadowy desert, unfrequented woods,
> I better brook than flourishing peopled towns.
> Here I can sit alone, unseen of any,
> And to the nightingale's complaining notes
> Tune my distresses, and record my woes.
> *Two Gentlemen of Verona, act* 5. *sc.* 4.

As the foregoing distinction between intense and moderate, holds in pleasure only, every degree of pain being softened by time, custom is a catholicon[7] for pain and distress of every sort; and of that regulation the final cause requires no illustration.

Another final cause of custom will be highly relished by every person of humanity, and yet has in a great measure been overlooked; which is, that custom hath a greater influence than any other known cause, to put the rich and the poor upon a level: weak pleasures, the share of the latter, become fortunately stronger by custom; while voluptuous pleasures, the share of the former, are continually losing ground by satiety. Men of fortune, who possess palaces, sumptuous gardens, rich fields, enjoy them less than passengers do. The goods of Fortune are not unequally distributed: the opulent possess what others enjoy.

And indeed, if it be the effect of habit, to produce the pain of want in a high degree while there < 420 > is little pleasure in enjoyment, a voluptuous life is of all the least to be envied. Those who are habituated to high feeding, easy vehicles, rich furniture, a crowd of valets, much deference and flattery, enjoy but a small share of happiness, while they are exposed to manifold distresses. To such a man, enslaved by ease and luxury, even the petty inconveniencies in travelling, of a rough road, bad weather, or homely fare, are serious evils: he loses his tone of mind, turns peevish, and would wreak his resentment even upon the common accidents of life. Better far to use the goods of Fortune with moderation: a man who by temperance and activity hath acquired a hardy constitution, is, on the one hand, guarded against external accidents; and, on the other, is provided with great variety of enjoyment ever at command.

I shall close this chapter with an article more delicate than abstruse, namely, what authority custom ought to have over our taste in the fine arts. One particular is certain, that we chearfully abandon to the authority of custom things that nature hath left indifferent. It is custom, not nature, that hath established a difference between the right hand and the left, so as to make it awkward and disagreeable to use the left where the right is commonly used. The various colours, tho' they affect us differently, are all of

7. A universal formula.

them agreeable in their purity: but custom has regulated that matter in another manner; a black skin upon a human being, is to <421> us disagreeable; and a white skin probably no less so to a negro. Thus things, originally indifferent, become agreeable or disagreeable by the force of custom. Nor will this be surprising after the discovery made above, that the original agreeableness or disagreeableness of an object, is, by the influence of custom, often converted into the opposite quality.

Proceeding to matters of taste, where there is naturally a preference of one thing before another; it is certain, in the first place, that our faint and more delicate feelings are readily susceptible of a bias from custom; and therefore that it is no proof of a defective taste, to find these in some measure influenced by custom: dress and the modes of external behaviour, are regulated by custom in every country: the deep red or vermilion with which the ladies in France cover their cheeks, appears to them beautiful in spite of nature; and strangers cannot altogether be justified in condemning that practice, considering the lawful authority of custom, or of the *fashion* as it is called: it is told of the people who inhabit the skirts of the Alps facing the north, that the swelling they universally have in the neck is to them agreeable. So far has custom power to change the nature of things, and to make an object originally disagreeable, take on an opposite appearance.

But as to every particular that can be denominated proper or improper, right or wrong, cu-<422>stom has little authority, and ought to have none. The principle of duty takes naturally place of every other; and it argues a shameful weakness or degeneracy of mind, to find it in any case so far subdued as to submit to custom.

These few hints may enable us to judge in some measure of foreign manners, whether exhibited by foreign writers or our own. A comparison between the ancients and the moderns, was some time ago a favourite subject: those who declared for ancient manners, thought it sufficient that these manners were supported by custom: their antagonists, on the other hand, refusing submission to custom as a standard of taste, condemned ancient manners as in several instances irrational. In that controversy, an appeal being made to different principles, without the slightest attempt to establish a common standard, the dispute could have no end. The hints above given tend to establish a standard for judging how far the authority of custom ought to be held lawful; and for the sake of illustration, we shall apply that standard in a few instances.

Human sacrifices, the most dismal effect of blind and grovelling superstition, wore gradually out of use by the prevalence of reason and humanity. In the days of Sophocles and Euripides, traces of that practice were still recent; and the Athenians, through the prevalence of custom, could without disgust suffer human sacrifices to be represented in <423> their theatre, of which the *Iphigenia* of Euripides is a proof. But a human sacrifice, being altogether inconsistent with modern manners as producing horror instead of pity, cannot with any propriety be introduced upon a modern stage. I must therefore condemn the *Iphigenia* of Racine,[8] which, instead of the tender and sympathetic passions, substitutes disgust and horror. Another objection occurs against every fable that deviates so remarkably from improved notions and sentiments; which is, that if it should even command our belief by the authority of history, it appears too fictitious and unnatural to produce a perception of reality:* a human sacrifice is so unnatural, and to us so improbable, that few will be affected with the representation of it more than with a fairy tale. The objection first mentioned strikes also against the *Phedra* of that author: the queen's passion, for her stepson, transgressing the bounds of nature, creates aversion and horror rather than compassion. The author in his preface observes, that the queen's passion, however unnatural, was the effect of destiny and the wrath of the gods; and he puts the same excuse in her own mouth. But what is the wrath of a heathen God to us Christians? we acknowledge no destiny in passion; and if love be unnatural, it never can be relished. A supposition like what our author lays hold of, may possibly co-<424>ver slight improprieties; but it will never engage our sympathy for what appears to us frantic or extravagant.

Neither can I relish the catastrophe of that tragedy. A man of taste may peruse, without disgust, a Grecian performance describing a sea monster sent by Neptune to destroy Hippolytus: he considers, that such a story

---

* See chap. 2. part 1. sect. 7.

8. Jean Racine (1639–99): French tragedian and friend of Molière, La Fontaine, and Boileau. *Iphigénie,* 1674; *Phèdre,* 1677.

might agree with the religious creed of Greece; and may be pleased with the story, as what probably had a strong effect upon a Grecian audience. But he cannot have the same indulgence for such a representation upon a modern stage; because no story that carries a violent air of fiction can ever move us in any considerable degree.

In the *Coëphores* of Eschylus,* Orestes is made to say, that he was commanded by Apollo to avenge his father's murder; and yet if he obey'd, that he was to be delivered to the furies, or be struck with some horrid malady: the tragedy accordingly concludes with a chorus, deploring the fate of Orestes, obliged to take vengeance against a mother, and involved thereby in a crime against his will. It is impossible for any modern to bend his mind to opinions so irrational and absurd, which must disgust him in perusing even a Grecian story. Again, among the Greeks, grossly superstitious, it was a common opinion that the <425> report of a man's death was a presage of his death; and Orestes, in the first act of *Electra,*[9] spreading a report of his own death in order to blind his mother and her adulterer, is even in that case affected with the presage. Such imbecility can never find grace with a modern audience: it may indeed produce some compassion for a people afflicted with absurd terrors, similar to what is felt in perusing a description of the Hottentotes; but such manners will not interest our affections, nor attach us to the personages represented. <426>

---

* Act 2. [Aeschylus (525–456 B.C.): founder of Greek tragedy. Seven of his tragedies survive, of which *Choephori* is one.]

9. Sophocles (496–406 B.C.), born in Athens. Seven of his plays survive, of which *Electra* is one.

External Signs of Emotions
and Passions

So intimately connected are the soul and body, that every agitation in the former, produceth a visible effect upon the latter. There is, at the same time, a wonderful uniformity in that operation; each class of emotions and passions being invariably attended with an external appearance peculiar to itself.* These external appearances or signs, may not improperly be considered as a natural language, expressing to all beholders emotions and passions as they arise in the heart. Hope, fear, joy, grief, are display'd externally: the character of a man can be read in his face; and beauty, which makes so deep an impression, is known to result, not so much from regular features and a fine complexion, as from good nature, good sense, sprightliness, sweetness, or other mental quality, expressed upon the countenance. Tho' perfect skill in that language be rare, yet what is generally known is sufficient for <427> the ordinary purposes of life. But by what means we come to understand the language, is a point of some intricacy: it cannot be by sight merely; for upon the most attentive inspection of the human face, all that can be discerned, are figure, colour, and motion, which singly or combined, never can represent a passion, nor a sentiment: the external sign is indeed visible; but to understand its meaning we must be able to connect it with the passion that causes it, an operation far beyond the reach of eye-sight. Where then is the instructor to be found that can unveil this secret con-

---

* Omnis enim motus animi, suum quemdam a natura habet vultum et sonum et gestum. *Cicero, l. 3. De oratore.* [III.57.216: "For nature has assigned to every emotion a particular look and tone of voice, and a bearing of its own."]

nection? If we apply to experience, it is yielded, that from long and diligent observation, we may gather, in some measure, in what manner those we are acquainted with express their passions externally: but with respect to strangers, we are left in the dark; and yet we are not puzzled about the meaning of these external expressions in a stranger, more than in a bosom-companion. Further, had we no other means but experience for understanding the external signs of passion, we could not expect any degree of skill in the bulk of individuals: yet matters are so much better ordered, that the external expressions of passion form a language understood by all, by the young as well as the old, by the ignorant as well as the learned: I talk of the plain and legible characters of that language: for undoubtedly we are much indebted to experience, in deciphering the <428> dark and more delicate expressions. Where then shall we apply for a solution of this intricate problem, which seems to penetrate deep into human nature? In my mind it will be convenient to suspend the enquiry, till we are better acquainted with the nature of external signs, and with their operations. These articles therefore shall be premised.

The external signs of passion are of two kinds, voluntary and involuntary. The voluntary signs are also of two kinds: some are arbitrary, some natural. Words are obviously voluntary signs: and they are also arbitrary; excepting a few simple sounds expressive of certain internal emotions, which sounds being the same in all languages, must be the work of nature: thus the unpremeditated tones of admiration are the same in all men; as also of compassion, resentment, and despair. Dramatic writers ought to be well acquainted with this natural language of passion: the chief talent of such a writer, is a ready command of the expressions that nature dictates to every person, when any vivid emotion struggles for utterance; and the chief talent of a fine reader, is a ready command of tones suited to these expressions.

The other kind of voluntary signs, comprehends certain attitudes and gestures that naturally accompany certain emotions with a surprising uniformity; excessive joy is expressed by leaping, dancing, or some elevation of the body: excessive grief, by <429> sinking or depressing it: and prostration and kneeling have been employ'd by all nations and in all ages to signify profound veneration. Another circumstance, still more than uniformity, demonstrates these gestures to be natural, viz. their remarkable conformity or resemblance to the passions that produce them.* Joy, which is a chearful elevation of mind, is expressed by an elevation of body: pride, magnanimity, courage, and the whole tribe of elevating passions, are expressed by external gestures that are the same as to the circumstance of elevation, however distinguishable in other respects; and hence an erect posture is a sign or expression of dignity:

> Two of far nobler shape, erect and tall,
> Godlike erect, with native honour clad,
> In naked majesty, seem'd lords of all.
>
> *Paradise lost, book* 4.

Grief, on the other hand, as well as respect, which depress the mind, cannot for that reason be expressed more significantly than by a similar depression of the body; and hence, *to be cast down,* is a common phrase, signifying to be grieved or dispirited.† <430>

One would not imagine who has not given peculiar attention, that the body should be susceptible of such variety of attitude and motion, as readily to accompany every different emotion with a corresponding expression. Humility, for example, is expressed naturally by hanging the head; arrogance, by its elevation; and langour or despondence, by reclining it to one side. The expressions of the hands are manifold: by different attitudes and motions, they express desire, hope, fear; they assist us in promising, in inviting, in keeping one at a distance; they are made instruments of threatening, of supplication, of praise, and of horror; they are employ'd in approving, in refusing, in questioning; in showing our joy, our sorrow, our doubts, our regret, our admiration. These expressions, so obedient to passion, are extremely difficult to be imitated in a calm state: the ancients, sensible of the advantage as well as difficulty of having these expressions

---

* See chap. 2. part 6.

† Instead of a complimental speech in addressing a superior, the Chinese deliver the compliment in writing, the smallness of the letters being proportioned to the degree of respect; and the highest compliment is, to make the letters so small as not to be legible. Here is a clear evidence of a mental connection between respect and littleness: a man humbles himself before his superior, and endeavours to contract himself and his handwriting within the smallest bounds.

at command, bestow'd much time and care, in collecting them from observation, and in digesting them into a practical art, which was taught in their schools as <431> an important branch of education. Certain sounds are by nature allotted to each passion for expressing it externally. The actor who has these sounds at command to captivate the ear, is mighty: if he have also proper gestures at command to captivate the eye, he is irresistible.

The foregoing signs, tho' in a strict sense voluntary, cannot however be restrained but with the utmost difficulty when prompted by passion. We scarce need a stronger proof than the gestures of a keen player at bowls: observe only how he writhes his body, in order to restore a stray bowl to the right track. It is one article of good breeding, to suppress, as much as possible, these external signs of passion, that we may not in company appear too warm, or too interested. The same observation holds in speech: a passion, it is true, when in extreme, is silent;* but when less violent it must be vented in words, which have a peculiar force not to be equalled in a sedate composition. The ease and security we have in a confident, may encourage us to talk of ourselves and of our feelings: but the cause is more general; for it operates when we are alone as well as in company. Passion is the cause; for in many instances it is no slight gratification, to vent a passion externally by words as well as by gestures. Some passions, when at a certain height, impel us <432> so strongly to vent them in words, that we speak with an audible voice even when there is none to listen. It is that circumstance in passion which justifies soliloquies; and it is that circumstance which proves them to be natural.† The mind sometimes favours this impulse of passion,

---

* See chap. 17.

† Tho' a soliloquy in the perturbation of passion is undoubtedly natural, and indeed not unfrequent in real life; yet Congreve, who himself has penned several good soliloquies, yields, with more candour than knowledge, that they are unnatural; and he only pretends to justify them from necessity. This he does in his dedication of the *Double Dealer*, in the following words. "When a man in a soliloquy reasons with himself, and *pro's* and *con's*, and weighs all his designs; we ought not to imagine, that this man either talks to us, or to himself: he is only thinking, and thinking (frequently) such matter as it were inexcusable folly in him to speak. But because we are concealed spectators of the plot in agitation, and the poet finds it necessary to let us know the whole mystery of his contrivance, he is willing to inform us of this person's thoughts: and to that end is forced to make use of the expedient of speech, no other better way being yet invented for the communication of thought."

by bestowing a temporary sensibility upon any object at hand, in order to make it a confident. Thus in the *Winter's Tale*,* Antigonus addresses himself to an infant whom he was ordered to expose,

> Come, poor babe,
> I have heard, but not believ'd, the spirits of the dead, <433>
> May walk again; if such things be, thy mother
> Appear'd to me last night; for ne'er was dream
> So like a waking.

The involuntary signs, which are all of them natural, are either peculiar to one passion, or common to many. Every vivid passion hath an external expression peculiar to itself; not excepting pleasant passions, witness admiration and mirth. The pleasant emotions that are less vivid, have one common expression; from which we may gather the strength of the emotion, but scarce the kind: we perceive a chearful or contented look; and we can make no more of it. Painful passions, being all of them violent, are distinguishable from each other by their external expressions: thus fear, shame, anger, anxiety, dejection, despair, have each of them peculiar expressions; which are apprehended without the least confusion: some painful passions produce violent effects upon the body, trembling, for example, starting, and swooning; but these effects, depending in a good measure upon singularity of constitution, are not uniform in all men.

The involuntary signs, such of them as are display'd upon the countenance, are of two kinds: some are temporary, making their appearance with the emotions that produce them, and vanishing with these emotions; others, being formed gradually by some violent passion often recurring, become permanent signs of that passion, and serve <434> to denote the disposition or temper. The face of an infant indicates no particular disposition, because it cannot be marked with any character, to which time is necessary: even the temporary signs are extremely awkward, being the first rude essays of Nature to discover internal feelings; thus the shrieking of a new-born

---

* Act 3. sc. 6. [Act 3, sc. 3.]

infant, without tears or sobbings, is plainly an attempt to weep; and some of these temporary signs, as smiling and frowning, cannot be observed for some months after birth. Permanent signs, formed in youth while the body is soft and flexible, are preserved entire by the firmness and solidity that the body acquires; and are never obliterated even by a change of temper. Such signs are not produced after the fibres become rigid; some violent cases excepted, such as reiterated fits of the gout or stone through a course of time: but these signs are not so obstinate as what are produced in youth; for when the cause is removed, they gradually wear away, and at last vanish.

The natural signs of emotions, voluntary and involuntary, being nearly the same in all men, form an universal language; which no distance of place, no difference of tribe, no diversity of tongue, can darken or render doubtful: even education, tho' of mighty influence, hath not power to vary nor sophisticate, far less to destroy, their signification. This is a wise appointment of Providence: for if these signs were, like words, <435> arbitrary and variable, the thoughts and volitions of strangers would be entirely hid from us; which would prove a great or rather invincible obstruction to the formation of societies: but as matters are ordered, the external appearances of joy, grief, anger, fear, shame, and of the other passions, forming an universal language, open a direct avenue to the heart. As the arbitrary signs vary in every country, there could be no communication of thoughts among different nations, were it not for the natural signs, in which all agree: and as the discovering passions instantly at their birth, is essential to our well-being, and often necessary for self-preservation, the author of our nature, attentive to our wants, hath provided a passage to the heart, which never can be obstructed while eye-sight remains.

In an enquiry concerning the external signs of passion, actions must not be overlooked: for tho' singly they afford no clear light, they are upon the whole the best interpreters of the heart.* By <436> observing a man's con-

* The actions here chiefly in view, are what a passion suggests in order to its gratification. Beside these, actions are occasionally exerted to give some vent to a passion, without any view to an ultimate gratification. Such occasional action is characteristical of the

duct for a course of time, we discover unerringly the various passions that move him to action, what he loves, and what he hates. In our younger years, every single action is a mark, not at all ambiguous, of the temper; for in childhood there is little or no disguise: the subject becomes more intricate in advanced age; but even there, dissimulation is seldom carried on for any length of time. And thus the conduct of life is the most perfect expression of the internal disposition. It merits not indeed the title of an universal language; because it is not thoroughly understood but by those of penetrating genius or extensive observation: it is a language, however, which every one can decipher in some measure; and which, joined with the other external signs, affords sufficient means for the direction of our conduct with regard to others: if we commit any mistake when such light is afforded, it never can be the effect of unavoidable ignorance, but of rashness or inadvertence.

Reflecting on the various expressions of our emotions, we recognise the anxious care of Nature to discover men to each other. Strong emotions, as above hinted, beget an impatience to express <437> them externally by speech and other voluntary signs, which cannot be suppressed without a painful effort: thus a sudden fit of passion, is a common excuse for indecent behaviour or opprobrious language. As to involuntary signs, these are altogether unavoidable: no volition nor effort can prevent the shaking of the limbs nor a pale visage, in a fit of terror: the blood flies to the face upon a sudden emotion of shame, in spite of all opposition:

> Vergogna, che'n altrui stampo natura,
> Non si puo' rinegar: che se tu' tenti

---

passion in a high degree; and for that reason, when happily invented, has a wonderfully good effect:

> *Hamlet.* Oh most pernicious woman!
> Oh villain, villain, smiling damned villain!
> My tables—meet it is I set it down,
> That one may smile, and smile, and be a villain;
> At least I'm sure it may be so in Denmark.   [*Writing.*
> So, uncle, there you are.
>   *Hamlet, act* I. *sc.* 8. [Act I, sc. 5.]

Di cacciarla dal cor, fugge nel volto.

Pastor Fido, act 2. *sc.* 5.[1]

Emotions indeed properly so called, which are quiescent, produce no remarkable signs externally. Nor is it necessary that the more deliberate passions should, because the operation of such passions is neither sudden nor violent: these however remain not altogether in obscurity; for being more frequent than violent passion, the bulk of our actions are directed by them. Actions therefore display, with sufficient evidence, the more deliberate passions; and complete the admirable system of external signs, by which we become skilful in human nature.

What comes next in order is, to examine the effects produced upon a spectator by external signs <438> of passion. None of these signs are beheld with indifference; they are productive of various emotions, tending all of them to ends wise and good. This curious subject makes a capital branch of human nature: it is peculiarly useful to writers who deal in the pathetic; and to history-painters it is indispensable.

It is mentioned above, that each passion, or class of passions, hath its peculiar signs; and with respect to the present subject it must be added, that these invariably make certain impressions on a spectator: the external signs of joy, for example, produce a chearful emotion; the external signs of grief produce pity; and the external signs of rage, produce a sort of terror even in those who are not aimed at.

Secondly, It is natural to think, that pleasant passions should express themselves externally by signs that to a spectator appear agreeable, and painful passions by signs that to him appear disagreeable. This conjecture, which Nature suggests, is confirmed by experience. Pride possibly may be thought an exception, the external signs of which are disagreeable, tho' it be commonly reckoned a pleasant passion: but pride is not an exception, being in reality a mixed passion, partly pleasant partly painful; for when a proud man confines his thoughts to himself, and to his own dignity or importance,

1. That cannot be orecome
   That's naturall: For if I drive it from
   My heart, it flies into my face.
   (*Il Pastor Fido,* trans. Sir Richard Fanshawe)

the passion is pleasant, and its external signs agreeable; but as pride chiefly <439> consists in undervaluing or contemning others, it is so far painful, and its external signs disagreeable.

Thirdly, It is laid down above, that an agreeable object produceth always a pleasant emotion, and a disagreeable object one that is painful.* According to this law, the external signs of a pleasant passion, being agreeable, must produce in the spectator a pleasant emotion: and the external signs of a painful passion, being disagreeable, must produce in him a painful emotion.

Fourthly, In the present chapter it is observed, that pleasant passions are, for the most part, expressed externally in one uniform manner; but that all the painful passions are distinguishable from each other by their external expressions. The emotions accordingly raised in a spectator by external signs of pleasant passions, have little variety: these emotions are pleasant or chearful, and we have not words to reach a more particular description. But the external signs of painful passions produce in the spectator emotions of different kinds: the emotions, for example, raised by external signs of grief, of remorse, of anger, of envy, of malice, are clearly distinguishable from each other.

Fifthly, External signs of painful passions, are some of them *attractive,* some *repulsive.* Of <440> every painful passion that is also disagreeable† the external signs are repulsive, repelling the spectator from the object: and the passion raised by such external signs may be also considered as repulsive. Painful passions that are agreeable produce an opposite effect: their external signs are attractive, drawing the spectator to them, and producing in him benevolence to the person upon whom these signs appear; witness distress painted on the countenance, which instantaneously inspires the spectator with pity, and impels him to afford relief. And the passion raised by such external signs may also be considered as attractive. The cause of this difference among the painful passions raised by their external signs may be readily gathered from what is laid down, chap. 2. part 7.

It is now time to look back to the question proposed in the beginning,

---

* See chap. 2. part 7.
† See passions explained as agreeable or disagreeable, chap. 2. part 2.

How we come to understand external signs, so as to refer each sign to its proper passion? We have seen that this branch of knowledge cannot be derived originally from sight, nor from experience. Is it then implanted in us by nature? The following considerations will incline us to answer the question in the affirmative. In the first place, the external signs of passion must be natural; for they are invariably the same in every country, and among the different tribes of men: pride, for example, is always <441> expressed by an erect posture, reverence by prostration, and sorrow by a dejected look. Secondly, we are not even indebted to experience for the knowledge that these expressions are natural and universal: for we are so framed as to have an innate conviction of the fact: let a man change his habitation to the other side of the globe, he will, from the accustomed signs, infer the passion of fear among his new neighbours, with as little hesitation as he did at home. But why, after all, involve ourselves in preliminary observations, when the doubt may be directly solved as follows? That if the meaning of external signs be not derived to us from sight, nor from experience, there is no remaining source whence it can be derived but from nature.

We may then venture to pronounce, with some degree of assurance, that man is provided by nature with a sense or faculty that lays open to him every passion by means of its external expressions. And we cannot entertain any reasonable doubt of this, when we reflect, that the meaning of external signs is not hid even from infants: an infant is remarkably affected with the passions of its nurse expressed on her countenance; a smile chears it, a frown makes it afraid: but fear cannot be without apprehending danger; and what danger can the infant apprehend, unless it be sensible that its nurse is angry? We must therefore admit, that a child can read anger in its nurse's <442> face; of which it must be sensible intuitively, for it has no other mean of knowledge. I do not affirm, that these particulars are clearly apprehended by the child; for to produce clear and distinct perceptions, reflection and experience are requisite: but that even an infant, when afraid, must have some notion of its being in danger, is evident.

That we should be conscious intuitively of a passion from its external expressions, is conformable to the analogy of nature: the knowledge of that language is of too great importance to be left upon experience; because a foundation so uncertain and precarious, would prove a great obstacle to the formation of societies. Wisely therefore is it ordered and agreeably to the system of Providence, that we should have nature for our instructor.

Manifold and admirable are the purposes to which the external signs of passion are made subservient by the author of our nature: those occasionally mentioned above, make but a part. Several final causes remain to be unfolded; and to that task I proceed with alacrity. In the first place, The signs of internal agitation display'd externally to every spectator, tend to fix the signification of many words. The only effectual means to ascertain the meaning of any doubtful word, is an appeal to the thing it represents: and hence the ambiguity of words expressive of things that are not objects of external sense; for in that case an <443> appeal is denied. Passion, strictly speaking, is not an object of external sense: but its external signs are; and by means of these signs, passions may be appealed to with tolerable accuracy: thus the words that denote our passions, next to those that denote external objects, have the most distinct meaning. Words signifying internal action and the more delicate feelings, are less distinct. This defect with regard to internal action, is what chiefly occasions the intricacy of logic: the terms of that science are far from being sufficiently ascertained, even after much care and labour bestow'd by an eminent writer;* to whom however the world is greatly indebted, for removing a mountain of rubbish, and moulding the subject into a rational and correct form. The same defect is remarkable in criticism, which has for its object the more delicate feelings; the terms that denote these feelings being not more distinct than those of logic. To reduce the science of criticism to any regular form, has never once been attempted: however rich the ore may be, no critical chymist has been found, to analyse its constituent parts, and to distinguish each by its own name.

In the second place, Society among individuals is greatly promoted by that universal language. Looks and gestures give direct access to the heart; and lead us to select, with tolerable accuracy, the <444> persons who are worthy of our confidence. It is surprising how quickly, and for the most part how correctly, we judge of character from external appearance.

Thirdly, After social intercourse is commenced, these external signs,

* Locke.

which diffuse through a whole assembly the feelings of each individual, contribute above all other means to improve the social affections. Language no doubt is the most comprehensive vehicle for communicating emotions: but in expedition, as well as in power of conviction, it falls short of the signs under consideration; the involuntary signs especially, which are incapable of deceit. Where the countenance, the tones, the gestures, the actions, join with the words in communicating emotions, these united have a force irresistible: thus all the pleasant emotions of the human heart, with all the social and virtuous affections, are, by means of these external signs, not only perceived but felt. By this admirable contrivance, conversation becomes that lively and animating amusement, without which life would at best be insipid: one joyful countenance spreads chearfulness instantaneously through a multitude of spectators.

Fourthly, Dissocial passions, being hurtful by prompting violence and mischief, are noted by the most conspicuous external signs, in order to put us upon our guard: thus anger and revenge, especially when sudden, display themselves on the <445> countenance in legible character.* The external signs again of every passion that threatens danger raise in us the passion of fear: which frequently operating without reason or reflection, moves us by a sudden impulse to avoid the impending danger.†

In the fifth place, These external signs are remarkably subservient to morality. A painful passion, being accompanied with disagreeable external signs, must produce in every spectator a painful emotion: but then if the passion be social, the emotion it produces is attractive, and connects the

---

* Rough and blunt manners are allied to anger, by an internal feeling, as well as by external expressions resembling in a faint degree those of anger: therefore such manners are easily heightened into anger; and savages for that reason are prone to anger. Thus rough and blunt manners are unhappy in two respects: first, they are readily converted into anger; and next, the change being imperceptible because of the similitude of their external signs, the person against whom the anger is directed is not put upon his guard. It is for these reasons a great object in society, to correct such manners, and to bring on a habit of sweetness and calmness. This temper has two opposite good effects. First, it is not easily provoked to wrath. Next, the interval being great between it and real anger, a person of that temper who receives an affront, has many changes to go through before his anger be inflamed; these changes have each of them their external sign; and the offending party is put upon his guard, to retire, or to endeavour a reconciliation.

† See chap. 2. part 1. sect. 6.

<446> spectator with the person who suffers. Dissocial passions only, are productive of repulsive emotions, involving the spectator's aversion, and frequently his indignation. This beautiful contrivance makes us cling to the virtuous, and abhor the wicked.

Sixthly, Of all the external signs of passion, those of affliction or distress are the most illustrious with respect to a final cause. They are illustrious by the singularity of their contrivance; and also by inspiring sympathy, a passion to which human society is indebted for its greatest blessing, that of providing relief for the distressed. A subject so interesting, deserves a leisurely and attentive examination. The conformity of the nature of man to his external circumstances, is in every particular wonderful: his nature makes him prone to society; and society is necessary to his well-being, because in a solitary state he is a helpless being, destitute of support, and in his manifold distresses destitute of relief: but mutual support, the shining attribute of society, is of too great moment to be left dependent upon cool reason; it is ordered more wisely, and with greater conformity to the analogy of nature, that it should be enforc'd even instinctively by the passion of sympathy. Here sympathy makes a capital figure; and contributes, more than any other means, to make life easy and comfortable. But however essential the sympathy of others may be to our well-being, one beforehand would not readily conceive how it could be <447> raised by external signs of distress: for considering the analogy of nature, if these signs be agreeable, they must give birth to a pleasant emotion leading every beholder to be pleased with human woes; if disagreeable, as they undoubtedly are, ought they not naturally to repel the spectator from them, in order to be relieved from pain? Such would be the reasoning beforehand; and such would be the effect were man purely a selfish being. But the benevolence of our nature gives a very different direction to the painful passion of sympathy, and to the desire involved in it: instead of avoiding distress, we fly to it in order to afford relief; and our sympathy cannot be otherwise gratified but by giving all the succour in our power.* Thus external signs of distress, tho' disagreeable, are attractive: and the sympathy they inspire is a powerful cause,

---

* See chap. 2. part 7.

impelling us to afford relief even to a stranger as if he were our friend or relation.* <448>

The effects produced in all beholders by external signs of passion, tend so visibly to advance the social state, that I must indulge my heart with a more narrow inspection of this admirable branch of the human consti-tution. These external signs, being all of them resolvable into colour, figure, and motion, should not naturally make any deep impression on a spectator: and supposing them qualified for making deep impressions, we have seen above, that the effects they produce are not such as might be expected. We cannot therefore account otherwise for the operation of these external signs, but by ascribing it to the original constitution of human nature: to improve the social state, by making us instinctively rejoice with the glad of heart, weep with the mourner, and shun those who threaten danger, is a contri-vance no less illustrious for its wisdom than for its benevolence. With re-spect to the external signs of distress in particular, to judge of the excellency of their contrivance, we need only reflect upon seve-<449>ral other means seemingly more natural, that would not have answered the end purposed. What if the external signs of joy were disagreeable, and the external signs of distress agreeable? This is no whimsical supposition, because there ap-pears not any necessary connection between these signs and the emotions produced by them in a spectator. Admitting then the supposition, the ques-tion is, How would our sympathy operate? There is no occasion to delib-erate for an answer: sympathy would be destructive, and not beneficial: for supposing the external signs of joy disagreeable, the happiness of others

---

* It is a noted observation, that the deepest tragedies are the most crouded; which in a slight view will be thought an unaccountable bias in human nature. Love of novelty, desire of occupation, beauty of action, make us fond of theatrical representations; and when once engaged, we must follow the story to the conclusion, whatever distress it may create. But we generally become wise by experience; and when we foresee what pain we shall suffer during the course of the representation, is it not surprising that persons of reflection do not avoid such spectacles altogether? And yet one who has scarce recovered from the distress of a deep tragedy, resolves coolly and deliberately to go to the very next, without the slightest obstruction from self-love. The whole mystery is explained by a single observation, That sympathy, tho' painful, is attractive, and attaches us to an object in distress, the opposition of self-love notwithstanding, which would prompt us to fly from it. And by this curious mechanism it is that persons of any degree of sensibility are attracted by affliction still more than by joy.

would be our aversion; and supposing the external signs of grief agreeable, the distresses of others would be our entertainment. I make a second supposition, That the external signs of distress were indifferent to us, and productive neither of pleasure nor of pain. This would annihilate the strongest branch of sympathy, that which is raised by means of sight: and it is evident, that reflective sympathy, felt by those only who have great sensibility, would not have any extensive effect. I shall draw nearer to truth in a third supposition, That the external signs of distress being disagreeable, were productive of a painful repulsive emotion. Sympathy upon that supposition would not be annihilated: but it would be rendered useless; for it would be gratified by flying from or avoiding the object, instead of clinging to it and affording relief: the condition of man would in reality be worse than if sympathy were totally era-<450>dicated; because sympathy would only serve to plague those who feel it, without producing any good to the afflicted.

Loath to quit so interesting a subject, I add a reflection, with which I shall conclude. The external signs of passion are a strong indication, that man, by his very constitution, is framed to be open and sincere. A child, in all things obedient to the impulses of nature, hides none of its emotions: the savage and clown, who have no guide but pure nature, expose their hearts to view, by giving way to all the natural signs. And even when men learn to dissemble their sentiments, and when behaviour degenerates into art, there still remain checks, that keep dissimulation within bounds, and prevent a great part of its mischievous effects: the total suppression of the voluntary signs during any vivid passion, begets the utmost uneasiness, which cannot be endured for any considerable time: this operation becomes indeed less painful by habit; but luckily, the involuntary signs cannot, by any effort, be suppressed, nor even dissembled. An absolute hypocrisy, by which the character is concealed and a fictitious one assumed, is made impracticable; and nature has thereby prevented much harm to society. We may pronounce, therefore, that Nature, herself sincere and candid, intends that mankind should preserve the same character, by cultivating simplicity and truth, and banishing every sort of dissimulation that tends to mischief.
<451>

Sentiments

Every thought prompted by passion, is termed *a sentiment.** To have a general notion of the different passions, will not alone enable an artist to make a just representation of any passion: he ought, over and above, to know the various appearances of the same passion in different persons. Passions receive a tincture from every peculiarity of character; and for that reason it rarely happens, that a passion, in the different circumstances of feeling, of sentiment, and of expression, is precisely the same in any two persons. Hence the following rule concerning dramatic and epic compositions, That a passion be adjusted to the character, the sentiments to the passion, and the language to the sentiments. If nature be not faithfully copied in each of these, a defect in execution is perceived: there may appear some resemblance; but the picture upon the whole will be insipid, through want of grace and delicacy. A painter, in order to represent the various attitudes of the body, ought to be intimately acquainted <452> with muscular motion: no less intimately acquainted with emotions and characters ought a writer to be, in order to represent the various attitudes of the mind. A general notion of the passions, in their grosser differences of strong and weak, elevated and humble, severe and gay, is far from being sufficient: pictures formed so superficially have little resemblance, and no expression; yet it will appear by and by, that in many instances our artists are deficient even in that superficial knowledge.

In handling the present subject, it would be endless to trace even the ordinary passions through their nice and minute differences. Mine shall be

* See Appendix, § 32.

an humbler task; which is, to select from the best writers instances of faulty sentiments, after paving the way by some general observations.

To talk in the language of music, each passion hath a certain tone, to which every sentiment proceeding from it ought to be tuned with the greatest accuracy: which is no easy work, especially where such harmony ought to be supported during the course of a long theatrical representation. In order to reach such delicacy of execution, it is necessary that a writer assume the precise character and passion of the personage represented; which requires an uncommon genius. But it is the only difficulty; for the writer, who, annihilating himself, can thus become another person, need be in no pain about the sentiments that belong to the as-<453>sumed character: these will flow without the least study, or even preconception; and will frequently be as delightfully new to himself as to his reader. But if a lively picture even of a single emotion, require an effort of genius, how much greater the effort to compose a passionate dialogue with as many different tones of passion as there are speakers? With what ductility of feeling must that writer be endued, who approaches perfection in such a work; when it is necessary to assume different and even opposite characters and passions, in the quickest succession? Yet this work, difficult as it is, yields to that of composing a dialogue in genteel comedy, exhibiting characters without passion. The reason is, that the different tones of character are more delicate and less in sight, than those of passion; and, accordingly, many writers who have no genius for drawing characters, make a shift to represent, tolerably well, an ordinary passion in its simple movements. But of all works of this kind, what is truly the most difficult, is a characteristical dialogue upon any philosophical subject: to interweave characters with reasoning, by suiting to the character of each speaker, a peculiarity not only of thought, but of expression, requires the perfection of genius, taste, and judgement.

How nice dialogue-writing is, will be evident, even without reasoning, from the miserable compositions of that kind found without number in all <454> languages. The art of mimicking any singularity in gesture or in voice, is a rare talent, though directed by sight and hearing, the acutest and most lively of our external senses: how much more rare must the talent be, of imitating characters and internal emotions, tracing all their different tints, and representing them in a lively manner by natural sentiments properly expressed? The truth is, such execution is too delicate for an ordinary genius; and for that reason, the bulk of writers, instead of expressing a passion as one does who feels it, content themselves with describing it in the language of a spectator. To awake passion by an internal effort merely, without any external cause, requires great sensibility: and yet that operation is necessary, no less to the writer than to the actor; because none but those who actually feel a passion, can represent it to the life. The writer's part is the more complicated: he must add composition to passion; and must, in the quickest succession, adopt every different character. But a very humble flight of imagination, may serve to convert a writer into a spectator; so as to figure, in some obscure manner, an action as passing in his sight and hearing. In that figured situation, being led naturally to write like a spectator, he entertains his readers with his own reflections, with cool description, and florid declamation; instead of making them eye-witnesses, as it were, to a real event, <455> and to every movement of genuine passion.* Thus most of our plays appear to be cast in the same mould; personages without character, the mere outlines of passion, a tiresome monotony, and a pompous declamatory style.†

This descriptive manner of representing passion, is a very cold entertainment: our sympathy is not raised by description; we must first be lulled

---

* In the *Aeneid,* the hero is made to describe himself in the following words: *Sum pius Aeneas, fama super aethera notus.* Virgil could never have been guilty of an impropriety so gross, had he assumed the personage of his hero, instead of uttering the sentiments of a spectator. Nor would Xenophon have made the following speech for Cyrus the younger, to his Grecian auxiliaries, whom he was leading against his brother Artaxerxes: "I have chosen you, O Greeks! my auxiliaries, not to enlarge my army, for I have *Barbarians* without number; but because you surpass all the *Barbarians* in valour and military discipline." This sentiment is Xenophon's; for surely Cyrus did not reckon his countrymen Barbarians. [*Aeneid* 1.378–79: "I am Aeneas the good . . . my fame is known in the heavens above." Kames elides the passage which, in full, reads: "I am Aeneas the good, who carry with me in my fleet my household goods, snatched from the foe; my fame is known in the heavens above."]

† Chez Racine tout est sentiment; il a su faire parler *chacun pour soi,* et c'est en cela qu'il est vraiment unique parmi les auteurs dramatiques de sa nation. *Rousseau.* ["In Racine sentiment is everything: he knows how to make each one speak for itself, and in that respect he is quite unique among our national dramatists." *La Nouvelle Héloïse* II. Lettre xvii, 1761.]

into a dream of reality, and every thing must appear as passing in our sight.*
Unhappy is the player of genius who acts a capital part in what may be
termed a *descriptive tragedy:* after assuming the very passion that is to be
represented, how is he <456> cramped in action, when he must utter, not
the sentiments of the passion he feels, but a cold description in the language
of a bystander? It is that imperfection, I am persuaded, in the bulk of our
plays, which confines our stage almost entirely to Shakespear, notwithstanding his many irregularities. In our late English tragedies, we sometimes
find sentiments tolerably well adapted to a plain passion: but we must not,
in any of them, expect a sentiment expressive of character; and, upon that
very account, our late performances of the dramatic kind are for the most
part intolerably insipid.

Looking back upon what is said, I am in some apprehension of not being
perfectly understood; for it is not easy to avoid obscurity in handling a
matter so complicated: but I promise to set it in the clearest light, by adding
example to precept. The first examples shall be of sentiments that appear
the legitimate offspring of passion; to which shall be opposed what are descriptive only, and illegitimate: and in making this comparison, I borrow
my instances from Shakespear and Corneille, who for genius in dramatic
composition stand uppermost in the rolls of fame.

Shakespear shall furnish the first example, being of sentiments dictated
by a violent and perturbed passion: <457>

> *Lear.* ———— ———— Filial ingratitude!
> Is it not, as if this mouth should tear this hand
> For lifting food to't?—But I'll punish home;
> No, I will weep no more—In such a night,
> To shut me out!—Pour on, I will endure.
> In such a night as this! O Regan, Gonerill,
> Your old kind father, whose frank heart gave all—
> O! that way madness lies; let me shun that;
> No more of that.—
> *Kent.* Good, my Lord, enter here.

---

* See chap. 2. part 1. sect. 7.

Lear. Pr'ythee, go in thyself, seek thine own ease,
This tempest will not give me leave to ponder
On things would hurt me more:—but I'll go in;
In, boy, go first. You houseless poverty—
Nay, get thee in; I'll pray, and then I'll sleep.—
Poor naked wretches, wheresoe'er you are,
That bide the pelting of this pitiless storm!
How shall your houseless heads, and unfed sides,
Your loop'd and window'd raggedness defend you
From seasons such as these?—O I have ta'en
Too little care of this! take physic, Pomp;
Expose thyself to feel what wretches feel,
That thou may'st shake the superflux to them,
And show the heavens more just.

King Lear, act 3. *sc.* 5.[1]

I give another example of the same kind, expressing sentiments arising from remorse and despair:

Othello. Lo! I have a weapon:
A better never did itself sustain
Upon a soldier's thigh. I've seen the day, <458>
That with this little arm, and this good sword,
I've made my way through more impediments
Than twenty times your stop. But, oh vain boast!
Who can controul his fate? 'tis not so now.
Be not afraid, though you do see me weapon'd;
Here is my journey's end, here is my butt,
The very sea-mark of my outmost sail.
Do you go back dismay'd? 'tis a lost fear.
Man but a rush against Othello's breast,
And he retires. Where should Othello go?
Now—how dost thou look now? Oh ill-starr'd wench!
Pale as thy smock! when we shall meet at compt,
This look of thine will hurl my soul from heav'n,
And fiends will snatch at it. Cold, cold, my girl;
Ev'n like thy chastity. O cursed slave!

___

1. Act 3, sc. 4.

Whip me, ye devils,
From the possession of this heav'nly sight;
Blow me about in winds, roast me in sulphur,
Wash me in steep-down gulfs of liquid fire—
Oh, Desdemona! Desdemona! dead! dead! oh! oh!

Othello, act 5. *sc.* 9.[2]

The sentiments here display'd flow so naturally from the passions represented, that we cannot conceive any imitation more perfect.

With regard to the French author, truth obliges me to acknowledge, that
he describes in the style of a spectator, instead of expressing passion like
one who feels it; which naturally betrays him into a tiresome monotony,
and a pompous decla-<459>matory style.* It is scarce necessary to give ex-

---

2. Act 5, sc. 2.

* This criticism reaches the French dramatic writers in general, with very few exceptions: their tragedies, excepting those of Racine, are mostly, if not totally, descriptive.
Corneille led the way; and later writers, imitating his manner, have accustomed the
French ear to a style, formal, pompous, declamatory, which suits not with any passion.
Hence to burlesque a French tragedy, is not more difficult than to burlesque a stiff sol-
emn fop. The facility of the operation has in Paris introduced a singular amusement,
which is, to burlesque the more successful tragedies in a sort of farce, called *a parody.*
La Motte [Antoine Houdard de la Motte, *A Critical Discourse on Homer's Iliad,* 1714],
who himself appears to have been sorely galled by some of these productions, acknowledges, that no more is necessary to give them currency but barely to vary the *dramatis
personae,* and instead of kings and heroes, queens and princesses, to substitute tinkers
and tailors, milkmaids and seamstresses. The declamatory style, so different from the
genuine expression of passion, passes in some measure unobserved, when great personages are the speakers; but in the mouths of the vulgar, the impropriety, with regard to
the speaker as well as to the passion represented, is so remarkable as to become ridiculous.
A tragedy, where every passion is made to speak in its natural tone, is not liable to be
thus burlesqued: the same passion is by all men expressed nearly in the same manner:
and, therefore, the genuine expressions of a passion cannot be ridiculous in the mouth
of any man who is susceptible of the passion.
    It is a well known fact, that to an English ear, the French actors appear to pronounce
with too great rapidity: a complaint much insisted on by Cibber [Colley Cibber, *Apology
for the Life of Mr. Colley Cibber, Comedian,* 1740] in particular, who had frequently heard
the famous Baron upon the French stage. This may in some measure be attributed to
our want of facility in the French tongue; as foreigners generally imagine, that every
language is pronounced too quick by natives. But that it is not the sole cause, will be
probable from a fact directly opposite, that the French are not a little disgusted with the

amples, for he never varies from that tone. I shall however take two passages
at a venture, in order to be confronted with those transcribed above. In the
tragedy of *Cinna*, Aemilia, after the <460> conspiracy was discovered, having nothing in view but racks and death to herself and her lover, receives
a pardon from Augustus, attended with the brightest circumstances of magnanimity and tenderness. This is a lucky situation for representing the passions of surprise and gratitude in their different stages, which seem naturally to be what follow. These passions, raised at once to the utmost <461>
pitch, and being at first too big for utterance, must, for some moments, be
expressed by violent gestures only: as soon as there is vent for words, the
first expressions are broken and interrupted: at last we ought to expect a
tide of intermingled sentiments, occasioned by the fluctuation of the mind
between the two passions. Aemilia is made to behave in a very different
manner: with extreme coolness she describes her own situation, as if she
were merely a spectator; or rather the poet takes the task off her hands:

> Et je me rens, Seigneur, à ces hautes bontés:
> Je recouvre la vûe auprès de leurs clartés.
> Je connois mon forfait qui me sembloit justice;
> Et ce que n'avoit pû la terreur du supplice,
> Je sens naitre en mon ame un repentir puissant,
> Et mon cœur en secret me dit, qu'il y consent.
> Le ciel a résolu votre grandeur suprême;
> Et pour preuve, Seigneur, je n'en veux que moi-même,
> J'ose avec vanité me donner cet éclat,
> Puisqu'il change mon cœur, qu'il veut changer l'état.
> Ma haine va mourir, que j'ai crue immortelle;
> Elle est morte, et ce cœur devient sujet fidele;

---

languidness, as they term it, of the English pronunciation. May not this difference of
taste be derived from what is observed above? The pronunciation of the genuine language
of a passion, is necessarily directed by the nature of the passion, particularly by the
slowness or celerity of its progress: plaintive passions, which are the most frequent in
tragedy, having a slow motion, dictate a slow pronunciation: in declamation, on the
contrary, the speaker warms gradually; and as he warms, he naturally accelerates his pronunciation. But as the French have formed their tone of pronunciation upon Corneille's
declamatory tragedies, and the English upon the more natural language of Shakespear,
it is not surprising that custom should produce such difference of taste in the two nations.

Et prenant désormais cette haine en horreur,
L'ardeur de vous servir succede à sa fureur.   *Act* 5. *sc.* 3.[3]

In the tragedy of *Sertorius,* the Queen, surprised with the news that her lover was assassinated, instead of venting any passion, degenerates into a <462> cool spectator, and undertakes to instruct the bystanders how a queen ought to behave on such an occasion:

> *Viriate.* Il m'en fait voir ensemble, et l'auteur, et la cause.
> Par cet assassinat c'est de moi qu'on dispose,
> C'est mon trône, c'est moi qu'on pretend conquerir;
> Et c'est mon juste choix qui seul l'a fait perir.
> Madame, après sa perte, et parmi ces alarmes,
> N'attendez point de moi de soupirs, ni de larmes;
> Ce sont amusemens que dédaigne aisement
> Le prompt et noble orgueil d'un vif ressentiment.
> Qui pleure, l'affoiblit; qui soupire, l'exhale:
> Il faut plus de fierté dans une ame royale;
> Et ma douleur soumise aux soins de le venger, &c.
>
> *Act* 5. *sc.* 3.[4]

---

3. Corneille: *Cinna,* act 5, sc. 3.

[Emilia]
I yield, Sir, to this generosity.
Its crystal radiance gives me back my sight.
What appeared justified is now a crime.
And—what death's terror had no power to do—
I feel in me burgeon repentance' flower,
And my heart's prompting gives assent to it.
Heaven has decided your supremacy,
And I, my lord, am the best proof 'tis so.
I dare give this decisive evidence:
Heaven changes me; then it can change the State.
My hate I thought undying ebbs to death;
It's dead. And with a new fidelity
I swear that, from now on, my eagerness
To serve you will replace my enmity.
(trans. John Cairncross)

4. Corneille, *Sertorius,* act 5, sc. 3: "I have been brought to see both the author and the cause. It is I who am destroyed by this murder; it is my throne, I whom they aim to

So much in general upon the genuine sentiments of passion. I proceed to particular observations. And, first, passions seldom continue uniform any considerable time: they generally fluctuate, swelling and subsiding by turns, often in a quick succession;* and the sentiments cannot be just unless they correspond to such fluctuation. Accordingly, a climax never shows better than in expressing a swelling passion: the following passages may suffice for an illustration.

> *Oroonoko.* ——— ——— Can you raise the dead?
> Pursue and overtake the wings of time? <463>
> And bring about again, the hours, the days,
> The years, that made me happy? *Oroonoko, act 2. sc. 2.*[5]

> *Almeria.* ——— ——— How hast thou charm'd
> The wildness of the waves and rocks to this?
> That thus relenting they have giv'n thee back
> To earth, to light and life, to love and me?
> *Mourning Bride, act 1. sc. 7.*

> I would not be the villain that thou think'st
> For the whole space that's in the tyrant's grasp,
> And the rich earth to boot. *Macbeth, act 4. sc. 4.*[6]

The following passage expresses finely the progress of conviction.

> Let me not stir, nor breathe, lest I dissolve
> That tender, lovely form, of painted air,

---

conquer, and my just choice who alone has perished. Madame, after such a loss, amidst such alarms, don't waste your sighs and tears on me; they are a diversion which disdains the prompt and noble pride of a burning resentment. Whoever weeps becomes weak; whoever sighs, expires; the royal soul must show more pride; and my grief must submit to the attentions of vengeance."

* See chap. 2. part 6.

5. *Oroonoko, or the Royal Slave,* by Aphra Behn, inspired Thomas Southern's *Oroonoko,* 1695; later revised by Garrick as *Isabella, or the Fatal Marriage,* 1741.

6. Act 4, sc. 3. Read "East" for "earth."

So like Almeria. Ha! it sinks, it falls;
I'll catch it ere it goes, and grasp her shade.
'Tis life! 'tis warm! 'tis she! 'tis she herself!
It is Almeria! 'tis, it is my wife!

Mourning Bride, act 2. sc. 6.

In the progress of thought, our resolutions become more vigorous as well as our passions:

If ever I do yield or give consent,
By any action, word, or thought, to wed
Another Lord; may then just heav'n show'r down, &c.

Mourning Bride, act 1. sc. 1. <464>

And this leads to a second observation, That the different stages of a passion, and its different directions, from birth to extinction, must be carefully represented in their order; because otherwise the sentiments, by being misplaced, will appear forc'd and unnatural. Resentment, for example, when provoked by an atrocious injury, discharges itself first upon the author: sentiments therefore of revenge come always first, and must in some measure be exhausted before the person injured think of grieving for himself. In the *Cid* of Corneille, Don Diegue having been affronted in a cruel manner, expresses scarce any sentiment of revenge, but is totally occupied in contemplating the low situation to which he is reduced by the affront:

O rage! ô desespoir! ô vieillesse ennemie!
N'ai-je donc tant vecu que pour cette infamie?
Et ne suis-je blanchi dans les travaux guerriers,
Que pour voir en un jour fletrir tant de lauriers?
Mon bras, qu'avec respect toute l'Espagne admire,
Mon bras, qui tant de fois a sauvé cet empire,
Tant de fois affermi le trône de son Roi,
Trahit donc ma querelle, et ne fait rien pour moi!
O cruel souvenir de ma gloire passée!
Oeuvre de tant de jours en un jour effacée!
Nouvelle dignité fatale à mon bonheur!
Precipice elevé d'où tombe mon honneur!
Faut il de votre éclat voir triompher le Comte,

Et mourir sans vengeance, ou vivre dans la honte?
Comte, sois de mon Prince à present governeur,
Ce haut rang n'admet point un homme sans honneur; <465>
Et ton jaloux orgueil par cet affront insigne,
Malgré le choix du Roi, m'en a sû rendre indigne.
Et toi, de mes exploits glorieux instrument,
Mais d'un corps tout de glace inutile ornement,
Fer jadis tant à craindre, et qui dans cette offense,
M'as servi de parade, et non pas de defense,
Va, quitte desormais le dernier des humains,
Passe pour me venger en de meilleures mains.

Le Cid, act 1. *sc.* 7.[7]

7. Corneille, *The Cid,* act 1, sc. 4:

[Don Diego]
O fury! O despair! O hostile age!
Have I then lived so long only for this?
Have I grown grey in warlike feats to see
My laurels faded in a single day?
My strong right arm the whole of Spain admires,
That arm which has so often saved the realm,
So many times buttressed a tottering throne,
Betrays me in my need, avails me nought.
O cruel memory of my past renown!
So many days in one day blotted out!
New honour fatal to my happiness!
O lofty heights from which my honour falls!
Must the count's triumph dim my glory's rays?
Must I die unavenged or die in shame?
Count, be the prince's tutor. That high rank
Cannot be held by a dishonoured man;
Your jealous pride has, by this grave affront,
Made me, despite the king, unfit for it.
And now an age-chilled body's ornament,
Once so much feared but used in this affront
Only for decoration, not defence,
Go, leave henceforth the lowest of the low.
Pass, to avenge me, into better hands.
(trans. John Cairncross)

These sentiments are certainly not the first that are suggested by the passion of resentment. As the first movements of resentment are always directed to its object, the very same is the case of grief. Yet with relation to the sudden and severe distemper that seized Alexander bathing in the river Cydnus, Quintus Curtius[8] describes the first emotions of the army as directed to themselves, lamenting that they were left without a leader, far from home, and had scarce any hopes of returning in safety: their King's distress, which must naturally have been their first concern, occupies them but in the second place according to that author. In the *Aminta* of Tasso, Sylvia, upon a report of her lover's death, which she believed certain, instead of bemoaning the loss of her beloved, turns her thoughts upon herself, and wonders her heart does not break:

> Ohime, ben son di sasso,
> Poi che questa novella non m'uccide.
>
> *Act* 4. *sc.* 2.[9] <466>

In the tragedy of *Jane Shore,* Alicia, in the full purpose of destroying her rival, has the following reflection:

> Oh Jealousy! thou bane of pleasing friendship,
> Thou worst invader of our tender bosoms;
> How does thy rancour poison all our softness,
> And turn our gentle natures into bitterness?
> See where she comes! Once my heart's dearest blessing,
> Now my chang'd eyes are blasted with her beauty,
> Loathe that known face, and sicken to behold her.
>
> *Act* 3. *sc.* I.

These are the reflections of a cool spectator. A passion while it has the ascendant, and is freely indulged, suggests not to the person who feels it, any sentiment to its own prejudice: reflections like the foregoing, occur not readily till the passion has spent its vigor.

A person sometimes is agitated at once by different passions; and the

8. Quintus Curtius Rufus: nothing is known of his dates or life, except that he flourished as a rhetorician ca. A.D. 50. The extant parts of his *History of Alexander* are regarded by scholars as inaccurate. The reference is to Book X.

9. Tasso, *Aminta,* act 4, sc. 2: "Alas! Now I am made of stones, since this news does not kill me."

mind in that case, vibrating like a pendulum, vents itself in sentiments that partake of the same vibration. This I give as a third observation:

> *Queen.* 'Would I had never trod this English earth,
> Or felt the flatteries that grow upon it.
> Ye've angels faces, but Heav'n knows your hearts.
> What shall become of me now! wretched lady!
> I am the most unhappy woman living.
> Alas! poor wenches, where are now your fortunes?
> [*To her women.* <467>
> Shipwreck'd upon a kingdom, where no pity,
> No friends, no hope! no kindred weep for me!
> Almost, no grave allow'd me.　　　*Henry* VIII. *act* 3. *sc.* 1.

> *Othello.* Oh devil, devil!
> If that the earth could teem with woman's tears,
> Each drop she falls, would prove a crocodile.
> Out of my sight.
> 　　*Desdemona.* I will not stay t'offend you.　　　　　[*going.*
> 　　*Lodovico.* Truly, an obedient lady:
> I do beseech your Lordship, call her back.
> 　　*Oth.* Mistress—
> 　　*Des.* My Lord.
> 　　*Oth.* What would you with her, Sir?
> 　　*Lod.* Who, I, my Lord?
> 　　*Oth.* Ay; you did wish that I would make her turn.
> Sir, she can turn and turn, and yet go on;
> And turn again. And she can weep, Sir, weep;
> And she's obedient: as you say, obedient;
> Very obedient—proceed you in your tears—
> Concerning this, Sir,—oh well-painted passion!—
> I am commanded home—get you away,
> I'll send for you anon—Sir, I obey the mandate,
> And will return to Venice.—Hence, avaunt!
> [*Exit Desdemona.*
> *Othello,* act 4. *sc.* 6.[10]

10. Act 4, sc. 1.

> *Aemilia.* Oh! my good Lord, I would speak a word with you.
> *Othello.* Yes, 'tis Aemilia—By and by—She's dead.
> 'Tis like she comes to speak of Cassio's death;
> The noise was high.—Ha! no more moving?
> Still as the grave. Shall she come in? were't good? <468>
> I think she stirs again—No—what's the best?
> If she come in, she'll, sure, speak to my wife;
> My wife! my wife! What wife! I have no wife;
> Oh insupportable! oh heavy hour!   *Othello, act 5. sc. 7.*[11]

A fourth observation is, That nature, which gave us passions, and made them extremely beneficial when moderate, intended undoubtedly that they should be subjected to the government of reason and conscience.* It is therefore against the order of nature, that passion in any case should take the lead in contradiction to reason and conscience: such a state of mind is a sort of anarchy, which every one is ashamed of, and endeavours to hide or dissemble. Even love, however laudable, is attended with a conscious shame when it becomes immoderate: it is covered from the world, and disclosed only to the beloved object:

> Et que l'amour souvent de remors combattu
> Paroisse une foiblesse, et non une vertu.
>   *Boileau, L'art poet. chant.* 3. *l.* 101.[12]

> O, they love least that let men know their love.
>   *Two Gentlemen of Verona, act* 1. *sc.* 3.[13]

Hence a capital rule in the representation of immoderate passions, that they ought to be hid or dissembled as much as possible. And this holds in <469> an especial manner with respect to criminal passions: one never counsels

---

* See chap. 2. part 7.

11. Act 5, sc. 2.

12. That, struggling oft, his Passions we may find,
    The Frailty, not the Virtue of his Mind.

13. Act 1, sc. 2.

the commission of a crime in plain terms: guilt must not appear in its native colours, even in thought: the proposal must be made by hints, and by representing the action in some favourable light. Of the propriety of sentiment upon such an occasion, Shakespear, in the *Tempest,* has given us a beautiful example, in a speech by the usurping Duke of Milan, advising Sebastian to murder his brother the King of Naples:

> *Antonio.* ———— ———— What might,
> Worthy Sebastian,—O, what might—no more.
> And yet, methinks, I see it in thy face,
> What thou shouldst be: th' occasion speaks thee, and
> My strong imagination sees a crown
> Dropping upon thy head.   *Act* 2. *sc.* 1.

There never was drawn a more complete picture of this kind, than that of King John soliciting Hubert to murder the young Prince Arthur:

> *K. John.* Come hither, Hubert. O my gentle Hubert,
> We owe thee much; within this wall of flesh
> There is a soul counts thee her creditor,
> And with advantage means to pay thy love.
> And, my good friend, thy voluntary oath
> Lives in this bosom, dearly cherished.
> Give me thy hand, I had a thing to say—
> But I will fit it with some better time. <470>
> By Heav'n, Hubert, I'm almost asham'd
> To say what good respect I have of thee.
>   *Hubert.* I am much bounden to your Majesty.
>   *K. John.* Good friend, thou hast no cause to say so yet—
> But thou shalt have—and creep time ne'er so slow,
> Yet it shall come for me to do thee good.
> I had a thing to say—but let it go;
> The sun is in the heav'n; and the proud day,
> Attended with the pleasures of the world,
> Is all too wanton and too full of gawds,
> To give me audience. If the midnight-bell
> Did with his iron-tongue and brazen mouth
> Sound one into the drowsy race of night;

If this same were a church-yard where we stand,
And thou possessed with a thousand wrongs;
Or if that surly spirit Melancholy
Had bak'd thy blood, and made it heavy-thick,
Which else runs tickling up and down the veins,
Making that idiot Laughter keep mens eyes,
And strain their cheeks to idle merriment,
(A passion hateful to my purposes);
Or if that thou couldst see me without eyes,
Hear me without thine ears, and make reply
Without a tongue, using conceit alone,
Without eyes, ears, and harmful sound of words;
Then, in despite of broad-ey'd watchful day,
I would into thy bosom pour my thoughts.
But ah, I will not—Yet I love thee well;
And, by my troth, I think thou lov'st me well.
    Hubert. So well, that what you bid me undertake,
Though that my death were adjunct to my act,
By Heav'n, I'd do't.
    K. John. Do not I know, thou wouldst? <471>
Good Hubert, Hubert, Hubert, throw thine eye
On yon young boy. I'll tell thee what, my friend;
He is a very serpent in my way.
And, wheresoe'er this foot of mine doth tread,
He lies before me. Dost thou understand me?
Thou art his keeper.   *King John, act* 3. *sc.* 5.[14]

As things are best illustrated by their contraries, I proceed to faulty sentiments, disdaining to be indebted for examples to any but the most approved authors. The first class shall consist of sentiments that accord not with the passion; or, in other words, sentiments that the passion does not naturally suggest. In the second class, shall be ranged sentiments that may belong to an ordinary passion, but unsuitable to it as tinctured by a singular character. Thoughts that properly are not sentiments, but rather descrip-

14. Act 3, sc. 3.

tions, make a third. Sentiments that belong to the passion represented, but are faulty as being introduced too early or too late, make a fourth. Vicious sentiments exposed in their native dress, instead of being concealed or disguised, make a fifth. And in the last class, shall be collected sentiments suited to no character nor passion, and therefore unnatural.

The first class contains faulty sentiments of various kinds, which I shall endeavour to distinguish from each other; beginning with sentiments that are faulty by being above the tone of the passion: <472>

> *Othello.* ———— ———— O my soul's joy!
> If after every tempest come such calms,
> May the winds blow till they have waken'd death!
> And let the labouring bark climb hills of seas
> Olympus high, and duck again as low
> As hell's from heaven!   *Othello, act 2. sc. 6.*[15]

This sentiment may be suggested by violent and inflamed passion, but is not suited to the calm satisfaction that one feels upon escaping danger.

> *Philaster.* Place me, some god, upon a pyramid
> Higher than hills of earth, and lend a voice
> Loud as your thunder to me, that from thence
> I may discourse to all the under-world
> The worth that dwells in him.
>   *Philaster of Beaumont and Fletcher, act 4.*[16]

Second. Sentiments below the tone of the passion. Ptolemy, by putting Pompey to death, having incurred the displeasure of Caesar, was in the utmost dread of being dethroned: in that agitating situation, Corneille makes him utter a speech full of cool reflection, that is in no degree expressive of the passion.

> Ah! si je t'avois crû, je n'aurois pas de maitre,
> Je serois dans le trône où le Ciel m'a fait naître;

---

15. Act 2, sc. 1.
16. Beaumont and Fletcher, *Philaster*, 1611.

> Mais c'est une imprudence assez commune aux rois,
> D'écouter trop d'avis, et se tromper au choix.
> Le Destin les aveugle au bord du précipice,
> Où si quelque lumiere en leur ame se glisse, <473>
> Cette fausse clarté dont il les eblouit,
> Le plonge dans une gouffre, et puis s'evanouit.
>
> *La mort de Pompée, act* 4. *sc.* 1.[17]

In *Les Freres ennemies* of Racine, the second act is opened with a love-scene: Hemon talks to his mistress of the torments of absence, of the lustre of her eyes, that he ought to die no where but at her feet, and that one moment of absence is a thousand years. Antigone on her part acts the coquette; pretends she must be gone to wait on her mother and brother, and cannot stay to listen to his courtship. This is odious French gallantry, below the dignity of the passion of love: it would scarce be excusable in painting modern French manners; and is insufferable where the ancients are brought upon the stage. The manners painted in the *Alexandre* of the same author are not more just: French gallantry prevails there throughout.

Third. Sentiments that agree not with the tone of the passion; as where a pleasant sentiment is grafted upon a painful passion, or the contrary. In the following instances the sentiments are too gay for a serious passion.

> No happier task these faded eyes pursue;
> To read and weep is all they now can do.
>
> *Eloisa to Abelard, l.* 47. <474>

Again,

---

17. Ah! Had thy good Advice Belief obtain'd
  Without a Master Ptolemy had Reign'd,
  But Kings still chuse (Govern'd by some ill Fate)
  The worst Advice after a long debate;
  Destiny blinds them, or if any Light
  Seem to inform, it but deceives their Sight,
  And with delusive Glimmerings leads them on,
  Till they have Reach'd their own Destruction.
      (*Pompey the Great.*)

Heav'n first taught letters for some wretch's aid,
Some banish'd lover, or some captive maid;
They live, they speak, they breathe what love inspires,
Warm from the soul, and faithful to its fires;
The virgin's wish without her fears impart,
Excuse the blush, and pour out all the heart;
Speed the soft intercourse from soul to soul,
And waft a sigh from Indus to the pole.

Eloisa to Abelard, l. 51.

These thoughts are pretty: they suit Pope, but not Eloisa.

Satan, enraged by a threatening of the angel Gabriel, answers thus:

Then when I am thy captive talk of chains,
Proud limitary cherub; but ere then
Far heavier load thyself expect to feel
From my prevailing arm, though Heaven's King
Ride on thy wings, and thou with thy compeers,
Us'd to the yoke, draw'st his triumphant wheels
In progress through the road of heav'n *star-pav'd.*

Paradise lost, book 4.

The concluding epithet forms a grand and delightful image, which cannot be the genuine offspring of rage.

Fourth. Sentiments too artificial for a serious <475> passion. I give for the first example a speech of Piercy expiring:

O, Harry, thou hast robb'd me of my growth:
I better brook the loss of brittle life,
Than those proud titles thou hast won of me;
They wound my thoughts, worse than thy sword my flesh.
But thought's the slave of life, and life time's fool;
And time, that takes survey of all the world,
Must have a stop. *First part, Henry* IV. *act* 5. *sc.* 9.[18]

18. Act 5, sc. 4. Read "youth" for "growth" in the first line.

Livy inserts the following passage in a plaintive oration of the Locrenses, accusing Pleminius the Roman legate of oppression.

> In hoc legato vestro, nec hominis quicquam est, Patres Conscripti, praeter figuram et speciem; neque Romani civis, praeter habitum vestitumque, et sonum linguae Latinae. Pestis et bellua immanis, quales fretum, quondam, quo ab Sicilia dividimur, ad perniciem navigantium circumsedisse, fabulae ferunt.*

The sentiments of the *Mourning Bride* are for the most part no less delicate than just copies of nature: in the following exception the picture is beautiful, but too artful to be suggested by severe grief.

> *Almeria.* O no! Time gives increase to my afflictions.
> The circling hours, that gather all the woes < 476 >
> Which are diffus'd through the revolving year,
> Come heavy laden with th' oppressive weight
> To me; with me, successively, they leave
> The sighs, the tears, the groans, the restless cares,
> And all the damps of grief, that did retard their flight.
> They shake their downy wings, and scatter all
> The dire collected dews on my poor head;
> Then fly with joy and swiftness from me.   *Act* I. *sc.* I.

In the same play, Almeria seeing a dead body, which she took to be Alphonso's, expresses sentiments strained and artificial, which nature suggests not to any person upon such an occasion:

> Had they, or hearts, or eyes, that did this deed?
> Could eyes endure to guide such cruel hands?
> Are not my eyes guilty alike with theirs,
> That thus can gaze, and yet not turn to stone?
> —I do not weep! The springs of tears are dry'd,

---

* Titus Livius, I. 29. § 17. ["In this legatus of yours {. . .} there is nothing of a human being, conscript fathers, except his form and outward appearance, nothing of a Roman citizen except his bearing and garments and the sound of the Latin language. He is a pest-bringing monster, like those of which myths say that, in order to destroy mariners, they once had their abode on this side and that of the strait by which we are separated from Sicily." Kames omits a phrase here indicated by braces.]

And of a sudden I am calm, as if
All things were well; and yet my husband's murder'd!
Yes, yes, I know to mourn: I'll sluice this heart,
The source of wo, and let the torrent loose.   *Act* 5. *sc.* 11.

Lady Trueman. How could you be so cruel to defer giving me that joy
which you knew I must receive from your presence? You have robb'd my
life of some hours of happiness that ought to have been in it.
                                                Drummer, act 5.[19]

Pope's Elegy to the memory of an unfortunate lady, expresses delicately
the most tender concern and sorrow that one can feel for the deplorable
fate <477> of a person of worth. Such a poem, deeply serious and pathetic,
rejects with disdain all fiction. Upon that account, the following passage
deserves no quarter; for it is not the language of the heart, but of the imagination indulging its flights at ease; and by that means is eminently discordant with the subject. It would be a still more severe censure, if it should
be ascribed to imitation, copying indiscreetly what has been said by others:

> What though no weeping loves thy ashes grace,
> Nor polish'd marble emulate thy face?
> What though no sacred earth allow thee room,
> Nor hallow'd dirge be mutter'd o'er thy tomb?
> Yet shall thy grave with rising flow'rs be drest,
> And the green turf lie lightly on thy breast:
> There shall the morn her earliest tears bestow,
> There the first roses of the year shall blow;
> While angels with their silver wings o'ershade
> The ground, now sacred by thy reliques made.[20]

Fifth. Fanciful or finical sentiments. Sentiments that degenerate into
point or conceit, however they may amuse in an idle hour, can never be the
offspring of any serious or important passion. In the *Jerusalem* of Tasso,
Tancred, after a single combat, spent with fatigue and loss of blood, falls
into a swoon; in which situation, understood to be dead, he is discovered

19. Joseph Addison, *The Drummer*, 1715, a prose comedy.
20. Alexander Pope, *Elegy to the Memory of an Unfortunate Lady*, 1717.

by Erminia, who was in love with him to distraction. A more happy situation cannot be imagined, to raise grief in an <478> instant to its height; and yet, in venting her sorrow, she descends most abominably into antithesis and conceit, even of the lowest kind:

> E in lui versò d'inefficabil vena
> Lacrime, e voce di sospiri mista.
> In che misero punto hor qui me mena
> Fortuna? a che veduta amara e trista?
> Dopo gran tempo i' ti ritrovo à pena
> Tancredi, e ti riveggio, e non son vista,
> Vista non son da te, benche presente
> E trovando ti perdo eternamente.   *Canto* 19. *st.* 105.[21]

Armida's lamentation respecting her lover Rinaldo,* is in the same vicious taste.

> *Queen.* Give me no help in lamentation,
> I am not barren to bring forth complaints:
> All springs reduce their currents to mine eyes,
> That I, being govern'd by the wat'ry moon,
> May send forth plenteous tears to drown the world,
> Ah, for my husband, for my dear Lord Edward.
>   *King Richard* III. *act* 2. *sc.* 2.

> *Jane Shore.* Let me be branded for the public scorn,
> Turn'd forth, and driven to wander like a vagabond,
> Be friendless and forsaken, seek my bread

---

* Canto 20. stan. 124. 125, & 126.

21. Her springs of teares she looseth foorth, and cries
    "Hither why bringst thou me, ah fortune blinde?
    Where dead (for whom I liu'd) my comfort lies,
    Where warre, for peace; trauell for rest I finde;
    Tancred, I haue thee, see thee, yet thine eies
    Lookte not upon thy loue and handmaide kinde,
    Undoe their doores, their lides fast closed seuer,
    Alas, I finde thee for to lose thee euer."
    (*Gerusalemme liberata,* trans. Edward Fairfax)

Upon the barren wild, and desolate waste,
Feed on my sighs, and drink my falling tears;
Ere I consent to teach my lips injustice,
Or wrong the orphan who has none to save him.

Jane Shore, act 4. <479>

Give me your drops, ye soft-descending rains,
Give me your streams, ye never-ceasing springs,
That my sad eyes may still supply my duty,
And feed an everlasting flood of sorrow.

Jane Shore, act 5.

Jane Shore utters her last breath in a witty conceit:

Then all is well, and I shall sleep in peace—
'Tis very dark, and I have lost you now—.
Was there not something I would have bequeath'd you?
But I have nothing left me to bestow,
Nothing but one sad sigh. Oh mercy, Heav'n!   [*Dies.*

Act 5.

Gilford to Lady Jane Gray, when both were condemned to die:

Thou stand'st unmov'd;
Calm temper sits upon thy beauteous brow;
Thy eyes that flow'd so fast for Edward's loss,
Gaze unconcern'd upon the ruin round thee,
As if thou hadst resolv'd to brave thy fate,
And triumph in the midst of desolation.
Ha! see, it swells, the liquid crystal rises,
It starts in spight of thee—but I will catch it,
Nor let the earth be wet with dew so rich.

Lady Jane Gray, act 4. *near the end.*

The concluding sentiment is altogether finical, unsuitable to the importance of the occasion, and even to the dignity of the passion of love. <480>

Corneille, in his *Examen of the Cid,** answering an objection, That his

---

* Page 316.

sentiments are sometimes too much refined for persons in deep distress, observes, that if poets did not indulge sentiments more ingenious or refined than are prompted by passion, their performances would often be low, and extreme grief would never suggest but exclamations merely. This is in plain language to assert, that forc'd thoughts are more agreeable than those that are natural, and ought to be preferred.

The second class is of sentiments that may belong to an ordinary passion, but are not perfectly concordant with it, as tinctured by a singular character.

In the last act of that excellent comedy, *The Careless Husband*,[22] Lady Easy, upon Sir Charles's reformation, is made to express more violent and turbulent sentiments of joy, than are consistent with the mildness of her character:

> *Lady Easy.* O the soft treasure! O the dear reward of long-desiring love.——Thus! thus to have you mine, is something more than happiness; 'tis double life, and madness of abounding joy.

If the sentiments of a passion ought to be suited to a peculiar character, it is still more necessary that actions be suited to the character. In the 5th act of the *Drummer,* Addison makes his gardener act even below the character of an ignorant credulous rustic: he gives him the behaviour of a gaping idiot. <481>

The following instances are descriptions rather than sentiments, which compose a third class.

Of this descriptive manner of painting the passions, there is in the *Hippolytus* of Euripides, act 5. an illustrious instance, namely, the speech of Theseus, upon hearing of his son's dismal exit. In Racine's tragedy of *Esther,* the Queen hearing of the decree issued against her people, instead of expressing sentiments suitable to the occasion, turns her attention upon herself, and describes with accuracy her own situation:

22. Colley Cibber.

Juste Ciel! tout mon sang dans mes veines se glace.

Act i. *sc.* 3.[23]

Again,

Aman. C'en est fait. Mon orgueil est forcé de plier. L'inexorable Aman est reduit à prier.   *Esther, act* 3. *sc.* 5.[24]

Athalie. Quel prodige nouveau me trouble et m'embarrasse?
La douceur de sa voix, son enfance, sa grace,
Font insensiblement à mon inimitié
Succeder—Je serois sensible à la pitié?

Athalie, act 2. *sc.* 7.[25]

Titus. O de ma passion fureur desesperée!

Brutus of Voltaire, act 3. *sc.* 6.[26]

What other are the foregoing instances but describing the passion another feels? <482>

A man stabbed to the heart in a combat with his enemy expresses himself thus:

So, now I am at rest:—
I feel death rising higher still, and higher,
Within my bosom; every breath I fetch
Shuts up my life within a shorter compass:
And like the vanishing sound of bells, grows less
And less each pulse, 'till it be lost in air.   *Dryden.*

23. "Heavens above! My blood has turned to ice."
24. "It's true. My pride is forced to bend. The unrelenting Aman is reduced to prayer."
25. What miracle disturbs and baffles me?
    The sweetness of his voice, his youth, his charm
    Make hatred imperceptibly give way
    To what? To feeling pity? Can that be?
         (*Athaliah*, trans. John Cairncross)
26. "Oh the despairing fury of my passion!"

Captain Flash, in a farce composed by Garrick, endeavours to hide his fear by saying, "What a damn'd passion I am in."

An example is given above of remorse and despair expressed by genuine and natural sentiments. In the fourth book of *Paradise lost,* Satan is made to express his remorse and despair in sentiments, which, though beautiful, are not altogether natural: they are rather the sentiments of a spectator, than of a person who actually is tormented with these passions.

The fourth class is of sentiments introduced too early or too late.

Some examples mentioned above belong to this class. Add the following from *Venice preserv'd,* act 5. at the close of the scene between Belvidera and her father Priuli. The account given by Belvidera of the danger she was in, and of her husband's threatening to murder her, ought naturally to have alarmed her relenting father, and to have < 483 > made him express the most perturbed sentiments. Instead of which, he dissolves into tenderness and love for his daughter, as if he had already delivered her from danger, and as if there were a perfect tranquillity:

> Canst thou forgive me all my follies past?
> I'll henceforth be indeed a father; never
> Never more thus expose, but cherish thee,
> Dear as the vital warmth that feeds my life,
> Dear as those eyes that weep in fondness o'er thee:
> Peace to thy heart.

Immoral sentiments exposed in their native colours, instead of being concealed or disguised, compose the fifth class.

The Lady Macbeth, projecting the death of the King, has the following soliloquy.

> ———— ———— The raven himself's not hoarse
> That croaks the fatal entrance of Duncan
> Under my battlements. Come all you spirits
> That tend on mortal thoughts, unsex me here,
> And fill me from the crown to the toe, top-full
> Of direct cruelty; make thick my blood,

Stop up th' access and passage to remorse,
That no compunctious visitings of nature
Shake my fell purpose. *Macbeth, act* I. *sc.* 7.[27]

This speech is not natural. A treacherous murder was never perpetrated even by the most har-<484>dened miscreant, without compunction: and that the lady here must have been in horrible agitation, appears from her invoking the infernal spirits to fill her with cruelty, and to stop up all avenues to remorse. But in that state of mind, it is a never-failing artifice of self-deceit, to draw the thickest veil over the wicked action, and to extenuate it by all the circumstances that imagination can suggest: and if the crime cannot bear disguise, the next attempt is to thrust it out of mind altogether, and to rush on to action without thought. This last was the husband's method:

Strange things I have in head, that will to hand;
Which must be acted ere they must be scann'd.

Act 3. *sc.* 5.[28]

The lady follows neither of these courses, but in a deliberate manner endeavours to fortify her heart in the commission of an execrable crime, without even attempting to colour it. This I think is not natural; I hope there is no such wretch to be found as is here represented. In the *Pompey* of Corneille,* Photine counsels a wicked action in the plainest terms without disguise:

Seigneur, n'attirez point le tonnerre en ces lieux,
Rangez vous du parti des destins et des dieux,
Et sans les accuser d'injustice, ou d'outrage;
Puis qu'ils font les heureux, adorez leur ouvrage; <485>
Quels que soient leurs decrets, déclarez-vous pour eux,
Et pour leur obéir, perdez le malheureux.
Pressé de toutes parts des coléres celestes,

---

* Act I. sc. I.
27. Act I, sc. 5. Read "direst cruelty" for "direct cruelty."
28. Act 3, sc. 4.

Il en vient dessus vous faire fondre les restes;
Et sa tête qu' à peine il a pû dérober,
Tout prête dechoir, cherche avec qui tomber.
Sa retraite chez vous en effet n'est qu'un crime;
Elle marque sa haine, et non pas son estime;
Il ne vient que vous perdre en venant prendre port,
Et vous pouvez douter s'il est digne de mort!
Il devoit mieux remplir nos vœux et notre attente,
Faire voir sur ses nefs la victoire flotante;
Il n'eût ici trouvé que joye et que festins,
Mais puisqu'il est vaincu, qu'il s'en prenne aux destins.
J'en veux à sa disgrace et non à sa personne,
J' exécute à regret ce que le ciel ordonne,
Et du même poignard, pour César destiné,
Je perce en soupirant son cœur infortuné.
Vous ne pouvez enfin qu' aux dépens de sa tête
Mettre à l'abri la vôtre, et parer la tempête.
Laissez nommer sa mort un injuste attentat,
La justice n'est pas une vertu d'état.
Le choix des actions, ou mauvaises, ou bonnes,
Ne fait qu' anéantir la force des couronnes;
Le droit des rois consiste à ne rien épargner;
La timide équité détruit l'art de regner;
Quand on craint d'être injuste on a toûjours à craindre,
Et qui veut tout pouvoir doit oser tout enfraindre,
Fuir comme un deshonneur la vertu qui le pert,
Et voler sans scrupule au crime qui lui sert.[29]

29. Act I, sc. I:

Side with the Gods, declare yourself for Fate,
Draw not on us their Thunder and their Hate,
Ask not how firstly, wherefor they chastise,
But worship him whom they would have to Rise,
Approve of their dresses, applaud their Will,
And whom they frown on in Obedience kill.
By divine vengeance on all side persu'd
Pompey invokes your Aegypt in the fewd;
His head that he has shifted so to save,

In the tragedy of *Esther,** Haman acknowledges, <486> without disguise, his cruelty, insolence, and pride. And there is another example of the same kind in the *Agamemnon* of Seneca.† In the tragedy of *Athalie,*‡ Mathan, in cool blood, relates to his friend many black crimes he had been guilty of, to satisfy his ambition.

In Congreve's *Double-dealer,* Maskwell, instead of disguising or colouring his crimes, values himself upon them in a soliloquy:

Cynthia, let thy beauty gild my crimes; and whatsoever I commit of treachery or deceit, shall be imputed to me as a merit.—Treachery! what

---

Falling your Royal Company would have;
His present coming I unfriendly deem,
Th'effect of Hatred rather than Esteem;
'Tis to Destroy you, hither now to fly,
And can you doubt if he deserve to Dye?
He should have come with Bays upon his brows,
And with Success have seconded our Vows;
With Feasts and Triumphs then we had receiv'd him,
'Tis his own Fate, not we that have deceiv'd him,
Not him, but his ill Fortune we neglect,
For to his person we would pay Respect;
Caesar subdu'd, by the same Sword had Dy'd,
With which less willingly we pierce his side;
Under his Ruine you must shelter take,
And in this Storm his Death your harbour make,
Which though the World should reckon as a Crime,
Is but a Just compliance with the time;
The strict regard of Justice does annoy
The power of Crowns, and policy Destroy;
'Tis the Prerogative of Kings to spare
Nothing when they their own Destruction fear;
He wants no Danger whom the care of Right
Keeps from Injustice when 'tis requisite;
Who to his Royal Power no bound, would have
To his own Conscience must not be a slave.

                    (*Pompey the Great*)

* Act 2. sc. 1.
† Beginning of act 2.
‡ Act 3. sc. 3. at the close.

treachery? Love cancels all the bonds of friendship, and sets men right
upon their first foundations.   *Act* 2. *sc.* 8.

In French plays, love, instead of being hid or disguised, is treated as a
serious concern, and of greater importance than fortune, family, or dignity.
I suspect the reason to be, that in the capital of France, love, by the easiness
of intercourse, has dwindled down from a real passion to be a connection
that is regulated entirely by the mode or fashion.* This may in some measure excuse <487> their writers, but will never make their plays be relished
among foreigners:

> *Maxime.* Quoi, trahir mon ami?
> *Euphorbe.* —L'amour rend tout permis,
> Un véritable amant ne connoît point d'amis.
>   *Cinna, act* 3. *sc.* 1.[30]

> *Cesar.* Reine, tout est plaisible, et la ville calmée,
> Qu'un trouble assez leger avoit trop allarmée.
> N'a plus à redouter le divorce intestin
> Du soldat insolent, et du peuple mutin.
> Mais, ô Dieux! ce moment que je vous ai quittée,
> D'un trouble bien plus grand à mon ame agitée,
> Et ces soins importuns qui m'arrachoient de vous
> Contre ma grandeur même allumoient mon courroux.
> Je lui voulois du mal de m'être si contraire,
> De rendre ma presence ailleurs si necessaire.
> Mais je lui pardonnois au simple souvenir
> Du bonheur qu'à ma flâme elle fait obtenir.

---

* A certain author says humorously, "Les mots mêmes d'amour et d'amant sont ban-
nis de l'intime société des deux sexes, et relegués avec ceux de *chaine* et de *flame* dans les
Romans qu'on ne lit plus." And where nature is once banished, a fair field is open to
every fantastic imitation, even the most extravagant. ["Even the words for love and loving
are banished from intimate society between the sexes, and replaced by those of bond and
passion from the Roman authors whom no one any longer reads."]

    30. [Maxime]
       What, betray my friend?

      [Euphorbus]
      All's fair in love; a true lover knows no friends.

C'est elle dont je tiens cette haute espérance,
Qui flate mes desirs d'une illustre apparence,
Et fait croire à César qu'il peut former de vœux,
Qu'il n'est pas tout-à-fait indigne de vos feux,
Et qu'il peut en pretendre une juste conquête,
N'ayant plus que les Dieux au dessus de sa tête.
Oui, Reine, si quelqu' un dans ce vaste univers
Pouvoit porter plus haut la gloire de vos fers;
S'il étoit quelque trône où vous pouissiez paroître
Plus dignement assise en captivant son maître, <488>
J'irois, j'irois à lui, moins pour le lui ravir,
Que pour lui disputer le droit de vous servir;
Et je n'aspirerois au bonheur de vous plaire,
Qu'après avoir mis bas un si grand adversaire.
C'etoit pour acquerir un droit si précieux,
Que combattoit par tout mon bras ambitieux,
Et dans Pharsale même il a tiré l'epée
Plus pour le conservir, que pour vaincre Pompée.
Je l'ai vaincu, Princesse, et le Dieu de combats
M'y favorisoit moins que vos divins appas.
Ils conduisoient ma main, ils enfloient mon courage,
Cette pleine victoire est leur dernier ouvrage,
C'est l'effet des ardeurs qu'ils daignoient m'inspirer;
Et vos beaux yeux enfin m'ayant fait soûpirer,
Pour faire que votre ame avec gloire y réponde,
M'ont rendu le premier, et de Rome, et du monde;
C'est ce glorieux titre, à présent effectif,
Que je viens ennoblir par celui de captif;
Heureux, si mon esprit gagne tant sur le vôtre,
Qu'il en estime l'un, et me permette l'autre.

Pompée, act 4. *sc.* 3.[31]

31. My queen, this Storm is laid without much harm,
    A great Commotion gave a great Alarm;
    But when I left you I began to find
    A greater Tumult in my Troubled mind.
    Love, my most powerful passion made me hate
    Success and greatness, Curse the cruel fate

The last class comprehends sentiments that are unnatural, as being suited to no character nor passion. These may be subdivided into three branches: first, sentiments unsuitable to the constitution of man, and to the laws of his nature; second, inconsistent sentiments; third, sentiments that are pure rant and extravagance.

————

> That rais'd me, since thus great I cannot spare
> My self one hour of Joy, but some new Care
> Still calls me from you, yet I straight again
> Am reconcil'd to Fortune, and restrain
> My Causeless passion, nay, adore my Bays,
> Since they my Hopes as well as Person raise
> To that auspicious height from whence I see,
> So fair a prospect of Felicity,
> That I dare hope Requital of my Flame,
> Though my Ambitious Love make you his Aim.
> You may now Caesar with like ardour meet,
> Kings cast their Crown and Sceptres at my feet
> But if the world a Monarch yet contains,
> Who more deserves the Glory of your Charms
> On whose high Throne you might with greater State
> Give Laws to Nations, and Dispose of Fate,
> By Force of Arms I would my Title prove,
> His Rival less for Empire than for Love,
> Nor should I hope you would my Flames allow,
> Till I had made so great a Rival bow;
> These were the Ambitious hopes which have thus farr
> Engag'd your Caesar in a Civil Warr,
> And that I might this glorious right maintain,
> I conquer'd Pompey on Pharsalia's Plain;
> When e'er I fought, your Beauty did afford
> Strength to my Arm, and Sharpness to my Sword,
> And all the fair Success I had in Arms,
> Were the Effects of your Bright Beauties Charms,
> Which in my Breast did first this Passion move,
> And now has Rais'd me Equal to your Love,
> Since I without a Rival am become
> Master of all the World and Head of Rome:
> These are my Titles that my Valour gave,
> Which love innobles by the name of Slave,
> And I am more than Blest if you approve
> And perfect the success of humble love.
>   (*Pompey the Great*)

When the fable is of human affairs, every event, every incident, and every circumstance, ought to be natural, otherwise the imitation is imperfect. <489> But an imperfect imitation is a venial fault, compared with that of running cross to nature. In the *Hippolytus* of Euripides,* Hippolytus, wishing for another self in his own situation, How much (says he) should I be touched with his misfortune! as if it were natural to grieve more for the misfortunes of another than for one's own.

> *Osmyn.* Yet I behold her—yet—and now no more.
> Turn your lights inward, Eyes, and view my thought.
> So shall you still behold her—'twill not be.
> O impotence of sight! mechanic sense
> Which to exterior objects ow'st thy faculty,
> Not seeing of election, but necessity.
> Thus do our eyes, as do all common mirrors,
> Successively reflect succeeding images.
> Nor what they would, but must; a star or toad;
> Just as the hand of chance administers!
>
> *Mourning Bride, act* 2. *sc.* 8.

No man, in his senses, ever thought of applying his eyes to discover what passes in his mind; far less of blaming his eyes for not seeing a thought or idea. In Moliere's *L'Avare,*† Harpagon being robbed of his money, seizes himself by the arm, mistaking it for that of the robber. And again he expresses himself as follows:

> Je veux aller querir la justice, et faire donner la question à toute ma maison; à servantes, à valets, à fils, à fille, et à moi aussi.[32] <490>

This is so absurd as scarce to provoke a smile, if it be not at the author.

Of the second branch the following are examples.

---

* Act 4. sc. 5.
† Act 4. sc. 7.
32. "I'll call the police, and have all my household put to the torture, maids, valets, son, daughter, even myself" (trans. George Graveley and Ian Maclean, Oxford University Press, 1968).

———— ———— Now bid me run,
And I will strive with things impossible.
Yea get the better of them.   *Julius Caesar, act 2. sc. 3.*[33]

Vos mains seules ont droit de vaincre un invincible.
                                        Le Cid, act 5. sc. last.[34]

Que son nom soit beni. Que son nom soit chanté.
Que l'on celebre ses ouvrages
Au de la de l'eternité.   *Esther, act 5. sc. last.*[35]

Me miserable! which way shall I fly
Infinite wrath and infinite despair?
Which way I fly is hell: myself am hell;
And in the *lowest* deep, a *lower* deep
Still threatening to devour me, opens wide;
To which the hell I suffer seems a heav'n.
                                        Paradise lost, book 4.

Of the third branch, take the following samples.

Lucan, talking of Pompey's sepulchre,

———— ———— Romanum nomen, et omne
Imperium Magno est tumuli modus. Obrue saxa
Crimine plena deûm. Si tota est Herculis Octe,
Et juga tota vacant Bromio Nyseia; quare <491>
Unus in Egypto Magno lapis? Omnia Lagi
Rura tenere potest, si nullo cespite nomen

33. Act 2, sc. 1.
34. [Don Rodrigue]
    Your hands alone have the right to vanquish the invincible.

35. "May his name be blessed. May his name be sung. May his works be celebrated
{for all times and for all ages,} unto eternity." Kames omits the phrase in braces.

Haeserit. Erremus populi, cinerumque tuorum,
Magne, metu nullas Nili calcemus arenas.   *L. 8. l. 798.*

Thus in Row's translation:

> Where there are seas, or air, or earth, or skies,
> Where-e'er Rome's empire stretches, Pompey lies.
> Far be the vile memorial then convey'd!
> Nor let this stone the partial gods upbraid.
> Shall Hercules all Oeta's heights demand,
> And Nysa's hill for Bacchus only stand;
> While one poor pebble is the warrior's doom
> That fought the cause of liberty and Rome?
> If Fate decrees he must in Egypt lie,
> Let the whole fertile realm his grave supply,
> Yield the wide country to his awful shade
> Nor let us dare on any part to tread,
> Fearful we violate the mighty dead.[36]

The following passages are pure rant. Coriolanus, speaking to his mother,

> What is this?
> Your knees to me? to your corrected son?
> Then let the pebbles on the hungry beach
> Fillop the stars; then let the mutinous winds
> Strike the proud cedars 'gainst the fiery sun:
> Murd'ring impossibility, to make
> What cannot be, slight work.   *Coriolanus, act* 5. *sc.* 3.

> *Caesar.* ——— ——— Danger knows full well,
> That Caesar is more dangerous than he. <492>
> We were two lions litter'd in one day,
> And I the elder and more terrible.
>
> *Julius Caesar, act* 2. *sc.* 4.[37]

---

36. Kames uses Nicholas Rowe's verse translation of Lucan, 1718. In the Latin text Kames transposes "tumuli est" in line 2, and reads "Egypto Magno" for "Egypto Magni."
37. Act 2, sc. 2.

Almahide. This day—
I gave my faith to him, he his to me.
   Almanzor. Good Heav'n, thy book of fate before me lay
But to tear out the journal of this day.
Or if the order of the world below,
Will not the gap of one whole day allow,
Give me that minute when she made that vow.
That minute ev'n the happy from their bliss might give,
And those who live in grief a shorter time would live,
So small a link if broke, th' eternal chain
Would like divided waters join again.

Conquest of Granada, act 3.

   Almanzor. ——— ——— I'll hold it fast
As life: and when life's gone, I'll hold this last.
And if thou tak'st it after I am slain,
I'll send my ghost to fetch it back again.

Conquest of Granada, part 2. act 3.

   Lyndiraxa. A crown is come, and will not fate allow,
And yet I feel something like death is near.
My guards, my guards—
Let not that ugly skeleton appear.
Sure Destiny mistakes; this death's not mine;
She doats, and meant to cut another line.
Tell her I am a queen—but 'tis too late;
Dying, I charge rebellion on my fate;
Bow down, ye slaves— <493>
Bow quickly down and your submission show;
I'm pleas'd to taste an empire ere I go.   *[Dies.*

Conquest of Granada, part 2. act 5.

   Ventidius. But you, ere love misled your wand'ring eyes,
Were, sure, the chief and best of human race,
Fram'd in the very pride and boast of nature,
So perfect, that the gods who form'd you wonder'd

> At their own skill, and cry'd, A lucky hit
> Has mended our design.   *Dryden, All for love, act* 1.

Not to talk of the impiety of this sentiment, it is ludicrous instead of being lofty.

The famous epitaph on Raphael is no less absurd than any of the foregoing passages:

> Raphael, timuit, quo sospite, vinci
> Rerum magna parens, et moriente mori.[38]

Imitated by Pope in his Epitaph on Sir Godfrey Kneller:

> Living, great Nature fear'd he might outvie
> Her works; and dying, fears herself might die.

Such is the force of imitation; for Pope of himself would never have been guilty of a thought so extravagant.

So much upon sentiments: the language proper for expressing them, comes next in order. <494>

---

38. The correct text is

> Ille hic est Raphael, timuit quo sospite vinci
> Rerum magna parens, et moriente mori

The epitaph was composed by Cardinal Pietro Bembo (1470–1547), for the tomb of his great friend Raphael (1483–1520) in Santa Maria Rotonda (The Pantheon) in Rome. A favored translation in the eighteenth century was by William Harrison (1685–1713), minor poet and friend of both Swift and Addison:

> Here Raphael lies, by whose untimely end
> Nature both lost a rival and a friend.

Language of Passion

Among the particulars that compose the social part of our nature, a propensity to communicate our opinions, our emotions, and every thing that affects us, is remarkable. Bad fortune and injustice affect us greatly; and of these we are so prone to complain, that if we have no friend nor acquaintance to take part in our sufferings, we sometimes utter our complaints aloud, even where there are none to listen.

But this propensity operates not in every state of mind. A man immoderately grieved, seeks to afflict himself, rejecting all consolation: immoderate grief accordingly is mute: complaining is struggling for consolation.

> It is the wretch's comfort still to have
> Some small reserve of near and inward wo,
> Some unsuspected hoard of inward grief,
> Which they unseen may wail, and weep, and mourn.
> And glutton-like alone devour.
>
> *Mourning Bride, act* i. *sc.* i.

When grief subsides, it then and no sooner finds a tongue: we complain, because complaining <495> is an effort to disburden the mind of its distress.*

---

* This observation is finely illustrated by a story which Herodotus records, *b.* 3. Cambyses, when he conquered Egypt, made Psammenitus the King prisoner; and for trying his constancy, ordered his daughter to be dressed in the habit of a slave, and to be employ'd in bringing water from the river; his son also was led to execution with a halter about his neck. The Egyptians vented their sorrow in tears and lamentations; Psammenitus only, with a downcast eye, remained silent. Afterward meeting one of his

Surprise and terror are silent passions for a different reason: they agitate the mind so violently as for a time to suspend the exercise of its faculties, and among others the faculty of speech.

Love and revenge, when immoderate, are not more loquacious than immoderate grief. But when these passions become moderate, they set the tongue free, and, like moderate grief, become <496> loquacious: moderate love, when unsuccessful, is vented in complaints; when successful, is full of joy expressed by words and gestures.

As no passion hath any long uninterrupted existence,* nor beats always with an equal pulse, the language suggested by passion is not only unequal but frequently interrupted: and even during an uninterrupted fit of passion, we only express in words the more capital sentiments. In familiar conversation, one who vents every single thought, is justly branded with the character of *loquacity;* because sensible people express no thoughts but what make some figure: in the same manner, we are only disposed to express the strongest pulses of passion, especially when it returns with impetuosity after interruption.

I formerly had occasion to observe,† that the sentiments ought to be tuned to the passion, and the language to both. Elevated sentiments require elevated language: tender sentiments ought to be clothed in words that are soft and flowing: when the mind is depressed with any passion, the sentiments must be expressed in words that are humble, not low. Words being intimately connected with the ideas they represent, the greatest harmony is required between them: to express, for example, an humble sentiment in high-sounding words, is disagreeable by a discordant mixture <497> of

---

companions, a man advanced in years, who, being plundered of all, was begging alms, he wept bitterly, calling him by his name. Cambyses, struck with wonder, demanded an answer to the following question: "Psammenitus, thy master Cambyses is desirous to know, why, after thou hadst seen thy daughter so ignominiously treated and thy son led to execution, without exclaiming or weeping, thou shouldst be so highly concerned for a poor man, no way related to thee?" Psammenitus returned the following answer: "Son of Cyrus, the calamities of my family are too great to leave me the power of weeping; but the misfortunes of a companion, reduced in his old age to want of bread, is a fit subject for lamentation."

* See chap. 2. part 3.

† Chap. 16.

feelings; and the discord is not less when elevated sentiments are dressed in low words:

> Versibus exponi tragicis res comica non vult.
> Indignatur item privatis ac prope socco
> Dignis carminibus narrari coena Thyestae.
>
> *Horace, Ars poet. l. 89.*[1]

This however excludes not figurative expression, which, within moderate bounds, communicates to the sentiment an agreeable elevation. We are sensible of an effect directly opposite, where figurative expression is indulged beyond a just measure: the opposition between the expression and the sentiment, makes the discord appear greater than it is in reality.*

At the same time, figures are not equally the language of every passion: pleasant emotions, which elevate or swell the mind, vent themselves in strong epithets and figurative expression; but humbling and dispiriting passions affect to speak plain:

> Et tragicus plerumque dolet sermone pedestri
> Telephus et Peleus: cum pauper et exul uterque;
> Projicit ampullas et sesquipedalia verba,
> Si curat cor spectantis tetigisse querela.
>
> *Horace, Ars poet. l. 95.*[2]

Figurative expression, being the work of an enli-<498>vened imagination, cannot be the language of anguish or distress. Otway, sensible of this, has painted a scene of distress in colours finely adapted to the subject: there is scarce a figure in it, except a short and natural simile with which the speech is introduced. Belvidera talking to her father of her husband:

> Think you saw what past at our last parting;
> Think you beheld him like a raging lion,

---

* See this explained more particularly in chap. 8.

1. "A theme for Comedy refuses to be set forth in verses of Tragedy; likewise the feast of Thyestes scorns to be told in strains of daily life that well nigh befit the comic sock."

2. "So, too, in Tragedy Telephus and Peleus often grieve in the language of prose, when, in poverty and exile, either hero throws aside his bombast and words a foot and a half long, should he want his lament to touch the spectator's heart."

Pacing the earth, and tearing up his steps,
Fate in his eyes, and roaring with the pain
Of burning fury; think you saw his one hand
Fix'd on my throat, while the extended other
Grasp'd a keen threat'ning dagger; oh, 'twas thus
We last embrac'd, when, trembling with revenge,
He dragg'd me to the ground, and at my bosom
Presented horrid death; cry'd out, My friends!
Where are my friends? swore, wept, rag'd, threaten'd, lov'd;
For he yet lov'd, and that dear love preserv'd me
To this last trial of a father's pity.
I fear not death, but cannot bear a thought
That that dear hand should do th' unfriendly office;
If I was ever then your care, now hear me;
Fly to the senate, save the promis'd lives
Of his dear friends, ere mine be made the sacrifice.

Venice preserv'd, act 5.

To preserve the foresaid resemblance between words and their meaning, the sentiments of active and hurrying passions ought to be dressed in words <499> where syllables prevail that are pronounced short or fast; for these make an impression of hurry and precipitation. Emotions, on the other hand, that rest upon their objects, are best expressed by words where syllables prevail that are pronounced long or slow. A person affected with melancholy, has a languid and slow train of perceptions: the expression best suited to that state of mind, is where words, not only of long, but of many syllables, abound in the composition; and for that reason, nothing can be finer than the following passage.

In those deep solitudes, and awful cells,
Where heav'nly-pensive Contemplation dwells,
And ever-musing Melancholy reigns.

Pope, Eloisa to Abelard.

To preserve the same resemblance, another circumstance is requisite, that the language, like the emotion, be rough or smooth, broken or uniform. Calm and sweet emotions are best expressed by words that glide softly:

surprise, fear, and other turbulent passions, require an expression both rough and broken.

It cannot have escaped any diligent inquirer into nature, that in the hurry of passion, one generally expresses that thing first which is most at heart:* which is beautifully done in the following passage. <500>

> Me, me; adsum qui feci: in me convertite ferrum,
> O Rutuli, mea fraus omnis.   *Aeneid* ix. 427.[3]

Passion has often the effect of redoubling words, the better to make them express the strong conception of the mind. This is finely imitated in the following examples.

> ———— ———— Thou sun, said I, fair light!
> And thou enlighten'd earth, so fresh and gay!
> Ye hills and dales, ye rivers, woods, and plains!
> And ye that live, and move, fair creatures! tell,
> Tell, if ye saw, how came I thus, how here.——
>   *Paradise lost, book* viii. 273.

> ———— ———— Both have sinn'd! but thou
> Against God only; I, 'gainst God and thee:
> And to the place of judgement will return.
> There with my cries importune Heaven, that all
> The sentence, from thy head remov'd, may light
> On me, sole cause to thee of all this wo;
> Me! Me! only just object of his ire.
>   *Paradise lost, book* x. 930.

Shakespear is superior to all other writers in delineating passion. It is difficult to say in what <501> part he most excels, whether in moulding

---

* Demetrius Phalereus (of Elocution, sect. 28) justly observes, that an accurate adjustment of the words to the thought, so as to make them correspond in every particular, is only proper for sedate subjects; for that passion speaks plain, and rejects all refinements.

3. Me, me, he cry'd, turn all your Swords alone
   On me; the Fact confess'd, the Fault my own.
                    (trans. Dryden)

every passion to peculiarity of character, in discovering the sentiments that proceed from various tones of passion, or in expressing properly every different sentiment: he disgusts not his reader with general declamation and unmeaning words, too common in other writers: his sentiments are adjusted to the peculiar character and circumstances of the speaker; and the propriety is no less perfect between his sentiments and his diction. That this is no exaggeration, will be evident to every one of taste, upon comparing Shakespear with other writers in similar passages. If upon any occasion he fall below himself, it is in those scenes where passion enters not: by endeavouring in that case to raise his dialogue above the style of ordinary conversation, he sometimes deviates into intricate thought and obscure expression:* sometimes, to <502> throw his language out of the familiar, he employs rhyme. But may it not in some measure excuse Shakespear, I shall not say his works, that he had no pattern, in his own or in any living language, of dialogue fitted for the theatre? At the same time, it ought not to escape observation, that the stream clears in its progress, and that in his later plays he has attained the purity and perfection of dialogue; an observation that, with greater certainty than tradition, will direct us to arrange

---

* Of this take the following specimen.

> They clepe us drunkards, and with swinish phrase
> Soil our addition; and, indeed it takes
> From our atchievements, though perform'd at height,
> The pith and marrow of our attribute.
> So, oft it chances in particular men,
> That for some vicious mole of nature in them,
> As, in their birth, (wherein they are not guilty,
> Since Nature cannot chuse his origin),
> By the o'ergrowth of some complexion
> Oft breaking down the pales and forts of reason;
> Or by some habit, that too much o'er-leavens
> The form of plausive manners; that these men
> Carrying, I say, the stamp of one defect,
> (Being Nature's livery, or Fortune's fear),
> Their virtues else, be they as pure as grace,
> As infinite as man may undergo,
> Shall in the general censure take corruption
> From that particular fault.   *Hamlet, act* 1. *sc.* 7.

[Act 1, sc. 4. Read "Fortune's star" for "Fortune's fear."]

his plays in the order of time. This ought to be considered, by those who rigidly exaggerate every blemish of the finest genius for the drama ever the world enjoy'd: they ought also for their own sake to consider, that it is easier to discover his blemishes, which lie generally at the surface, than his beauties, which cannot be truly relished but by those who dive deep into human nature. One thing must be evident to the meanest capacity, that where-ever passion is to be display'd, Nature shows itself mighty in him, and is conspicuous <503> by the most delicate propriety of sentiment and expression.*

I return to my subject from a digression I cannot repent of. That perfect harmony which ought to subsist among all the constituent parts of a dialogue, is a beauty, no less rare than conspicuous: as to expression in particular, were I to give instances, where, in one or other of the respects above mentioned, it corresponds not precisely to the characters, passions, and sentiments, I might from different authors collect volumes. Following therefore the method laid down in the chapter of sentiments, I shall confine my quotations to the grosser errors, which every writer ought to avoid.

And, first, of passion expressed in words flowing in an equal course without interruption.

In the chapter above cited, Corneille is censured for the impropriety of his sentiments; and here, for the sake of truth, I am obliged to attack <504> him a second time. Were I to give instances from that author of the fault under consideration, I might transcribe whole tragedies; for he is no less faulty in this particular, than in passing upon us his own thoughts as a spectator, instead of the genuine sentiments of passion. Nor would a comparison between him and Shakespear upon the present article, redound more to his honour, than the former upon the sentiments. Racine is here less incorrect than Corneille; and from him therefore I shall gather a few

---

* The critics seem not perfectly to comprehend the genius of Shakespear. His plays are defective in the mechanical part; which is less the work of genius than of experience, and is not otherwise brought to perfection but by diligently observing the errors of former compositions. Shakespear excels all the ancients and moderns, in knowledge of human nature, and in unfolding even the most obscure and refined emotions. This is a rare faculty, and of the greatest importance in a dramatic author; and it is that faculty which makes him surpass all other writers in the comic as well as tragic vein.

instances. The first shall be the description of the sea-monster in his *Phaedra,* given by Theramene, the companion of Hippolytus. Theramene is represented in terrible agitation, which appears from the following passage, so boldly figurative as not to be excused but by violent perturbation of mind:

> Le ciel avec horreur voit ce monstre sauvage,
> Le terre s'en émeut, l'air en est infecté,
> Le flot, qui l'apporta, recule epouvanté.[4]

Yet Theramene gives a long pompous connected description of that event, dwelling upon every minute circumstance, as if he had been only a cool spectator:

> A peine nous sortions des portes de Trézéne,
> Il étoit sur son char. Ses gardes affligés,
> Imitoient son silence, autour de lui rangés.
> Il suivoit tout pensif le chemin de Mycénes.
> Sa main sur les chevaux laissoit flotter les rênes. < 505 >
> Ses superbs coursiers qu'on voyoit autrefois
> Pleins d'une ardeur si noble obéir à sa voix,
> L'œil morne maintenant et la tête baissée,
> Sembloient se conformer à sa triste pensée, &c.
>
> *Act 5. sc. 6.*[5]

4. The heavens beheld the monster, horror-struck;
   It poisoned all the air; it rocked the earth.
   The wave that brought it in recoiled aghast.

5. Scarce were we issuing from Troezen's gates;
   He drove his chariot; round about him ranged,
   Copying his silence, were his cheerless guards.
   Pensive, he followed the Mycenae road,
   And let the reins hang loose upon his steeds.
   These haughty steeds, that once upon a time,
   Noble, high-spirited, obeyed his voice,
   Now dull of eye and with a dejected air
   Seemed to conform to his despondent thoughts.
               (*Phaedra,* trans. John Cairncross)

The last speech of Atalide, in the tragedy of *Bajazet,* of the same author, is a continued discourse; and but a faint representation of the violent passion which forc'd her to put an end to her own life:

> Enfin, c'en est donc fait. Et par mes artifices,
> Mes injustes soupcons, mes funestes caprices,
> Je suis donc arrivée au douloureux moment,
> Où je vois, par mon crime, expirer mon amant.
> N'étoit-ce pas assez, cruelle destinée,
> Qu'à lui survivre, hélas! je fusse condamnée?
> Et falloit-il encore que, pour comble d'horreurs,
> Je ne pusse imputer sa mort qu'à mes fureurs!
> Oui, c'est moi, cher amant, qui t'arrache la vie;
> Roxane, ou le Sultan, ne te l'ont ravie.
> Moi seule, j'ai tissu le lien malheureux
> Dont tu viens d'éprouver les detestables nœuds.
> Et je puis, sans mourir, en souffrir la pensée?
> Moi, qui n'ai pû tantôt, de ta mort menacée,
> Rétentir mes esprits, prompts à m'abandonner!
> Ah! n'ai-je eu de l'amour que pour t'assassiner?
> Mais c'en est trop. Il faut par un prompt sacrifice,
> Que ma fidelle main te venge, et me punisse.
> Vous, de qui j'ai troublé la gloire et le repos,
> Héros, qui deviez tous revivre en ce héros,
> Toi, mere malheureuse, et qui dès notre enfance,
> Me confias son cœur dans une autre esperance, < 506 >
> Infortuné Visir, amis désespérés,
> Roxane, venez tous contre moi conjurez,
> Tourmenter à la fois une amante eperdue;   [*Elle se tue.*
> Et prenez la vengeance enfin qui vois est dûe.
>
> *Act 5. sc. last.*[6]

---

6. Racine, *Bajazet,* end of act 5. "Well, it is all over. Through my pretence, my unjust suspicions, my disastrous whims, I have reached the painful moment when I see my lover die because of my crimes. Cruel fate, was it not enough that I should be condemned to survive him? To complete this horror, did I have to ascribe his death only to my mad passion? Yes, dear love, it is I who took your life. Neither Roxane nor the Sultan took it from you. I alone fashioned the unfortunate tie whose bond has stricken you with mis-

Tho' works, not authors, are the professed subject of this critical undertaking, I am tempted by the present speculation, to transgress once again the limits prescribed, and to venture a cursory reflection upon that justly-celebrated author, That he is always sensible, generally correct, never falls low, maintains a moderate degree of dignity without reaching the sublime, paints delicately the tender affections, but is a stranger to the genuine language of enthusiastic or fervid passion.

If in general the language of violent passion ought to be broken and interrupted, soliloquies ought to be so in a peculiar manner: language is intended by nature for society; and a man when alone, tho' he always clothes his thoughts in words, seldom gives his words utterance, unless when prompted by some strong emotion; and even then by starts and intervals only.* Shakespear's soliloquies may be justly established as a model; for it is not easy to conceive any model more perfect: of his many incomparable soliloquies, I confine myself to the two following, being different in their manner. <507>

> *Hamlet.* Oh, that this too too solid flesh would melt,
> Thaw, and resolve itself into a dew!
> Or that the Everlasting had not fix'd
> His canon 'gainst self-slaughter! O God! O God!
> How weary, stale, flat, and unprofitable
> Seem to me all the uses of this world!
> Fie on't! O fie! 'tis an unweeded garden,
> That grows to feed: things rank and gross in nature
> Possess it merely.—That it should come to this!
> But two months dead! nay, not so much; not two;—

---

fortune. Can I bear to think of it without dying; I, who, a little while ago, when threatened with your death, did not manage to keep myself from fainting. Did I love you only to stab you? But it is too much: I must sacrifice myself, quickly; let my obedient hand avenge you and punish me. All you others, whose glory and peace I have disturbed, past heroes who should have lived again in this hero; you, unhappy mother, who, from early childhood, entrusted me with his heart, hoping better things for him; unfortunate Vizier; desperate friends; Roxane, all called up, here, before me, come and torment a stricken lover. [She stabs herself.] Take at last what revenge is due you!" (Trans. Y. M. Martin.)

* Soliloquies accounted for, chap. 15.

So excellent a king, that was, to this,
Hyperion to a satyr: so loving to my mother,
That he permitted not the winds of heav'n
Visit her face too roughly. Heav'n and earth!
Must I remember—why, she would hang on him,
As if increase of appetite had grown
By what it fed on; yet, within a month—
Let me not think—Frailty, thy name is *Woman!*
A little month! or ere those shoes were old,
With which she followed my poor father's body,
Like Niobe, all tears—Why she, ev'n she—
(O heav'n! a beast that wants discourse of reason,
Would have mourn'd longer—) married with mine uncle,
My father's brother; but no more like my father,
Than I to Hercules. Within a month!—
Ere yet the salt of most unrighteous tears
Had left the flushing in her gauled eyes,
She married—Oh, most wicked speed, to post
With such dexterity to incestuous sheets!
It is not, nor it cannot come to good.
But break, my heart, for I must hold my tongue.

Hamlet, act I. *sc.* 3.[7] <508>

Ford. Hum! ha! is this a vision? is this a dream? do I sleep? Mr. Ford, awake; awake, Mr. Ford; there's a hole made in your best coat, Mr. Ford! this 'tis to be married! this 'tis to have linen and buck baskets! Well, I will proclaim myself what I am; I will now take the leacher; he is at my house; he cannot 'scape me; 'tis impossible he should; he cannot creep into a half-penny purse, nor into a pepper-box. But lest the devil that guides him should aid him, I will search impossible places; tho' what I am I cannot avoid, yet to be what I would not, shall not make me tame.

Merry Wives of Windsor, act 3. *sc. last.*[8]

These soliloquies are accurate and bold copies of nature: in a passionate soliloquy one begins with thinking aloud; and the strongest feelings only,

7. Act I, sc. 2.
8. Act 3, sc. 5.

are expressed; as the speaker warms, he begins to imagine one listening, and gradually slides into a connected discourse.

How far distant are soliloquies generally from these models? So far indeed as to give disgust instead of pleasure. The first scene of *Iphigenia* in Tauris discovers that princess, in a soliloquy, gravely reporting to herself her own history. There is the same impropriety in the first scene of *Alcestes,* and in the other introductions of Euripides, almost without exception. Nothing can be more ridiculous: it puts one in mind of a most curious device in Gothic paintings, that of making every figure explain itself by a written label issuing from its mouth. The description which a parasite, in <509> the *Eunuch* of Terence,* gives of himself, makes a sprightly soliloquy: but it is not consistent with the rules of propriety; for no man, in his ordinary state of mind and upon a familiar subject, ever thinks of talking aloud to himself. The same objection lies against a soliloquy in the *Adelphi* of the same author.† The soliloquy which makes the third scene, act third, of his *Heicyra,* is insufferable; for there Pamphilus, soberly and circumstantially, relates to himself an adventure which had happened to him a moment before.

Corneille is not more happy in his soliloquies than in his dialogue. Take for a specimen the first scene of *Cinna.*

Racine also is extremely faulty in the same respect. His soliloquies are regular harangues, a chain completed in every link, without interruption or interval: that of Antiochus in *Berenice*‡ resembles a regular pleading, where the parties *pro* and *con* display their arguments at full length. The following soliloquies are equally faulty: *Bajazet,* act 3. sc. 7.; *Mithridate,* act. 3. sc. 4. & act 4. sc. 5.; *Iphigenia,* act 4. sc. 8.

Soliloquies upon lively or interesting subjects, but without any turbulence of passion, may be carried on in a continued chain of thought. If, for example, the nature and sprightliness of the subject prompt a man to speak his thoughts in the <510> form of a dialogue, the expression must

---

* Act 2. sc. 2.
† Act 1. sc. 1.
‡ Act 1. sc. 2.

be carried on without break or interruption, as in a dialogue between two persons; which justifies Falstaff's soliloquy upon honour:

> What need I be so forward with Death, that calls not on me? Well, 'tis no matter, Honour pricks me on. But how if Honour prick me off, when I come on? how then? Can Honour set a leg? No: or an arm? No: or take away the grief of a wound? No. Honour hath no skill in surgery then? No. What is Honour? A word.—What is that word *honour?* Air; a trim reckoning.—Who hath it? He that dy'd a Wednesday. Doth he feel it? No. Doth he hear it? No. Is it insensible then? Yea, to the dead. But will it not live with the living? No. Why? Detraction will not suffer it. Therefore I'll none of it; honour is a mere scutcheon; and so ends my catechism.
>
> *First part, Henry* IV. *act* 5. *sc.* 2.[9]

And even without dialogue, a continued discourse may be justified, where a man reasons in a soliloquy upon an important subject; for if in such a case it be at all excusable to think aloud, it is necessary that the reasoning be carried on in a chain; which justifies that admirable soliloquy in *Hamlet* upon life and immortality, being a serene meditation upon the most interesting of all subjects. And the same consideration will justify the soliloquy that introduces the 5th act of Addison's *Cato.* <511>

The next class of the grosser errors which all writers ought to avoid, shall be of language elevated above the tone of the sentiment; of which take the following instances.

> *Zara.* Swift as occasion, I
> Myself will fly; and earlier than the morn
> Wake thee to freedom. Now 'tis late; and yet
> Some news few minutes past arriv'd, which seem'd
> To shake the temper of the King.—Who knows
> What racking cares disease a monarch's bed?
> Or love, that late at night still lights his lamp,
> And strikes his rays through dusk, and folded lids,
> Forbidding rest, may stretch his eyes awake,

9. Act 5, sc. 1.

And force their balls abroad at this dead hour.
I'll try.   *Mourning Bride, act* 3. *sc.* 4.

The language here is undoubtedly too pompous and laboured for describing so simple a circumstance as absence of sleep. In the following passage, the tone of the language, warm and plaintive, is well suited to the passion, which is recent grief: but every one will be sensible, that in the last couplet save one, the tone is changed, and the mind suddenly elevated to be let fall as suddenly in the last couplet:

> Il déteste à jamais sa coupable victoire,
> Il renonce à la cour, aux humains, à la gloire;
> Et se fuïant lui-même, au milieu des deserts,
> Il va cacher sa peine au bout de l'univers; <512>
> *Là, soit que le soleil rendît le jour au monde,*
> *Soit qu'il finît sa course au vaste seine de l'onde,*
> Sa voix faisoit redire aux echos attendris,
> Le nom, le triste nom, de son malheureux fils.
>
> *Henriade, chant.* viii. 229.[10]

Language too artificial or too figurative for the gravity, dignity, or importance, of the occasion, may be put in a third class.

Chimene demanding justice against Rodrigue who killed her father, instead of a plain and pathetic expostulation, makes a speech stuffed with the most artificial flowers of rhetoric:

> Sire, mon pere est mort, mes yeux ont vû son sang
> Couler à gros bouillons de son généreux flanc;
> Ce sang qui tant de fois garantit vos murailles,
> Ce sang qui tant de fois vous gagna des battailes,
> Ce sang qui, tout sorti, fume encore de courroux

---

10. Voltaire, *Henriade*, 8.229: "He ever detests his guilty victory; he renounces the court, his fellow human beings, even glory; and fleeing from himself to the midst of the wilderness, he seeks to hide his sorrows at the farthest ends of the universe; there, whether the sun restores daylight to the world, or sets beneath the vast net of waves, his voice can call out again to the tender echoes, the name, the sad name of his wretched son."

> De se voir répandu pour d'autres que pour vous,
> Qu'au milieu des hazards n'osoit verser la guerre,
> Rodrigue en votre cour vient d'en couvrir la terre.
> J'ai couru sur le lieu sans force, et sans couleur:
> Je l'ai trouvé sans vie. Excusez ma douleur,
> Sire; la voix me manque à ce recit funeste,
> Mes pleurs et mes soupirs vous diront mieux le reste.[11]

And again,

> Son flanc étoit ouvert, et, pour mieux m'emouvoir,
> Son sang sur la poussiére écrivoit mon devoir; <513>
> Ou plûtôt sa valeur en cet état réduite
> Me parloit par sa plaie, et hâtoit ma pursuite,
> Et pour se faire entendre au plus juste des Rois,
> Par cette triste bouche elle empruntoit ma voix.[12]

Act 2. *sc.* 9.

---

11. *The Cid,* act 2, sc. 8.

> My father's dead. My eyes have seen his blood
> Gush from his great, his noble-hearted side,
> This blood so oft the safeguard of your walls,
> This blood, so oft battle-victorious,
> This blood, though spilt, that reeks with anger still
> At being shed for others than yourself,
> That even war's hazards did not dare to draw,
> Rodrigo in your court covers the earth
> With it. I hurried thither, pale, distraught.
> I found him lifeless, Sire; forgive my grief.
> My voice fails as I tell this fearful tale.
> My tears, more eloquent, can say the rest.

12. His flank was open wide. The more to stir me on,
> His blood had writ my duty in the dust.
> Rather, his valour, now reduced so low,
> Spoke to me through his wound, called for revenge.
> And, to appeal to the most just of kings,
> Borrowed by these unspeaking lips my voice.
>   (*The Cid*)

Nothing can be contrived in language more averse to the tone of the passion than this florid speech: I should imagine it more apt to provoke laughter than to inspire concern or pity.

In a fourth class shall be given specimens of language too light or airy for a severe passion.

Imagery and figurative expression are discordant, in the highest degree, with the agony of a mother, who is deprived of two hopeful sons by a brutal murder. Therefore the following passage is undoubtedly in a bad taste.

> *Queen.* Ah, my poor princes! ah, my tender babes!
> My unblown flow'rs, new appearing sweets!
> If yet your gentle souls fly in the air,
> And be not fixt in doom perpetual,
> Hover about me with your airy wings,
> And hear your mother's lamentation.
>
> *Richard* III. *act* 4. *sc.* 4.

Again,

> *K. Philip.* You are as fond of grief as of your child. <514>
> *Constance.* Grief fills the room up of my absent child,
> Lies in his bed, walks up and down with me,
> Puts on his pretty looks, repeats his words,
> Remembers me of all his gracious parts,
> Stuffs out his vacant garment with his form;
> Then have I reason to be fond of grief.
>
> *King John, act* 3. *sc.* 6.[13]

A thought that turns upon the expression instead of the subject, commonly called *a play of words,* being low and childish, is unworthy of any composition, whether gay or serious, that pretends to any degree of elevation: thoughts of this kind make a fifth class.

13. Act 3, sc. 4.

In the *Amynta* of Tasso,* the lover falls into a mere play of words, demanding how he who had lost himself, could find a mistress. And for the same reason, the following passage in Corneille has been generally condemned:

> *Chimene.* Mon pere est mort, Elvire, et la premiere épée
> Dont s'est armée Rodrigue a sa trame coupée.
> Pleurez, pleurez, mes yeux, et fondez-vous en eau,
> La moitié de ma vie a mis l'autre au tombeau,
> Et m'oblige à venger, après ce coup funeste,
> Celle que je n'ai plus, sur celle que me reste.
>
> *Cid, act* 3. sc. 3.[14] <515>

> To die is to be banish'd from myself:
> And Sylvia is myself; banish'd from her,
> Is self from self; a deadly banishment!
>
> *Two Gentlemen of Verona, act* 3. sc. 3.[15]

> *Countess.* I pray thee, Lady, have a better cheer:
> If thou ingrossest all the griefs as thine,
> Thou robb'st me of a moiety.
>
> *All's well that ends well, act* 3. sc. 3.[16]

> *K. Henry.* O my poor kingdom, sick with civil blows!
> When that my care could not with-hold thy riots,
> What wilt thou do when riot is thy care?

---

* Act 1. sc. 2.

14. My father's dead, Elvira. The first sword
Rodrigo wielded cut his thread of life.
Weep, weep, my eyes, dissolve. Half of my life
Has sent the other half down to the tomb,
And forces mee thereafter to avenge
The one that's gone on the surviving one.
    (*The Cid,* trans. John Cairncross)

15. Act 3, sc. 1.
16. Act 3, sc. 2.

O, thou wilt be a wilderness again,
Peopled with wolves, thy old inhabitants.

Second part Henry IV. *act* 4. *sc.* 11.[17]

Cruda Amarilli, che col nome ancora
D'amar, ahi lasso, amaramente insegni.

Pastor Fido, act 1. *sc.* 2.[18]

Antony, speaking of Julius Caesar:

O world! thou wast the forest of this hart:
And this, indeed, O world, the heart of thee,
How like a deer, striken by many princes,
Dost thou here lie! *Julius Caesar, act* 3. *sc.* 3.[19]

Playing thus with the sound of words, which is still worse than a pun, is
the meanest of all con-<516>ceits. But Shakespear, when he descends to a
play of words, is not always in the wrong; for it is done sometimes to denote
a peculiar character, as in the following passage:

K. Philip. What say'st thou, boy? look in the lady's face.
Lewis. I do, my Lord, and in her eye I find
A wonder, or a wond'rous miracle;
The shadow of myself form'd in her eye;
Which being but the shadow of your son,
Becomes a sun, and makes your son a shadow.
I do protest, I never lov'd myself
Till now infixed I beheld myself
Drawn in the flatt'ring table of her eye.
Faulconbridge. Drawn in the flatt'ring table of her eye!
Hang'd in the frowning wrinkle of her brow!
And quarter'd in her heart! he doth espy

17. Act 4, sc. 5.
18. O Amarillis, Authresse of my flame,
(Within my mouth how sweet now is thy name!
But in my heart how bitter!)

19. Act 3, sc. 1.

Himself Love's traitor: this is pity now,
That hang'd, and drawn, and quarter'd, there should be,
In such a love so vile a lout as he.

King John, act 2. *sc.* 5.[20]

A jingle of words is the lowest species of that low wit; which is scarce
sufferable in any case, and least of all in an heroic poem: and yet Milton
in some instances has descended to that puerility:

And brought into the world a world of woe.
——— Begirt th' Almighty throne <517>
Beseeching or besieging ———
Which tempted our attempt ———
At one slight bound high overleap'd all bound.
——— ——— With a shout
Loud as from numbers without number.[21]

One should think it unnecessary to enter a caveat against an expression
that has no meaning, or no distinct meaning; and yet somewhat of that
kind may be found even among good writers. Such make a sixth class.

Sebastian. I beg no pity for this mould'ring clay
For if you give it burial, there it takes
Possession of your earth:
If burnt and scattered in the air; the winds
That strow my dust, diffuse my royalty,
And spread me o'er your clime; for where one atom
Of mine shall light, know there Sebastian reigns.

Dryden, Don Sebastian King of Portugal, act 1.

Cleopatra. Now, what news, my Charmion?
Will he be kind? and will he not forsake me?
Am I to live or die? nay, do I live?
Or am I dead? for when he gave his answer,
Fate took the word, and then I liv'd or dy'd.

Dryden, All for love, act 2.

---

20. Act 2, sc. 1.
21. Milton, *Paradise Lost:* 9.11; 5.868; 1.642; 4.181; 3.346.

If she be coy, and scorn my noble fire,
   If her chill heart I cannot move;
   Why, I'll enjoy the very love,
And make a mistress of my own desire.

        Cowley, poem inscribed, The Request. <518>

His whole poem, inscribed, *My picture,* is a jargon of the same kind.

——— ——— 'Tis he, they cry, by whom
Not men, but war itself is overcome.   *Indian Queen.*

Such empty expressions are finely ridiculed in the *Rehearsal:*

Was't not unjust to ravish hence her breath,
And in life's stead to leave us nought but death.

        Act 4. *sc.* 1.

End of the FIRST VOLUME.